Domingos Álvares,

African Healing, and

the Intellectual History of

the Atlantic World

Domingos Álvares,

African Healing, and

the Intellectual History of

the Atlantic World

JAMES H. SWEET

The University of North Carolina Press   Chapel Hill

All rights reserved. Manufactured in the United States of America.
Designed by Courtney Leigh Baker and set in Arno Pro and
Quadraat Sans by Rebecca Evans. The paper in this book meets
the guidelines for permanence and durability of the Committee
on Production Guidelines for Book Longevity of the Council on
Library Resources. The University of North Carolina Press has
been a member of the Green Press Initiative since 2003.

Library of Congress Cataloging-in-Publication Data
Sweet, James H. (James Hoke)
Domingos Álvares, African healing, and the intellectual
history of the Atlantic world / James H. Sweet.
p. cm.   Includes bibliographical references and index.
ISBN 978-0-8078-3449-7 (cloth : alk. paper)
ISBN 978-1-4696-0975-1 (pbk. : alk. paper)
1. Álvares, Domingos, ca. 1710. 2. Slaves—Brazil, Northeast—
Biography. 3. Healers—Brazil, Northeast—Biography.
4. Healers—Portugal—Biography. 5. Atlantic Ocean Region—
History—18th century. 6. Slave-trade—Africa, West—
History—18th century. 7. Inquisition—Portugal—History—
18th century. 8. Medicine, Magic, mystic, and spagiric.
9. Witchcraft. 10. Voodooism. I. Title.
HT869.A58S84 2011
909'.049607092—dc22
[B]   2010032661

cloth   15 14 13 12 11 5 4 3 2 1
paper   17 16 15 14 13 5 4 3 2 1

This mis-shapen knave—
His mother was a witch, and one so strong
That could control the moon, make flows and ebbs,
And deal in her command without her power.
... [T]his demi-devil—
For he's a bastard one—
... [T]his thing of darkness, I
Acknowledge mine.

PROSPERO, referring to his slave Caliban,
in William Shakespeare's *The Tempest*

Contents

Illustrations, Maps, and Tables

TABLES

Acknowledgments

The idea for this book took shape roughly ten years ago. I had recently arrived in Miami with a new job, a young family, and an eager self-assurance about the future. Shortly after beginning the research and writing, I received news that my maternal grandmother had died in Honolulu. The years since her death have been punctuated by yet more loss. Between 2001 and 2008, my stepmother, my father, and my grandfather died. In South Africa, my wife Margaret lost the matriarch and patriarch of her extended family, as well as her aunt. Each of these deaths was keenly felt. However, the accumulation of loss served to bring the surviving family closer together, fortified by the shared bonds of the past. Likewise, the births of children insured the regeneration of the past in the present. My son Aidan was born in 2003, adding untold joy (and noise) to our house. As he and his sister Aly have grown, their smallest gestures and idiosyncrasies reflect upon their parents, their grandparents, and the ancestors they never knew. By continuing to impose themselves in our lives in these ways and others, the deceased force us to consider what makes us whole. Whether in Honolulu, Charlotte, Miami, Milledgeville, or Johannesburg, we are bound by the ancestors and kin we too easily forget in our daily strivings. Without their collective sustenance and support, I never could have completed this book.

The process of thinking and writing about Domingos Álvares has taught me much about the enduring power that can be derived from family and friends. In this way, he has been a therapeutic companion over these last ten years, constantly reminding me of the things that matter most. Ironically, for Margaret, Alexandra, and Aidan, Domingos has been a much less salutary figure. Like the mercurial trickster that he could sometimes be, Domingos kept me away from my family's dinner table on far too many nights. For the lost time we can never get back, I am truly sorry. All I can do is promise to make up for it. In the meantime, thank you for your patience and sacrifices. None of this could have been possible without you. Your love and laughter sustain me always.

The web of kin that extends beyond the boundaries of Madison, Wisconsin, has become increasingly important to me. My mother Lyn and my brothers Gray and Jason are my bedrock. In body, I may be absent, but my spirit is always grounded on Wensley Drive. Lifelong friends also remain crucial pillars of support in Charlotte—Kenny Hugo, Todd McMasters, Tony Scott, and Mike Shildt. In South Africa, inspiration comes from my in-laws Gertrude, James, Joseph, Mary, and Martha Marble. With deep admiration and affection I remember A.B.C. and Kay Motsepe, whose legacies survive in the remarkable achievements of their children and grandchildren, as well as in my own marriage. If not for their blessing and Ous Kuki's selfless generosity, my marriage to Margaret never would have happened. To Ous Tshepo and Cyril, we can never thank you enough for the love and attention you have given us and our children over the years. Your unwavering support and encouragement have strengthened us in more ways than we can count. We will continue to aspire to your exemplary high standards.

Though family is the foundation upon which this project rests, I could not have completed it without the support of numerous colleagues and friends. A remarkable number of people took time out of their busy schedules to read the entire manuscript. Walter Hawthorne, Florencia Mallon, Joe Miller, Luis Parés, Terry Rey, Jim Sidbury, Tom Spear, and Cameron Strang offered comments and critiques that have made the book immeasurably better than it was in its earlier drafts. I am indebted to each of them for their generosity and goodwill. In addition, the twelve students in my graduate seminar on the history of the African diaspora in fall 2009 read the full manuscript, as did the graduate students in Jim Sidbury's spring 2010 Atlantic history seminar at the University of Texas. Their suggestions were enormously helpful as I made my final revisions. Elaine Maisner at the University of North Carolina Press has shown amazing patience with me as she shepherded the book through the writing and editorial process. She is a brilliant editor and cultivator of talent, but what separates Elaine from her peers is her loyalty, decency, and common sense. I can't thank her enough for her trust and support.

Other colleagues listened to my ideas or read chapters over the years. I first tested the idea of the book in a public talk at Florida International University in Miami. There, Felice Lifshitz's enthusiastic endorsement spurred me forward. Akin Ogundiran also offered early suggestions on Yoruba and Mahi materials. My colleagues at the University of Wisconsin have been instrumental in offering their encouragement and advice. Florence Bernault, Neil Kodesh, and David McDonald read some of the early chapters. Likewise Teju Olaniyan offered important feedback. Every year, professors and graduate students in African history at Northwestern University exchange ideas with the Africanist historians in Madison during a spring workshop. Jon Glassman, David Schoenbrun, and Butch Ware, along with their students, read the first three chapters of the manuscript. Their incisive comments strengthened these early chapters considerably. Emmanuel Akyeampong, Matthew Restall, Reinaldo Roman, and David Sartorius invited me to their respective campuses to deliver lectures on some of my early findings. I thank them for the opportunity to share my work with them and their colleagues. Several of my Brazilianist colleagues also offered advice, source material, and encouragement. Luis Nicolau Parés generously shared with me some of his field notes from Benin and directed me in some of the finer points of Sakpata devotion. Mariza de Carvalho Soares and I traded notes on the various iterations of "Mina" identity in Brazil. And finally Mary Karasch read my proposals with great interest, supporting my various bids for funding the project.

The research for this book could not have been possible without the support of the National Endowment for the Humanities and the Graduate School at the University of Wisconsin. Their generous funding allowed me to make crucial trips to Portugal and Brazil. Likewise, I wish to thank Jim Delehanty of UW's African Studies Program, who graciously agreed to finance the production of the maps for the book. During the writing stages, I was the beneficiary of several residential fellowships. I wrote the first half of the manuscript as the Walter Hines Page fellow at the National Humanities Center, where Geoff Harpham, Kent Mulliken, and the staff provide a unique space for creative, interdisciplinary exchanges that result in only the very best scholarship. My year at the NHC was probably the most productive and stimulating of my career, in no small part because of the numerous opportunities to receive feedback on my work. To thank everyone would be an impossible task; however, Robert Beachy, Glenda Gilmore, Jan Goldstein, Randall Jelks, Ben Kiernan, Sarah Shields, and Rachel Weil were especially thoughtful critics. I also had the opportunity to share some of the early chapters with various seminars and working groups in the Triangle area. Holly Brewer, Emily Burrill, Chris Lee, Lisa Lindsay, Lydia Lindsey, John Sweet, Carlton Wilson, and Peter Wood offered particularly helpful comments. Finally, several people merit thanks for insuring that my social life remained well lubricated. Robert Beachy, Emily Burrill, Randall Jelks, and Chris Lee shared good drinks and better conversation. The James Joyce Pub in Durham was the place I went to feed my passion for football; it also happened to be Jeffrey Kerr Ritchie's self-proclaimed "local." By sheer coincidence we met there one Saturday morning. Our shared professional interests almost always took a backseat to the more pressing issues of politics and who was going to win the Premiership.

I completed the manuscript during a year spent as a fellow at the Institute for Historical Studies at the University of Texas at Austin. The institute benefits from the visionary leadership of Julie Hardwick, who, in only a few years, has built one of the most vibrant and competitive fellowship programs in academia. Her energy and creativity are the motor forces that drive the institute. Meanwhile, Courtney Meador insures that the day-to-day operations run smoothly, performing her duties with alacrity and good cheer. Among the fellows, Nancy Appelbaum, Ruben Flores, and Dave Kinkela were my most frequent interlocutors and social companions. I also enjoyed the rich camaraderie of UT faculty, including Erika Bsumek, Jorge Cañizares, Toyin Falola, Frank Guridy, Bob Olwell, Jim Sidbury, and Ann Twinam. Cañizares and Sidbury were particularly welcoming, inviting me to take part in their graduate seminar on Atlantic history. After hours, Sidbury introduced me to the Elephant Room, where we shared a love of good jazz and stout beer. Coincidentally, Matt Childs was also on fellowship at UT during my time in Austin. Not only was he a careful reader of my work, but he graciously introduced me to "his" Austin—from afternoon pitchers at Dog and Duck to 4:00 A.M. chorizo con huevos at Las Cazuelas. It is rare that I find genuine kinship in my daily professional life, but Sidbury and Childs, along with Jorge Cañizares and Toyin Falola, revealed themselves as kindred spirits in a variety of ways. I respect them immensely as scholars, but my year in Austin made me respect them even more as people. I thank them for their friendship.

Finally, I wish to recognize a handful of other colleagues who have been a part of my extended family for many years. Jean Rahier and Mariama Jaiteh remain among my closest friends, despite the great distance from Madison to Miami. I could never repay their loyalty and love. Likewise, Terry Rey and his family are extraordinarily close to me. Our daughters, Aly and Thoraya, have grown up together and are still best of friends, even from afar. Terry flew from Philadelphia to stand as Aidan's godfather. I know of nobody better equipped to teach my son about life, loss, and love. Last but not least, twenty-five years ago Colin Palmer saw in me a spark of ability that I could not see myself. His interventions transformed my life. Colin has endured a series of unimaginable setbacks over the last several years. Despite these difficulties, he has remained upbeat and remarkably productive. I am inspired by his grace, dignity, and amazing resilience.

Ultimately, the collective support of family and friends is the generator for any "history." Individual accomplishments are possible only through the selflessness, generosity, and sacrifices of others. Domingos Álvares understood this nearly 300 years ago. I can only hope this book serves as a testament to the collective strength and good fortune of those who supported me.

Domingos Álvares,

African Healing, and

the Intellectual History of

the Atlantic World

Introduction

Early on the morning of August 12, 1743, in the jails of the Portuguese Holy Office in Lisbon, guards awakened Domingos Álvares, removed him from his cell, and delivered him to the custody of Inquisitor Manuel Varejão e Távora. In the presence of two deputies and a notary, Távora asked Domingos to confess his sins. Domingos answered that he had nothing more to confess. Távora immediately ordered Domingos into the building's cellar, the Sala do Tormento, where "the doctors, surgeons, and other ministers in the execution of the torment were called and sworn in." The deputies stripped Domingos naked and threw him on the rack (*potro*). In a last attempt to elicit a confession, the notary warned Domingos that "if the torment killed him or broke his bones . . . it would be his fault, and his fault alone, and not that of the Inquisitors and other ministers, who judged his case according to its merits." The notary's report gives no indication that Domingos responded. Lying face up on the wooden rack, eight leather cords tied snugly around his arms and legs, Domingos waited for the executioner to turn the wheel, tightening the cords of the apparatus. With each turn, a new order of pain—first, the strangling of circulation and subsequent deadening of the hands and feet; next, the penetration of the straps through the naked flesh, lacerating down to the bone; finally, if necessary, the tightening of the straps until they crushed the very bone. After fifteen minutes of this excruciating torture, Domingos cried out for Jesus and the Virgin Mary, prompting Távora to bring an end to the proceedings. Just eleven days later, the Inquisitors sentenced Domingos to public whipping and four years exile in the Portuguese village of Castro Marim; he was judged guilty of heresy, apostasy, and entering into a pact with the Devil.[1]

How did Domingos Álvares, a recently manumitted African slave, find himself in such a dire predicament? What were the circumstances that led to his arrival in Lisbon, the bizarre accusations against him, and his eventual banishment to a Portuguese frontier outpost? The answers to these questions lie at the intersection of some of the most salient issues relating to the history of the eighteenth-century Atlantic world, a world Domingos traveled far more extensively than most people of his time. From 1730 to

1750, he journeyed from the interior of West Africa, to the sugarcane breaks of northeastern Brazil, to the cosmopolitan, urban setting of Rio de Janeiro, to the Inquisitorial jails of Lisbon, and finally to the rural hamlets of southern Portugal. Though Domingos' itinerant life may seem exceptional, it was this constant uprooting and crossing of borders that opens windows onto broader sets of human experiences that defined the Atlantic world. By carefully following Domingos' movements and experiences in this vast, interconnected world, we can begin to piece together the series of events that eventually led to his Portuguese imprisonment and exile.

I first became aware of Domingos' remarkable story more than ten years ago when I stumbled upon his massive Inquisition file in the Portuguese national archives. The file contains more than 600 pages of manuscript material, covering two different Inquisition cases, recounting events on three different continents. As I transcribed all of the documents included in the cases, a disjointed, fragmented narrative of Domingos' life began to emerge from the manuscript pages. Yet the story that ultimately unfolded is more than a simple biographical sketch; these two Inquisition cases provide a unique perspective on the breadth and scope of the South Atlantic world during the first half of the eighteenth century. Domingos himself delivered dozens of pages of confessions and answers to interrogatories put forth by Inquisitors. Though filtered through the institutional apparatus of the Portuguese Holy Office, these pages reveal much about Domingos' understandings of the worlds he traveled. In addition to Domingos' own ideas and versions of events, nearly four dozen others recounted their interactions with Domingos throughout the Atlantic world. These witnesses came from all parts—Allada, Recife, Rio, Languedoc, Seville, Tavira, and Faro—and from all walks of life—slaves, market women, sugar planters, merchants, housewives, ship's captains, soldiers, and priests. The brief life histories and testimonies provided by each of these individuals give us invaluable insights on the various social, political, cultural, and economic landscapes that Domingos encountered. At the same time, taken as a whole, these eyewitness accounts reflect the ways local histories connected with much larger Atlantic forces of empire, slavery, mercantilism, and colonialism.

Even though the Inquisition documents are remarkably complete in recording nearly twenty years of Domingos' life, crucial gaps remain. In order to frame the varied contexts and questions that emanate from Domingos' lived experiences, I supplement the Inquisition cases with a range of other sources, including oral traditions, ethnography, genealogy, maps, colonial legal documents, slave trade data, censuses, Catholic parish records, news-

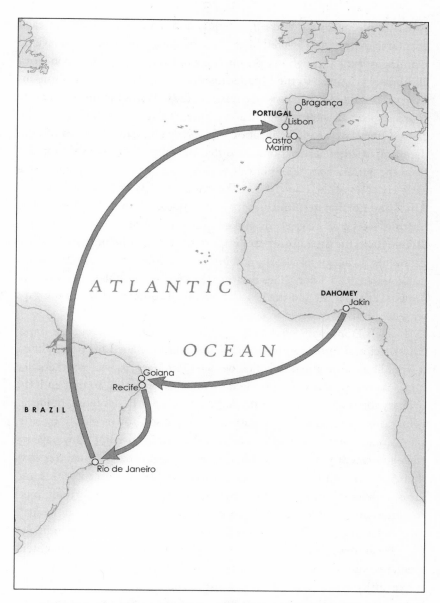

MAP I.1 Travels of Domingos Álvares, 1730–1750. Map created by the University of Wisconsin Cartography Lab.

papers, travel accounts, and other Inquisition materials. My goal in each chapter is to provide a layered history, one that begins at the micro level of Domingos, runs through the peculiarities of local and regional concerns, and finally connects to the broader histories of the Atlantic. In some instances, Domingos' social world comes vividly to life, as the supplementary sources speak directly to people and incidents outlined in the Inquisition cases. Often, this cross-fertilization of sources illustrates the breadth and depth of Atlantic connections. In other instances, Domingos disappears from the narrative for brief periods of time. This is particularly true in the early chapters of the book, where the evidence of Domingos' life in West Africa and northeastern Brazil is frustratingly sparse. In these sections, the histories are far more episodic and conjunctural. While I am able to place Domingos in the broad context of important and well-documented historical events, I cannot always outline his specific roles in the events as they unfolded. Instead, I draw lines between the evidentiary dots specific to Domingos' experiences and the broader historical contexts, filling in the gaps with details from other sources.

Though Domingos eventually became a subject of Portuguese imperial power and European institutions sometimes shaped his possibilities, it would be shortsighted to conclude that Domingos, as well as others like him, was completely circumscribed by these institutions. To that end, the primary focus of this "Black Atlantic" history is not Enlightenment ideals, colonial legal systems, Christianity, or Portuguese Crown rule. To be sure, these are important topics deserving of the ample attention they have received in recent years. Scholars in a variety of fields have shown the ways that Africans and their descendants engaged European institutions and ideas, employing them for their own ends, ultimately transforming metropolitan imperatives into thoroughly American ones. There can be little doubt that this new "Atlantic" scholarship has recast our understanding of the African-descended contribution to ideas about encounter, enlightenment, revolution, and independence.[2]

Nevertheless, these approaches largely fail to accommodate African historical perspectives, either on their own terms or as integral parts of a tightly braided Atlantic world. As one historian recently put it, "If the category of the Atlantic is to mean anything, it ought to include Africa, but there seems to be no room for this often overlooked fourth continent in most new versions of the Atlantic."[3] Even as Atlantic scholars lament the absence of Africa and Africans from the field, they often fail to recognize the ways that categories for analyzing the Atlantic remain preponderantly

American and European. In the developing "Atlantic" episteme, many of the questions that animated old-style colonial and imperial histories are simply recycled in a framework that continues to privilege the European-American nexus. By definition, "Atlantic" Africans march down the inevitable path of Americanization, an Americanization in dialogue with European ideas and institutions but very rarely African ones. In this way, Africans are often mechanically inserted into historical processes that are predetermined by the boundaries of European empire and colonialism. "Atlantic" Africans speak European languages, dress in European-style clothes, marry in the Catholic Church, and lodge legal complaints in colonial Crown courts. Ironically, this reduction of the "Atlantic" to European colonial processes now even proliferates in the scholarship on Africa in the form of "Eurafricans," "African Christians," and "Atlantic creoles." Thus, the Americanization of Africans begins in Africa, rendering them uniquely equipped to address the challenges of enslavement and colonialism in the Americas.[4] As these Africans move forward into the Atlantic, some of them embrace the principles of liberty and equality articulated in the Declaration of Independence, the Declaration of the Rights of Man and of the Citizen, and other Enlightenment- and revolutionary-era philosophies. In short, Africans are almost seamlessly woven into the narrative of Western democratic triumphalism, their political challenges framed as crucial to our understandings of liberty, equality, and freedom.

All of this is well and good for understanding revolutionary and emancipatory outcomes, but it does little to reveal the impacts of African institutions and ideas on the making of the Americas (let alone on Europe), especially in the years prior to 1750. Nor does it take into account the ways that processes of empire building, social dislocation, and transculturation, often understood as exceptional to the Americas, unfolded in parallel and overlapping fashion in West Africa. This erasure of African categories of knowledge reduces the history of the Atlantic to a European-American anachronism, assuming that the only "Black Atlantic" history worth telling is one in which African aspirations are expressed through colonial American languages and institutions. It bears remembering that between 1500 and 1820, more than three out of four immigrants to the Americas was African.[5] Millions of these enslaved Africans never learned European languages or ways of negotiating colonial bureaucracies of church and state. Others understood these institutions but rejected them in favor of those they found more efficacious. Surely, the histories of these Africans deserve to be told, if not for a fuller understanding of the ideas and institutions that shaped their own lives, then to better contextualize the historical processes that resulted in a polysemic, interconnected, and entangled Atlantic world.

In this early eighteenth-century Atlantic world, European dominance was rarely a foregone conclusion, particularly in those colonial spaces where Africans and their descendants figured prominently in the overall population. By offering alternate ways of thinking about family, religion, medicine, economics, and politics, Africans like Domingos Álvares contested the very legitimacy of European imperial power. For Portuguese authorities, Domingos constituted a threat far exceeding the boundaries of simple "criminality"; he was their worst colonial nightmare. As a healer, Domingos performed crucial social and political roles in society. His primary function was that of an intellectual, "a function that [was] directive, organizational, or educative." Thus, it was not so much the individual "quality and content" of Domingos' behaviors that rendered him powerful. Rather, it was his position "within the ensemble of social relations," his ability to extract broader political meanings from "illness," imparting these meanings to his clients and building new communities around ideas of collective redemption and well-being.[6]

Wherever he traveled, Domingos offered this political discourse of health and healing as an alternative to imperialist discourses. He often operated under a different episteme and communicated in an African vernacular indecipherable to most Europeans. Nevertheless, Domingos spoke a universally understood language of anti-imperial, anticolonial political contestation that echoed far and wide in the Atlantic world. Both consciously and unconsciously, he engaged the most potent political issues of the day— colonialism, mercantilism, warfare, slavery, religious disputes, and contentious kingship.

Tracing Domingos' travels provides a unique opportunity to reveal conjunctural conflict and accommodation in the forging of the Atlantic world. In isolation, political struggles in Abomey, Rio de Janeiro, or Castro Marim might seem purely local, and indeed, the peculiarities of local histories and environments bear heavily on the possibilities presented to Domingos at any given moment. At the same time, the conceptual tools for analyzing new political contingencies, forged first in Africa and then through the various encounters that followed, never faded from Domingos' memory. Like a palimpsest, Domingos accrued new ways of reading the worlds he encountered, layering these ideas one on top of the other. But the "parchment" and the original etchings were definitively African, shaped by twenty years of formative experiences in his homeland. As a vehicle for social and political empowerment, Domingos carried various Africas to Brazil and various Africas and Brazils to Portugal, calling upon those traditions that best suited the circumstances of the moment. In this way, local histories of Africa also became Brazilian and Portuguese histories. Likewise, Brazilian and Portuguese histories became African. Sewn together through a series of forced migrations, Domingos' African, Brazilian, and Portuguese histories collectively became Atlantic.

Domingos' Atlantic experience began in a small village in the central region of contemporary Benin. Though the Portuguese monitored Domingos for almost ten years and produced hundreds of pages of manuscript material on his activities, there are only a handful of substantive references to Africa in the official correspondence. Throughout the documents, Domingos is most often described as being from the "Costa da Mina," but this referent is little help since the term "Mina" encompassed a broad region from Ghana to Nigeria.[7] More useful are two descriptions, one from an African woman and the other from Domingos himself, that point toward a homeland in the region of present-day Benin now commonly known as Mahi. In 1742, an African woman from Allada described Domingos as "Cobú," a reference to the Agonli-Cové region, about forty miles northeast of Abomey.[8] Shortly thereafter, in 1743, Domingos testified that he was "thirty-four years old more or less . . . born in Nangon on the Mina Coast." "Nangon" is almost certainly Naogon, a village that lies only one mile from the town of Cové, in the center of the Agonli-Cové region.[9] Together, these scraps of evidence strongly suggest that Domingos Álvares was born in the village of Naogon sometime around 1710.[10]

This was an inauspicious time to come into the world. Domingos' entire passage from infancy to adulthood unfolded in the shadow of Dahomean military expansion, and he witnessed firsthand the panic, flight, famine, and disease triggered by violent warfare. What did these threats mean to him? How did they shape his life? What kinds of transformations did Agonli-Cové experience during this period? The answers to these questions are only partially addressed in European documentary sources, and even then, in fragmented fashion. In order to piece together the historical changes wrought by the empire of Dahomey, I combine European sources with Dahomean oral traditions, as well as an examination of specific Fon-Gbe terms found in the Inquisition documents. As several generations of Africanist historians have shown, these multiple, overlapping methodological approaches are the most effective means of capturing the internal histories of precolonial African societies. However, the methodologies of oral tradition and linguistics can be pushed one step further by considering accounts from the lives of enslaved Africans in the Americas. If read carefully, the voices and actions of the enslaved can reveal much about their earlier experiences in Africa, thereby enriching our knowledge not only of slave life in the Americas but also of Africa itself. Thus, the quest for understanding Domingos' African background is dialectical to understanding his experiences in Brazil and in the broader Atlantic. Domingos' spiritual, social, and political consciousness was forged in conflict with the empire of Dahomey. The impacts of these Dahomean conflicts resonated broadly across the Atlantic world, inspiring Domingos to deploy crucial elements of his African past in a continuing struggle for freedom, while at the same time responding to the changing conditions of new Atlantic environments.

Dahomey

You have nearly all the people of this family in your country.
They knew too much magic. We sold them because they made too much trouble.
—Dahomean informant remembering why a certain clan
was sold away to slavery in the Americas, 1930s, quoted in Melville J.
Herskovits, *Dahomey: An Ancient West African Kingdom*

In late March 1727, English ship captain William Snelgrave steered the galley
Katherine toward the shore near the West African port of Ouidah with the
intention of purchasing slaves. Snelgrave, a veteran captain of more than
twenty years, had traded extensively at Ouidah, most recently in 1720. Upon
anchoring his ship and forging the several miles inland to the English fort,
he discovered a "dismal" scene. The land was decimated, buildings burned,
and fields strewn with human remains. Just three weeks earlier, the army
of Dahomey had overrun the port city. In the ensuing chaos, thousands
of people fled. Others were captured and made prisoners of war. Among
the prisoners were "about forty . . . white Men, English, French, Dutch and
Portuguese," who occupied the various European forts at Ouidah. After
being marched nearly forty miles inland to Allada, one of the European
prisoners, the governor of the Royal African Company, was given an audience with the king of Dahomey, Agaja. Apologizing for the inconveniences
suffered by the Europeans, Agaja explained that "he was very sorry for what
had happen'd, for he had given Orders to his Captains . . . to use the white
Men well; but he hoped they would excuse what had befallen them, which
was to be attributed to the Fate of War: Confessing, he was much surprized
when he was first informed, so many white People were made Prisoners,
and soon after brought to his Camp. That in the Confusion of Things he
had not regarded them so much as he ought; but for the future, they should
have better Treatment."

The Europeans returned to their forts, where Snelgrave found them in
a miserable and uncertain state. Assessing the situation, Snelgrave decided
there was little hope for conducting business at Ouidah. The *Katherine*

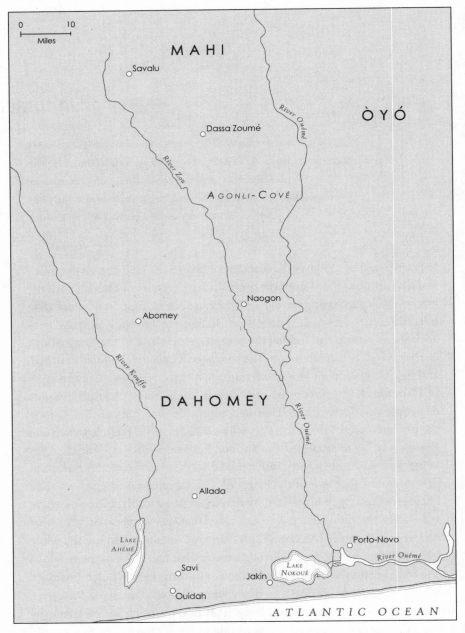

MAP 1.1 Dahomey, Òyó, and Mahi. Map created by the University of Wisconsin Cartography Lab.

lifted anchor and sailed twenty miles down the coast to the port of Jakin, arriving on the morning of April 3. Snelgrave had not conducted business in Jakin before, but he knew its bad reputation. All details of the trading arrangement needed to be established before Snelgrave went ashore since the ruler of Jakin "had formerly plaid base Tricks with some Europeans, who had not taken such a Precaution." In order to secure his interests, Snelgrave sent the ship's surgeon ashore to negotiate the terms of trade. By nightfall, an agreement was reached and Snelgrave retired to a house that would serve as his trading factory.

The following day, on April 4, a royal messenger arrived at Snelgrave's door inviting him to meet with King Agaja at his camp in Allada. Given what he had witnessed at Ouidah, Snelgrave received Agaja's invitation with trepidation. He said that he would consider the proposal and provide a response the following day. Recognizing Snelgrave's unease, the messenger threatened that if he did not go to Allada, "he would highly offend the King" and would "not be permitted to trade, besides other bad Consequences [that] might follow." Four days later Snelgrave abandoned his camp at Jakin and struck out for Allada. Over the course of two days, Snelgrave rode more than forty miles in a hammock carried by a team of twelve servants. Accompanying Snelgrave were the Duke of Jakin and a Dutch captain, also in hammocks, "which is the usual way of travelling in this Country for Gentlemen either white or black." A retinue of 100 slaves attended to the men's needs. As they traveled, Snelgrave again witnessed the carnage of war—the burned-out remains of towns and villages, bones littered across the fields.

Immediately upon arriving in Allada, Snelgrave was greatly perturbed by the numerous flies that swarmed the area. Though he was given several servants to keep the flies away when he was eating, he observed that "it was hardly possible to put a bit of Meat into our Mouths without some of those Vermin with it." The source of these flies was a mystery to Snelgrave until later that afternoon, when, approaching the king's gate, he saw "two large Stages, on which were heaped a great number of dead Men's Heads, that afforded no pleasing sight or smell." Snelgrave's interpreter informed him that these were the heads of 4,000 Huedas who had been sacrificed by the Dahomeans to their "God" as gratitude for their victory at Ouidah. The following evening, Snelgrave witnessed the arrival of yet more prisoners of war, 1,800 "Tuffoes" brought before Agaja to determine their fate. Many were sacrificed in the same manner as the 4,000 Huedas. Others were kept as slaves for Agaja's own use. And still others were reserved for sale to Europeans. In a public ceremony, Agaja's soldiers received 800 cowry shells for each male prisoner of war; for women and children, 400 cowries each. In addition, soldiers received 200 cowries for each enemy head they returned.[1] Snelgrave claimed that some soldiers appeared at the court with "three, or more Heads hanging on a String." Over time, these amounted to thousands of skulls that Agaja collected with "designs to build a Monument with them."

After several days in Allada, Snelgrave met with Agaja and expressed his desire to "fill my ship with Negroes; by which means I should return into my own Country in a short time; where I should make known how great and powerful a King I had seen." Agaja agreed that he would trade, but not before settling on a "Custom," or fee to conduct trade. Snelgrave cleverly argued that because Agaja was a "far greater Prince" than King Huffon of Ouidah, he should not command a fee as high as that which was customary under Hueda rule. Agaja retorted that "as he was a greater Prince, he might reasonably expect the more Custom," but since Snelgrave was the first English captain to arrive after the conquest of Ouidah, he would treat him "as a young Wife or Bride, who must be denied nothing at first." Snelgrave was asked to name his price and eventually requested a fee one-half of that previously charged by Huffon. Moreover, he asked that the king deliver three male slaves for every female and that he be given the right to reject any slaves that he found unfit. Agaja agreed, noting that he "designed to make Trade flourish" and that he would "protect the Europeans that came to his Country." Over the next several months, some 600 slaves were dispatched from Allada to Jakin, until Snelgrave finally filled the *Katherine*'s 300-ton hull. On July 1, 1727, the *Katherine* set sail for Antigua. During the seventeen-week passage, 50 of the enslaved Africans died from disease, dehydration, and malnutrition. The remaining 550 of Agaja's prisoners of war began their new lives as Caribbean slaves, cultivating cane to fulfill England's insatiable desire for sugar.[2]

Dahomey's conquest of Ouidah represents the apex of its military power under Agaja. Its army was the best-trained, best-equipped military in the region, consisting of 10,000 regular troops, as well as various apprentices, servants, and hangers-on. In addition to its victory over Ouidah, it had already conquered Weme (1710s) and Allada (1724). Agaja, who had been military commander under the former king (his brother, Akaba), was proud of his accomplishments in propelling Dahomey to regional dominance. In recounting his military prowess, Agaja told several Europeans that his father and grandfather had fought fewer than a dozen battles combined. His brother had fought only 79 battles. He, on the other hand, had fought more than 200 battles and was still counting.[3]

The victory at Ouidah was particularly gratifying for Agaja, in no small part because it provided Dahomey with direct access to the spoils of European trade. No longer would Dahomey have to accede to the wishes of Hueda middlemen. As Agaja's exchange with Snelgrave illustrates, Dahomey was eager to cultivate good relations with its European counterparts, but consolidation of the victory at Ouidah would prove to be much more difficult than Agaja anticipated. The early promise of easy wealth was thwarted by years of warfare and disruptions in the interior. The exiled Hueda, who fled to the west during the 1727 invasion, continued to contest Dahomean supremacy at Ouidah. More ominous still was the Kingdom of Òyó, the Yoruba-speaking kingdom to the northeast of Dahomey whose mounted cavalry struck fear into even the most hardened Dahomean soldiers. Just one year before Dahomey took Ouidah, Òyó had invaded Dahomey, killed and enslaved large numbers of soldiers, and burned the capital city of Abomey to the ground, forcing Agaja to flee to the bush. Agaja attempted to enter into negotiations with Òyó in 1727, but these negotiations failed. Beginning in 1728 and continuing for three years, Òyó marched on Dahomey every dry season in an attempt to overthrow Agaja. In 1728 and 1729, Òyó troops were thwarted in their attempts to take the Dahomean capital, and they retreated north in order to avoid the floods of the rainy season. By 1730, however, Òyó conquered Abomey, forcing Agaja to transfer his capital to Allada. The Kingdom of Òyó would remain a thorn in Agaja's side for years to come, occupying his attentions in the north even as rivals in the south conspired to cut him out of the trade with Europeans.

The accounts of Europeans in Agaja's court are well known to historians.[4] So too are the contours of the political and military history that propelled Dahomey into a regional power in the first half of the eighteenth century.[5] Less well known are the impacts of warfare and slavery on those who were the victims of Agaja's military aggression. The overwhelming emphasis in European accounts of Dahomean military expansion rests on the savagery of the aggressors: fields scattered with bones, heads on strings, and gruesome scenes of human sacrifice. To be sure, this bloodshed and killing are important for understanding the dynamics of political power in the region, but violence was also critical in shaping the social and cultural identities of people. Peoples displaced by violence often reconstituted themselves in alliance with others in similar circumstances. These exile societies were multilingual, polytheistic, and ethnically heterogeneous. Nevertheless, they usually spoke a common lingua franca, shared religious ideas, and sought common ways to resist the overwhelming power of Dahomey. As such, these new identities born of violence could be grafted onto those identities that were already very much regional in character.

The foundation of this regional culture emerged out of a series of migrations that began around the year 1000 C.E., continuing through the period of Agaja. The result of these overlapping migrations was a confluence of Ewe, Adja, Fon, Gun, and proto-Yoruba into a contiguous cultural area with a broadly shared linguistic structure (Gbe-speaking), shared sense of lineage and history (through the ancestral homeland at Tado, in present-day Togo), and shared religious system (centered on vodun). Geographically, this region was bounded roughly by the Volta River in the west and the Ouémé River in the east, although these boundaries were porous, allowing for the influx of strong Yoruba influences from the east and Islamic influences from the north. The horrific violence of the 1700s is a reminder that we should take care not to confuse cultural similarity with political cohesion. Nevertheless, it seems clear that migration, trade, and warfare had facilitated shared sociocultural affinities among peoples, even if they did not necessarily conceive of themselves as sharing a common "identity." In short, the Gbe-speaking region was, at the same time, culturally similar and politically heterogeneous prior to the arrival of Europeans.[6]

European commerce increased the pace of social and cultural exchange, as the demand for slaves transformed local economic and political configurations. The Portuguese established regular trade in the region in the sixteenth century. By the end of the seventeenth century, the Dutch, English, and French also exchanged goods along the coast. Europeans delivered cowry shells (from the Indian Ocean), iron bars, guns, tobacco, rum, and linen in exchange for gold, small quantities of palm oil and ivory, and thousands of slaves. In the 1690s, roughly 10,000 slaves a year left the Bight of Benin, and by the first decades of the eighteenth century, the trade peaked at more than 18,000 souls exported annually.[7] Overall, an estimated 400,000 Africans departed the Slave Coast between 1700 and 1725, more than from any other region in Africa.[8] Trade on such a massive scale drew attention well beyond the immediate coastline. In the early 1700s, Islamic merchants from the far northern interior purportedly traveled three months on horseback in order to trade slaves at Ouidah and Jakin.[9] By 1715, one French trader stated that between twenty and thirty different African nationalities were sold at Ouidah.[10]

Though Ouidah was the hub for the region's economic expansion and

"A Mahi Village." Lithograph from J. A. Skertchly, *Dahomey as It Is; Being a Narrative of Eight Months' Residence in That Country*... (London: Chapman and Hall, 1874).

the epicenter of cultural exchange, the impacts of these transformations reverberated deep into the interior. Nowhere were these changes felt more than in the region of Agonli-Cové, sixty miles from the coast. Situated halfway between the Yoruba kingdom at Ketu and the Fon at Abomey, Agonli-Cové had long been a cultural crossroads. Not only was it a way station for east-west Fon and Yoruba migrations that had been ongoing for hundreds of years, but its location near the confluence of the Ouémé and Zou Rivers meant that people and goods from as far north as the Niger River tributaries could easily reach the area. During the seventeenth and early eighteenth centuries, the region never fell under the full dominion of either the Yoruba or the Fon kingdom. Indeed, the area from Agonli-Cové north to Dassa and Savé was something of a political no-man's-land. Eighteenth-century observers described the region as a series of "independent states" set "amongst their Mountains and Woods."[11] However, with the rise of Dahomean militarism and empire, these acephalous groups eventually united into a "confederacy" that came to be known as "Mahi."[12]

The word "Mahi" (or "Malli," "Maki," "Maxi") was a Fon term of derision used by the kings of Dahomey to describe all of the inhabitants of the region between Dahomey and Òyó. It can be translated roughly as "those who divide the market" or "those who revolt."[13] The term first appeared in European documents in 1732, coinciding roughly with the Dahomean army's first major assaults on the region.[14] Caught in the middle of the Dahomey-Ọ̀yọ́ disputes of the late 1720s, the diffuse peoples of Mahi found themselves at the geographic center of a protracted war. The loose social and political structures of these peoples made them particularly vulnerable to enslavement. Thus, Mahi was considered "ideal terrain for slave hunting."[15] Though the Mahi retained cultural allegiances to the Gbe-speaking peoples, they, along with the Ọ̀yọ́ and many others on the Slave Coast, feared Dahomey's increasing power and rejected the legitimacy of their conquests of Allada and Ouidah. By 1730, many Mahi, including the peoples of the Agonli-Cové region, entered into an alliance with Ọ̀yọ́. This alliance was, quite possibly, the determining factor in Ọ̀yọ́'s ability to finally take Abomey, forcing Agaja to flee to Allada. In retaliation, Agaja sent his army into Mahi territory in May 1731, and it remained there until March 1732. During these raids, many villages were destroyed. The survivors were enslaved or became refugees, fleeing northward, where they eventually entered into an alliance with the Jagun, a Yoruba dynastic group centered at Yaka. This alliance of exiles became part of the "Mahi confederacy." Thus, "Mahi" was transformed from a term of derision into a marker of mutual protection, an "ethnic" identity born in the fires of war, in resistance to the privations wrought by the army of Dahomey.[16]

The formation of a broad Mahi identity, in common cause against Dahomey, should not distract attention from real and meaningful differences that continued to define peoples like those in Agonli-Cové. The political expediency of collective action did not necessarily translate into full social and cultural transformations. From an ethnographic perspective, the profound disturbances of warfare resulted in "a veritable cocktail of races" in the region.[17] Mahi simply became a broad "meta-ethnic" expression of many smaller units of identity, including Savalus, Iannos, and Agonlis.[18] These local signifiers of identity retained deep sociocultural importance. Even today, when one asks people of Agonli-Cové, "What are you?," they will often answer that they are Agonli rather than Mahi, despite hundreds of years of "official" recognition as Mahi.[19] In the eighteenth century, as Mahi identity was just emerging, these narrower divisions remained all the more salient. In Brazil, eighteenth-century documents describe Africans as Sabaru (Savalu), Agolin (Agonli), and so on.[20] To complicate matters further, some Africans identified themselves primarily by their village of origin. Thus, the layers of identity could run concentrically from natal kin to meta-ethnic signifiers like "Mahi," or even broader still to regions of provenance like the "Costa da Mina." These identities operated like Russian dolls, one inside the other, the utility of each determined by context and circumstance.[21]

IF WARFARE AND forced migrations resulted in the formation of new political identities like "Mahi," these tensions also created circumstances for the transformation of spiritual identities. Until the reign of Agaja, spirituality tended to be mostly localized, with peoples performing devotions to deities in accordance with their own distinct histories and needs. These deities, usually described as "fetishes" by Europeans, were actually voduns. Though the term "vodun" is now widely understood in the Gbe-speaking region to mean "god," voduns are best understood as forces or powers.[22] These powers made themselves known by means of supernatural revelations, indicating, among other things, where a temple or shrine should be established. The power of the vodun could only be invoked in these specially designated local spaces, where devotees called the power to earth in a series of carefully choreographed rituals. These rituals consisted of specific orations, dances, and offerings of food, drink, and goods. Successful invocation resulted in the possession of the devotees by their patron deity. If the vodun was kept happy and sated, it promised wealth, peace, and prosperity to its devotees. But if it was scorned or ignored, it could unleash havoc on communities. Though voduns tended to be localized in the eighteenth century, the most powerful ones drew large numbers of adherents who promoted their spread across the region. Likewise, migration of vodun devotees led to the transfer of shrines to new locales. Origins remained paramount, as devotees continued to recognize that the power of the vodun emanated from the earliest shrines. Thus, while it was understood that voduns had lineages that were place-specific, there was already a proliferation of overlapping voduns across the Gbe-speaking region in the years prior to the rise of Dahomey.

The mythical founders of the Gbe-speaking peoples, Mawu and Lisa, eventually spawned hundreds of voduns as their descendants, but their immediate lineage included those associated with the most basic elements of nature: the sky, the earth, and the sea.[23] In the 1690s, Englishman Willem Bosman observed that some of these were "Publick Deities which are worshipped and prayed to throughout the whole Country."[24] Other notable "fetishes" of the seventeenth and eighteenth centuries included "some lofty high Trees," thunder, and snakes.[25] Devotees of the snake, Dangbe, have drawn the inordinate attention of European observers since the seventeenth century. Local tradition has it that Ouidah adopted the snake as its royal deity at the birth of the kingdom of Hueda.[26] Offerings to Dangbe "commonly comprized of Money, some Pieces of Silk or Stuff, all sorts of European and African Commodities, all sorts of Cattel, and good Eatables and Drinks."[27] In exchange for these offerings, "whenever any Calamity threatens their Country, by imploring the Snake's Assistance, they are always delivered from it." Unfortunately for the Hueda, Dangbe's good fortune ran out in 1727. When Agaja's warriors sacked the kingdom, they found "great numbers" of domesticated snakes in the houses. Seizing the snakes, the soldiers "held them up by the middle, and spoke to them in this manner: *If you are Gods, speak and save your selves*: Which the poor Snakes not being able to do, the *Dahomes* cut their Heads off, ripped them open, broiled them on Coals, and eat them."[28] In this way, the conquests of Dahomey were as much spiritual assaults as they were military conquests.

The brazen rejection of Ouidah's snake vodun was in accordance with the Dahomeans' belief that conquered peoples' deities were inferior. Temporal failures were understood to be directly related to the failures of the gods. Hence, there was little to fear in desecrating the snake, or, for that matter, any other voduns that crossed the path of the Dahomean military machine. The only "true" power in the region was the secular power of the Dahomean army, and its spiritual blessing came directly from the king and his ancestors. Hence, the sacrificial heads of conquered enemies were offered not to the voduns but rather to the deceased royal ancestors of Agaja.[29] Yet the virulence of the soldiers' response to the snakes—talking to them, mocking them, eating them—reveals a deep-seated ambivalence, even fear, that the voduns might seek vengeance against them. Despite a widespread, deeply held belief in the power of the voduns, the Dahomean monarchy suppressed this spiritual world in the interest of military dominance. As long as Dahomean military outcomes remained positive, the forsaking of the voduns was perfectly logical. But when the tides turned against them, as they did after 1727, the very voduns that had been the objects of the soldiers' scorn became the solutions to their problems.

According to myth, there were no voduns in Dahomey until Agaja demanded that they be brought into the kingdom. Until that time, women of Dahomey gave birth to goats, and goats gave birth to humans. In order to alleviate this imbalance in nature, eleven voduns were carried en masse from the Fon heartland in Adja to Abomey. Among these were Hevioso, Gu, Dā, Fa, and Legba. Only upon summoning the voduns and showing them devotion were natural reproductive capacities restored, humans giving birth to humans, goats to goats.[30] Thus, regional history was rewritten, attributing the birth and regeneration of a new people to Agaja's embrace of a pan-Dahomean cast of divinities. Contrary to the myth, the term "vodun" was in wide circulation in the region from as early as 1658, when Capuchin missionaries in Allada equated "vodun" with "god."[31] The myth also distorts the well-known origins and proliferation of some of these voduns through-out the region. For example, Hevioso, the vodun of thunder, originated in the small village of Hevie, halfway between Abomey and Ouidah.[32] It later spread southward to Ouidah, overlapping with worship of the vodun of the sea, before migrating westward into the Adja heartland.[33] Other voduns had originated in Yorubaland before spreading across the region, some even to Abomey.

Taken literally, the myth explains that neglect of the voduns had resulted in an upside-down world of humans bearing goats and goats bearing hu-mans. In reality, however, the myth seems to be a response to a political order that was inverted in topsy-turvy fashion, as the kingdom of Dahomey quickly lost traction against its rivals and pressed to seek new solutions. De-spite inconsistencies, the myth holds one ringing truth: Until the rise of the empire of Dahomey, there was no formal, centralized acknowledgment of the deities diffused throughout the region. Only when Dahomeans began co-opting the local deities of the peoples they conquered did the official pantheon of vodun actually emerge.[34]

After the conquest of Ouidah in 1727, Dahomey suffered a series of ca-lamities. First, it had difficulties subduing the conquered Hueda along the coast. Second, the kingdom of Òyó marched on Abomey from the north-east. Third, Òyó's Mahi allies presented stiff new challenges in the interior. These setbacks were not interpreted as mere happenstance. Indeed, politi-cal challenges intertwined with spiritual ones. This abrupt shift in political fortunes was deemed, quite literally, as much a threat to the survival of the kingdom "as if humans were bearing goats." Reproduction and regeneration were at stake as the nascent empire teetered. In response, Agaja instituted a policy of appropriating the deities of conquered peoples, importing their shrines and priests to Abomey, where they were integrated into the official royal pantheon.[35] On the one hand, this policy served to expand the spiri-tual power of the kingdom, drawing strength from each new vodun brought to the king's court. On the other hand, the new policy served to placate the deities of conquered peoples. It is no small coincidence that the timing of this move came in the aftermath of Agaja's soldiers' dining on the remains of Ouidah's snakes. The fact that Hueda would not be vanquished was testa-ment to the vengeance of one of its most potent spiritual forces.[36] But the real motivation behind this shift in policy was the immediate political threat presented by vodun priests and their devotees. As the case of Hevioso suggests, some of these localized deities transcended their immediate origins, gaining wide followings across the region. As priests gathered more and more followers, they increasingly threatened the political legitimacy of the monarchy at Abomey. Agaja hoped that the policy of assimilation would insure the loyalty of the priests and their growing congregations, but he feared that potential rivals were plotting to overthrow him. In 1732, Snelgrave observed that Agaja had "grown exceedingly cruel towards his People, being always suspicious, that Plots and Conspiracies are carrying on against him."[37] Particularly suspect in these plots were the priests and devotees of Sakpata, the vodun of the earth.

"Sakpata" is a generic term for a larger group of deities associated with the land; however, by the eighteenth century it was understood primarily to be the vodun of smallpox. European traders recognized smallpox in the Bight of Benin as early as the first half of the seventeenth century.[38] Some scholars have assumed that Europeans introduced the disease into the region, but this seems unlikely since smallpox emerged in North Africa as early as 10,000 B.C., spreading along trade routes east to India and south to sub-Saharan Africa.[39] Dahomean history also seems to confirm that the origins of the disease were in the interior since the major centers for Sakpata devotion lie north and east of Abomey. Regardless of its origins, it is clear that by the early eighteenth century, the disease had devastating impacts on Dahomey. Snelgrave noted that Agaja himself was "pitted with the Small Pox."[40] According to oral tradition, shortly after Agaja came to power in 1716, Dahomean warriors moved against Hondji, southwest of Abomey. There, the soldiers were decimated by smallpox, the mortality from the disease being greater than that caused by their enemies. In response, Agaja sent envoys to the major shrine of Sakpata in Mahi, where they collected the knowledge necessary to establish a Sakpata shrine at Abomey.[41] Despite this tentative embrace of the vodun, the relationship between the monarchy and Sakpata remained strained. Outbreaks of smallpox in the region were noted in thirteen different years between 1708 and 1734. During years of epidemic, nearly half of the population could become infected, resulting in population declines that approached 10 percent a year.[42] Compounding the losses from disease, periodic famines also killed "many thousands" in the region.[43] Agaja possessed one of the most feared armies in the world, but he was powerless against the forces of the earth vodun, which could give or take life at its own caprice.

The only mortals capable of intervening under such dire circumstances were Sakpata priests. Individuals afflicted with smallpox went to the priests in search of ways to placate the angry god. The priests prescribed offerings to the vodun, medicines for the sick, and so on. When people died from the disease, the priests were the only ones to handle the bodies, and they were responsible for arranging proper ritual burials. For those who escaped ghastly death from the pox, the priests prepared feasts of ritual thanks at which the survivors swore their devotion to the vodun. The healing skills of the priests attracted people from across the region, especially those who were forcibly exiled by warfare, permanently or temporarily alienated from their homelands. As congregations swelled, Sakpata priests gained tremendous political power. New adherents included not only commoners but also local chiefs and elders, whose affiliation with Sakpata undoubtedly shaped their political outlooks.[44] Logic demanded that Agaja's reign of terror not be disentangled from the simultaneous terrors wrought by smallpox, famine, and dislocation. Sakpata unleashed its wrath as punishment for the evils and injustices of Dahomean militarism. Disease, hunger, and exile were mere symptoms of a much broader calamity. One way of appeasing the vodun was for people to join forces in opposition to the Dahomean army. Balance could be restored to the land by defeating the imperial usurpers and restoring rightful chiefs to their kingdoms. In this way, Sakpata represented a potential cure, not only to immediate maladies like smallpox but also to larger ones like the imperial ambitions of Dahomey.

Agaja responded to the challenges of Sakpata in the most practical way he could, given the untenable circumstances. The king might have preferred to eradicate all worship of Sakpata, killing the priests and destroying their shrines. But this would have risked a much broader political uprising among Sakpata devotees. Moreover, Agaja probably genuinely feared the ire of the vodun, which had already demonstrated its ability to punish him on more than one occasion. Still, the temporal challenges of the Sakpata priests were intolerable. Their political power was matched by growing economic power. As payment for their services, the priests collected many of the offerings made at the shrines. This practice was noted by Europeans as early as the late seventeenth century, when Bosman observed that "these Roguish Priests sweep all the mentioned Offerings to themselves, and doubtless make themselves very Merry with them."[45] The priests also claimed the possessions of the deceased. As a result of these collections, a French trader observed that vodun priests were "nearly all rich and chiefs of villages."[46] Hence, the challenge of Sakpata was thoroughgoing—political, social, cultural, and economic. Indeed, for many in the region, Sakpata appeared to be the only true "king of the earth." As Melville Herskovits put it, "The King of Dahomey could brook no competitor, not even 'the King of the Earth,' and hence the King of the Earth must be banished."[47] Since Agaja could not kill the Sakpata priests, he decided to neutralize them by selling them into the Atlantic slave trade.

BY THE TIME OF Dahomey's conquest of Ouidah in 1727, the young man who years later would become Domingos Álvares was around eighteen years old and had already completed a series of initiations that marked him as an adult. As an adolescent, he endured a rite of passage in which he had "one tooth filed on the top part of the jaw, and in correspondence on the bottom part he has two that are so far apart that he seems to be lacking one tooth." There is no contemporary evidence that the peoples from central or northern Benin filed their teeth during the eighteenth century. Modern anthropological evidence, however, suggests that dental modification was common among adolescents in Dahomey in the 1930s. Boys between the ages of twelve and fifteen subjected themselves to tooth removal and tooth filing mostly for aesthetic reasons, although for men who had not submitted to this ritual, it was said that "his oxen have horns that are not separated."[48] Domingos was also marked with piercings in both ears and on the left side of his nose. As early as the seventeenth century, Jesuit priest Alonso de Sandoval noted that the only physical sign of "Lecumies barbas" was the piercing on the left side of their nose.[49] More strikingly, in 1793, English slave trader Archibald Dalzel wrote that among the "Mahees . . . some bore the ears, others the nose, thrusting a bead or a cowrie into the aperture."[50] Finally, like all young men in the region, Domingos would have submitted to ritual circumcision. In 1705, Bosman noted that male circumcision was "customary" in the region.[51] Likewise, Dalzel observed that the operation was "universally practiced" on young men, "whose caresses are not admitted of by the females till they have undergone this amputation."[52]

Domingos carried the physical markers of his African youth with him for the rest of his life, but he was just as deeply marked by his lived experiences in Agonli-Cové. Years later, he would recall that "his parents are already dead, and they were called in the language of his land, the father Afnage and the mother, Oconon."[53] Each of these names suggests strong linkages to the world of vodun. Afnage is likely some variation of the group of voduns associated with Sakpata. According to Herskovits, "nenge" is a surname for Dada Zodji, the original Sakpata deity.[54] In a list of names of the various descendant qualities or manifestations of Sakpata from the 1930s, he noted that Avimadye was the chief of the pantheon (*dokpwégâ*), concerning himself mostly with the dead.[55] The name "Avimanje" literally means "no tears must fall," reflecting Sakpata's reputation for inflicting death with impunity, particularly on those who neglect him. When Sakpata takes a life, however capricious the death may seem, nobody should grieve for the victim. Thus, Avimanje represents one of the strongest and enduring manifestations of Sakpata.[56] Even today, one of the most well-known Sakpata priests in Benin is named Avimandje-Non.[57] Moreover, the vodun Avimanje continues to be worshipped in the Jeje temples of Afro-Brazilian Candomblés in Bahia and Rio de Janeiro.[58] That Domingos remembered his father by the name of this powerful Sakpata quality was not unusual. During the initiation process, devotees "died" a ritual death and were resurrected as the embodiment of the vodun, taking on their language, traits, and even name.[59]

Domingos' mother's name, "Oconon," means "possessor/mother of the land" in the Fon-Gbe language.[60] Her partnership with Afnage reinforces the notion that each was a servant of Sakpata, the "king of the land." Together, they no doubt formed a potent spiritual alliance. "Oconon" is also closely related to "Bokonon," which means "diviner" in the Fon language.[61] Like the priests of Sakpata, diviners were under immense scrutiny during the reign of Agaja. According to oral history, Agaja hated and feared the traditional Fon system of divination with *gbo* (empowerment objects) because "it permitted too many alliances against him." As a result, he replaced the *gbo* diviners with diviners of Fá, a Yoruba system that involved the casting of sixteen cowries or palm nuts in order to "read" someone's fate.[62] It seems likely that Domingos' parents were practitioners of this proscribed form of divination with *gbo*. In fact, given their esoteric knowledge of the earth, the voduns of Sakpata were said to possess "so many *gbo* that a person cannot call the names of them all." By virtue of their direct communications with the vodun, Sakpata priests were among the most prolific manufacturers of *gbo*.[63] This linking of Sakpata priests to *gbo* production only highlights the marginality of the earth voduns under the reign of Agaja. Though the Dahomean myth reveals nothing of what happened to the diviners of *gbo*, we can surmise that they were subject to expulsion, in much the same fashion as occurred with the priests of Sakpata.[64]

Taken together, the names of Domingos' parents suggest important roles in the leadership of a Sakpata congregation. Most tellingly, "Afnage" (or its variations) stands at the head of the Sakpata pantheon and is most often represented in a position of leadership in ritual settings. His marriage to "Oconon" reflects the normal pattern of shared male/female leadership in the healing communities of the Gbe-speaking region.[65] In short, Domingos' parents were more than simple devotees of the vodun; they quite likely were priests (vodunon). If so, Domingos stood to inherit his parents' role as a spiritual leader, the position of vodunon being tied to lineage.[66] The responsibilities of the vodunon were considerable. As the "possessor of the vodun," the priest embodied the vodun as the living link to the spirit world. The vodun "chose" the priest (or one of his earlier direct ancestors) by means of supernatural revelations, indicating how and where to establish the original altar to invoke the vodun. The priest passed this knowledge on to devotees, whose worship and offerings propitiated the vodun, but it was always the priest who orchestrated ritual and provided ultimate authority on the esoteric knowledge necessary to satisfy the vodun and bring harmony to the community.

The content of Domingos' spiritual training is mostly unknowable, but the context is not. Under the best of circumstances, much of the vodunon training was esoteric and hidden from view. Apprentices learned an array of chants, orations, myths, rhythms, dietary restrictions, and medicines that were peculiar to their deity. Devotees of Sakpata even learned an arcane form of Yoruba as their primary ritual language.[67] But the social ruptures of the eighteenth century must have thrown "normal" practices into disarray. We can imagine that in early childhood Domingos was able to absorb much of the knowledge that was at the core of his parents' belief system. This was a time of relative peace in Agonli-Cové. Domingos would have been raised around the shrine and among the congregants of Sakpata, with the knowledge that he would one day succeed his father as the congregation's spiritual leader. After 1727, however, sea changes in the social and political terrain radically transformed the role of the priesthood. Refugees, exiles, the starving, and the diseased swelled membership of Sakpata congregations. Political pressures mounted as Agaja began to proscribe the vodun and its adherents. The gravity of these social and political power struggles with Dahomey could not have been lost on Domingos. Since he later claimed that his parents were "already dead," we can assume that he witnessed their passing. Their deaths only heightened his awareness of the sociopolitical tensions, hastening his graduation into the ranks of the priesthood and thrusting him into the role of community leader. Exactly how and when he took the mantle of vodunon is unclear. What seems likely, though, is that by the time Òyó and Dahomey began their warfare in 1728, Domingos Álvares was already a powerful spiritual and political leader, one of those Sakpata priests and manufacturers of *gbo* who was a prime target for enslavement by Agaja and the army of Dahomey.

IN THE IMMEDIATE YEARS leading up to Domingos Álvares' enslavement, Agonli-Cové and the other parts of the region that would later come to be known as Mahi were undergoing rapid transformations. In 1730, William Snelgrave described the condition of the Dahomean interior, beginning with a reference to Agaja: "He is only a great King in name for want of Subjects, by reason of his having destroyed in so cruel a manner the Inhabitants of all the Places he has conquered. This has obliged many hundred thousands to fly from his Arms, into foreign Countries; that are by Situation secured from his rambling Bands, either by great Rivers, Mountains or Lakes."[68] Those taking flight sought safety, food, and shelter; they also found a spiritual refuge. In the "Rivers, Mountains or Lakes" northeast of Dahomey, communities grew around leaders who promised delivery from the maladies that plagued the land. These communities welcomed people who spoke different languages, who privileged worship of some deities over others, and who even declared themselves members of other kingdoms like Hueda, Allada, and so on. Yet the peoples of these "new" emerging communities shared two important traits in common. First, despite their cultural differences, there were overarching similarities that allowed for mutual understandings and integration. We have already seen how religious ideas overlapped, a process that was only quickened by forced migration. The same can be said of language. By the late eighteenth century, the *"lingua geral*, or general tongue, . . . [was] spoken not only in Dahomy-proper, but in Ouidah, and the other dependent states; and likewise in Mahee, and several neighbouring provinces."[69] This commonly spoken language was crucial in the realization of these new communities, facilitating a range of new, shared ideas, cobbled together from old, diverse ones.

The second trait shared by these exiles is more obvious—the disdain, even hatred, of Dahomean banditry. This social and political ill encompassed an array of other ailments—diseases, hunger, and so on—that found redress in the worship of Sakpata. As these religious communities surged in power in the late 1720s, Dahomey could not ignore the social, political, and spiritual threats that emanated from them. When Agaja sent his army into "Mahi" in 1731 and 1732, thousands of formerly exiled peoples were once again set in motion, along with new refugees. Many were killed, some escaped to the north, and still others were enslaved. Though few of the enslaved men and women could have been prepared for the deep sense of alienation that would follow them to the coast, through the Middle Passage, and on to the Americas, those who had already endured forced exile had some distinct advantages over those who had not. The lessons of constructing new identities out of the ashes of the old were only the beginning. A religious leader like Domingos Álvares had a clear sense of where he was from (Naogon) and where his core beliefs originated (his "kinsmen"), but he was also imminently cognizant of the plurality of social, cultural, and political ideas that made communities like his possible. The glue that ultimately held together these "new" communities of exiles and refugees was the belief that healing was the most viable means of addressing the misuse of power. That this belief had wide-ranging political implications was one possible outcome of successful healing, but it was not necessarily the primary focus. Rather, the ultimate goals were balance, reciprocity, and community stability.

When Domingos Álvares was enslaved, sometime between 1728 and 1732, his healing techniques were already proven in addressing the illegitimacy of one of the most powerful armies in the world. Nothing about his enslavement would have challenged his belief in the power of vodun. Indeed, his enslavement was a direct consequence of that power, an admission on the part of Dahomey that Sakpata priests "knew too much magic." They were sold away because "they made too much trouble."[70] Thus, unlike many other enslaved Africans, Domingos Álvares entered slavery from a position of relative power, cast out because he represented a potent spiritual and political threat. Though it would be foolish to assume that he was content with his fate, it seems safe to conclude that Domingos met his enslavement with measured resignation. Dahomey set him in motion toward an unknown fate, but as was proven in Naogon and across Mahi, exile was not the equivalent of social death. He was multilingual, polytheistic, and flexible in his understandings of kinship. These skills would serve him well wherever he went. Domingos was also, quite probably, the "possessor of the vodun," a stature that compelled him to address abuses of power through communities of healing. He would settle elsewhere and establish a new community, confident in the conviction that if Sakpata could deliver people from the ailments of Dahomey, it would certainly deliver them from whatever maladies might lay ahead.

2

Passages

> Oh, ancestors, do all in your power that princes and nobles who today rule
> never be sent away from here as slaves to Ame'íkâ [America]. . . . We pray you to do
> all in your power to punish the people who bought our kinsmen, whom we shall
> never see again. Send their vessels to Ouidah harbor. When they come, drown
> their crews, and make all the wealth of their ships come back to Dahomey.
> —Prayer recited during the sacrifice of a goat to the spirits of
> unknown ancestors, Dahomey, 1930s, quoted in Melville J.
> Herskovits, *Dahomey: An Ancient West African Kingdom*

After his capture and enslavement in the interior of Benin, traders pushed
and prodded Domingos Álvares toward the coast along with other convicts,
outcasts, and prisoners of war. At the outset of the journey, Domingos probably knew some of his fellow captives. If this was the case, we can imagine
that he retained his leadership role, offering words of hope and encouragement to his comrades. While still on familiar terrain, they might have enter-
tained thoughts of escape or rescue by friends and family, but these hopes
faded quickly as they trekked away from their home environments. Hands
bound from behind, tied one to the other, the newly enslaved marched over
land for much of the journey. Given their proximity to the Ouémé and Zou
Rivers, it is likely that they spent some portion of the journey in canoes,
coursing southward toward Lake Nokoué, the lagoon basin leading to the
port at Jakin. Traveling by canoe would have been a relief from the misery
of walking in chains, prodded and beaten by their Dahomean captors. Since
famine was widespread in the region, the enslaved were fed precious little.
Exhaustion and hunger left the captives vulnerable to disease. Some also
bore the wounds of battle. Assuming their passage to the coast was unob-
structed, the sixty-mile journey would have lasted around a week. For those
who survived the trek, recent memories of death, destruction, and loved
ones left behind must have taken a steep psychological toll.

Upon their arrival at Jakin, Domingos and the other enslaved captives
were held in warehouses owned by the local chief. There, they awaited

European merchants who would inspect them, negotiate a price, and eventually dispatch them to the Americas. Before the Europeans could begin trading, however, the ruler of Jakin required that they agree to a "customs" payment. This payment was divided into two parts, one that went directly to the Jakin chief and another that was passed on to Agaja in recognition of Jakin's tributary status with Dahomey. The right to trade did not come cheap. In 1731, for example, the captain of the French slave ship *Diligent* paid the ruler of Jakin two lengths of silk, one barrel of flour, one barrel of wine, and the value of eight slaves. In addition, the French captain agreed to pay King Agaja his customary duty, the equivalent value of ten slaves.[1]

The customs negotiations completed, the ruler of Jakin invited the Europeans to his warehouses to begin their trade. Armed guards stood watch over Domingos and his fellow captives, who were still bound and stripped naked for inspection. The arrival of white men at the warehouse must have shocked and terrified many of the captives. Though most had never before seen Europeans, they knew them from their chilling reputations as bloodthirsty cannibals. The Mahi and the Òyó would have been especially frightened since "those in-land *Negroes* which come from the Country beyond *Ardra* [Allada] . . . imagine, that [Europeans] buy them and carry them off only in order to eat them."[2] The warehouse guards did nothing to dampen these rumors, taunting the captives with threats that the white men would soon arrive to buy them and eat them.[3]

However fanciful and cruel the cannibal stories, they contained some crucial elements of truth: European traders greedily consumed the bodies of enslaved Africans in exchange for a variety of merchandise. In parts of West Central Africa, it was believed that European trade goods were literally manufactured from the body parts of captives taken away in slave ships—wine was blood, cheese was brain, gunpowder was crushed bone, and so on. Contemporary memories of the slave trade in the Bight of Benin are no less evocative. There, oral tradition recalls that the corpses of slaves were floated out into the Atlantic Ocean in order to serve as bait for collecting cowry shells. Live cowries attached themselves to the cadavers in order to feed on them. After some time, the decomposing bodies were reeled in to the beach and left to sit in the open air until the cowries died. The cowry shells were then collected from the corpses and circulated as currency.[4] Even though the oral tradition is apocryphal, it accurately reflects the social, economic, and corporeal realities of Africans caught up in the slave trade. African bodies were systematically depleted, "eaten" away by their

European captors and transformed into all varieties of food, money, clothing, and other commodities.

The prepurchase inspection process only amplified the worst fears of those enslaved Africans who believed the Europeans intended to eat them. Normally, the ship's surgeon assessed the physical condition of the captives, examining their eyes, ears, noses, mouths, and genitals. Through interpreters, the doctor asked the Africans to prove a full range of motion in all of their members by waving their arms, bending their knees, running, jumping, and so on. Once the surgeon completed his examination, the merchants took over—poking, prodding, searching for defects. European traders preferred young males and, more often than not, got their way, departing with cargoes that, on average, contained two males for every female. Portuguese traders were particularly insistent that their slaves be adolescent males. Indeed, they believed that "children ten to fifteen years old" were "the best captives." In the absence of accurate birth dates, the Portuguese estimated the age of male slaves by examining their beards. Any young man not yet showing evidence of facial hair—judged by the Europeans to occur around the age of twenty-four in Africans—was placed in the preferred category.[5] In response to these preferences, African merchants tried to mask any evidence of facial hair by closely shaving the beards of their male captives. After shaving them, they rubbed the men's faces with a pumice stone until "the skin is plain and soft as if it never had hair." Despite these extreme measures, Portuguese merchants were not easily fooled. As part of their inspection, the Portuguese sometimes ran their tongues across the faces of the enslaved, searching for even the faintest signs of stubble.[6] This practice was not solely for determining age; traders also believed they could discover illness or disease by the taste of the captives' sweat. Domingos Álvares and his male compatriots were likely subjects of this treatment by Portuguese traders. For those who imagined they were destined to sate the appetites of white cannibals, the poking, prodding, and tasting of their skin only would have deepened their sense of foreboding.

Once the sorting was complete and the slaves chosen, the bargaining began. Trade was conducted according to a gold standard, but all manner of goods were traded in exchange for slaves—spirits, guns, cowries, cloth, sugar, and tobacco. Portuguese merchants had a distinct advantage since most of them sailed to Africa directly from Brazil, where they could acquire trade goods not usually carried by their European competitors. Sweet, second-rate tobacco, unsuitable for the European market, was the most frequently traded consumer item carried by Portuguese merchants to the

"Slave Market." *Top*: A slave trader examines a man before purchasing him. The accompanying description reads: "An Englishman licking a Negro's chin to be sure of his age and to determine by the taste of his sweat if he is sick." *Bottom*: Newly purchased slaves are rowed out to the waiting ship. Meanwhile, the "Negroes on shore . . . wail and scream on seeing their relatives and friends embark." Lithograph from M. Chambon, *Le guide du commerce de l'Amérique principalement par le port de Marseille* (Avignon: J. Mossy, 1777), vol. 2, pl. XI. Courtesy Wisconsin Historical Society Library, image number WHi-74285.

Bight of Benin. Portuguese traders also smuggled significant amounts of gold dust into the region. Until the conquest of Ouidah, the Portuguese tended to trade most of this gold with other Europeans, but after 1727, Agaja expressed a strong preference for gold in exchange for slaves.[7] With their virtual monopoly on tobacco and gold, the Portuguese became the preferred clients of African merchants and the envy of their European competitors. In 1728, the director of the English fort at Ouidah complained that Agaja "sends for the Portuguese Captains and sells all the fine slaves for gold . . . and what they won't buy for gold, these he sends down here to dispose of for goods, by which means he engrosses all the gold into his own hands."[8] Leveraging their market advantage, Portuguese traders demanded only the highest-quality captives, so much so that prime, young males like Domingos Álvares came to be known simply as "Portuguese slaves" or "gold slaves."[9]

In the late 1720s and early 1730s, "Portuguese slaves" were valued at between six and seven ounces of gold.[10] Portuguese merchants no doubt purchased Domingos Álvares for that amount or its equivalent in tobacco. After being transferred to the possession of the Europeans, Domingos' flesh would have been seared with a hot branding iron, either on his shoulder or on his chest, a mark identifying him as the property of his new owners. Along with other men, women, and children, he would have then been herded into another warehouse to await shipment. The duration of their stay in the warehouse depended largely on the volume of slaves brought to the coast. European traders usually waited until the warehouse was nearly full before transporting individuals to the waiting ships since food and water were more easily accessible on shore. This process of purchasing slaves, filling the warehouse, and transferring slaves to awaiting ships could take two to three months, even under ideal circumstances. If there was an interruption in the interior trade, it could take many more months, even a year, to fill a ship.

Between 1727 and 1732, Europeans complained bitterly about the state of affairs in the Bight of Benin. The old trade structures at Ouidah were "almost ruined," and continuous warfare in the interior interrupted established commercial routes, choking the flow of slaves down to the coast. While Agaja held a monopoly over the slave trade, he refused to serve as a middleman, as the Hueda had done previously. In 1730, the viceroy of Brazil charged that Dahomey "impedes the passage of slaves and robs the negros that go to the interior to buy them."[11] In the same year, Snelgrave observed that Agaja "drives no regular trade in slaves, but only sells such as he takes in his wars."[12] As long as Dahomey produced large numbers of war captives, Europeans were content. But when Dahomey's military fortunes dimmed, trade slowed significantly and Europeans became impatient. The protests began as early as 1728, when Portuguese traders complained that slave ships were delayed on the coast while waiting to fill their holds. During this time, "eight to nine ships . . . waited a very long time, some for almost a year, others for eight, nine, and ten months," before they could depart for Brazil.[13]

Maintaining the enslaved on the coast for extended periods presented serious health risks for the Africans. The close quarters of their captivity, combined with the squalid conditions of the warehouses, created a ripe environment for contagious diseases. In 1728, the director of the English fort at Ouidah feared "the risk of mortality occasioned by the smallpox, flux, fevers and other distempers incident in this part of the country."[14] European surgeons tended to these ailments the best they could, using purgatives and bleedings, but the doctors often encountered resistance from their African captives, who preferred their own methods of healing. In 1738, a Dutch factor reported that "when slaves get holes in their legs, either as a result of disease or worms or accidents, they recover much more quickly by taking the medicines of their own land than by being compelled against their will to take European medicine."[15]

Long delays also resulted in shortages of food onboard the waiting ships. Portuguese slave traders normally carried adequate provisions to sustain their crews and human cargoes for the entirety of the six-to-seven-month round-trip journey from Brazil to Benin. Lengthy layovers on the African coast forced them to stop in the islands of São Tomé and Principe for food and water. In 1728, for example, seven of ten ships arriving in Pernambuco from the Mina Coast had to lay over in São Tomé.[16] These problems persisted in years that followed. In 1730, the frustrated viceroy of Brazil wrote to his superiors in Lisbon, concluding that the trade on the Mina Coast was "lost." Furthermore, "the ships survive only by taking many fewer slaves than their holds can carry and their voyages have lasted one year and some 15 to 16 months, because of the difficult means of gathering slaves . . . it being necessary that they then stop in the islands of Principe and Sam Thomê in order to restore their provisions."[17]

Despite numerous complaints about the "ruinous" state of trade at the Benin ports, European ships continued to travel there by the dozens. In June 1730, fourteen ships traded in the region, half of them Portuguese — five at Jakin and two at Ouidah. The following June, fifteen European ships arrived at the coast, nine of them Portuguese—six at Jakin and three at Ouidah.[18] Though traders may have encountered some inconveniences in gathering slaves, there is no indication that the overall numbers of Africans departing Benin decreased in any significant way. Still, the long delays on the coast must have had their impacts on the enslaved. Not only was their physical health threatened, but idle time and solitude no doubt weighed heavily on their mental health.

Some of the enslaved probably found the isolation and uprooting from family to be unbearably traumatic. In stable societies of the Gbe-speaking region, an individual's social identity was defined largely by his or her place among family and kin. Wealth, power, and prestige were measured primarily in people, not land or money. Thus, a premium was placed on enlarging the kinship unit—through polygynous marriages, childbirth, adoption, and even the enslavement of outsiders. Together, these extended families built dwellings, tended cattle, harvested crops, engaged in trade, cooked, raised children, and protected the community in times of war. Reciprocal responsibilities meant that individuality was not only frowned upon but dangerous. Crimes committed by individuals were attributed to the kin group; individual economic debts were the responsibility of the group; and so on. When breaches in the code of conduct occurred, the community decided collectively on a proper course of action, always with the aim of restoring balance and cohesiveness to the clan. In short, a person was a person only insofar as he or she was a member of a kinship group, and the kin group was defined by the number and quality of people in its ranks.

As many scholars have observed, to be alienated from the collective wealth, power, and protection of the natal lineage group was tantamount to social death, a virtual erasure of one's personhood.[19] Although this alienation was no doubt deeply felt by many enslaved Africans, we must take care not to romanticize or homogenize African forms of kinship, particularly in war-torn regions like Dahomey. For example, we know that violence and instability characterized much of the Gbe-speaking region during the 1720s and 1730s, constantly threatening networks of natal kin. Moreover, as suggested in the previous chapter, ideologies of lineage could also be built around healing communities. Domingos Álvares' parents were already dead, and he likely presided over a congregation, many of whom were similarly alienated from their natal lineages and homelands. Under these trying circumstances, new communities mimicked patterns of reciprocity that characterized natal kinship units. These attempts to restore some sense of normalcy and stability were only natural.[20]

To be sure, there were steep psychic costs to such re-creations. Blood ties could never be fully replaced, and neither could lost friends. Nevertheless, as they sat in the fetid conditions of the warehouse, and later aboard ship during the Middle Passage, Domingos Álvares and other enslaved Africans went about the process of resurrecting their social selves. They inquired about one another's homelands, families, spiritual beliefs, and conditions of original enslavement in the interior. By sharing the individual stories of their collective suffering, new bonds emerged. Friendships formed and families were made in the bowels of slave ships. Some of these relationships survived for years, even in the Americas. Others died more quickly, as the enslaved were scattered beyond the range of effective and sustainable communication. It is impossible to know exactly where Domingos Álvares fit in the matrix of this emerging, new social order. We can imagine that some were drawn to his spiritual power and charisma, while others were just as likely repelled by his powers. As long as they were still on African soil, the social and political specter of Agaja loomed, and if Agaja had reason to fear Sakpata, others did too. Only when they moved away from the coast and toward their new lives as slaves would social and political imperatives shift more decisively.

DEPARTING THE WAREHOUSE at Jakin, Domingos Álvares again marched in chains, three miles over land, forging several streams that ran parallel to the coast, before finally reaching the Atlantic Ocean. The sight of the sea was probably yet one more new and frightful source of anxiety for Domingos. Most interior peoples had never before laid eyes on the ocean. Indeed, some of the enslaved Òyó who accompanied Domingos might have feared dying at their first glimpse of the ocean's vastness. In 1727, Snelgrave reported that the "national Fetiche" of Òyó was the sea, and the Òyó "were prohibited by their Priests from ever seeing it, under no less a Penalty than Death; which they made the People believe, would by their God, if they were so presumptuous, be inflicted on them."[21] Domingos probably did not share this belief; however, the turbulence of the surf and the prospect of crossing through the waves to the awaiting slave ship must have at least given him pause. All along the coast, sandbars created enormous breaks in the surf. Waves six to eight feet tall were not uncommon. Even Europeans who were experienced with the sea described the so-called Slave Coast as "seething like a boiling cauldron."[22] At Jakin, two sandbars created a surf of three waves, each wave larger than the previous one.[23] Shackled in twos in order to prevent them from jumping overboard, the enslaved were loaded onto canoes piloted by

"A Capsize off Whydah." The violence of the surf along the Slave Coast frightened slaves and traders alike. Lithograph from J. A. Skertchly, *Dahomey as It Is; Being a Narrative of Eight Months' Residence in That Country . . .* (London: Chapman and Hall, 1874).

expert African oarsmen. The boat's crew timed their departure in accordance with the waves, attacking the smaller ones at their crest, rising into the air, and crashing down before quickly rowing to the next swell. In this way, they avoided the fury of the largest waves, which could easily capsize the canoes, sending the human cargo to a watery grave at the bottom of the sea. After clearing the surf, the oarsmen paddled the canoe to the waiting slave ship, anchored less than a hundred yards from the shore. There, the captives were off-loaded and introduced to the crowded, cramped hold of the slave ship that would be their home for months to follow.

The horrors of the slave ship have been well chronicled in scholarly works, slave narratives, and even film.[24] However, none of these mediums can fully capture the extent and duration of suffering. For the healthy, the Middle Passage was an extreme test of physical and mental endurance. For those already ill or weak, it was often a death sentence. Under optimal conditions, early eighteenth-century Portuguese slave ships made the crossing from the Mina Coast to Pernambuco in a month's time. Relative to French and English ships, which commonly required four months to reach the Caribbean, the journey to northeastern Brazil was a mere hop.[25] Yet conditions were still abysmal. In 1793, a Portuguese doctor described the environment:

> Shackled in the holds of ships, the black slaves . . . are far more deprived than when on land. First of all, with two or three hundred slaves placed under the deck, there is hardly room enough to draw a breath. No air can reach them, except through the hatch gratings and through some square skylights so tiny that not even a head can pass through them. . . . Second, the slaves are afflicted with a very short ration of water, of poor quality and lukewarm because of the climate— hardly enough to water their mouths. The suffering that this causes is extraordinary, and their dryness and thirst cause epidemics which, beginning with one person, soon spread to many others. Thus, after only a few days at sea, they start to throw the slaves into the ocean. Third, they are kept in a state of constant hunger. Their small ration of food, brought over from Brazil on the outward voyage, is spoiled and damaged, and consists of nothing more than beans, corn, and manioc flour, all badly prepared and unspiced.[26]

Ships departed the Mina Coast, heading south-southeast, opposite their desired destination of Brazil. The reason for this apparent diversion was the warm-water Guinea Current, a strong oceanic freeway, some 300 miles wide, that flowed east-southeast along the African shoreline. Escaping the current quickly was of paramount importance. Ships usually waited for the current to ease or for westbound storms to neutralize its worst effects before departing the Mina Coast.[27] Otherwise, the current could easily drag ships hundreds of miles south toward the Central African coast. In 1733 and 1734, Portuguese captain José da Costa Ferreira sailed his corsair into the teeth of the current, tacking for five months between the island of Fernando Po (present-day Bioko Island) and the African coast. Unable to break free of the tidal pull and running short of provisions, he finally admitted defeat and deposited his cargo of 700 starving, dehydrated slaves on African soil before returning to Bahia with an empty ship.[28] Ships that successfully wrested themselves from the current usually arrived in proximity of the São Tomé islands within two weeks of their departure from the Mina Coast.[29] Those that needed provisions or convalescence for the ill laid over in the islands. Others bypassed the islands and turned directly for Brazil.

Given the paucity of information on eighteenth-century Portuguese slaving voyages, there is no way of re-creating Domingos Álvares' Middle

TABLE 2.1 Age and Sex of African Slaves Who Arrived in Rio de Janeiro from Ouidah Aboard the *Nossa Senhora da Thalaia e Santo Antônio*, 1715

Age	Male	Female	Total
Under 8 years	6	6	12
8–14	8	1	9
15–24	19	19	38
25–35	34	15	49
Older than 35	2	2	4
Total	69	43	112

Source: Luis Lisanti Filho, ed., *Negócios coloniais: uma correspondência do século XVIII* (Brasília: Ministério da Fazenda, 1973), 2:50–52, 170–84.

Passage experiences with any specificity. Nevertheless, the details of one slaving journey from Ouidah to Rio de Janeiro in 1714–15 (see table 2.1) are illustrative of broader trends, providing us a glimpse of the possible conditions endured by Domingos Álvares and his fellow captives. In September 1714, Lisbon merchant Francisco Pinheiro outfitted the three-masted *galera Nossa Senhora da Thalaia e Santo Antônio* for a slaving venture aimed at collecting 400 Africans on the Costa da Mina. The ship departed Lisbon on September 19. The ship's captain, Jozeph Vieira Marques, opened trading in Ouidah on December 10, exchanging cloth and iron bars for five slaves. As the days passed, he expanded his trade to include gold dust, cowry shells, and rum (*aguardente*), but slaves arrived at the coast only in twos and threes. As a result, Marques had difficulty filling the ship's hold. After a month, only eighty-eight Africans had been purchased for Pinheiro, a pace that slowed even more dramatically in the weeks that followed. Between January 10 and February 1, Marques purchased only twenty-eight slaves for the ship's owner. Then, on the afternoon of February 1, a bolt of lightning struck the ship, splitting the forward mast and killing the boatswain. The mast was repaired, but the ship ultimately departed Ouidah with only 173 Africans onboard—116 on Pinheiro's account and 57 belonging to other merchants and crew members of the ship. This shortfall in the desired number of slaves meant that the captives did not have to endure the "tight packing" that might have otherwise been their fate. Still, they suffered much of the same discomfort and humiliation experienced by others enslaved on the Mina Coast. For example, all of Pinheiro's 116 slaves had the letters "FP" (for "Francisco Pinheiro") seared onto their right breasts. The ship finally pulled out of Ouidah on February 8, 1715, arriving in the islands of São Tomé on February 26, where the crew collected provisions. After an eight-day layover, the ship sailed for Rio de Janeiro, a journey that lasted thirty-nine days. Altogether, from the time the ship departed Ouidah until the time it arrived in Rio, sixty-five days passed. During this time, smallpox and ophthalmia plagued captives and crew. Of Pinheiro's 116 slaves, 4 died at sea, leaving 112 for market.

Upon their arrival in Rio, these 112 slaves—69 males and 43 females—were quickly prepared for sale.[30] Nearly half of the cargo were males between the ages of fifteen and thirty-five. Almost a fifth (21) were under the age of fourteen, and 12 of these were under the age of eight. Four infants—3 boys and 1 girl—were not a part of the "official" count, but they were noted in the inventory when they were sold along with their mothers. Including these babies, 22 percent of those onboard the *Thalaia* were children under the age of fourteen. In addition, 1 woman was "eight months pregnant." Only 4 of the Africans were over the age of thirty-five.

Two days after their arrival in Rio, Pinheiro's slaves went to market. More than two-thirds (76) of the Africans sold in just three days. Of these, only 1 had any notable defect, a man with smallpox who still fetched a reasonable sum of 120 mil-réis.[31] The remaining 36 Africans, many of whom exhibited symptoms of malnutrition and disease, sold more slowly over the course of the next month. Nine were designated as "thin [*magro*]"; 5 had serious eye problems, including 4 who were blind in at least one eye; 4 were generically "sick [*doente*]"; 1 had smallpox; and 1 young man, who "fell ill at sea," died after eleven days in Rio. Thus, by the time all of the slaves sold, nearly 20 percent of those who had departed the Benin coast only three months earlier were either dead or afflicted with some notable physical defect. It is important to recognize that even among the (relatively) healthy, some sold at reduced prices, including 2 "bearded" men (*barbados*). Though these men were not described as "old [*velho*]"—that is, over thirty-five—they probably were deemed to be beyond effective working age, underscoring the economic desirability of younger "Portuguese slaves" so esteemed by traders on the African coast.[32]

Statistically, the *Nossa Senhora da Thalaia* was a fair representation of eighteenth-century Portuguese slave ships. If anything, its relatively small cargo, quick crossing of the Atlantic, and low rate of mortality resulted in a more favorable outcome for its African captives than was the case on many Portuguese slave ships. As such, we can assume that the conditions endured by Domingos Álvares were at least as grim as those suffered by the Africans on the *Thalaia*. The Atlantic crossing to Pernambuco, Domingos' final destination, would have been about ten days shorter than the journey to Rio de Janeiro. However, most Portuguese ships making the Middle Passage in the 1720s and 1730s were far more crowded than the *Thalaia* was in 1715. Between 1728 and 1732, the time of Domingos' crossing, slave ships arriving at Pernambuco from the Mina Coast carried an average of 243 captives, although some, like the *Nossa Senhora da Vida e Santo Antônio*, arrived with as many as 546 slaves onboard.[33] Mortality rates during the passage from Benin to Brazil could be devastatingly high. In 1736, Bahian slave trader João da Costa Lima packed more than 800 Africans onto his ship at Jakin. Lacking food and water, more than 400 died before Lima disembarked the remaining slaves on the island of "Zambores" (Sherbro Island) off the coast of Sierra Leone.[34] Even in the nineteenth century, mortality rates commonly approached 10 percent.[35] If we assume a low-end 10 percent mortality rate to Pernambuco during the time of Domingos' crossing, of the 267 enslaved Africans on an average ship departing the Bight of Benin, 27 would have died and at least as many would have suffered injury or illness. For slave traders, disease, suffering, and the loss of human life were simply part of the cost of doing business.

The traders' perspectives, as seen through the cold calculations of debits and credits recorded in shipboard ledgers, are of only limited use in recovering African understandings of the Middle Passage. On the main deck, captain and crew ordered their lives with maps, charts, hourglasses, and astrolabes. "Science" measured the passage of time, movement across space, and responses to disease and hunger. Below decks, spatial and temporal referents ceased to exist, replaced by disorientation, disease, and death.[36] For Domingos, bound in darkness in the belly of the ship, where temperatures reached 120 degrees during the day, the kaleidoscope of illnesses, psychoses, and delirium would have rendered traditional diagnoses practically useless. Perhaps he recognized smallpox in some of his shipmates, but how to disentangle it from dehydration, dysentery, ophthalmia, and so on? The symptoms of this new Atlantic illness were beyond anything he could have imagined in his homeland. The relentless, day-to-day, universal suffering was a new order of evil. Even maladies we recognize as mundane realities of seafaring life, like the dizziness and nausea of seasickness, must have been viewed as just one more symptom of this new and often deadly curse.

Enslaved Africans addressed the suffering at the hands of their European captors in a variety of ways—some of them violent, others not. Wherever they could, captives smuggled stolen weapons into the holds of ships—

axes, knives, hammers, scissors, and even guns. Others fashioned weapons from nails, scrap iron, and wood they found onboard. Mahi and Òyó soldiers no doubt viewed their enslavement as little more than an extension of warfare with Dahomey. As such, they sought opportunities to overpower the ship's crew and reclaim their freedom. The first significant waves of Mahi and Òyó slaves (1728–32) coincided with an upsurge in the number of shipboard slave revolts in the Bight of Benin. While Portuguese slave trade records are incomplete for this period, French documents indicate that in the years 1728 and 1729, at least six of the twenty-five ships that traded in the Bight of Benin experienced slave revolts.[37] The most successful insurrection aboard a French ship occurred in 1732 when captives on the *Parfait* succeeded in sinking the ship while it was still anchored near shore.[38] Similar rebellions took place onboard English ships during the same time period.[39]

While violence was an option for some, others on slave ships survived by investing their energies in the weak, the elderly, and the very young, urging them to remain strong while trying to do the same themselves. The youngest victims of the trade—like the twelve children under the age of eight on the *Nossa Senhora de Thalaia*—were especially vulnerable. Their anguished cries of loneliness and separation from loved ones must have been wrenching for the men and women who accompanied them.[40] Under such dire conditions, the imperative to rebuild community was of paramount importance. Emotional ties forged on slave ships often persisted in the Americas.[41] In the early nineteenth century, English traveler Henry Koster emphasized the depth of affection demonstrated by shipmates in Brazil: "The Negroes show much attachment to their wives and children, to their other relations if they should chance to have any, and to their *malungos* or fellow-passengers from Africa."[42] In short, shipmate bonds were a balm against the horrors of the Middle Passage, a ray of hope for the future, and, in some cases, the core of a new community, a new family in the Americas.

Still others on slave ships searched for ways to remedy the onboard suffering, raining curses on those responsible for this new, all-encompassing form of evil. One eighteenth-century commentator familiar with the slave trade claimed that one in four Africans who arrived in the Americas were accused of "sorcery" in their homelands.[43] Though probably an exaggeration, such a claim highlights European perceptions of African powers and the potential for categories of resistance beyond the grasp of most Europeans. In 1696, a French slave ship departed Goree Island. Among its cargo were "several negresses quite proficient in the diabolical sciences." After seven weeks at sea and despite favorable winds, the ship inexplicably sat listless off Goree, "as if it were nailed to the same spot several leagues from land." Provisions dwindled and slaves died, forcing the crew to throw the emaciated bodies overboard. Some of the dying slaves accused one woman of orchestrating their murders, claiming that she threatened to "eat their hearts." The ship's surgeon performed autopsies on several of the dead and found that their internal organs were "dry and empty." In order to elicit a confession from the suspect, the captain ordered her tied to a cannon and whipped by one of the crewmen. She responded to the beating with stoic silence, as if the blows had no effect on her. Angered by her defiant resolve, the ship's surgeon seized a cord and "applied some lashes with all his might." Still unmoved by the blows being inflicted upon her, the "negresse" told the surgeon that since he had mistreated her without cause, she would also eat away his heart. Within two days the surgeon was dead. Angry and terrified, the captain considered his next move. He contemplated having the "negresse" strangled or thrown into the sea, but he feared that her compatriots might take even more extreme measures against the ship. In desperation, he decided to negotiate with her. If she agreed to cease her curses and allow the ship to progress, the captain would free her and some of her co-conspirators, delivering them back to the African coast. The woman agreed to this arrangement and was returned to her homeland along with several others. The ship replenished its provisions, and the voyage continued to the French islands without further incident.[44]

Given the range of skills possessed by Domingos Álvares, we can imagine that he tried to employ similar strategies, appealing to voduns or ancestors to provide solutions to the collective suffering of those onboard the slave ship. Some of these attempts to alleviate suffering would have been interpreted as sorcery or witchcraft by the ship's crew. However, we must be careful not to adopt the optic of the enslavers. Impeding the progress of a ship and poisoning the crew were acts of criminal malevolence in the eyes of European traders, but from the point of view of enslaved Africans, these were powerful antidotes, medicines in the fight against warfare, enslavement, and so on. Though Domingos was uniquely prepared to address many of the symptoms associated with enslavement and the Middle Passage, the depth and scope of shipboard suffering must have been vexing for him. Moreover, because he was shackled in darkness for much of the journey, there was little he could do to address the individual ailments of his comrades. This isolation prevented a clear diagnosis of European malevolence and thwarted access to the medicines that might have alleviated it.[45] Addressing this powerful new illness would require new knowledge, new approaches, and new techniques, none of which could be gained in the belly of the ship. Only when he arrived on terra firma, freed from the confines of the ship, would Domingos Álvares be able to comprehend fully the meaning of his enslavement, expanding his repertoire of responses to address slavery's worst effects.

LANGUISHING IN THE bowels of the slave ship day after day, Domingos Álvares could not know exactly how or when the Middle Passage would come to an end. In the absence of any understanding of seaborne travel, time, space, and forward motion seemingly melted away. For those fleeting moments when the ship's crew allowed Domingos on deck for feeding and exercise, the vastness of the ocean must have seemed eternal, never-ending. After a month at sea, arrival at Pernambuco must have come as a relief. Although the mental and physical suffering of the passage was behind them, the ultimate fate of Domingos and his shipmates still remained unclear. None of them had yet performed a single task as a slave. In fact, up to that point, their treatment was more akin to that of prisoners than that of slaves. The precise meanings and contours of their enslavement would become clearer only over the days and months that followed. From the perspective of the enslavers, the fate of the Africans was far less ambiguous. Slaves arrived in Pernambuco for one purpose only: to work—especially in tilling the fields and cutting the cane of the dozens of sugar plantations in the region. African slaves were the economic engine that generated wealth for ambitious planters and the Portuguese Crown. Without them, the sugar plantations would cease to produce.

Domingos' arrival in Pernambuco coincided with a regional crisis that would transform the social and economic landscape of the region until at least the end of the eighteenth century.[46] For years, Pernambuco had been a major center of sugar production. During the seventeenth century, it was one of the wealthiest captaincies in Brazil; however, a series of factors led to an economic downturn beginning as early as the 1670s. International competition, especially from the Caribbean, resulted in a glut of sugar in European markets, pushing prices downward. In Lisbon, the price of one arroba of sugar (approximately 32 pounds) fell from 3$800 réis in 1654 to 1$300 réis in 1688.[47] As a result of Caribbean competition, sugar prices in Brazil remained flat over the course of the eighteenth century. Meanwhile, the discovery of vast amounts of gold in Brazil's interior sent the prices of goods and services soaring. For example, slave prices quadrupled in the first three decades of the eighteenth century. Prior to the discovery of gold, the average slave sold for 40 to 50 mil-réis. By the middle of the 1730s, slaves sold for 200 mil-réis.[48] As prices of slaves and other goods rose and sugar prices fell, many planters were pushed to the edge of insolvency. In the mid-1720s, indebted sugar planters appealed to the Crown for a temporary provision prohibiting the seizure of their mills, noting that the inability to "cultivate and grind" would prejudice the royal treasury by diminishing the duties it collected. The Crown granted the concession in July 1726.[49] By 1731, colonial officials in Pernambuco complained of a more general "ruin to the people and commerce of the captaincy" caused by competition in Bahia, Rio, and Minas Gerais.[50] Similarly, in 1733, the town council of Recife lamented that the captaincy was "reduced to a miserable state."[51]

One of the results of Pernambuco's shifting economic fortunes was a rapid and steep decline in the African slave trade to the region. In 1731, the governor of Pernambuco, Duarte Sodré Pereira, observed that trade with the Mina Coast was "coming to an end." According to Pereira, it had been many months since slave merchants departed Pernambuco to trade in Benin, with the exception of "one small ship." Pereira claimed that when he began his term as governor in 1727, fifteen or sixteen Pernambuco ships traded yearly at the Mina Coast, a number that was now reduced to no more than five per year.[52] Slave trade data seem to bear out Pereira's claims. Between 1726 and 1730, an average of 2,311 slaves arrived yearly in Pernambuco from the Mina Coast. By 1731, the number dropped to 859, and in 1732, it fell to just 763.[53] For those few Africans arriving into the captaincy, slave merchants demanded payment in gold, thereby privileging buyers with connections to the interior mining regions. Merchants reluctantly agreed to exchange slaves for sugar once the gold trade was exhausted, but planters could not produce enough sugar to pay the high costs of slaves.[54] Low returns on sugar, combined with unaffordable slave prices, created a vicious cycle of economic futility. In order to remain solvent, many planters sold their existing interests in African slaves, taking advantage of the high prices offered by miners in the southern interior of the country or by their agents in Rio de Janeiro. However, selling away prime slaves to the mines reduced the quality of labor on the farms and plantations. As the governor of Pernambuco saw it, only inferior slaves who were not "capable for Rio de Janeiro served on the sugar plantations, manioc farms, and tobacco farms."[55]

If Pernambuco suffered the ill effects of the gold boom and international pricing pressures, sugar-growing regions to its north endured even greater hardships. The captaincy of Itamaracá, centered on Itamaracá Island and the inland parish of Goiana, was one such region. Though Itamaracá was a distinct administrative unit, the province functioned economically as an extension of Pernambuco, with more than 250 sugar plantations (*engenhos*) dotting the region between Recife and Goiana. In a 1750 census of the region's *engenhos*, Itamaracá accounted for thirty-five of them—six on the island and twenty-nine in the interior around Goiana.[56] Located roughly forty miles north of Recife, Goiana was connected to the Portuguese fleet trade solely through its relationship with Pernambuco, the Crown prohibiting direct trade between Itamaracá and Portugal or Africa. As such, planters in Goiana were dependent on Pernambucan agents to conduct their trade. Two-masted ships (*sumacas*) departed Recife with slaves and supplies, sailing roughly twenty-five miles north up the Atlantic coast and then west up the Goiana River. The ships set anchor about three miles south of the village of Goiana. Barges and canoes then ferried sugar down the river from Goiana to the waiting ships, which transported the sugar to market at Recife.[57]

When the sugar economy thrived, the contiguous relationship between Recife (58 *engenhos*), Olinda (63 *engenhos*), Igarassu (35 *engenhos*), and Itamaracá worked well for the northern province, as it traded on a relatively equal footing with its neighbors. However, as fortunes waned and gold became the monetary standard, Itamaracá became economically isolated. This was especially true of the inland parishes, which were distant from the economic hub of Recife and even more distant from the circuits of the gold mines. When prices of slaves skyrocketed in the eighteenth century, planters nearest to Recife were better-situated to purchase the leftover "refuse" slaves that were unsuitable for the mines. Planters in more distant regions like Goiana sometimes were shut out of the market altogether. Even when they could penetrate the market, transportation costs erased any hopes of profit. In 1725, the prior of the Carmelite convent at Goiana noted that many of the most prominent *engenhos* of the region were "deserted" and "almost all are inoperable because of the necessity of the owners to sell them in order to save their lives."[58] Some indebted planters simply abandoned their properties to creditors, fleeing for the mines "with the few slaves that they were able to hide from seizure."[59] The impacts of seizure and abandonment on Goiana's economy had long-term implications. Nearly a quarter of a century later, in 1750, one-fourth of its *engenhos* were still inoperable (*fogo morto*).[60]

Desperate to break its deepening economic crisis, Itamaracá appealed directly to the Portuguese king for relief. Beginning in the 1710s, officials requested a royal concession that would allow them to send ships directly from Itamaracá to Angola and the Mina Coast to buy slaves. Provincial officials emphasized that most of the Africans arriving in Pernambuco were

Map of Itamaracá. Engenho Tapirema is to the right at the end of the Tapirema River. Olinda and Recife (Pernambuco) are to the left, where the "Capübari" River meets the Atlantic coast. Antonio Horacio Andreas, *Provincia di Pernambuco*, lithograph, Nella Stamperia degl'Eredi del Corbelleti [1698?]. Courtesy Fundação Biblioteca Nacional, Rio de Janeiro, Brazil.

destined for the mines, and the leftover slaves could only be purchased at excessive prices beyond the means of most Itamaracá sugar planters. By sidestepping the gold merchants at Recife, planters hoped they could control slave prices and save their sugar-growing enterprises. The Crown, recognizing that the gold trade at Pernambuco and points south was "prejudicial" to Itamaracá, granted its request for direct trade with Africa in 1713, offering a six-year concession that was renewed three times through 1731.[61] Ships began trading directly between Itamaracá and Africa in September 1721 and continued through July 1730 before the commerce came to an end.[62]

During his roughly seven years in the Pernambuco region, Domingos labored on two sugar properties, the first in the northern hinterlands near Goiana and the other just outside of Recife. Domingos arrived in Itamaracá just as the last of the concessionary ships made their way directly from the Mina Coast. Whether he arrived in Brazil on one of these ships or whether he came through Recife is difficult to know. What is clear is that his stay in Itamaracá was brief. In his only reference to his time in the province, Domingos stated that he was baptized on "Engenho da Tapirema in the parish of Goyana, bishopric of Pernambuco." Engenho Tapirema was an old sugar estate in the interior hinterlands of Itamaracá, located along the

Tapirema River. Like many other *engenhos* in the region, it suffered financial difficulties in the eighteenth century. In the early 1700s, Manoel Cavalcante, the military commander (*alcaide-mor*) of Goiana, purchased Tapirema for 20,000 cruzados (8,000 mil-réis), a price far below the estimated startup cost of 15,000 mil-réis for a medium-sized *engenho* during the period.[63] When Cavalcante purchased Tapirema, it was burdened with a 2,400 mil-réis lien owed to the royal treasury. Cavalcante agreed to pay the debt within six years, but the mill was inoperable. To make matters worse, of the thirty-three *engenhos* in Itamaracá, only three mills crushed "extremely limited amounts of cane." As a result of these difficulties, Cavalcante was unable to pay his debt within the allotted six years. Shortly thereafter, Cavalcante died, leaving the struggling *engenho* to his wife, Sebastianna de Carvalho. In 1731, the lien still remained and the royal treasury ordered that the property be sold or rented out in order to satisfy the debt. In 1732, a portion of Tapirema was rented out to one Lázaro Maciel de Azevedo for 100 mil-réis per year, the proceeds going to serve the debt owed to the Crown.[64]

The economic struggles of Tapirema, and the sugar crisis more generally, had a profound impact on Domingos Álvares, shaping his early understandings of Brazilian slave society. In particular, Domingos' stay in Itamaracá taught him crucial lessons about the complicated relationship between slavery, labor, and religion. Even as he was still recovering from the exhaustion of the Middle Passage, Domingos confronted the sobering reality of his fate in the cane fields. The work of cutting cane defined the rhythm of the sugar plantation for nearly ten months out of the year. Awakened before dawn, slaves set off for the fields in gangs of two, usually one man and one woman. Men cut the cane while women bundled it. Bent at the waist under the hot sun, fighting off snakes, rats, and other vermin, Domingos would have been expected to cut up to 4,200 cane stalks every day. These stalks were bundled, loaded onto oxcarts, and carried to the nearest mill to be pressed. Once the daily cutting quota was complete, slaves were free to spend the remainder of the day as they wished, although other chores— weeding, ditch digging, fence repair, construction projects, and so on— could impinge on these meager freedoms.[65]

Under the best of circumstances, sugar labor was relentless, backbreaking work. During times of economic depression like those suffered at Tapirema in the eighteenth century, slave masters often demanded more output from their slaves even as they deprived them of basic necessities like food and clothing. In 1710, the Portuguese Crown ordered sugar planters in Pernambuco to provide their slaves with adequate food or give them a free day during the week to cultivate their own gardens, an indication that hunger was widespread among slaves in the province.[66] Newly arrived Africans like Domingos were particularly vulnerable to these deprivations since the cultivation of gardens required resources (tools, seed, water, and so on) and growing time before they would produce a crop. Commenting on the plight of the recently arrived, Jesuit priest André João Antonil wrote in 1711: "The new slaves should receive great care, because they still do not have the means to make a living like those who plant their own gardens." Yet even those who possessed the industry to plant their own garden plots were "only recognized as slaves in the distribution of labor and forgotten in sickness and in the distribution of clothing."[67] In short, slave masters often shirked their obligations to sustain the physical health and well-being of their slaves so long as those slaves could continue to work.

DURING HIS FIRST DAYS on Engenho Tapirema, Domingos would have known little more than the scythe and the cane stalk. He did not speak the Portuguese language. He was unfamiliar with the flora, fauna, and geography of the region. And he was isolated from the social structures that resonated most deeply with him. In the midst of such exhaustion, isolation, and anguish, there appeared to be few protectors of African interests; however, one of them was the Catholic Church. From the perspective of the Church, the principal justification for slavery was the redemption of African souls. As such, Catholic priests urged masters to take great care in teaching their slaves the beliefs and sacraments of the faith. The Portuguese Crown reinforced Catholic doctrine, demanding that slaves be baptized and indoctrinated.[68] Nearly all of the large sugar planters built chapels on their properties for precisely this purpose. For many planters, the *engenho* chapel was simply a façade to protect against the rebukes of Church and Crown, although others took the proselytizing mission more seriously. At the very least, most slave masters insured that their slaves were baptized, although it remains unclear how deeply these and other Catholic teachings penetrated among the enslaved, particularly among first-generation Africans.[69]

One of Domingos' first experiences in the weeks following his arrival in Brazil was his baptism by Father Antônio at the *engenho's* chapel, dedicated to Nossa Senhora da Conceição. The fact that Domingos remembered so many details of his baptism—the name of the chapel, the name of the presiding priest, the name of his godfather—more than ten years later in Lisbon suggests that he did not view the ritual with cynical skepticism or indifference. On the contrary, he seemed to embrace it fully. The migration of voduns across the Gbe-speaking region and their integration into the fabric of local societies had prepared him to be tolerant, even welcoming, of new beliefs. His own persecution and enslavement only reinforced this imperative for tolerance. Unlike the institutional Catholic Church, Domingos did not subscribe to a doctrine of "one God, one faith." Rather, his spiritual worldview, and that of many other Africans, was flexible, integrative, and imminently responsive to the vagaries of historical change.

Of course, tolerance had its limits, and there was ample reason to be suspicious of the Catholic Church in Brazil. The Jesuits, Benedictines, and Carmelites were among the largest slaveholders in the colony, employing Africans in sugar planting, gardening, ranching, and other laborious tasks. In addition, individual priests often owned slaves, utilizing them as personal body servants. Some of these priests could be as cruel and ruthless as any other slaveowners. For example, between 1746 and 1749 at the Benedictine monastery in Olinda, a number of slaves ran away because of the beatings and torture they suffered at the hands of Father Salvador dos Santos.[70] Yet many other Catholic priests expressed genuine interest in the spiritual and physical well-being of Africans. Indeed, priests hounded slaveowners to provide Africans with adequate food, shelter, and clothing. They agitated for the end of torture and cruel treatment. And they called for proper Christian burials of the dead.[71] In some instances, they even argued that the bodies and souls of Africans were more important than the property rights of slave masters.

To provide just one example from Pernambuco, in 1710, Bishop Manuel Álvares da Costa wrote to King João V regarding the treatment of ailing slaves by their masters. The bishop complained that when slaves fell ill, their masters simply "cast them into the woods, leaving them at the disposition of nature." In this way, planters avoided financial responsibility for the upkeep of unproductive workers. If the slaves recovered from their illnesses, the masters retrieved them and put them back to work. But if their illnesses were terminal, the slaves "died there without cure or sacraments as if they were brutes." Frustrated that planters ignored his admonishments, the bishop asked the king to issue a law that would strip slaveowners of all property claims if they released their slaves into the woods. Thus, any slave that recovered his health would remain free. The bishop also suggested that any person "who, with Christian charity wants to take such sick slaves in order to cure them, applying to them corporal and spiritual medicines, thus improving the slave's health, the slave will remain under the dominion of the person who took him under his own account and cured him." The king rejected both suggestions, implicitly endorsing the planters' economic interests over the interest of slave salvation.[72] Nevertheless, the advocacy by Catholic priests on behalf of slaves reflected a strong commitment to protecting the spiritual and physical well-being of the enslaved, even in the face of stiff planter opposition. In this way, many Catholic priests were agents of transformation, "healers" in much the same vein that Domingos Álvares had been in Naogon.

The hierarchy of worship in the Church also must have resonated with Domingos. Catholic priests were the transmitters of ritual knowledge to their congregations, in much the same fashion as the "possessors of the vodun [vodunon]." In this respect, Domingos probably viewed his baptismal priest, Father Antônio, as a peer—an equal—each possessing the esoteric knowledge to transport and activate their respective deities, all in the interest of maintaining the well-being of the larger community of worshippers. Other slaves on Tapirema, including Domingos' godfather Gaspar Pereira, facilitated his initiation into the community of Catholic worshippers at the chapel of Nossa Senhora da Conceição.[73] From Domingos' perspective, the collective worship of God could very well have appeared as a new healing community that promised redemption from the pains of enslavement. Beyond similarities in the function and structure of a benevolent priesthood, other elements, including much of the ritual behavior and practices, would have been familiar to Domingos.

The gateway to Catholicism for enslaved Africans was the sacrament of baptism. Under normal circumstances, adults were required to demonstrate a thorough understanding of the mysteries of the faith before they could be baptized. These mysteries included such abstract and counterintuitive concepts as the Holy Trinity, the Virgin Mary, heaven, hell, and so on. Recognizing the difficulties in conveying the mysteries of the faith to newly arrived Africans, Church officials authorized a special, abbreviated catechism to accommodate "the rudeness of their understanding and the barbarity of their speech." In his 1707 edict to Brazilian Catholics, Bahian archbishop Sebastião Monteiro da Vide described this catechism:

> For greater security in regard to the Baptism of the brute and raw
> slaves, and those of unknown language, such as are those who come
> from Mina . . . [they] will be asked only the following questions:
>   Do you want to wash your soul with holy water?
>   Do you want to eat the salt of God?
>   Will you cast all the sins out of your soul?

Will you commit no more sins?
Do you want to be a child of God?
Will you cast the devil out of your soul?[74]

For Domingos, the choreography of Catholic baptism and indoctrination would have appeared strikingly similar to the rituals conducted in the initiation of new members into vodun communities in Naogon. First, in order for one to qualify for baptism, the Catholic Church required a basic understanding of the transformative power of devotion to God, particularly against the evils of Satan. This basic knowledge was a minimal prerequisite for the baptismal candidate to follow the line of questioning in the abbreviated catechism. A similar period of instruction in the forms of proper worship was the first step in the initiation process of Sakpata devotees and was administered in seclusion with other novitiates. Inherent in understanding worship was a mastery of a certain arcane, ritual language. For devotees of Sakpata, this ritual language was an ancient form of Yoruba. For Africans embracing Catholicism in Brazil, the ritual language was Portuguese at first and perhaps some Latin later on. The second ritual similarity between Catholic baptism and vodun initiation related to the symbolic washing away of sin. Baptismal water was resonant of palm oil, water, alcohol, and salt anointed on the heads of Sakpata initiates to ritually cleanse them and invoke the vodun.[75] Third, the taking of salt, which in Catholic doctrine connoted "the food of divine wisdom," adhered closely to the ritual practice of eating a vodun's favorite foods during initiation rituals.[76] That salt was understood as a "necessity of life" in Dahomey only reinforced the tie between worship of the new Christian God and the temporal well-being of his followers.[77] Fourth, the culmination of the baptismal ritual resulted in a "new" person with a new name, just as was the case in initiation rituals in vodun. Indeed, Domingos only became "Domingos" after his initiation into the Christian fold. He no doubt continued to identify himself by his African name, probably reflective of one of the major qualities of Sakpata. Nevertheless, he likely recognized and respected the ritual significance of the new name given to him by the Catholic priests. After all, the new name was a badge of honor, a signal of initiation into the dominant community of worshippers in his new Brazilian homeland. The irony of his new name, meaning "of the Lord," might have been lost on him, yet it was a mirror image of his African name, directly reflective of a quality of the religion's major deity.

As a result of these crucial confluences in the structure of spiritual be-lief and ritual practice, Domingos Álvares probably viewed God as just one more powerful deity to integrate into an ever-expanding pantheon of vo-duns. Like his own congregation in Naogon, the Catholic Church appeared to be a receptacle for a variety of voduns, expressed in the numerous saints, their altars with representations of deities in human form, and the distinct rituals of worship and prayer that accompanied each one. Despite these obvious similarities, many elements of Catholicism remained a mystery to Domingos. Once enslaved Africans were baptized, it was expected that their owners would continue their religious education, teaching them the Articles of the Faith, the Our Father, the Hail Mary, the Ten Command-ments, and so on. Nevertheless, many masters did not "teach the doctrine point by point, and at leisure, as required for ignorant people, but rather all at once, and with a great deal of haste."[78] As a result, many baptized Afri-cans remained ignorant of Church doctrine. In 1711, Father Antonil noted that African slaves "do not know who their creator is, what they are to be-lieve, what law they are to protect, how they are to commit themselves to God, [or] why Christians go to Church." When Africans knelt to pray, they asked "to whose ears" they were speaking. Additionally, they asked where their souls went when they left their bodies at death.[79] In short, the abstrac-tion of the mysteries and the rigidity of the doctrine baffled many Africans, whose experiences with the spiritual world were often more personal (that is, ancestral) and grounded in the day-to-day realities of healing.[80]

As a recent arrival from the Mina Coast, Domingos Álvares probably shared many of these uncertainties about the finer details of the Catholic faith. Domingos' embrace of God's community would have been tentative, contingent on the rewards and bounties offered by the deity, just as was the practice with other deities in the pantheon of vodun. There are indica-tions that he continued to build on his knowledge of Catholic ritual even after his baptism. For example, though he never completely grasped laws and precepts like the Ten Commandments, he did learn to recite the Lord's Prayer and the Hail Mary, precisely the kinds of arcane ritual orations that were at the core of so many vodun ceremonies. Even though nourishing and appeasing God were important for Domingos, his primary obligation remained with Sakpata, and he no doubt yearned to build a new healing community in Goiana. Despite these desires, grinding work and isolation seemed to dominate Domingos' existence at Tapirema. Only the failing for-tunes of his masters rescued him from this impoverished, rural oblivion and delivered him to a more cosmopolitan setting. Sometime around 1733, when the financial crisis at Engenho Tapirema reached a crescendo and a portion of the property was rented out, Sebastianna de Carvalho dispatched Domingos to her sister and brother-in-law in Recife, where Domingos once again started a new life.[81]

3

Recife

Today he cures; tomorrow he kills.
—Description of Domingos Álvares during his time in Recife

When Domingos Álvares arrived in Recife around 1733, he encountered a scene far different from the bedraggled, rural environment of Engenho Tapirema. If Tapirema and its immediate surroundings were isolated, parochial, and increasingly destitute, Recife was the region's cosmopolitan hub, boasting a population of around 10,000 people.[1] During the colonial period, the urban center of the city consisted of two contiguous settlements, one on the island of Santo Antônio and the other on the island of Recife. The Capibaribe River bisected these two settlements at the Atlantic Ocean. The city was connected by a bridge of wooden planks, built on pillars of rock and shell. On either side of the bridge were dozens of houses, buildings of three and four stories, churches with high towers, fortresses, and a major port served by the Portuguese fleets.[2]

The streets of Recife bustled with commerce, not only from legitimate trade in sugar, gold, and slaves but also from a thriving informal economy. Throughout the city, one could find a "multiplicity of peddlers, hawkers, sailors, black men, and black women who in the public streets . . . and its suburbs walk around with . . . packages, trays, boxes, and various other containers selling all quality of goods to the people."[3] While most of these men and women made no pretense about the impermanence of their work, others posed as legitimate craftspeople. For example, in 1732, the *juiz de fora* complained to the Crown of the "excessive number of goldsmiths in Olinda and Recife and other places in the captaincy, the majority of them mulattoes and blacks, which results in the appearance of counterfeit money and thievery."[4] Enterprising Africans and Afro-Brazilians were a constant cause for concern among the Portuguese, who feared that slaves, in particular, had an unfair market advantage on the untaxed goods they sold. Ironically, it may have been colonial authorities who put Africans in the streets in the first place. In the early 1720s, members of the Recife town council

Maurício de Nassau Bridge, Recife. Antonio Horacio Andreas, *Prospetto della citta Maurizea capitale della provincia di Pernambuco*, lithograph, Nella Stamperia degl'Eredi del Corbelleti [1698?]. Courtesy Fundação Biblioteca Nacional, Rio de Janeiro, Brazil.

(*câmara*) were accused of sending their slaves into the streets to sell manioc, oil, and wine at "exorbitant prices." The apparent objective of the town council members, many of whom were themselves merchants, was to avoid taxes normally paid to the Crown on such products.[5] The king tried to put a stop to the practice, but black peddlers continued selling their wares in the streets. Members of the town council denied they were to blame, claiming that goods appeared on the streets because of the "continuous thievery" of black slaves.[6] The council reported that slaves stole goods from their merchant masters, passing the contraband items on to friends and relatives to fence in the city's streets. Though the colonial government passed laws in 1749 and 1781 prohibiting the activities of street hawkers, there was little compliance, and the informal economy of slaves and freed blacks thrived deep into the nineteenth century.[7]

Domingos likely witnessed the commotion of Recife's urban center upon his arrival into the port. The sights of Africans moving freely about the city, the sounds of familiar languages, and the smells of West African cooking in the streets must have excited his senses, perhaps even awakening memories of his homeland. Unfortunately, his stay in the city center was short-lived. After being turned over to the possession of his new master, Jacinto de Freitas da Silva, Domingos embarked in a canoe piloted by one of the many enslaved boatsmen who traversed the rivers and waterways of the region. As the canoe moved upstream along the Capibaribe River and the city center faded from view, Domingos would have recognized the familiar sight of sugar plantations on either side of the river's banks—Torre, Madalena, Monteiro—grand *engenhos* that stretched one after the other for as far as the eye could see. The canoe transported Domingos five miles up the Capibaribe, depositing him at a large sugar *engenho* called Casa Forte. Casa Forte was an old and storied estate that had been in existence since the middle of the sixteenth century. The plantation possessed fertile soils, fine backlands, and a number of houses and buildings, including a chapel dedicated to Nossa Senhora das Necessidades.[8] Jacinto de Freitas almost certainly expected that Domingos would work in the production of sugar, most likely cutting cane, but Domingos had other ideas.

LIKE MOST SLAVES, Domingos bristled under the coercion and abuse of chattel slavery, but he rejected plantation labor on several additional grounds. In his homeland, agricultural labor was generally the preserve of women. While men engaged in warfare, hunting, and religious pursuits, women tended and harvested crops. Males controlled female agricultural labor through a well-entrenched system of polygamous marriage. Men paid money (cowry shells) and cloth to a woman's family in exchange for her labor and child-bearing capacities. As a result of these social arrangements, one Western observer in eighteenth-century Dahomey noted that "the women . . . support the men either by their work or their trade."[9] Thus, women were a primary source of labor, wealth-building, and social status for men. Indeed, a man's "greatness and power" could be measured in direct proportion to the number of wives he possessed.[10]

Though Domingos Álvares was just reaching the age of marriage when he was enslaved, he would have been socialized to see agricultural labor as "women's" work. The social emasculation of enslavement in the cane fields was exaggerated further by the likelihood that Domingos was a vodun priest, denied the right to engage in the vocation that Sakpata ordained for him. In the social hierarchy of his homeland, his role as a *vodunon* meant that he possessed knowledge surpassing that of most people. In this respect, he was much more of a public intellectual than a laborer. However, his knowledge and power were contingent on having a community of worshippers who could pay tribute to the vodun. Without a group of devotees, Domingos was powerless—quite literally a priest without a flock. As Domingos became familiar with the neighboring *engenhos* of Casa Forte, as well as the flora and fauna of the region, he demanded the right to heal freely, unencumbered by the constraints of plantation slavery.

Given the decline in the African slave trade in the early 1730s and the frequent outbreaks of disease in Pernambuco, there was ample incentive for Jacinto de Freitas to encourage Domingos' healing skills. In the 1740s, one commentator in Pernambuco noted that "the multitude of slaves from Guiné, Mina, and Angola, who continually enter this port . . . very rarely arrive without contagious diseases to which they are subject in the climates of those lands, for example, scurvy . . . cachexia, scabies, leprosy, diarrhea, dysentery, dropsy, ophthalmia, etc."[11] Moreover, in the period leading up to Domingos' arrival in Recife, economic depression in the sugar industry affected the collective health of enslaved workers in profoundly negative ways. For example, in 1725, a number of sugar planters testified that Recife "experienced a great loss of slaves from contagion and diseases . . . and because of the punishment of a severe famine, which obliged [the planters] to sustain life with bad food, many slaves died."[12] Anecdotal evidence from plantation inventories bears out the claim of widespread loss of life. In 1726, fifty-six adult slaves lived on the Benedictine plantation Engenho Musurepe. By 1730, five were dead from "smallpox and other illnesses," while two others died of "old" age, leaving a total of forty-nine adults on the property. Thus, even on efficient, well-run properties that should have been sheltered from the worst effects of the depression, losses were significant.[13]

At first, Domingos probably performed cures only on the slaves at Casa Forte, but as his reputation spread, he became "widely known as a healer and, as such, was procured by all sorts of people."[14] Jacinto de Freitas apparently hired out Domingos to sugar planters on neighboring properties, allowing him to heal on a case-by-case basis, collecting the earnings from his cures. This practice was not at all unusual and was a tacit acknowledgment of African expertise in medicine and healing. Even the Benedictines sometimes hired African healers on their properties in Olinda.[15] This informal economy in African healing also served to accommodate the seemingly disparate demands of enslaved healers and slave masters. Though Domingos might have resisted the labor of sugar cultivation, he was effective in healing slaves who were integral to the production of sugar. In this way, Domingos actually contributed to the perpetuation of slavery and the sugar economy in a time of deep depression. Moreover, Domingos could earn cash for his master through his cures. For his part, Domingos gained relief from the daily drudgery of sugar labor, freeing him to make new social con-

TABLE 3.1 Origin of African Slaves Who Arrived in
Pernambuco, 1722–1732

Year	Mina	Angola	Cacheu
1722	1,957		
1723	3,693	339	
1724	2,505	678	150
1725	1,650	678	
1726	2,733	291	
1727	2,684	770	
1728	2,803	1,728	
1729	1,426		
1730	1,910		
1731	859	291	
1732	763		
Total	22,983	4,188	150

Sources: For Mina and Cacheu, 1722–31: AHU, Conselho Ultramarino, Pernambuco, Caixa 42, Document 3786; for Mina, 1732: AHU, Conselho Ultramarino, Pernambuco, Caixa 44, Document 4007; for Angola: Klein data set, 1723–71.

nections through healing. Ultimately, this arrangement seemed to be a win-win proposition for both Domingos and Jacinto de Freitas.

During his travels across Pernambuco, Domingos would have encountered *engenhos* like Massangano, Samba, Catumba, and Chango—all names that reflected the overwhelming African influences on colonial Brazilian society.[16] Perhaps more important for Domingos, he found on these *engenhos* significant numbers of Africans who shared mutually intelligible cultures and histories. Between 1722 and 1732, more than 27,000 enslaved Africans disembarked in Recife, with over 84 percent of them coming from the same broad region known as the Costa da Mina (see table 3.1).[17] Most of the so-called Mina slaves were from areas south and west of Domingos' homeland in Agonli-Cové. When these Ouidahs, Ardas, and others encountered Domingos in Recife, they sometimes emphasized their differences rather than their similarities. For example, one of Domingos' African compatriots, a woman named Thereza Arda, testified that Jacinto de Freitas and her master, Zacharias de Britto, were close friends. As a result of this friendship, Thereza accompanied Britto to Casa Forte and "saw Domingos there many times." Describing her relationship to Domingos, Thereza declared that "we are supposed to be from the same Mina Coast, however, I am from the Arda nation and Domingos is from Cobû, which are different lands."[18]

The precise contours of difference outlined in this terse statement are difficult to unravel. Allada (Arda), widely regarded as the traditional cradle of social and political power in the Gbe-speaking region, was conquered by Dahomey in 1724. Thereza may have been staking a claim to social superiority etched in the deep history of the Bight of Benin, distancing herself from the rustic newcomer. She also may have viewed the Cobu as enemies from a "different land," closer to the Yoruba than to traditional Gbe speakers. Whatever the case, we can be sure that Thereza's reference was more than a simple acknowledgment of distinct geographic homelands. Arriving from an acephalous political group as a healer and a feared enemy of Agaja, Domingos was a consummate "outsider"—alone, dangerous, and perhaps even feared.

At the same time, Domingos shared much in common with the majority of Minas in Pernambuco's slave population. Although some of the enslaved probably had been members of the Dahomean army, the overwhelming majority had been vanquished by Dahomey, just as Domingos had been. When Dahomey conquered Allada and Ouidah, it delivered thousands of war prisoners to Europeans for enslavement and transport to the Americas. As discussed in chapter 1, those who survived Dahomey's invasions often fled to communities like the one that Domingos likely presided over in Naogon, facilitating exchanges in language, religion, and so on. Once reconvened in places like Pernambuco, the enslaved of Dahomey shared a great deal of common cultural ground on which to build new communities.

One of the key ingredients in the formation of these new communities was a shared language. The *"língua geral,"* spoken in Dahomey, Ouidah, Mahi, and "neighbouring provinces," also became the lingua franca of many Brazilian slave communities in the eighteenth century.[19] References to enslaved Africans speaking the "Mina language" abound in eighteenth-century Brazilian documents, but perhaps the clearest indicator of the language's adherence in Brazil is the publication of Antônio da Costa Peixoto's *Obra nova da língua geral de Mina* (New Volume of the General Language of Mina) (1741).[20] Born and raised in Entre-Douro-e-Minho, Portugal, Peixoto left his homeland in the early eighteenth century to join dozens of other Portuguese men seeking their fortunes in the mining districts of Brazil. There, Peixoto learned the Mina language from local African slaves, penning a Mina/Portuguese grammar as early as 1731. Ten years later, he published an expanded version of the grammar in Portugal. In the prologue of the 1741 edition, Peixoto explained his motivation in writing the volume, asserting that "in this America and Minas [Gerais] . . . if slaveowners, and even those who do not own slaves, would learn this language there would not be so much insult, ruin, damage, thievery, death, and finally, atrocities, which many of these miserable ones have experienced: and it seems to me that they would be able to avoid some of these disorders if there was greater curiosity and less laziness on the parts of residents and inhabitants of these countries."[21]

One part Mina/Portuguese dictionary and one part basic phrase book, Peixoto's remarkable volume not only demonstrates the continuity of an African creole language from the Bight of Benin to Brazil but also shines important light on the worldview of Brazil's so-called Mina slaves. Quantitatively, the language that Peixoto records is mostly Fon (Gbe) with minor inflections from Yoruba and other neighboring languages.[22] As such, the language accurately reflects the diversity of Mina populations on either side of the Atlantic. Peixoto clearly points to this diversity in his discussion of the various ethnic and regional identities represented in Brazil. For example, he notes that the Gun (*guno*) are the same as the "Mina people," the Gun here referring to the peoples along the coast of Benin, including the Hula, Hueda, and even Allada, who fled Dahomey's invasions eastward toward Porto Novo. This corroborates the earlier argument that most Mina slaves arriving in Brazil in the 1720s came from regions south and west of Abomey. Even more interesting, Peixoto reveals that the *gamlimno* (Agonli-nu) are the same as the "Cobu people."[23] Again, the distinction between "Cobu people" and "Mina people" underscores the differences between the two groups in Brazil, at least during the late 1720s and early 1730s.[24] Given that "Cobu" is the final entry in the list of ethnonyms that Peixoto provides, at least one scholar has speculated that Peixoto's informant was actually Cobu.[25] If this was the case, Peixoto's grammar gives us even deeper insight into Domingos Álvares' worldview than we might have otherwise imagined.

Perhaps most intriguing, the *Obra nova* links the history and culture of the Bight of Benin to Brazil. For instance, Peixoto includes many translations relating to religion and spirituality. In most of his examples, Christian ideas are translated into the lexicon of vodun. Thus, God, "Nosso Senhor," is "*hihávouvódum*," literally "the white man's vodun."[26] "Catholic priest," or "Padre," is translated as "Avóduno," or *vodunon*.[27] Prayer beads (*avódumgê*), Lent (*avódumcu*), Easter (*avódumnhi*), Sunday (*avódumzambe*), and Saint's Day (*avódumzampê*) also have "vodun" as their root words.[28] Even the Devil (*leba*) is glossed from the vodun deity Legba.[29] The implications of these renderings for enslaved Minas should be clear enough: Brazilian

Catholicism was largely grafted onto the structures and meanings of vodun. For someone like Domingos Álvares, who very likely *was* a *vodunon*, the translation of "Catholic priest" as "Avóduno" would have confirmed the priest as a colleague and intellectual peer, one who seemed to possess a new and powerful vodun. For other enslaved Minas, Catholicism represented a set of beliefs similar to vodun, offering new forms of healing and redemption. The acquisition of Catholic knowledge and subsequent initiation into the religion (baptism) were therefore likely understood as entry into a new healing community that might alleviate worldly ills.

The historical linkages between Dahomey and Brazil in Peixoto's *Obra nova* are by no means limited to the topic of religion. In his rendering of dialogues between Brazilian slave masters and Mina slaves, Peixoto records important memories of enslavement. For example:

> SLAVE MASTER: The white man's land does not have war [*hiháboutó mématimaguam*]. . . .
> SLAVE: The white man's land is no good [*hihábouthómé manhôhā*].
> SLAVE MASTER: Why is it no good [*anihutu hinharam*]?
> SLAVE: Whites punish so many slaves [*hi hà bouno, hé nachuhé acrú susû*].[30]

Here, we see a transparent reference to warfare in Dahomey, seemingly as a justification for the enslavement of Africans in Brazil. The Mina slave does not contest the slave master's assertion regarding warfare, but he rejects the master's insinuation that enslavement saved Africans from a grimmer fate. Indeed, the slave seems to suggest that the warfare of Africa is preferable to the slavery of Brazil.

Though Peixoto's work assumes European superiority, the volume also belies a deep uncertainty about that superiority, not just culturally but also politically and economically. The very idea that slaveowners should master the Mina language is perhaps the clearest indicator that distinct, powerful Mina communities existed in Brazil. According to Peixoto, these communities might threaten the "order" of colonialism and slavery if slave masters did not demonstrate "greater curiosity and less laziness." Of course, for Domingos Álvares, the tens of thousands of Mina slaves that arrived in Pernambuco in the 1720s and 1730s were not the same objects of surveillance and fear that they were for the Portuguese. Rather, these large numbers of Mina slaves represented a deep vein of untapped potential for broader community building. The *língua geral* was an extraordinarily useful, and perhaps necessary, foundation for these new communities, but their actual construction would require a re-articulation of spiritual, kinship, and political institutions that were historically resonant to enslaved Minas yet relevant to their new social condition in Brazil.

In his conversations with his Mina compatriots and through exchanges with Luso-Brazilians, Domingos would have quickly learned that he was not the only healer in the region. In fact, the range of therapeutic possibilities in Recife and its environs seemed practically endless. Many of these therapies had Central African origins. Until the early eighteenth century, roughly four out of five Africans arriving in Pernambuco came from the broad region usually known to the Portuguese simply as "Angola."[31] As table 3.1 demonstrates, even in the 1720s and 1730s, Central Africans constituted almost one-fifth of African arrivals in Pernambuco. Given their cultural dominance in slave communities throughout the seventeenth century and their continuing importance in the eighteenth century, Central Africans re-created a number of healing rituals, adapting them to the peculiarities of Brazilian slave society.[32] There were groups of *calundeiros*, experts in the ritual healing of Central Africa, who called the spirits of their ancestors to possess their bodies and provide remedies for various ailments.[33] There were congregations devoted to "Caçûtû," an oracle who took the form of a black goat in spirit-possession rituals.[34] And there were practitioners of rituals known as *quibando*, divinations used to determine past events, like the origins of illness, thievery, and so on.[35]

In addition to Central African therapeutic forms, there were others based on native Brazilian and Portuguese beliefs. In the late 1730s the "cult of *jurema*" spread rapidly through indigenous communities of northeastern Pernambuco, making its way south of Recife by the middle of the eighteenth century. Based on a set of ancient indigenous beliefs, the *jurema* ritual combined dancing and the ingestion of a hallucinogenic drink, made from the roots of the *jurema* (mimosa) tree, to initiate a trancelike state. As the healing cult spread, it eventually came to include peoples of African and Portuguese ancestry, as well as Indians. The result of this new ethnic mixture was a transformation in ritual practice. For example, in 1781, members of the *jurema* cult in Una, near Serinhaém, integrated some Christian elements into their rituals. Before drinking the *jurema*, they consecrated the ritual beverage by dipping a crucifix into it.[36]

As might be expected, the Catholic Church also provided various healing options including baptism, ritual devotion to saints, and so on. In addition to these everyday, institutionalized forms of therapeutic healing, there were more extraordinary ones like exorcism. In the first decade of the eighteenth century, Father Alberto de Santo Tomás, a Catholic missionary, passed through Bahia and Pernambuco, where "he tried in his sermons and conversations, as well as in confession, to exhort and admonish people that they should not consult the Negro fetishers, nor some other person they might understand had dealings with the Devil, and that in order to free themselves from evil, they should use the exorcisms of the Church, which were the most secure and efficacious remedy."[37] Of course, the ritualized casting out of evil spirits by Catholic priests was not that far removed from the work of African *calundeiros* or *vodunons*, who called upon their ancestors to perform similar functions. In this way, Father Alberto actually Africanized Catholic doctrine in order to remain a viable and salient option for those seeking therapeutic remedies.

In addition to performing frequent exorcisms, Father Alberto manufactured special *bolsas* for his followers. *Bolsas* were pouches made of cloth or leather usually worn around the neck on a cord or string. Most *bolsas* contained some combination of powerful substances from the natural world—bones, hairs, feathers, animal skins, roots, stones, powders, and so on—often accompanied by a folded piece of paper with Christian prayers written on it. Though similar pouches (*pátuas*) could be found in Portugal as early as the Middle Ages, by the eighteenth century, they were most often associated with African forms of "superstition." As such, they were almost always described as *bolsas de mandinga*. Depending on the combination of substances inside the *bolsa*, it protected the wearer from fists, knives, and/or gunshots. Some ensured victory in gambling and games of chance. Others protected slaves from beatings by their masters. And still others allowed slaves to escape bondage unnoticed by their masters.[38] Father Alberto prescribed a mixture of myrrh, gold dust, wax, salt, olive leaves, and rue that he placed in *bolsas* and distributed to sick people. According to the priest, if the ill wore the *bolsas* at all times, they would return to health. Father Alberto also performed other unorthodox cures, including enemas made from holy water that elicited hair, sand, bones, teeth, fishhooks, and other "filth" from the bodies of the sick. According to Father Alberto, his cures were so successful that when he passed through Recife, the town council wanted to recognize him with a special commendation to the king; however, the priest refused, attributing his success to the power of God.[39] Ultimately, Catholic authorities in Lisbon censured Father Alberto for the exorcisms and cures he performed in Brazil; however, this did not stop Catholic priests from continuing to integrate African forms into their rituals. Several years later, in 1714, Father Joseph Maurício distributed packets of consecrated hosts for residents of Serinhaém to carry in their *bolsas*, despite Church mandates that prohibited the desecration of consecrated hosts and other holy objects.[40]

Africans were not unaware of these subtle yet important transformations in Catholic rituals and were themselves open to integrating elements of Catholicism into their own belief systems. In 1740, a "new sect" of slaves and freedpeople formed their own house of worship on Rua da Praia in Recife. Their "abominable rites" consisted of "vile actions of filth and carnal copulation" before an image of the crucified Christ laid on the ground and covered with flowers. The Catholic priests who denounced the "sect" noted that all of the adherents promised "obedience" to the "provincial," who was followed in a strict hierarchy by "master novices," "novitiates," and "other titles similar to those that exist in the sacred Carmelite and Franciscan religions."[41] Though the priests placed a Catholic gloss on the hierarchy of the congregation, the six slaves (three men and three women) and one freedwoman who took part in the ceremonies likely viewed the hierarchy through a very different optic. Evidence is admittedly cryptic, but the hierarchy described by the Catholic priests closely mirrors the hierarchy of vodun—with the *vodunon* (chief priest), *vodunsi* (initiates), and novitiates. And the "vile actions" before an image covered with flowers (offerings?) are strongly suggestive of vodun rituals. The image of Christ at such an altar, as a revered ancestor or even as a new vodun, would not have been out of keeping with these rituals and is just one indication of the ways that vodun might have transformed in the context of Pernambuco slave society. Even if one rejects the suggestion that this was a vodun congregation, we still cannot ignore the community-building exercise implicit in the social hierarchy described by the Catholic priests. At the very least, the Recife congregation was an incipient community, a ranked social unit consisting mostly of slaves, marked by ritual kinship and cultural affinity.

If, in fact, the Recife "sect" practiced vodun, this would represent one of the first documented ritual communities in Pernambuco that hailed from the Dahomey region. We must remember that the wave of Mina slaves that arrived in the province in the first three decades of the eighteenth century, like Domingos Álvares, were only just beginning to gain a firm social and cultural foothold in the region. The terrain was already replete with Central African, Portuguese, and indigenous communities of healing. Building new therapeutic communities required new knowledge, some measure of freedom, access to resources, and time to gain a loyal following—all things that were denied to the vast majority of chattel slaves. Still, even as early as the 1720s, documents reveal isolated cases of what appear to be ritual practices imported from the Bight of Benin. For example, in 1725, a slave named Francisco was accused of divining and curing in Olinda. Francisco walked through the city streets with a snake inside of a calabash. When called upon by his clients, he removed the snake from the calabash and performed various actions with it. When the snake made a menacing move, Francisco pacified it with soothing gestures. Then he wrapped the snake around his head and spoke with it, learning the answers to his clients' questions. After performing his divination, Francisco put the snake back in the calabash and collected his fee.[42]

As discussed in chapter 1, the serpent vodun attracted numerous devotees in Dahomey, especially in Ouidah. That enslaved Africans in Brazil continued to appeal to this vodun for remedies for their worldly ills should not surprise us; however, it is important to emphasize that unlike Central African and Native American rituals, which had a long history in northeastern Brazil, rituals and beliefs of Dahomean origin did not yet have institutional foundations. Francisco's invocations of Dangbe were a radically corrupted version of the reciprocal, community-based worship that occurred in the Bight of Benin. Over time, he might have been able to build a core community of followers and an altar to Dangbe, similar to the one formed by the Recife "sect" in 1740. However, until Francisco could mobilize the resources to create such a community, he was resigned to his work as an itinerant healer, adrift from the social and spiritual networks that provided meaning to the lives of so many people from the Bight of Benin.

Apparently, Domingos found himself in a position similar to that of Francisco. Though Jacinto de Freitas allowed Domingos to cure, Freitas maintained control over Domingos' movements, dictating who, when, and where Domingos would cure. We can surmise that Domingos accepted this arrangement for a time. After all, there was much to learn about Recife, not just in terms of its people and their already-established ways of healing but also about the particular maladies that plagued the region and the herbal medicines that could be utilized to effect cures. Domingos was a quick study, integrating new knowledge from the traditions he encountered in his travels around the province. For example, he learned an effective cure for headache, malaise, and dizziness caused by the heat of the sun. This cure involved folding a cloth napkin, placing it on the head of the sick person, and then placing a full cup of water, upside down, on top of the napkin. The ill person was to sit in the sun until all of the water soaked through the napkin. Domingos later claimed that he learned this remedy from "whites" and observed that "generally, all the Christians do it."[43] In addition, he learned a cure for kidney stones that involved treatment with a little "stone" from the head of a jackfish (*xaréu*). Convinced of the efficacy of the remedy, Domingos added a jackfish stone to the sack of medicines that he carried around with him.[44] Finally, Domingos also maintained a keen interest in the Catholic Church. He confessed, took communion, and attended mass regularly, embracing the rituals of this increasingly familiar healing community.

In his most significant gesture toward the Church, Domingos submitted to the Sacrament of Confirmation, the final step in his initiation into the Catholic faith. Confirmation requires a renewal of the baptismal promise and a public declaration that the initiate will live as Christ's servant. Domingos' confirmation took place in the chapel dedicated to Saint Pantelão on Engenho Monteiro, adjacent to Casa Forte. Presided over by the bishop of Pernambuco, the confirmation ritual was a highly choreographed spectacle, much like his earlier baptism. Standing before the gathered parishioners, the bishop laid hands on Domingos, calling for the Holy Spirit to come down to him. The bishop then drew the sign of the cross on Domingos' forehead with consecrated oil, reciting aloud, "I seal thee with the sign of the cross and confirm thee with the chrism of salvation, in the name of the Father and of the Son and of the Holy Spirit," followed by, "Peace be unto you." Domingos replied, "And also with you."[45] At the conclusion of the ceremony, Domingos emerged a full-fledged initiate of Catholicism, embracing the protective capacities of God and the saints but also sealing his individual commitment to abide by the religion's precepts.

IN ALL OF THESE TRADITIONS—Central African, native Brazilian, Portuguese, and Catholic—Domingos found new therapeutic methods that resonated with him. However, none could fill the void of the community he left behind in Naogon. Once he gained his bearings in Recife, he demanded greater freedom to meet with associates on other properties, search for medicines in the hinterlands, and heal on his own account. But Jacinto de Freitas refused to make such allowances, instead adhering to the strict code of conduct that dictated planter behavior in northeastern Brazil. The social hierarchy of the sugar plantation insisted that planters (*senhores de engenho*) assert patriarchal lordship over their vassals, be they family members, tenant farmers (*lavradores de cana*), or slaves. Jesuit priest André João Antonil put it best in 1711 when he wrote: "To be *senhor de engenho* is a title to which many aspire, because it means to be served, obeyed, and respected by many

... and in Brazil to be a *senhor de engenho* is as esteemed as a title of nobility in Portugal."[46] In order to protect the *engenho*, and hence the broader system of sugar production, planters needed to maintain strict discipline and control, particularly over the masses of "brute" African slaves. Planters who failed in this charge not only risked losing their own considerable investments but also became a threat to the security of their fellow planters.[47] For Freitas to allow Domingos the freedom to heal implied the right to go into the hinterlands to collect medicines, an unacceptable example for other slaves. Moreover, the allowance of such freedoms meant the loss of control over Domingos' labor. So long as Freitas controlled Domingos' healing practices and put them to effective use in perpetuating sugar and slavery, there was a place for Domingos in the world of the sugar *engenhos*. But as soon as he asserted the right to utilize his powers to build new communities, the patriarchal standing of the planters was eroded and their power jeopardized.

The consequences of disciplinary leniency by slave masters could be seen in pockets across the region, but the urban center of Recife was a particularly stark example of the disorder that sugar planters feared. The planters' merchant rivals often allowed their slaves to move freely across the city. The fact that these slaves and freed blacks engaged in all manner of untaxed trade was a particularly grating insult to struggling and insolvent planters. Rural planters expressed their indignation with merchants in a variety of ways, most often complaining to the Crown in broad terms that sugar and slavery were "dead" in the region, supplanted by merchant interests. However, in other instances, unmonitored slaves and freed blacks became the targets of planter anxieties. In 1738, the planter Sebastião Antunes traveled from Rio Grande do Norte to Recife to conduct business. When he arrived in the city, he ordered his slave Francisco to purchase some baked goods from the slave women who sold food and drink in the city's plaza (*quitandeiras*). When Antunes bit into a piece of citron cake, he found that it was "full of hairs, and because of the nausea this caused, he did not want to eat it." Some days later, Antunes ordered Francisco to purchase more cakes from the women, and again Antunes found "a hair the length of a finger ... in the honey on top of the cake." Antunes removed the hair and ate the cake, but on "the last bite, he felt a hair from the back of his tongue down his throat," which caused vomiting, dry heaves, a burning tongue, and a sore throat. These pains in his tongue and throat persisted for days even after he returned to Rio Grande, expanding to his head and face, at times putting him "at death's door."

Certain that he had been poisoned, Antunes denounced the *quitandeiras* before the Inquisition. Antunes admitted that there was no reason why the women "would want to do such great damage to him." In fact, he had never even seen the women. Instead, he always sent Francisco to do his bidding, but Francisco "never had any conflicts with the women" either. Though Antunes acknowledged that his slave purchased the sweets and delivered them to him, he insisted it was the *quitandeiras*, four sisters and their mother, who were responsible for the decline of his health. Antunes was entirely unwilling to consider the possibility that Francisco had a role in his poisoning. For Antunes, it was simply unthinkable that Francisco would do him any harm.[48] Like most rural slave masters, Antunes probably saw himself as benevolent and paternal in his treatment of his slaves. Meanwhile, the slave women of Recife's unruly center were dangerous threats to law, order, and life.[49] In these and other subtle ways, rural slaveholders blindly clung to their "way of life" as peaceful and idyllic, while casting the freedoms of Afro-Brazilian urbanites as inherently dangerous, the antithesis of the "good order" demanded by the *senhores de engenho*.

Exacerbating the shadowy threats of Afro-Brazilian economic competition, poisoning, and generalized "disorder" was the fear of more overt forms of physical violence by roaming bands of Africans. For planters, the unmonitored movement of large numbers of slaves and freed blacks was a palpable threat. Ironically, it appears that most of the violence in Recife's streets, just as on the sugar plantations, involved slave versus slave.[50] For example, on September 22, 1737, around eleven o'clock in the evening on Rua da Senzala, several slaves had some "drunken disagreements" that led to a violent altercation. The details of the fracas are sketchy, but it seems that in the heat of an argument, Antônio Cacheu delivered a blow to an unnamed slave of José de Freitas. Bystanders separated the two men, but shortly thereafter, a small group returned seeking revenge against Antônio. At least four men commenced fighting, some with knives. In the ensuing melee, Antônio Cacheu was stabbed two times, once in the back and once on the right side of his head. He died at the scene. The alleged perpetrator of the crime, a slave named Bartholomeu, belonged to the merchant Antônio Lopes da Costa. When Costa learned that his slave had been arrested, he immediately went to the jail and protested, claiming the murder charge had to be false. Costa argued that "after eight o'clock at night nobody leaves my house, which is notorious among all of my neighbors."[51] Costa's emphasis on the public notoriety of the rules of his household was a forceful assertion of his status as a "good" slave master. Whether Costa was telling the truth or not, it remains clear that African slaves often enjoyed the pleasures, and the pains, of Recife's streets deep into the night.

It was precisely this free movement of enslaved Africans, particularly at night, that so concerned sugar planters, who were far more isolated in their rural outposts than were city dwellers. For years, runaway Africans terrorized Pernambuco planters. The *quilombo* of Palmares, a vast network of runaway communities that stretched across the southern part of the captaincy in the seventeenth century, remained etched in the historical memory of the region. Various militias, bush captains (*capitães-de-mato*), and volunteers destroyed the core of Palmares by 1694, but smaller *mocambos* (hideouts) persisted.[52] In 1729, the governor of Pernambuco, Duarte Sodré Pereira, reported to King João V that in the backlands of Pernambuco, runaway slaves still came together "to rob the residents." The runaways built houses "partly in water," where they created "sharpened wooden stakes like swords" to protect the settlements. According to Pereira, one of these *mocambos* had recently been destroyed. Twelve men and two women were captured during the raid, all of them returned to their masters.[53] Still, the problem persisted into the 1730s, as runaway slaves continued "robbing passersby in the streets, committing many murders." In response, the king authorized a company of forty men—twenty-five regular soldiers and fifteen Indian conscripts—to go into the hinterlands and destroy the *mocambos*. By 1736, "many" were arrested and "some killed." Others returned to their masters, while still others ran deeper into the backlands "for fear of punishment."[54]

Taking into account the seigneurial code of conduct in northeastern Brazil, combined with the widespread fear of slave crime and violence, it becomes clear why Jacinto de Freitas placed limitations on Domingos' healing practice. It would have been unfathomable for him to do otherwise, particularly during a time when sugar planters suffered through severe social and economic crises. During these desperate times, maintaining the *engenho* and the appearance of planter nobility was more important than ever. Of course, difficult times spelled opportunity for someone like Domingos, who simply refused to adhere to planter formalities. He began to steal away from Casa Forte in search of potential clients, defying his master's orders. Because of his itinerant ways, neighboring *senhores de engenho* increasingly viewed Domingos as a menace. The owner of Engenho Madalena, José Rodrigues Colaço, believed that Domingos threatened life and property on his plantation. One of Colaço's house slaves, a mixed-race woman (*parda*) named Caetana Maria do Espírito Santo, reported that "her masters and the rest of the family in the house" deeply feared Domingos and "everybody complained about him." Even worse, she observed that it was Domingos' "fame as a fetisher [*feiticeiro*]" that frightened everyone so deeply. In response to the threat posed by Domingos, Colaço issued a standing order to the overseer on his property: If Domingos appeared on Engenho Madalena, he was to be forcibly removed as quickly as possible.[55]

For Jacinto de Freitas, Domingos' disobedience was intolerable, but the rumors and innuendos that he harbored a *feiticeiro* were an outright humiliation, a demonstration of Freitas' inability to control his slaves and a stain on his good reputation. Freitas clamped down even harder on Domingos, punishing him and trying to limit his further movement. Yet the more proscriptions Freitas placed on Domingos, the more Domingos resisted. Soon, Freitas began experiencing unexplainable losses on his *engenho*. Cattle died. Slaves fell gravely ill. Even Freitas' family experienced disturbing assaults on their health. Any of these might have been explained away by the combination of drought, famine, and disease that were common in Recife in the mid-1730s; however, the startling rapidity with which Freitas incurred these losses demanded some other explanation. Because of "the great mortality of cattle, horses, and slaves on his *engenho*," Freitas began to suspect that the rumors were true: Domingos was a *feiticeiro*, and he was systematically destroying Freitas' *engenho* with his curses (*maleficios*).

The *maleficios* that Domingos allegedly unleashed on Freitas encompassed a range of meanings between "poison" and "fetish." Slave masters in colonial Brazil were acutely aware that Africans sometimes killed their enemies, but there was a great deal of uncertainty about how they actually accomplished this feat. In his 1711 commentary on Brazilian slavery, Father Antonil wrote that Africans "killed with poison or fetishes, not lacking among them notable masters in this art."[56] Antonil was correct: Africans killed their masters, other slaves, and even cattle in Brazil. But his comment points to a central tension in Brazilian understandings of African practice: Which "art" had Africans mastered—the art of poisons or the art of fetishes? Poison could easily be explained from a scientific perspective: The natural properties of the substance consistently provoked illness or death.[57] But the perpetrators of poisonings rarely announced their intentions to their enemies. By its very nature, poison was a quiet, stealthy killer. Since Africans possessed knowledge of plants and other substances that were often unknown to European pharmacists, let alone slave masters, they could easily conceal poisons among plant and animal objects that might be used for benign, everyday purposes. Because some of these hidden substances defied European classification as poisons, Europeans understood them as having some other power, the power of fetishes. Furthermore, slave masters knew that Africans engaged in arcane ritual practices in their own languages that escaped European comprehension, rituals that sometimes resulted in the manufacture of "fetishes" aimed at harming slave masters. When Jacinto de Freitas accused Domingos of killing with "*maleficios*," he acknowledged this blurry line between "science" and the "supernatural." In the absence of scientific proof that Domingos poisoned his property, he left open the possibility that Domingos possessed other, unexplainable powers that could result in the rapid and steep decline of his fortunes.

Whether or not Domingos actually poisoned his master's property and family is a matter of conjecture, but this elusive proof is entirely unimportant for understanding the damaging effects of the social conflicts that produced the accusation. Disputes over Domingos' freedom to heal were the root cause of the rancor between Domingos and Freitas. As these disputes escalated, each man likely believed that one was out to injure the other. Some of these injuries were real, like those resulting from beatings or poisoning. But others were far less obvious. For instance, Freitas knew nothing of the lines of reciprocity between vodun, *vodunon*, and *vodunsi* that compelled Domingos to build a new healing community. Likewise, Domingos had little understanding of the damage his behaviors had on Freitas' reputation as a *senhor de engenho*. Despite the invisibility of the social sanctions embodied in these curses, they were perceived as real, debilitating injuries by both men. Indeed, on some level, each threatened the other's very social existence. Thus, when Freitas began to incur such heavy losses on his *engenho*, it was only natural that he would turn to Domingos as the culprit. By this time, it was clear that Domingos wanted to destroy him. The illnesses and deaths on Casa Forte simply confirmed what Freitas already knew. In this way, the accusation that Domingos was a "fetisher" or a "witch" was a reflection of Domingos' similar understandings of Jacinto de Freitas as the source of his greatest suffering—a sort of witches' "hall of mirrors."[58] Ultimately, the circularity of witchcraft or fetishry accusations acted as a sort of resumé of the existing social tensions that characterized Casa Forte in the 1730s.

Though it would be easy to view Domingos' alleged actions against his master as simple resistance or revenge, this would be a narrow optic on these matters. In fact, the destruction of the *engenho* was entirely consistent with African understandings of healing. The most immediate barrier standing in the way of Domingos' redemption from social isolation and exile was

Jacinto de Freitas. After more than five years in Brazil, cut off from the life-giving sustenance of his home community, Domingos was desperate to re-constitute a new social network, a new group of kin, a new self. Slowly but surely, he was dying a social death, constrained as he was by the demands of plantation labor and its inherent lack of freedom. This long, drawn-out process reached a painful crescendo in Recife, where the promise of redemption was perceptible in the language, histories, and cultures of the many Mina slaves he encountered. In order to save himself from the continued suffering of social alienation, Domingos resorted to the strongest medicine possible, a medicine that would cure him of Jacinto de Freitas. For some, this cure would have been interpreted as murder and destruction of property, but for Domingos, there was little to distinguish "killing" from "curing." Some of his African compatriots understood clearly that the therapeutic continuum defied easy characterizations of "good" versus "evil" or "doctor" versus "witch." Thereza Arda succinctly summarized how African conceptions of healing encapsulated these apparent contradictions when she described Domingos in six simple words: "Today he cures; tomorrow he kills."[59] "Killing" simply formed one part of a larger bundle of healing powers that most Europeans extracted as "evil." For Domingos Álvares and other Africans, redemption from slavery and social death represented a powerful cure indeed.

UNABLE TO VANQUISH Domingos, Jacinto de Freitas eventually ordered him jailed and sold away from Pernambuco. Here, the parallels with Do-mingos' experiences in Dahomey are more than striking. Just as Agaja gov-erned over a fiercely contested and fragmented Dahomean empire, so too did Jacinto de Freitas barely hold on to an exploitative seigneurial way of life. The legitimacy of each man's authority was threatened by rapid social and economic changes. In the midst of these crises, the sociopolitical up-start Domingos Álvares challenged ill-gained power with the promise of healing, kinship, and social redemption. For Agaja and Freitas, Domingos' otherworldly powers were respected and feared, but precisely because of these powers, he threatened social order. As such, Domingos' continued physical presence in the community was rendered intolerable. Ultimately, Agaja and Freitas recognized that Domingos was more valuable to them alive than dead. Agaja feared that killing Domingos might unleash the ire of his followers, or worse, of Sakpata. Moreover, Agaja could accrue an eco-nomic benefit by selling Domingos into the slave trade. For his part, Freitas also might have feared the otherworldly ramifications of killing Domingos, but more important, he already owned an economic stake in Domingos. To kill him would have meant the loss of his original investment, not to mention whatever Domingos might elicit at auction. During times of economic depression, this was too high a price to pay for revenge. In the end, Freitas jailed Domingos and sold him away to a distant market. Just as the king of Dahomey could brook no competitor, neither could the kings of the cane.

4

Rio de Janeiro

There is in this city a great healer coming from Pernambuco.
—Alexandre, enslaved apprentice shoemaker in Rio de Janeiro, 1737

In 1727, Recife's jailer, Antônio de Azevedo Pereira, complained to the Crown that the city's jail was too small to accommodate its "innumerable" prisoners. As a result of this overcrowding, waves of "malignant diseases" tore through the jail and the inmates died "miserably." According to Pereira, if not for the "great charity and fervent zeal" with which the Jesuit priests assisted the inmates, many more would have died in the squalid, suffocating conditions.[1] Construction of a new, larger facility was completed in 1732; however, this did not alleviate the problem of overcrowding. In 1735, Pereira complained that the new jail was still overflowing with "the great number of delinquents" in the province.[2]

When Domingos Álvares arrived at the jail about a year later, in late 1736, he was a bitterly frustrated man. Since his arrival in Brazil, he had struggled unsuccessfully to re-create his social self through the construction of a new healing community. He had successfully negotiated his transformation from cane laborer to healer, but he was still a chattel slave, and his master sought to control all aspects of his healing practice. At every turn, Jacinto de Freitas thwarted Domingos' attempts to claim some measure of freedom and heal on his own terms. Eventually, Domingos provoked a confrontation with Freitas, a clash of wills that resulted in Domingos' removal from Casa Forte and his subsequent incarceration. Whatever fragmented friendships he had forged in Recife were now dashed, replaced by even greater social isolation in the pestilent confines of the jail. As Domingos sat in his cell, he likely wondered what lay ahead for him. The cramped, unsanitary conditions of his imprisonment were reminiscent of his earlier experiences on the West African coast at Jakin. Certainly, another Middle Passage did not await him, but his fate seemed frighteningly uncertain.

The Jesuit priests provided some relief during their missions to the jail, offering comfort, prayers, and perhaps even food and water. Domingos no doubt appreciated these interventions, but he was not naive. After more than five years in Brazil, he could see that the remedies of the Catholic Church were no match for the ills that plagued him and so many other enslaved Africans. Moreover, the Jesuits were among the largest slaveholders in Brazil. Though some of the Catholic priests were charitable and benevolent men, their God proved powerless in addressing the everyday problems of most Africans. Quoting biblical scripture, priests exhorted African slaves to "be obedient to them that are your lords according to the flesh" (Ephesians 6:5). In exchange for their earthly labors, God promised freedom in heaven, a "glorious" redemption from their Babylonian captivity.[3] Such abstract assurances often rang hollow for enslaved Africans. Faith alone and the promise of a better life in the hereafter would not suffice. Devotion required reciprocity, and if the Christian God could not deliver an improved quality of life, some other god might.

Domingos languished in the Recife jail for several months while Jacinto de Freitas searched for a buyer. Given Domingos' infamy in the region, finding a new owner proved to be a difficult task. Finally, in early 1737, Freitas sold Domingos to Manuel da Costa Soares, a forty-year-old resident of Recife who "made a living from his business of negros."[4] It is unclear whether Soares captained slave ships sailing for Africa or only engaged in Brazil's internal trade.[5] Either way, he seems to have been absent from Recife at the time of Domingos' disputes with Jacinto de Freitas. Thus, he had no knowledge of Domingos' reputation as a "*feiticeiro*," nor did he know of Freitas' eagerness to get rid of Domingos. As he took possession of Domingos and loaded him onto the waiting ship, Soares viewed him as just another "piece [*peça*]," an opportunity to profit from the diminishing fortunes of northeastern planters.

For Domingos, the sight of the slave ship must have been the realization of his worst fears. Already anguished from the isolation of his enslavement in Pernambuco, he again faced the dreadful prospect of mental and physical suffering in the bowels of the ship. The grim memories of the Middle Passage, seven years earlier, surely flooded back into his mind. Domingos steeled himself for the arduous journey, perhaps praying to his ancestors, voduns, and even God for his safe delivery to yet another unknown destination. As the ship raised anchor and departed from Recife, Domingos might have learned that he was heading for Rio de Janeiro, but he could not have fully understood what this meant. Once clear of land, there was nothing but the monotonous misery of the sea. Several days into the journey, the winds suddenly and inexplicably stopped blowing, impeding the ship's forward progress. Sailors feared such abrupt calms in the winds. Crews and cargoes could die at sea of starvation and thirst if the wind remained still for more than a few days. Many sailors held to a widespread belief that the wind was not naturally so capricious. Rather, ships suffered curses that prevented the wind from filling their sails. Only by breaking the curse could the ship resume its forward movement.

As the slave ship sat dead in the water, Manuel da Costa Soares "heard that Domingos was a *feiticeiro*." Soares ordered the crew to tie Domingos to the ship's mast and whip him in much the same fashion as the captain and crew targeted the "negresse" sorceror on the French slave ship off Goree in 1696 (see chapter 2). When the crew stripped Domingos of his clothing, "they removed some pouches [*bolsas*] from his neck in which . . . he carried fetishes." These fetishes were burned, and Domingos was whipped. Shortly thereafter, the winds stirred and the ship sailed on to Rio without further incident, confirmation for the crew that Domingos' empowered objects (*gbo*) were the source of the curse. Altogether, the thousand-mile journey from Recife to Rio normally lasted around fourteen days under the ideal conditions of the summer monsoon; however, the troubles during Domingos' passage indicate a journey of longer duration. When the ship finally arrived at Rio de Janeiro, a relieved Manuel da Costa Soares carried Domingos and his other slaves to a warehouse to await sale.[6]

Domingos' arrival in Rio created a buzz in the slave community. At least two of his former acquaintances from Recife now lived in Rio. Caetana Maria do Espírito Santo, the mixed-race woman formerly enslaved on Engenho Madalena, had earned her freedom and moved south to live in Rio's urban center. Thereza Arda had also left Recife when her master died, and she was subsequently sold to a new master in Rio. Upon learning of Domingos' arrival in Rio, both women stirred fabulous rumors about his powers. Thereza claimed that Domingos not only had killed cattle and slaves in Pernambuco but also had killed the wife and son of Jacinto de Freitas. Caetana was more succinct, asserting that Domingos had "killed almost all the people on [Freitas'] *engenho*." More shocking still, Thereza and Caetana insisted that Domingos had committed the ultimate crime of killing his master, the *senhor de engenho*, Jacinto de Freitas—this despite the fact that Freitas was very much alive in Pernambuco and did not die until more than twenty years later in 1759.[7]

In their exaggeration of Domingos' capacities to destroy slave master interests, Thereza and Caetana spoke to larger truths that resonated deeply with the African community of Rio de Janeiro. Their rumors articulated the aspirations and fantasies of an entire community, bounded by its desire to see the slave master get his just dues. As the rumors spread, the women's privileged, "insider" knowledge of Domingos' past created new networks of intimacy among those who shared the knowledge. The veracity of the stories was not nearly as important as their collective social impact. As historian Luise White puts it: "How people talk about . . . their experiences, with what words and imaginings, does not flow directly out of a folk past; the power of those images derives from their historical and cultural meanings . . . but also from the individuals' ability to use them to describe their lives, their conflicts, and their fears. The power of any particular piece of gossip lies in the importance of the contradictions it reveals; the power of a rumor lies in the contradictions it brings together and explains."[8] For the slave community of Rio de Janeiro, Domingos Álvares was at once a powerful healer and a potential redeemer from the cruelties and abuses of enslavement. Nothing revealed this more clearly than his alleged murder of the slave master. Thus, even before he entered the social world of Rio's slave community, Domingos' reputation preceded him, simultaneously marking him as powerful, feared, respected, and admired.

News of Domingos' skills quickly reached slaveowners. As might be expected, the descriptions of his "healing" powers transformed significantly as word spread from the enslaved to the enslavers. Slaves and freed blacks believed Domingos utilized his powers to kill his masters, perhaps the most powerful and efficacious solution to the ailments of the enslaved. However, the enslaved described Domingos to slave masters as simply a great healer, capable of curing all manner of physical illness. In this respect, Domingos represented a viable alternative to Portuguese doctors, pharmacists, and bleeders.

Shortly after Domingos' arrival, a skilled slave named Alexandre traveled to the house of a woman named Leonor de Oliveira Cruz to make her a pair of shoes. Recognizing that she was not well, Alexandre asked her about her ailment. Leonor complained that she suffered from a chronic illness that Portuguese doctors had failed to cure, an ailment that she now understood to be "*feitiços*." In response, the apprentice cobbler asked Leonor if she was aware that "there is in this city a great healer coming from Pernambuco."[9] Leonor had not heard of this powerful healer, but she owned a domestic slave who had recently arrived from Pernambuco. She asked her slave, the very same Thereza Arda, if she knew any such person. Thereza responded affirmatively, noting that Domingos had been "widely known" as a healer in

Pernambuco and was now in the house of the slave trader, Manuel da Costa Soares.

On Thereza's endorsement, Leonor de Oliveira consulted her husband, Manuel Pereira da Fonseca, requesting that he send for Domingos. Fonseca went to Soares' house to inquire about Domingos' services. After his experiences at sea, Soares was more than willing to let Fonseca take Domingos for a trial consultation. Meeting Domingos for the first time, an anxious Leonor asked if he possessed the power to cure her and divine the source of the evil she suffered. Domingos responded that he did not know how to divine, but he could cure her with his herbs. Fonseca was skeptical that Domingos could help his wife; however, Leonor went to her husband "with her hands raised in the air," begging him to purchase Domingos. Ultimately, Fonseca relented, granting his wife's wish and bringing Domingos to live with them in their house. Thus, in just a matter of weeks, Domingos completed a remarkable transformation from an imprisoned "*feiticeiro*" to a valued and desired "healer." The very same powers that had made him a danger also made him a valuable commodity, as Leonor viewed him as her last hope for restoring her health. Meanwhile, when the slave trader Soares sold Domingos to Fonseca, he "gave thanks to God" that he was able to get rid of the troublesome slave.[10]

If Domingos' passage from Recife represented the nadir of his Brazilian experience, fortune smiled brightly on him after his arrival in Rio. Remarkably, he was able to rekindle several of the nascent friendships he had forged more than a thousand miles away in Pernambuco. When he arrived at the house of his new master, he was no doubt extremely pleased to receive the welcome of his "partner," Thereza Arda.[11] Domingos also became fast friends with Fonseca's young house slave (*moleque*), Caetano. Soon, Domingos learned that another old acquaintance from Recife, Caetana Maria do Espírito Santo, also lived nearby, allowing him to meet and speak with her "numerous times."[12] The exhilaration and emotional sustenance drawn from these unlikely reunions must have been deeply satisfying. Having survived the shared experiences of slavery in Recife, followed by the profound uncertainties of uprooting and separation, Domingos, Thereza, and Caetana reconnected in Rio, seemingly against all odds. Out of such serendipity (or was it providence?) came opportunities to cement bonds anew and build on the links of the past, sharing "old" knowledge with "new" friends like Caetano. In this way, broadly conceived kinship ties could sometimes be maintained, even fortified, despite the duress of forced migration and integration into a new community. These connections provided vital

TABLE 4.1 Brazilian-Born versus African-Born Slaves
in Rio de Janeiro, 1737–1740

Brazilian-Born		African-Born	
Male	47	Male	153
Female	58	Female	118
Total	105	Total	271
	= 22.1%		= 77.9%
	Brazilian-born		African-born

Source: ACMRJ, Nossa Senhora da Candelária and Santíssimo Sacramento,
Óbitos, 1737–40.

Note: This sample is drawn from 107 different properties where all slaves are listed
clearly according to birthplace. Inventories that include any slaves listed without a
clear provenance are excluded from this sample.

sustenance from the places left behind, but more important, they formed
the foundation for new webs of kin in unfamiliar places.

As Domingos built on the goodwill of friends, old and new, he also
took advantage of the opportunities offered by Rio's vibrant urban setting.
Though it had not yet surpassed Salvador in population or political importance, Rio was rapidly becoming the principal city of Brazil. With more
than 20,000 inhabitants, Rio was roughly twice the size of Recife.[13] There
are no reliable population statistics for the city during this early period, but
estimates suggest that between one-third and one-half of the city's residents were enslaved.[14] The forms of slavery witnessed by Domingos in Rio
reflected very different mercantile and entrepreneurial imperatives than the
forms of slavery on northeastern sugar properties or in the interior mining
regions. Rio slaves toiled in a variety of unskilled jobs as porters, muleteers,
peddlers, factory workers, and small farmers, as well as in a variety of skilled
trades as masons, blacksmiths, goldsmiths, tailors, and cobblers. Given the
economic diversity of the city, slaves tended to be distributed evenly across
individual holdings. The average number of slaves on properties in Rio
totaled only 3.5 per household.[15] The sex ratios in these households were
remarkably balanced. Unlike other regions, where slave men often outnumbered slave women by a margin of more than two to one, sex ratios in Rio's
slave community were nearly even. Again, this balanced sex ratio can be
explained in large part by the array of occupations that were the preserve

TABLE 4.2 Origin and Sex of African Slaves Listed in Wills
and Testaments of Slaveholders in Rio de Janeiro, 1737–1740

Origin	Male	Female	Total
Angola	44	44	88 (34%)
Mina	33	34	67 (26%)
Benguela	27	14	41 (16%)
Ganguela	16	5	21 (8%)
Congo	6	3	9 (3.5%)
Cape Verde	8	1	9 (3.5%)
Monjollo	4	1	5 (2%)
Moçambique	2	1	3
Bamba	2	0	2
Fula	2	0	2
Massangano	1	1	2
Carabari	1	1	2
Libollo	1	0	1
Maxicongo	1	0	1
Mbaca	1	0	1
Benin	1	0	1
Cobu	1	0	1
São Tomé	1	0	1
Loango	0	1	1
Total	152 (58.9%)	106 (41.1%)	258

Source: ACMRJ, Nossa Senhora da Candelária and Santíssimo Sacramento,
Óbitos, 1737–40.

Note: This sample includes only those slaves with narrow designations of
identity where some degree of African regional accuracy can be determined.
Hence, "Guine" slaves are not included.

of slave and freed women in Rio—seamstress, laundress, cook, midwife,
hawker, prostitute, housekeeper, and so on.

The slave population of the city was also overwhelmingly African, with
Africans representing approximately three-quarters of all enslaved (see
table 4.1).[16] When Domingos arrived in Rio, the city was undergoing a shift
in the composition of this African population away from "Mina" slaves toward "Angola" and "Benguela" slaves, thereby ending a thirty-year cycle in
which Minas challenged Angolas for numerical dominance (see table 4.2).
As suggested by the slave-trade statistics for Recife, Mina slaves dominated

African arrivals in Brazil in the early part of the eighteenth century, especially in the Brazilian northeast. The trade in Mina slaves to Rio is not as well documented, but it seems clear that significant numbers of Minas also arrived in Rio during the first three decades of the eighteenth century. Many of these Africans were destined for the gold mines of Minas Gerais. Between 1725 and 1727, around 5,700 Africans from the Mina Coast and Cape Verde arrived yearly at Rio de Janeiro. Roughly 40 percent of these were transferred to the mines. The remainder stayed in Rio and its immediate hinterlands, although some went as far south as São Paulo.[17] Between 1724 and 1736, Mina slaves represented over 30 percent of all Africans buried in the parish of Candelária, one of Rio's two urban parishes.[18] However, by the time Domingos arrived in the city, Minas had declined to 26 percent of enslaved Africans. Similarly, between 1718 and 1726, 681 adult Minas were baptized in Rio, a number that fell to only 235 between 1744 and 1750.[19] Even as the numbers of Minas in the overall population diminished, the trade from Central Africa to Rio grew significantly. In a sample of 23,872 Africans arriving at Rio between 1731 and 1735, 90 percent came from Central Africa.[20] In spite of these shifts in the African slave population of Rio, Domingos Álvares still found that at least a quarter of the city's African slaves hailed from the Bight of Benin. In addition, there were many more freed Africans from the Mina Coast scattered across city.[21]

Even before he completely recognized the cosmopolitan breadth of Rio, Domingos would have been struck by the physical beauty of the city. Surrounded by majestic, rolling terrain, four major hills (morros) defined the parameters of colonial Rio de Janeiro. To the north, Morro de São Bento and Morro da Conceição formed one barrier. To the south, Morro do Castello and Morro de Santo Antônio created another natural boundary. Packed in between these hills, in an area of just over one square mile, were the majority of the city's residents—black and white, slave and free. The most significant buildings—forts, churches, governor's palace, customs house, mint, jail—stretched along the cobblestone streets of the waterfront, facing Guanabara Bay, while more humble residential sites tended to occupy the interior.

Domingos lived on Largo de Santa Rita in the northern end of the city, about four blocks from the waterfront.[22] A modest two-story, single-spired Catholic church, Igreja de Santa Rita, dominated the large public square. Along the sides of the square were small single-story residential dwellings. In order to accommodate commercial activity, many of these buildings opened onto the street, operating as places of business. These shops con-

Rio de Janeiro waterfront. Domingos lived behind the cluster of buildings at the far right of the image. Luís dos Santos Vilhena, *Prospecto da cidade de S. Sebastião de Rio de Janeiro . . .* , watercolor [1775]. Courtesy Fundação Biblioteca Nacional, Rio de Janeiro, Brazil.

nected to the proprietor's living quarters by a corridor to the back of the building, where there was usually another door connecting the kitchen to a backyard.[23] Altogether, at least seven people lived in the cramped confines of Manuel Pereira da Fonseca's house. The slaves—Domingos, Thereza, and Caetano—slept on the floor in the kitchen. The seventy-year-old, Portuguese-born Fonseca, his thirty-eight-year-old mixed-race (*parda*) wife, Leonor de Oliveira, and their two sons occupied the more privileged living spaces.

When Domingos stepped outside the door of his master's house, he encountered a contradictory social landscape, at once deeply exploitative and full of opportunities. Signs of African debasement permeated the city, cheek by jowl with expressions of fabulous wealth and privilege. Setting off on a brisk, one-hour walking tour of the northern half of the city, Domingos could easily witness the complex social arrangements that defined his new home. On his very doorstep, next to Igreja de Santa Rita, was the Cemitério dos Pretos Novos, or Cemetery for Newly Arrived Africans. Here, dead and dying Africans, recently arrived on ships from Cacheu, Ouidah, Jakin, Luanda, Benguela, and Mozambique, were unceremoniously buried in common graves.[24] The steady stream of corpses brought from the slave market on the city's waterfront was a stark reminder of the homeland, the

Middle Passage, and the corrosive effects of slavery on African bodies. The cruel and inhumane treatment of the dead also reminded the enslaved of the frightening consequences of isolation, rootlessness, and social death. For most Africans, including Domingos, burial demanded ritual preparation of the body and the performance of specific ceremonies by family and kin in order to insure that the soul of the deceased would rest peacefully. In the absence of proper burials, these were restless, angry souls, rendering Largo de Santa Rita a truly "haunted" space for many Africans. We can only speculate how Domingos responded to the frequent arrival of these unhappy spirits; however, we can be sure that they reinforced his desire to create a space for a new therapeutic community away from the aura of evil that hung over Largo de Santa Rita.[25]

Striking out from Largo de Santa Rita, heading northwest on Rua dos Ourives, Domingos traveled only one block before reaching the base of Morro da Conceição. Atop the hill was the imposing palace of the Catholic bishop, and at street level, the ecclesiastical jail (*aljube*), where the Church imprisoned those accused of crimes against the faith. The iron-grated windows of the jail opened up to the outside, sometimes allowing illicit exchanges between prisoners and passersby in the streets.[26] Turning right on Rua da Prainha and walking downhill toward the bay, Domingos traveled just one block before reaching the living quarters of his friend from Recife, the former slave Caetana Maria do Espírito Santo.[27] Another freed *parda* and friend of Domingos, Paula Rosada, lived at the bottom of Rua da Prainha in a warehouse (*trapixe*) on the waterfront where she sold baked goods (*quitandas*).[28] Turning right on Rua Nova de São Bento, Domingos passed the Convento de São Bento, the massive Benedictine property with its Baroque church atop the hill. At the bottom of Morro de São Bento, Domingos continued left onto Rua dos Quarteis, funneling toward the waterfront. At Rua Direita, he turned right toward the center of the city.

As he proceeded toward the political and commercial center, the dirt and mud roads changed to cobblestone, the houses grew larger, and business increased. The first major hub of activity along the waterfront was the customs docks (*cais da alfândega*) and warehouses. Here, ships arrived to transport all manner of goods in and out of the colony—wines from Portugal, gold from Minas Gerais, and slaves from Africa. Africans could be seen "seated nude in the street, waiting patiently for a passer-by to purchase them."[29] Some sat stoically, but others outwardly displayed their grief and misery. In 1748, one teenage boy "cried continuously and refused to eat." He later confessed to his master that "he thought they wanted to fatten him in

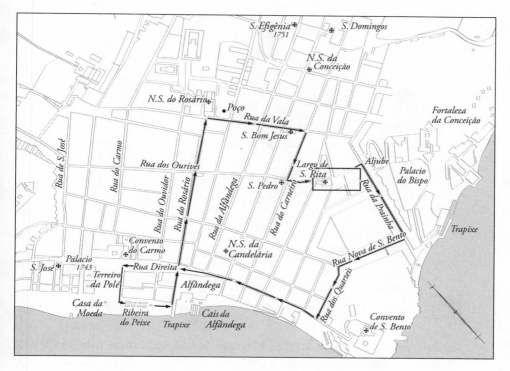

MAP 4.1 Street map of Rio de Janeiro delineating Domingos' path through the city. Map created by the University of Wisconsin Cartography Lab, adapted from *Planta da cidade de São Sebastião do Rio de Janeiro* (1758–60?). Courtesy Fundação Biblioteca Nacional, Rio de Janeiro, Brazil.

order to eat him."[30] In addition to the wrenching sight of the recently arrived slaves, Domingos might have encountered some of the king's slaves carrying deceased Africans in hammocks away from slave ships, destined to be buried a short walk up the hill at Santa Rita. Or he just as easily could have seen a wealthy slaveowner carried in a similar hammock by two of his African slaves.[31] The contrast of these two scenes could not have been more striking—one man treated like so much human waste, the other like a king, both dependent on African slaves to reach their final destinations.

Two blocks further south on Rua Direita, Domingos came to the main square of the city, known as Terreiro da Polé, where slaves were publicly punished at the tall whipping post in the center of the plaza. Only a few years later, in 1743, the square would be renamed Terreiro do Paço for the governor's palace that was already under construction on the southern edge of the square.[32] Just around the corner from the whipping post, on

Slaves carrying a woman in a sedan chair. Watercolor by Carlos Julião from *Riscos illuminados de figurinhos brancos e negros dos uzos do Rio de Janeiro e Serro do Frio* (Rio de Janeiro, 1960), pl. XIII. Courtesy Fundação Biblioteca Nacional, Rio de Janeiro, Brazil.

the waterfront, African men sold fish at the Ribeira do Peixe. Some of the stands were owned by whites, who staffed them with their slaves. Others, like the one owned by the freed Mina José Dias, were the small-scale enterprises of recently freed African entrepreneurs.[33] In addition to the fishmongers, other African men, and especially women, sold fruits, vegetables, and baked goods either as wandering hawkers or at fixed streetside markets (*quitandas*) surrounding the public square. Shadowing all this activity in Terreiro da Polé were some of the most sacred and hallowed institutions of the colonial administration—two Catholic churches, the colonial mint, the royal warehouses, and the nearly completed governor's house. Thus, white men (but few white women) moved in and out of the square. Depending on their station in life, some walked on their own, others walked with a slave carrying a parasol to protect them from the sun, and still others rode in a hammock or sedan carried by multiple slaves. In this way, the very act of moving about the city signified one's place in the social and economic hierarchy.[34]

Departing the hustle of Terreiro da Polé and rounding Ribeira do Peixe, Domingos encountered the next major thoroughfare, Rua do Rosário. Five blocks up Rosário was the church dedicated to Nossa Senhora do Rosário e São Benedito dos Homens Pretos. Completed in 1725, Our Lady of the Rosary was the church of choice for many of the city's *pretos* (Africans) and *crioulos* (Brazilian-born blacks). The church shared space with one of the city's largest garbage pits (*poço*), thereby insuring a constant foul smell, as well as untold health hazards.[35] Meanwhile, the city's most illustrious white families attended the Church of São José near the central square, as well as Nossa Senhora da Glória, the recently completed church overlooking the bay just south of the city. *Pardos* frequented Nossa Senhora da Conceição, several blocks northwest of Rosário.

The division of churches along racial and ethnic lines was no coincidence. Rather, it was the result of decades-long battles over hierarchies of worship between Africans and Portuguese, as well as among Africans of differing nations. From the first half of the seventeenth century, there existed in Rio a brotherhood of African and African-descended men and women, mostly Angolans, devoted to Our Lady of the Rosary and Saint Benedict. At the same time, there was a brotherhood consisting mostly of "Guiné" slaves devoted to Saint Dominic. The Church of São Sebastião housed both congregations. These brotherhoods played vital roles in the social lives of their members, but their most important public functions revolved around processions celebrating the Saint's Day and burials of brotherhood members. By the last decades of the seventeenth century, disputes with the Church over ecclesiastical powers, as well as conflicts between the brotherhoods over the use of church space and the efficacy of their respective saints, led to the brotherhoods being expelled from the Church of São Sebastião. In response, each brotherhood sought to build an independent church dedicated to its particular saint. In 1700, construction began on the Church of Our Lady of the Rosary, while just a few years later, only five blocks northwest, builders laid the first bricks for the Chapel of Saint Dominic (São Domingos).[36]

During Domingos' time in Rio, the Church of Our Lady of the Rosary and the Chapel of Saint Dominic were the centers of black Catholic life. In addition to cultivating devotion to its own saints, each church became the home for still other African brotherhoods dedicated to new saints. For example, beginning in 1734, the Church of the Rosary hosted a confraternity of "*pretos* Minas" dedicated to Saint Anthony of Mouraria. Another Mina brotherhood, this one dedicated to Our Lady of Lampadosa, also made the Church of the Rosary its home in the 1730s. Similarly, the Chapel of Saint Dominic housed a brotherhood of Minas devoted to Baby Jesus.[37] And in 1740, a brotherhood dedicated to Saints Elesbão and Efigênia also was installed at Saint Dominic.[38] Though there is no evidence that Domingos had any direct involvement with these confraternities, he might have had particular interest in the brotherhood of Saints Elesbão and Efigênia. Brazilian historian Anderson José Machado de Oliveira suggests that these saints were especially attractive to Africans from the Mina Coast, primarily because they reflected a similar duality to the creator divinities of vodun, Mawu and Lisa. Both sets of divinities represented the "sun and moon," foundational deities whose strikingly similar histories "could have incited Minas to associate such saints as their devotional symbols, establishing a profound dialogue between African ancestral gods and Catholic saints."[39] In Rio de Janeiro, the brotherhood of Elesbão and Efigênia initially included only Africans from the Mina Coast, Cape Verde, São Tomé, and Mozambique, expressly forbidding the admission of Angolans, creoles, *cabras*, and *mestiços*. The brotherhood quickly came to be dominated by "*pretos* Makis [Mahis]," suggesting a forceful Mahi presence in mid-eighteenth-century Rio. At the very least, Domingos would have found a nascent community of Mahi brethren upon which to forge new relationships out of a broad, common African past.

The importance of Catholic brotherhoods in Afro-Brazilian social and cultural life cannot be overstated. From the Church's perspective, the brotherhoods were a crucial means of introducing Africans to Catholicism, but for Africans, the brotherhoods were much more than an entrée into Portuguese or Brazilian religious ways. The brotherhoods represented an opportunity to build new communities of kin, even in a repressive slave society. Africans of various nations came together under the banner of larger meta-ethnic nations like Angola, Mina, and so on in order to worship ancestral figures (representations of saints) in shrines (altars) installed at Catholic churches. Indeed, the process by which Africans worshipped in the Catholic Church was very much in accordance with practices in their homelands. As Mary Karasch has noted, when new Africans arrived in Rio de Janeiro, they would learn that members of the brotherhoods

> organized ceremonies in the saint's honor, dressed the statue in
> proper clothing and symbols of sainthood, carried it in procession,
> paid a priest to say Mass at its altar, prayed "fervently" before other
> statues of the saint in the street, carried the saint's image on their

persons, and honored the image as long as it was forceful. . . . When the charm no longer fulfilled its purpose and dissension broke out because of witchcraft or sorcery and diseases plagued the brothers and their families, then one of the leaders led the brotherhood to a new saint, forming a new brotherhood.[40]

Given this clear overlap with the beliefs and practices of vodun, it is only natural to ask why someone like Domingos would not have been more attracted to the Catholic brotherhoods. The reasons are twofold. First, as already suggested in previous chapters, Domingos was open to integrating new deities into his system of belief, even those "voduns" of the Catholic Church. But during his years in Brazil, he had come to recognize that Catholicism ignored the everyday needs of the majority of Africans. God, Jesus, and the saints might have been effective in addressing some maladies; however, even the Catholic priests admitted that God could not free Africans from enslavement and the caprices of a master's power, except in the next life. Moreover, Catholic doctrine prohibited the worship of "false idols," those very voduns that might alleviate some of the pain and suffering that God could not address. By rigidly limiting the therapeutic options of Africans to God and the saints, the Catholic Church actually did the bidding of the masters, reinforcing the notion that African sources of healing, community building, and liberation were sinful, dangerous, and therefore illegal. In this way, the Catholic Church not only protected the purity of the faith but also worked to protect slave masters from some of the most potent forms of African resistance.

The second reason Domingos rejected the Catholic brotherhoods as a viable community of healing related to hierarchies of power within the brotherhoods themselves. If the Catholic Church reinforced the power of wealthy, white slaveowners, the black brotherhoods reinscribed this hierarchy, privileging financially solvent, freed blacks, sometimes even ones who were themselves slaveowners. To be a member of a brotherhood required the payment of yearly dues. For example, the yearly fee demanded by the brotherhood of Saints Elesbão and Efigênia was 480 réis in the mid-eighteenth century.[41] While this was a relatively small amount of money, equivalent to several days' wages for a skilled worker, it was still money that slaves had to raise on their own accord. Theoretically, of course, chattel slaves owned neither the time nor the labor that went into raising this money. For that matter, they did not even "own" the money itself, as masters held all claims over slaves' bodies and their property. As a result, only those slaves with masters who allowed them to have small businesses or time to collect alms could actually become members of the brotherhoods.

Theory aside, it was customary for many slaves to have such "privileges" in Rio, and the majority of brothers actually were enslaved; however, in order for the brotherhood to fulfill obligations to its members, it required far more income than the meager sums raised from yearly dues. Annual expenditures for burials and festivals alone could run into the hundreds of thousands of réis. Therefore, brotherhoods raised money by charging their members for the privilege of holding office. For example, the highest office in the brotherhood of Saints Elesbão and Efigênia, that of the *juiz*, required a payment of 12,000 réis. The *escrivão* (secretary) had to pay 10,000 réis. Regular members of the *mesa* (governing council) of the brotherhood— twelve men and twelve women—paid 2,000 réis each.[42] The only Africans who could afford these exorbitant fees were those who were freed, thereby creating a structure that inevitably placed wealthy freedmen in positions of religious power. As Mariza de Carvalho Soares aptly notes: "Freed blacks were not in the numerical majority of the brotherhood, but they were the ones who counted most, those who occupied the offices, those who made decisions, and consequently, the ones who were its greatest beneficiaries."[43]

As an enslaved African who was probably a vodun priest, Domingos Álvares must have questioned the legitimacy of the brotherhoods' governing structure. Not only did the brotherhoods reinforce hierarchies of economic power and freedom in the larger society, but they subverted hierarchies of worship in which voduns, priests, ancestors, and kin determined spiritual power through reciprocal exchanges. In the Catholic brotherhoods, the keys to power were not the ritual knowledge and devotion that invoked the goodwill of ancestors (saints). Rather, power was literally bought. In this way, temporal wealth determined spiritual power rather than the other way around. Though Domingos continued to share with the Catholic brothers their belief in the power of the saints, he would not submit to what he perceived as the false and ill-gained spiritual power of the brotherhoods' governing hierarchy.

Leaving behind the locations of black Catholic power and heading home along Rua da Vala, Domingos passed Igreja do Senhor Bom Jesus, the preferred church of his mistress, Leonor de Oliveira. Turning right onto Rua do Carneiro, Domingos walked one block before again reaching Rua dos Ourives. Pausing at the intersection just one block from his master's house, he would have seen the Church of São Pedro and across from it several residential dwellings owned by Francisco Gomes, a freed Mina slave and perhaps one of the wealthiest Africans in Rio. Gomes lived in the buildings with his wife, Rosa Mendes, also a former slave. The couple had no children of their own, although each had a son from a previous relationship. Next door lived Mendes' grown son, Antônio da Silva. In addition to the buildings he owned, Gomes rented a plot of land in the city's hinterlands on the farm of João Rosário. There, Gomes grew manioc, which he sold for profit. Among Gomes' most valuable assets were ten slaves—five adult Africans and their five children—nearly three times the number of slaves held by the average slaveholder in the city.

As a result of his economic fortune, Gomes enjoyed membership in three Catholic brotherhoods—São Domingos, Santo Antônio da Mouraria, and Santo Elesbão e Santa Efigênia. When he died in 1741, Gomes commanded a magnificent funeral, his body dressed in the garments of Saint Francis and carried through the streets of Rio by the brothers of all three confraternities. As if this were not enough, Gomes stipulated in his last will and testament that the brothers of the governing council of Nossa Senhora do Rosário also should accompany his body to its final resting place. In exchange for this honor, Gomes offered alms in the amount of 8,000 réis. With the arrival of the funeral procession at the Church of São Domingos, the residing priest performed the burial ceremony, along with four other priests. Gomes requested that in the days that followed the funeral forty masses should be said for his soul—twenty at his central parish church, Candelária, and twenty at the altar of Santo Elesbão and Santa Efigênia in the Church of São Domingos. For each mass at Candelária, he offered 400 réis alms, and for each at São Domingos, 300 réis. Beyond the outlay of funds for the elaborate funeral and masses in his memory, Gomes bequeathed 15,000 réis to Santo Elesbão and Santa Efigênia, 5,000 réis to São Domingos, and 5,000 réis to Santo Antônio da Mouraria.[44]

Though Gomes might have possessed exceptional wealth, he was by no means alone in this middling group of formerly enslaved, entrepreneurial African strivers. Scattered across the city were dozens of freed Africans engaged in a wide range of economic endeavors. Like Gomes, some lived in Rio and rented or owned agricultural properties outside of the city.[45] Others worked in the city as salespeople, like the aforementioned *quitandeiras* and fishmongers. And still others earned their livings in trades as barbers, seamstresses, and so on.[46] In short, this group of freed Africans was occupationally diverse, representing the breadth and scope of Rio's aspiring middling classes.

Slaveownership was one of the primary mechanisms of upward social mobility for freedpeople like Francisco Gomes. Indeed, dozens of formerly enslaved Africans in Rio became slaveowners themselves. Between 1737 and 1741, at least thirty-eight different freed men and women (*forros*) brought their own slaves to be baptized at Nossa Senhora da Candelária, Domingos' home parish.[47] It must be remembered that slavery was a socially sanctioned, deeply engrained institution not only in Brazil but also in the homelands of many Africans. Still, the widespread embrace of Brazilian-style chattel slavery by the formerly enslaved indicates a crucial shift toward the commodification of people. That such forms of human coercion and labor exploitation had been normalized across society demonstrates the corrosive effects of slavery on all people, even those who themselves had suffered its most debilitating consequences.

Compounding this situation, Rio's entrepreneurial, urban environment actually encouraged slavery as the most efficient means of capital accumulation. Even a cursory examination of the last wills and testaments during the late 1730s reveals how this system worked. Some small business owners utilized slave labor to operate the entirety of their enterprises. For example, the blacksmith João Ignácio Álvares employed fourteen male slaves and three females in his iron-forging business.[48] Each of Álvares' slaves gained valuable skills working in his foundry, thereby increasing his or her value. Álvares probably retained most of these slaves for his own use, but he always had the option of capitalizing on their increasing value by renting out one or two or by selling to other slaveowners at a healthy profit. Dotted throughout the inventories of slaveholders in Rio are references to lone blacksmiths, barbers, goldsmiths, *quitandeiras*, and shoemakers who worked for their masters essentially as independent contractors. Each of these slaves represented a potential source of income for the slaveowner, who could profit from his or her skills. Some slaveowners allowed their slaves to keep a portion of the profits from their business activities. For example, Thome da Souza owned two Africans, Lucas Mina and Luís Mina, who Souza allowed to work freely throughout the city "on his count and risk," taking a portion of the profits from their daily earnings.[49] In this way, small entrepreneurs could ascend the economic and social ladder on the backs of one or two skilled slaves. Some of these skilled slaves slowly earned the money to purchase their own freedom. Once manumitted, many of these former slaves also aspired to acquire a slave so they could train him or her in their skill, thereby quickening their own economic and social ascent and initiating the cycle all over again.

In some respects, the idea of building "wealth in people" in Brazil was similar to notions of wealth building in many parts of Africa, where polygamy, adoption, and enslavement were common mechanisms for acquiring economic power and social status.[50] However, there were important differences. Unlike in most parts of Africa, slaves in Brazil represented a potential source of capital growth, especially in urban areas where slave labor was equally distributed and market competition intense. Slaves accumulated or lost monetary value based on age, health, level of acculturation, and skills possessed. As such, the vagaries of the market could determine a slave's value, over and beyond his or her actual productive capacities. Ultimately, slave masters determined the amount of control they asserted over African slaves and the extent to which they would treat them as outright chattel or grant them certain "freedoms." In the majority of instances, slaves were dispensable, interchangeable cogs in labor-intensive enterprises, producing sugar, manioc, gold, bricks, and so on. Freedom in these settings was often elusive. But in those instances where small slaveholders owned one or two skilled slaves, they were often dependent on their slaves' loyalty and goodwill in order to profit from their skills. In these settings, capital accumulation adhered more closely to ideas of "wealth in people as wealth in knowledge," with slaves' value contingent on their willingness to share their intellectual capital with their masters.[51] The customary trade-off was the granting of greater freedom of movement, the ability to earn cash, and the potential promise of manumission.

Of course, slave masters determined if, when, and under what conditions they would manumit their slaves. Indeed, manumission records indicate that very few African slaves received unconditional manumissions — that is, manumissions without some monetary compensation or promise of future service. During Domingos' time in Rio, less than 5 percent of all manumissions were unconditional grants of freedom to African-born slaves, despite the fact that Africans represented roughly three-quarters of the slave population.[52] More than 75 percent of manumitted Africans paid their masters for their freedom papers, usually after years of uncompensated labor.[53] In this way, the vast majority of African manumissions were not grants of freedom so much as they were individuals purchasing their own slavery. This distinction is crucial because it places emphasis less on the act of granting "freedom" than on the transfer of "ownership" from the slave master to the slave, actually perpetuating the institution of chattel slavery. By granting small freedoms and holding out the promise of manumission, slave masters manipulated slaves to work harder and earn them ever greater profits.

In those instances where slave masters actually entered into contracts for their slaves' freedom, the master exerted total control over the transaction, dictating terms for the transfer of ownership that were almost always financially exploitative. During Domingos' time in Rio, Africans paid an average of 117,350 réis cash for their manumissions, slightly higher than the 100,000-réis average for healthy Africans found in property inventories during the period.[54] This average cash payment was exclusive of payments in kind (such as other slaves) and/or the possibility of future service. Nor did it include the years of service already devoted to the master.[55] Furthermore, this 117,350-réis average included payments for undervalued Africans who were old and infirm. For example, in 1743, Dorothea Criolla paid just 44,800 réis for the manumission of her husband, Domingos Angola, who was listed as "already old."[56] The price that healthy Africans paid to claim ownership of themselves commonly exceeded twice the actual market value of a healthy African slave; some even paid as much as three times the value of a prime slave.[57] In one extreme example, the wife of a slave barber named Antônio Mina paid 350,000 réis and an Angolan *moleque* named Matheus in order to free her husband from his master, Manuel Antônio de Carvalho. Thus, Carvalho not only walked away with the earnings from Antônio's years of service but also enjoyed the capital appreciation of Antônio's skill as a barber, pocketing roughly three-and-a-half times the average value of a male slave. In this way, slave masters actually increased their capacity to purchase slaves with the proceeds they received from manumissions.[58]

If financial windfalls did not necessarily result in the perpetuation of slavery, then the trading of one slave for another certainly did. When Antônio's wife offered the young Angolan, Matheus, as part of the transaction that earned her husband's freedom, she essentially exchanged her loved one's liberty for the enslavement of another. These forms of exchange were not altogether common. Slave masters preferred to receive cash, thereby allowing them the flexibility to reinvest their earnings according to their own wishes. Nevertheless, the trading of one slave for another clearly illustrates the way that manumission worked for the slaveholder's benefit, not simply reinforcing slavery but sometimes *expanding* it. Masters seemed particularly keen on trading experienced slaves, from whom they had already extracted years of service, for younger ones, thereby potentially doubling the productive capacity of their original investment. For example, in 1743, Angela Pereira da Glória noted that she bought her slave Maria Mina "when she came from her land still new and small." As a result of the "good service" she received from Maria, Pereira granted her freedom in exchange for 60 mil-réis in cash and a "newly arrived negra named Izabel, of the Angola nation."[59] In other words, after receiving years of "good service" and a cash payment equal to more than half the value of a prime slave, Angela Pereira was now poised to begin the cycle anew with the young Angolan slave, Izabel.

In still other instances, manumission's role in expanding slavery was even more explicit. In 1738, Manuel Ferram received two young Angolans, a "*moleque*," Francisco, and a "*molecona*," Maria, in exchange for the manumission of his slave, Marianna Angola.[60] Some years later, in 1753, Antônio dos Reis Franco received two Mina women in exchange for the manumission of his slave Marianna Mina.[61] It is crucial to recognize that even in these two-for-one exchanges, slaveholders probably received below-market value for manumission. In the economy of manumission, the cash value of slaves often far exceeded their actual value on the open market. This cost differential is illustrated perfectly in the case of the *parda* slave, Luzia, who paid her master 200,000 réis for her manumission—123,200 réis in cash and "76,800 in the value of slave named Francisco from the Benguella nation."[62] Luzia's value as an acculturated female slave was probably equivalent to that of the African man, Francisco. The 123,200 réis in cash was simply the manumission tariff, the steep value-added tax that many slaves paid in order to claim ownership rights over their own bodies.

Ultimately, whether through financial extortion or the expansion of chattel holdings, slave masters stood to benefit economically from manumission. Recognizing the ways that manumission facilitated the institution of slavery does not diminish the joy, opportunity, and expanded life chances of those individual Africans who achieved their freedom. However, our overarching assessment of manumission as a progressive, liberal legal mechanism should be tempered by the recognition that it often functioned as little more than a reification of slavery, a tool used by masters to exact a steep financial, human, and psychic toll on their slaves, especially Africans.

Though the legal mechanism of manumission often operated to reinforce African chattel slavery, the intimacy of Rio's urban environment sometimes influenced manumission decisions in ways that allowed for small openings in the institution of slavery, especially for women and children. These openings pointed toward freedom, but this was a freedom contingent on strict cultural and gendered conditions that actually underscored the very narrow limits of freedom in Brazilian society. Overall, Brazilian-born and female slaves were more than twice as likely to be manumitted as Africans and men.[63] The vast majority of Brazilian-born slaves spoke Portuguese, worshipped in the Catholic Church, and generally understood the customs and mores of their masters. Slave masters were most likely to free those with whom they shared certain cultural understandings and/or some deeper bonds of affection. These included female lovers and their shared children. Sprinkled throughout the manumission records are references to family ties between slaves and slave masters. These most often appear hidden behind terse phrases like "for the love I have for him/her" or "because I raised him/her from infancy." However, in other cases slave masters explicitly announced the manumission of their wives and children, as when João Rodrigues Álvares freed his Angolan wife from slavery, noting that "it was not just that his wife should be under subjection of slavery,"[64] or when Miguel Leite Pereira freed the *mulatinha* Eufrania, "recognizing that she is his daughter," born of his Mina Courana slave, Eugenia.[65] Even if one sets aside the inherent coercion of slaveowners' relations with their female slaves, it is clear that manumission came at the cost of certain other freedoms associated with Portuguese male power. The overwhelming privileging of acculturated slaves, women, and children in manumission decisions points to a system in which the patriarchal power of Portuguese-speaking white men was the society's ultimate measure of "freedom."

Baptismal records reveal similar intimate relationships between enslaved women and white men, further illuminating some of the gendered contingencies of slavery and freedom. In Domingos' home parish, three white men claimed paternity of enslaved children in baptismal records between May 1737 and September 1738. Among them was one Silvestre Martins, a Portuguese man who admitted to being married in his hometown of Vianna, even though he appeared at the baptismal font to claim paternity of his enslaved son, João, born of a relationship with a slave woman named Eugenia.[66] Clearly, Martins was undeterred by the stigma of his adultery. In claiming his child, he also tacitly acknowledged his relationship with Eugenia, who was the slave of another man. The web of relationships between Martins, his enslaved lover, his enslaved son, and Eugenia's master lays bare some of the complicated tensions between slavery and freedom in Rio's urban environment. Though the public acknowledgment of intimate relations between slaves and whites remained relatively rare, the compound effect of these relationships on the larger society meant that acculturated slaves, especially women and children, were the most likely to benefit from institutional mechanisms like manumission. Meanwhile, Africans and men were largely restricted from these legal mechanisms, unless they possessed extraordinary skills or resources. Indeed, African men were three times less likely to be manumitted than African women; four times less likely than Brazilian-born males; and an astonishing seven times less likely than Brazilian-born females.[67] If anything, the practice of manumitting Brazilian-born and female slaves, combined with a continuing influx of slaves from Africa, only hardened attitudes toward African men, rendering them the prototype of the lifelong chattel slave. In this way, the fixity of chattel slavery in urban Rio came to be defined primarily by provenance (African) and sex (male).

The combination of urban intimacy and social mobility in Rio sometimes resulted in perverse quirks in the institution of chattel slavery that further confound and challenge our understandings of slavery and freedom. In one notable case, a slaveholder named Joanna Soares owned a Cape Verdian slave, Domingas da Cruz, and her two *pardo* sons, Francisco and Vicente. Cruz earned her freedom, paying Soares 200,000 réis; however, her two sons remained enslaved. When the boys' white father, Leandro Álvares, died, he left 500,000 réis to apply equally toward their manumissions. The executor of Álvares' will immediately remitted 400,000 réis to Soares for this end. Unfortunately, Soares demanded the entire sum in order to free just one of the brothers. Thus, only Vicente went free. The remaining 100,000 réis from the bequest eventually went to Soares as a downpayment toward Francisco's manumission.

Meanwhile, the boys' mother, Domingas da Cruz, purchased a Ganguella slave of her own, a young *moleca* named Antônia. Cruz also owned small amounts of gold. Why Cruz chose to purchase her own slave when she apparently had the means to liberate her son and fulfill the final wishes of her children's father remains a mystery. To her credit, when Cruz died in October 1738, she left Antônia to her enslaved son, Francisco, "for the discharge of her conscience." Cruz lamented that Francisco sacrificed 150,000 réis of his inheritance in order to manumit her other son, Vicente. She hoped that the value of Antônia would allow her sons "both to remain equal . . . and free," as their father had requested in his final will.[68]

As a result of Cruz's bequest, the enslaved Francisco became a slaveowner himself, posing yet another difficult personal and financial dilemma. He could immediately sell Antônia and combine her proceeds with the 100,000 réis left over from his father's bequest, applying the money toward his own manumission. Or he could retain ownership of Antônia, utilizing her labor to earn the necessary funds to eventually purchase his freedom, an option that would have left him with a significant chattel asset on achieving his manumission. Francisco chose to sell Antônia quickly, receiving 80,000 réis, about half of the 150,000 réis his mother had hoped for. Francisco now had 180,000 réis invested toward his freedom. For reasons that remain unclear, Francisco's progress toward his manumission came to an abrupt halt after he sold Antônia. It seems likely that the demands of his masters blunted his attempts to earn his freedom. Perhaps his earnings as a skilled carpenter made him indispensable to Joanna Soares. Whatever the case, Francisco Álvares remained enslaved for nearly five more years before he reappears in the records. By this time, Joanna Soares and her husband were dead, having passed ownership of Francisco to their son, Bertholomeu dos Santos. Dos Santos agreed to free Francisco for 340,000 réis, minus the 180,000 réis already credited from his father's estate and the sale of Antônia. This left 160,000 réis that Francisco owed. On March 18, 1743, dos Santos agreed to free Francisco immediately, but only on the condition that he pay the remaining 160,000 réis within two years.[69] Assuming Francisco met the terms of his agreement with dos Santos, he would have achieved his mother's dying wish nearly seven years after her death. Altogether, Domingas da Cruz and her two sons would have paid Joanna Soares and her heirs 940,000 réis for their manumissions. Or, to put it another way, the value of the three was twelve times the value of their Ganguella slave, Antônia.

Francisco's ambivalent ownership and sale of Antônia, even though he was himself a slave, was not that unusual. In addition to inheritances, slaves became slaveowners in other ways in eighteenth-century Rio de Janeiro. For example, because it was customary for slaveowners to allow trusted, skilled slaves to work independently, only returning to their masters to share their profits, some slaves used their earnings to buy other slaves. During Domingos' time in Rio, André Nogueira Machado, a wealthy *oleiro* (potter/ brickmaker), owned a slave named Gonçalo. Gonçalo himself owned a slave named Francisca. When Francisca gave birth to a son, José, Gonçalo then became the owner of at least two slaves.[70] By definition, Machado also "owned" Francisca and José, but apparently he accommodated Gonçalo's assertions of ownership, separate from his claim to Gonçalo as a chattel slave.[71] The question that leaps to mind in this formulation is why Gonçalo simply would not use his earnings to purchase his own freedom. Clearly, he had the capacity to do so. Perhaps Machado refused his requests for manumission; however, the answer to this riddle also seems to lie partly in Gonçalo's relationship with Francisca. Two years after the birth of José, Gonçalo married Francisca, thereby becoming the husband of his "slave."[72]

Ultimately, these anomolies in the system of slavery, however common they may have become in Rio de Janeiro, amounted to very little for Do-

Street scene at Largo de Santa Rita in the 1840s, roughly a hundred years after Domingos lived there. The cemetery for newly arrived Africans lay adjacent to the church until 1769, when it was moved to Valongo. The fountain was built in 1839. From Louis Buvelot and Auguste Moreau, *O Rio de Janeiro pitoresco* (Rio de Janeiro: Heston and Rensburg, 1845). Courtesy Fundação Biblioteca Nacional, Rio de Janeiro, Brazil.

mingos Álvares. He was still an African slave, a male, and a recent arrival in the city. Nevertheless, he could see in Rio new possibilities that were notably absent from his earlier experiences in Pernambuco. Racial segregation, particularly at the street level, was almost imperceptible in Rio. Soldiers and local police insured that social decorum was maintained, protecting the city's wealthy residents from the "disorders of brute slaves of various nations... and similar people."[73] Otherwise, black and white, rich and poor, mixed freely across the dense urban space. If anything, the public "disorders" between slaves of various nations only underscored the extent to which the streets were an African domain.[74] This meant that Domingos had far greater access to other Africans than he had in the rural outskirts of Recife. Domingos also possessed an extraordinary skill that he quickly learned was in short supply, a skill that was even valued by many slave masters. Like dozens of other Africans, given the right situation, Domingos might be able to defy the odds and forge his own path to freedom; but he first had to heal his mistress, Leonor de Oliveira.

Arriving at Largo de Santa Rita, Domingos began his efforts to rid Leonor de Oliveira of her *maleficios*. Initially, his remedies seemed to have a salutary effect. Even Manuel da Fonseca commented that Domingos "applied some things that made [Leonor] feel better." But after a short time, Leonor's ailments returned. Meanwhile, the teenage son of Manuel and Leonor suffered an open wound on his leg that festered and refused to heal. Domingos traveled to the backwoods of Rio to collect herbs, which he used to make medicinal baths to treat the boy's leg. After a series of treatments, the wound did not heal; in fact, the infection grew worse. Manuel da Fonseca and Leonor de Oliveira began to suspect that Domingos was intentionally trying to harm them and their family. As a result, they curtailed his healing practice and restricted his freedom of movement. As had occurred with Jacinto de Freitas in Pernambuco, Domingos demanded the right to travel freely to collect his herbs; however, Fonseca steadfastly refused, believing that Domingos was out to do "evil."

As the conflict escalated, Domingos' anger deepened. One night after their masters were asleep, Thereza Arda asked Domingos why he would not provide remedies to cure their mistress and young master (*senhor moço*). Domingos provided an acid response: His mistress "did not show him enough kindness for him to cure her, but to kill her, yes." As for the young master, Domingos said he would give him something that would "carry his legs to hell." Despite Domingos' threats, the boy's leg evidently healed on its own, since he and his brother left Rio for the University of Coimbra only a few months later. Ironically, both went to Portugal to study for the priesthood.[75] As the young men prepared to depart for their theological studies, Domingos approached Leonor de Oliveira on several occasions, requesting permission to give the boys "something" that would "give them good fortune" in their travels. Leonor asked Domingos "if this was a thing of God or the Devil." Domingos responded that it was a thing of God. Believing that Domingos was incapable of doing good, Leonor refused his offer, and the boys traveled to Portugal without the benefit of Domingos' good luck charm.

Having lost the confidence of his masters, Domingos became increasingly agitated. He complained to "various people" that his masters did not want him to perform his cures and "treated him as a *feiticeiro*." Moreover, he argued that "they should find a person of respect to purchase him and give him his freedom, so he could have a public house where he could cure freely." The uncompromising stance taken by Domingos put him in a precarious position. He had already endured jail and exile more than once, so he was not unaware of the potential consequences of his resistance. In other parts of Brazil, slaves suspected of harming their masters with *feitiços* were brutally tortured. For example, in the town of Itú, about 200 miles southwest of Rio, the Africans Manuel Cabral and Thereza Mina were accused of killing people on their master's property in 1740. In order to elicit a confession from the two slaves, their master chained them around their necks and poured boiling wax and oil on them over the course of fifteen days.[76] If Domingos had heard of such cases, they did not deter him. Undaunted by the potential threat of Fonseca's retribution, Domingos held stubbornly to his demands for greater freedom.

After only six or seven months in Rio, Domingos' conflicts with Manuel da Fonseca and Leonor de Oliveira finally came to a head, prompting the governor of the captaincy, Mathias Coelho da Souza, to intervene.[77] It is not altogether clear what precipitated the governor's intervention. It simply might have been the accumulation of months of simmering tension, or perhaps there was another turn in Leonor's health. By the winter of 1737, she was in the early months of pregnancy, and it seems quite possible that symptoms of morning sickness would have been interpreted as the onset of yet another bout of *maleficios*.[78] Either way, it is notable that Domingos had come to the attention of the highest-ranking official in the captaincy, a clear indication of his powerful reputation in the city. Perhaps most surprising was the manner in which the governor imposed himself in the feud. Rather than ordering Domingos jailed or exiled, the governor urged Manuel da Fonseca to sell Domingos to another master who might adhere to the slave's wishes. The governor facilitated this process by linking Fonseca with a potential buyer.

In mid-1738, a man named José Cardoso de Almeida "experienced a great mortality among his slaves." After hearing rumors from other slaves that Domingos knew how to cure *feitiços*, Almeida approached the governor with a request to avail himself of Domingos' services. At the governor's urging, Fonseca released Domingos to the custody of Almeida, who carried Domingos to his farms in Rio's countryside. Accompanying Almeida and Domingos on their trek to the backlands were Almeida's wife and her brother, the Catholic priest Salvador Ferreira Mendes. It is unclear exactly why Mendes was invited; however, it seems logical to conclude that he was brought along to monitor the proceedings and to advise his brother-in-law on any irregularities that might offend the Catholic Church.

Domingos arrived at Almeida's properties with nothing more than a sack of leaves, roots, herbs, and powders. As his entourage stood back and watched, Domingos surveyed a large tract of land with several garden plots arranged on a hillside, each worked by a crew of slave laborers. Almost immediately, he looked uphill and shouted out the names of two slaves working on the more distant plot. How Domingos knew the slaves' names was a mystery to the bystanders since Domingos had never before been to the farms. Domingos advised that the two men should immediately be arrested; Almeida complied. Moving deliberately toward the upper property, Domingos asked to see the slaves' living quarters (*senzalas*). Arriving at the *senzala* of one of the detained men, Domingos ordered that a hole be dug in the middle of the earthen floor. There, they found a calabash containing "bones, roots, and many other things." Domingos announced to Almeida, "This here is what made your people sick and killed them." In response to this revelation, Almeida ordered the two offenders jailed in the Santa Cruz Fort, where one of them eventually died.

Returning to the lower property, Domingos called together all of the slaves on Almeida's farms and asked them to form a line. One by one, Domingos inspected the slaves, diagnosing whether they were infected with the evil cast by the two men. Some "did not have anything"; others had "the beginnings" of illness; and still others were "full" of *feitiços*. The sick were pulled aside to be healed. Domingos then ordered a large pot of water to be put on a fire. Opening his sack of medicinal plants, he poured the contents into the boiling cauldron, which resulted in a "fetid smell." Domingos then ordered the infected slaves to wash themselves with the water, but they refused. In response, Domingos dipped a little water out of the cauldron and cast it at one of the men in the line. The man immediately fell to the ground "like a dead person." Seeing this, Almeida's wife became distressed, believing that Domingos had killed her slave. In order to allay her fears, Domingos went to the aid of the man, assuring the mistress that her slave was not dead. Once propped up on his feet, the man immediately came back to life. Duly impressed by his powers, the remaining slaves submitted to Domingos' therapeutic baths.[79]

In addition to the baths, Domingos used his medicines to make infusions and drinks for Almeida's slaves. According to Almeida, these herbal remedies acted as purgatives, cleansing the ill people of their *feitiços*. Once the ailing slaves were purified, Domingos made a small cut on each person's arm and foot. Taking a pinch of herbs ground to the consistency of tobacco, he rubbed it into the bleedings, manipulating and massaging the wound until the herbs turned to powder and eventually disappeared. Domingos explained that this would seal the slaves, protecting them from any future attempts to infect them with *feitiços*. Ultimately, Domingos met with mixed success in his work on Almeida's farms. According to Almeida, "Among those that Domingos cured, some recovered and others died."[80]

More important for Almeida, who described himself simply as a "businessman," Domingos proved to be a remarkably profitable earner. After Domingos completed his work on the farms, Almeida allowed him to heal freely throughout the region. Observing that "in very few days Domingos could bring one dobra [12,800 réis] in earnings for his master," Almeida resolved to purchase him from Manuel Pereira da Fonseca. Almeida paid 150,000 réis for Domingos, about 25 percent above the average price paid for a healthy African slave in Rio in the 1730s.[81] Fonseca believed he was off-loading a dangerous and unproductive slave who was a potential threat to public safety. He was no doubt relieved to cut his losses and remove his family from harm's way. For Almeida, however, Domingos represented a tremendous economic opportunity. Even if Domingos only earned 12,800 réis per month, Almeida could recoup his initial investment of 150,000 réis in just under a year. The central question for Almeida was: How could he harness Domingos' skills and optimize his earning power while continuing to hold him in captivity?

5

Freedom

Freedom is not something that anybody can be given;
freedom is something people take and people are as free as they want to be.
—James Baldwin, *Nobody Knows My Name*

José Cardoso de Almeida quickly recognized that his ability to capitalize on Domingos' talents was contingent on the very freedoms Domingos had been demanding since he first laid foot in Brazil eight years earlier. Consequently, Almeida acquiesced to Domingos' wishes, granting him the right to move about the city unimpeded to conduct his healing practice. After having had three different slave masters in three different Brazilian provinces, Domingos could finally claim an important measure of autonomy, if not full freedom. From the outset, Almeida observed that "when [Domingos] went to the forest to search for herbs, he always went alone, spending the entire day and many times more, saying that it cost him dearly to find the herbs because he had to travel to all parts." At first, Domingos worked as an itinerant healer, joining the dozens of other enslaved and freed Africans who crisscrossed Rio and its hinterlands on a daily basis. As his reputation spread, Almeida fielded dozens of requests, receiving "letters from various people" across the region soliciting Domingos to cure their slaves. Within months, Almeida could no longer meet the rapidly increasing demand for Domingos' services. In order to maximize his profits from Domingos' growing fame, Almeida set him up in a "public house," a rental property in the western part of the city.[1] There, Domingos lived and cured all manner of people, sharing the profits with his master.

Though we do not know the precise details of the financial arrangement between Domingos and Almeida, under normal circumstances, Domingos would have been responsible for covering his own living expenses, including food, clothing, and some portion of the rent on his house. In addition, he would have paid Almeida a fixed daily rate, probably around half of his profits. All excess earnings were Domingos' to keep.[2] Domingos used some of these earnings to finance a separate arrangement with Almeida. Once

Domingos saved an agreed-upon amount of money, he would turn the money over to Almeida in exchange for his manumission. Just over a year later, in late 1739,[3] Almeida "received his requested amount and gave [Domingos] his manumission, leaving him in freedom."[4]

Taking the long view of Domingos' path to freedom in Brazil, we can draw several broad conclusions. First, Domingos' demands as a healer were clearly anathema to plantation culture. Until he became the slave of José Cardoso de Almeida, Domingos worked for slaveowners who were guided by a rural, planter ethos. As long as skilled slaves like Domingos maintained their proper place in the social and economic hierarchy, the master's way of life was safe. But Domingos transgressed this hierarchy when he demanded freedom of movement, freedom to heal, and so on. These freedoms were perceived to be real threats to the paternalistic, patriarchal power of the *senhores de engenho* and were simply intolerable. Second, if plantation settings were not amenable to someone with Domingos' skills, then urban areas like Rio were more so. Unlike agricultural regions dominated by conservative planters, Rio de Janeiro and its mining hinterlands were more entrepreneurial in spirit, laboratories for free-market ideas yet still driven by slave labor. The diversity of the economy and the growing middling class played crucial roles in facilitating new forms of slavery. Of course, the city had strong ties to the countryside, so the boundaries between urban and rural were permeable. Manuel Pereira da Fonseca, for example, owned a house in Rio, but his farms outside the city guided his economic interests and sociocultural compass. As a seventy-year-old man, his worldview was still guided largely by the desires and aspirations of the *senhores de engenho*, a way of life that Rio de Janeiro was rapidly leaving behind. Fonseca's stubborn determination to control Domingos' movements and his refusal to recognize Domingos' earning potential were partly a reflection of his own fading dreams.[5]

The future of slavery in Rio de Janeiro lay largely in relationships like that forged between Domingos and José Cardoso de Almeida. The fact that the governor intervened to facilitate Domingos' transfer from Fonseca to Almeida underscores some of the tensions in the transformation from a planter ethos to a market-driven one. The governor's intervention also highlights the "official" sanctioning of this transition at the highest levels of colonial government. Yet Domingos was not simply the object of manipulation for enterprising businessmen. It must be stressed that, in many respects, Domingos seized his own freedom. To the extent that he maintained control over a bundle of powers that was unavailable to his masters, they deeply feared him, and he manipulated these fears until he finally landed with a master who was responsive to his demands.[6] Nevertheless, the very nature of slavery was also changing, at least in urban settings like Rio. As time passed, the idea of hiring out slaves in a cash economy would become even more accepted and widespread. Almost a century later, in the late 1820s, an English traveler, the Reverend Robert Walsh, observed: "Many persons black and white about Rio live in the same manner. They possess a single slave, whom they send out in the morning, and exact at night a *patac* [320 réis]. They themselves do nothing, lying indolently about and living on this income."[7] By this time, roughly 88 percent of all property holders in Rio owned at least one slave, the majority utilized as cash-earning day laborers (*escravos de ganho*) in the urban economy.[8]

This newer, urban form of slavery was no less exploitative than plantation slavery; in fact, it was arguably more so. From a purely economic perspective, urban slaveowners sometimes stood to make far greater earnings from their individual slave investments than their planter counterparts. For example, Domingos earned 12,800 réis "in very few days" when Almeida first put him to work. As demand increased, so did Domingos' fee. By 1740, just a year after earning his manumission, he commanded 2 dobras (25,600 réis) to perform his cures, and by 1741, he demanded this amount for a simple diagnosis.[9] Based on these figures, Domingos almost certainly earned more than 30,000 réis per month when he was Almeida's slave, a truly astounding sum when one considers that the *annual* income created by a sugar plantation slave during the mid-eighteenth century was around 35,500 réis.[10] Thus, Domingos had the potential to earn as much in a month as a plantation slave could produce in a year. Even if the rental of the public house and Domingos' upkeep had remained entirely on Almeida's account, which was unlikely, Almeida still would have recouped Domingos' value within a year. If these earnings are combined with Domingos' manumission money, Almeida would have earned at least a 100 percent profit, and probably much more, in just over a year.[11] To be sure, Domingos was exceptional in his earnings potential, but his case further illustrates the direct relationship between slavery and exploitative capital accumulation, even in the first half of the eighteenth century.[12]

The question of what Domingos gained out of his relationship with Almeida is a little more complicated. The most obvious and simple answer is that he gained his freedom, but the contours of that freedom shifted over time. At first, Domingos was a vehicle for building Almeida's wealth, his freedom dependent on Almeida's willingness to allow him to move about freely earning income. Domingos probably could have run away or absconded with his earnings, yet he adhered to the terms of his slavery. Domingos' own definition of "freedom," which rested far more on his ability to build a therapeutic community through his healing practice than on economic independence, seems to explain why he accommodated Almeida's demands. Domingos was all too familiar with the limitations of trying to carry out his work in the rural environment. In Rio, the high population density, relative mobility of the enslaved and freed African populations, and greater access to his "Mina" kinsmen were far more conducive to the reconstitution of community (and self). Here, urban "slavery" and the master's desire for capital accumulation overlapped neatly with Domingos' primary demands—the "freedom" to heal and create new webs of kin. Ironically, then, by his own definition, Domingos gained an important measure of "freedom" as soon as he became Almeida's "slave."

This is not to say that Domingos never recognized the implications of individual economic freedom, but he had to *learn* the meaning of this freedom as an extraction of collective healing and community building. The commodification of his skills was a very different mode of exchange than what he was accustomed to in his homeland and as a plantation slave. In many respects, his service under José Cardoso de Almeida was an apprenticeship in the cash economy. The detached, depersonalized nature of curing for cash was alien to Domingos, whose healing practices in Benin were tied to reciprocal obligations of devotees, priests, and deceased ancestors. Nevertheless, Domingos quickly understood that his *individual* ability to generate cash was the key to the "freedom" of movement he so desperately desired as a necessary precondition to community building. Ironically, the skills that earned him his freedom in the cash economy often reinforced the enslavement of other Africans, as the majority of his clientele were slave owners seeking to heal their ailing slaves. Still, his healing practices had immediate salutary effects on Africans, some of whom surely recognized the broader implications of Domingos' powers as a potential source of community therapy.

Once Domingos gained his full legal freedom in 1739, he continued healing at the "public house" on Rua da Alfândega on the western outskirts of the city. Significantly, the house lay in close proximity to fertile spiritual grounds already frequented by Africans and their descendants, its location only blocks away from the churches and chapels of the city's black Catholic brotherhoods. The presence of Domingos' house in the midst of these Catholic spaces stood as a direct challenge to the Church's supremacy as the primary source of therapy for the region's African population. More-over, Domingos also attracted mixed-race and white clients to his healing center. One witness, Ignácio Correa Barbosa, who lived several houses away from Domingos' healing center, observed that "various white, *mulata*, and *negra* women" gathered at the house during the night to be cured. He also claimed that when the women departed the house, he overheard them saying, "I am bringing my roots and powders for good luck." According to Barbosa, Domingos' cures caused "great scandal" among his neighbors.[13]

The nighttime gatherings in the house on Rua da Alfândega eventually attracted the attention of the vicar of Nossa Senhora da Candelária, Ignácio Manuel da Costa Mascarenhas. In early 1740, Mascarenhas and one of his deputies raided the dwelling where Domingos lived and performed his cures. Arriving around sunset, they found "various sick people and many other *pretas* in the yard who were not sick." When the priests asked the people why they were gathered in the house, they answered that "they went there so the *preto* who lived there could cure them." Those who were not sick responded that they were there for Domingos to "close them so the *fetiços* would not enter their bodies." Searching the premises, the priests could not locate Domingos. Frustrated and angry, Mascarenhas pulled out a whip (*chicote*) and commenced beating Domingos' followers, chasing them from the house. As the ailing people spilled into the street, the priests shouted that Domingos had tricked them and warned them that they should never return to the house. Continuing his investigation the following morning, Father Mascarenhas again searched for Domingos around the house and surrounding neighborhood, but to no avail. Rumor had it that he had fled to the countryside west of the city, near the neighborhood of São Domingos. Mascarenhas traveled there to search for him on several occasions, but Domingos successfully evaded detection.[14]

In the aftermath of the raid, Domingos seemed to gain greater energy and purpose. Though the healing center on Rua da Alfândega was effectively shut down, Domingos quickly went about the task of rebuilding his practice. He stayed in São Domingos only a few days before he established a new healing center in a house on Rua de São José on the southern edge of the city. He set up another clinic in a rented building in Prainha, in the northern part of the city, only blocks from the place where he had lived as a slave when he first arrived in Rio. And he established a ritual space just south of the clinic on São José, in the countryside near the new parish church, Nossa Senhora da Glória. By late 1740, all three of these spaces

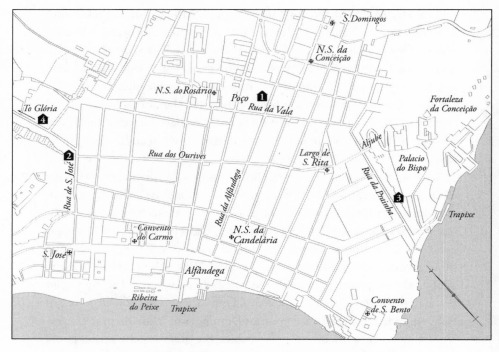

MAP 5.1 Domingos' healing centers and *terreiro* in Rio de Janeiro. (1) Domingos' original healing center, established when he was still the slave of José Cardoso de Almeida and later raided by Catholic priests. (2) The healing center in the southern part of the city; it rose to prominence after the priests invaded house #1. (3) The healing center at Prainha, near the house of his former master and mistress on Largo de Santa Rita. (4) Domingos' ritual space (*terreiro*) at Glória, located on the outskirts of the city just off the left edge of the map. Map created by the University of Wisconsin Cartography Lab, adapted from *Planta da cidade de São Sebastião do Rio de Janeiro* (1758–60?). Courtesy Fundação Biblioteca Nacional, Rio de Janeiro, Brazil.

operated simultaneously, Domingos splitting time between them as well as continuing his itinerant practice across the city and its hinterlands.

These were heady times for Domingos. Taking full advantage of his hard-earned freedom, he quickly and systematically went about the task of establishing a strong economic and social base. Clearly, Domingos was an astute businessman, but "business" was primarily a means to building new webs of kinship. His rental properties—the one that the priests raided in the western part of the city, plus those in the north and south—formed a ring around the edge of the city, connecting urban and rural in a therapeutic network that stretched across the region. His clinics were consistently "full of people" seeking cures, the majority of them slave masters with their ailing slaves. For these and other wealthy clients, Domingos demanded 2 dobras (25,600 réis) per cure. These steep prices might be explained, in part, by the miserable state of health in Rio. In 1737, the governor of Rio reported that 3,000 people in the captaincy died of some unspecified disease, probably smallpox.[15] Leprosy was also epidemic during the late 1730s and early 1740s. The disease prevailed mostly among "negros and commoners," infecting "more than 300 people" by 1740.[16] Regardless of the desperation generated by these epidemics and other illnesses, some of Domingos' clients balked at paying such excessive prices. When Maria de Jesus called Domingos to cure one of her domestic slaves on Rua do Ouvidor, Domingos diagnosed the enslaved woman's illness, but before curing her, he demanded his standard rate. In response, Maria de Jesus immediately kicked him out of her house, concluding that he was either a "*feiticeiro* or a trickster."[17] Others believed that Domingos simply duped them. Antônio da Costa Gouvea called Domingos to cure a slave on his *engenho* in the countryside. After paying for the cure, Gouvea concluded that Domingos was a *feiticeiro* "since the slave never improved from his cure."[18] Despite this handful of complaints, it is clear that the majority of Domingos' clients found his demands reasonable since he continued to draw dozens of new patients.

Domingos' urban clinics and itinerant practice thrived, but his real focus was the property in the southern countryside at the foot of Morro da Glória. Recently completed in 1739, Nossa Senhora da Glória was a spectacular Baroque-style Catholic church sitting atop a high hill that seemed to rise directly out of the sea. During this time, Glória was still very much a rural outpost, sparsely settled and several kilometers from Rio's urban center. The natural beauty of the area had attracted the spiritually inclined for over a hundred years. Indeed, legend held that as early as 1608, a man named Ayres had placed a small image of the Virgin Mary in a natural grotto on the hill, thereby consecrating the space.[19] The spiritual significance of the environment was not lost on Rio's African population. For Domingos, this majestic setting very likely represented the confluence of earth, sea, and sky voduns. In Dahomean thought, the god of the sea, Agbê, communicates with the creators "at the point where sea and sky meet, that is, at the horizon. Hence it is said that Agbê and his children are both in the sea and in the sky, because their home is where the two meet. And that is also why it is held that before a person dies, he must render account of his life to the ruler to whom the care of the earth was entrusted. In the sun, seen in the morning rising from the sea, and in the evening returning home once more, are the eyes of

Nossa Senhora da Glória. Watercolor by Henry Chamberlain from *Views and Costumes of the City and Neighbourhood of Rio de Janeiro, Brazil* (London, 1822).

Agbê."[20] Hence, Morro da Glória represented a potent passageway to the world of the sea and sky voduns, as well as a temporal symbol of the human life cycle. All that was required to tap this power and "render account" was the consecration of the space to the earth voduns.[21]

Here in this powerful spiritual space, just below the new Catholic church, Domingos established an altar under a large orange tree where he healed and made offerings to voduns every Saturday.[22] The construction of such an altar would have been unthinkable without previous knowledge, extensive training, and a bloodline tied to the priesthood of the vodun. Yet Domingos did not simply replicate a vodun altar from his homeland. Instead, he applied ritual knowledge learned in Naogon to the Brazilian setting in new and ingenious ways. The choice of the orange tree as the site of the altar was significant. Trees, deeply rooted in soil occupied by the earth voduns and other deceased ancestors, were powerful representations of the sustenance offered by the spirit world. In vodun and Brazilian Candomblé, the appearance of certain types of trees on auspicious sites is interpreted as a sign to build a shrine. In Dahomey, people believed that the *lokó* (silk cottonwood) tree could not be planted, instead growing only at the discretion of the vodun. Thus, its appearance was a provocation by the vodun to build an altar.[23] Similarly, prominent ficus and jack fruit trees have

Fetishes from the Guinea Coast. The importance of the "Fetisso Tree" and "Fetisso Mountain" are underscored by Domingos' decision to build his shrine at the base of an orange tree on Morro da Glória. Lithograph from C. Grafton Hardwicke and Tweeddale Argyll, *Voyages and Travels to Guinea and Benin*, vol. 3 of *A New General Collection of Voyages and Travels* (London: Thomas Astley, 1746).

become the locus of Candomblé worship in Brazil.[24] In early eighteenth-century Dahomey, Willem Bosman reported that trees were "pray'd to, and presented with Offerings, in time of Sickness, more especially Fevers, in order to restore the Patients to Health."[25] Domingos' decision to build his shrine under the orange tree was likely a direct acknowledgment of the bounty provided by the earth vodun, a symbol of his gratitude. The tree was also the invocation, the sign from the gods, that culminated the gathering of the vodun pantheon—earth, sea, and sky—in a single ritual setting.

In addition to the orange tree, Domingos' ritual space (*terreiro*) at Glória consisted of a small house, a yard where chickens were raised, and perhaps most important, a small group of initiates who assisted Domingos in his Saturday healing sessions. These initiates formed the core of a therapeutic community Domingos had been constructing ever since he was the slave of José Cardoso de Almeida, if not before. It seems likely that some of the people who were chased away from the house on Rua da Alfândega were among his first initiates, and they simply reconvened at the *terreiro* in Glória. New adherents apparently integrated the healing community through the urban clinics, deciding that they owed devotion to the voduns for returning them to health. In this way, the houses on Rua da Alfândega, on Rua de São José, and in Prainha served as gateways for potential initiates. This is not to say that all people healed at the clinics became initiates. As already noted, for the most part, these clinics served slave masters. The cash generated from curing "outsiders" subsidized the healing community at Glória since Domingos required cash to rent ritual space and housing, as well as to purchase daily necessities. In fact, there is suggestive evidence that Domingos returned to an African-style economy of barter and exchange with some of his former clients. Community "insiders" who made offerings of food and drink to the voduns were apparently exempt from the steep fees Domingos usually charged his clients. Such offerings speak to the "compositional" nature of wealth building for Domingos. By attracting knowledgeable followers who offered empowering substances to the voduns, Domingos created the necessary synergies to cultivate community health and well-being. In this way, wealth and power could not be measured by capital accumulation alone.[26]

Among the former slaves who constituted Domingos' broad, therapeutic community was a woman named Paula Rosada. Following her trajectory from ill client at one of his urban clinics to potential initiate provides us with a glimpse of the path that some of Domingos' adherents followed. Paula Rosada was a former slave, a freed *parda*, who complained of pains "like pin pricks" and tremors in her feet that prevented her from standing. According to Rosada, when Portuguese doctors failed to cure her, she began to suspect that she was infected with *maleficios*. Twice she went to the Convent of Saint Anthony to be blessed. When this also failed, she sought out Domingos, who she heard "knew how to cure *feitiços* and *maleficios*." Arriving at his clinic on Rua de São José, Rosada "found many other women—one white, other *pardas*, and the majority *negras*—who also went there to be cured." Domingos demanded that each woman bring *aguardente* (sugarcane liquor), which would be used in his cures. Pouring the *aguardente* into a cup, Domingos added some powders made from crushed roots that he had brought from the forest. He also squeezed juice from the fruit of *melão de São Caetano* (bitter melon) into the cup. Ordering Paula Rosada to grab the cup with her left hand, Domingos made a "blessing" over it with his right hand, speaking in a language that Rosada could not understand. After empowering the concoction with his words and gestures, Domingos ordered Rosada and the other women to drink. Almost immediately, Rosada gave a cough and vomited up "some hair." A short time later, she expelled "little bones that appeared to be from chickens and the talons of a hawk" from her rectum. As a result of this cure, Paula Rosada "felt much better" and resolved to stay at Domingos' house until she was completely free of the *maleficios* that had caused her illness.[27]

Though it might be tempting to dismiss Domingos' cure as some form of ritualized quackery, we should not lose sight of the actual medicines he employed. Paula Rosada presented with symptoms that today we might diagnose as type 2 diabetes. The pain and pin pricks in her feet, along with the tremors and difficulties walking, are classic symptoms of nerve damage caused by diabetes. Recent scientific research demonstrates that the fruit of *melão de São Caetano* (*Momordica charantia*) contains flavanoids and alkaloids that trigger insulin production in the pancreas, thereby making it an ideal herbal medicine for boosting blood-sugar levels. It has been used to treat diabetes, gout, and rheumatism for years in Africa and India.[28] It also continues to be used in herbal baths in Brazilian Candomblé.[29] Thus, whatever "*maleficios*" Paula Rosada might have expelled from her various orifices, her cure was likely due to the medicinal properties of the *melão de São Caetano*.

Domingos would have attributed the medicinal properties of the fruit to the power of the earth voduns, and his ritual blessings were almost certainly an invocation of that power. That it would take science 250 years to "rationalize" the pharmaceutical properties of *melão de São Caetano* reveals only one of the many fault lines separating early modern ideas from modern systems of knowledge. Domingos, and for that matter, most eighteenth-century folk, believed that illness could take the form of corporeal evil— hair, bones, sand, insects—that literally ate away bodies. The expulsion of this malevolence was powerfully tangible evidence of illness. To Domingos and his followers, the remedy worked because the voduns of the earth endowed *melão de São Caetano* with the ritual power to remove the corporeal evil that caused foot problems. The hair and bones were ample visual proof of this power. But Domingos' diagnosis and prescription were very much based on the "scientific" knowledge of trial and error. Ultimately, his cures were more effective (and "scientific") than any that could be offered by Portuguese doctors. Thus, early modern and African forms of healing were sometimes more "modern" and more advanced than what would emerge from Europe 100 or even 200 years later.[30]

Acknowledging the efficacy of Domingos' skills, Paula Rosada stayed on at his healing center for further therapy, remaining there for three weeks. During that time, Domingos administered purgatives consisting of the *pinhão* fruit (*Jatropha curcas*), crushed at night and put into a beverage consumed the following morning.[31] On another occasion, he prescribed infusions made from cow dung. Finally, on the Saturday before Easter, Domingos traveled with his patients to the ritual ground at Glória, where he planned "to remove the spirits that were in the bodies of the creatures." Arriving early in the morning, Rosada entered a house where Domingos was "passing black chickens over the heads of each of the black women who were already there." Rosada and her companions received the same treatment, which swept away the evil spirits from their heads.[32] Then, Domingos put some black powders on the heads of the women, prompting some to fall to the ground. Domingos announced that these had the "hidden spirit." Rosada was not among them. Moving outside into the yard under the tree, the ailing women gathered in front of a large "basin of water with a knife stabbed in the middle, and some calabashes." Each of the ill women—two whites and eight blacks—put their fingers into the mixture in the bowl, and "they began to convulse and jerk like filthy animals, running around the field." After some time, they fell to the ground "like dead people." Domingos then went to each of them, one at a time, putting his hand on their chests and saying some words that Rosada could not understand. Finally, brandishing one of his calabashes, Domingos announced that the evil spirit had gone away. He then made small cuts on the arms and soles of the feet of each person, putting black powders into the cuts "in order to close their bodies so the *feitiços* would not return."[33]

The content of Domingos' healing rituals begs further explanation, which will be provided later, but for now there are several crucial things to note about the experiences of Paula Rosada. Most important, her three weeks under Domingos' tutelage suggest a much deeper commitment than a simple healing session. After all, she "felt much better" after only her first days at the clinic. She easily could have left without further therapy. Her lengthy affiliation with Domingos' *terreiro* indicates that she was deeply impressed by his powers, so much so that she was moved to follow him. Indeed, Rosada seemed eager to explore the deeper mysteries of the vodun and the spiritual community presided over by Domingos. Though she failed to experience the state of possession and she eventually left his congregation, she still maintained a healthy respect for Domingos. In her later testimony, Rosada was quick to point out that Domingos charged 2 dobras only to slave masters, suggesting that she, and others like her, received preferential treatment. She also associated his work with that of the Catholic Church, noting that Domingos' house was "prepared with many images of saints and he showed himself to be very devoted." In short, Rosada, like many other slaves and former slaves, viewed Domingos as a man firmly committed to good deeds, especially the protection of the poor and enslaved.

Clearly, not all people saw Domingos in such a positive light. Some believed he was a fraud; others a simple fetisher. Among those with a poor opinion of Domingos was his former mistress Leonor de Oliveira Cruz. When Domingos traveled to his clinic in Prainha, he sometimes passed by the house of his former masters to visit with his enslaved comrades, Thereza Arda and Caetano. Domingos remained particularly friendly with the young man, Caetano, mentoring him and offering him advice. During this time, Leonor de Oliveira continued to suffer from various incurable ailments. When Domingos appeared at her house, he expressed what seemed to be genuine concern. According to Leonor, Domingos "showed a great desire to restore her health," urging her to come to his property at Glória, where he would use "fresh herbs gathered with the morning dew" to make drinks "that would remedy her ills." Leonor claimed that she found Domingos "repugnant," but "in order to obey her husband's desires to see her recover her health," she reluctantly agreed to travel to Glória as a desperate, last resort.[34]

In June 1740, Leonor de Oliveira and her slave, Thereza Arda, departed early one Saturday morning for Domingos' ritual ground. First, however, they made a short detour to hear morning mass at Leonor's church, Igreja do Bom Jesus. Whether Leonor sought God's blessing and protection for what lay ahead with Domingos, or whether she simply prayed for relief from her chronic pain, it is clear that, like many Brazilians, she adopted a multifaceted approach in addressing the maladies that ailed her. After mass, Leonor and Thereza walked through the center of the city to its southern outskirts, arriving at Glória around midday. There, ceremonies were already well under way. As they reached the *terreiro*, they found "three black women possessed by the Devil [*endemoninhadas*] shouting, and beyond these, one white, one *parda*, and many *negra* women walking in a circle" under the orange tree.[35] Domingos ordered a pause in the proceedings and directed Leonor to wait inside the house while he prepared the ritual bath anew.

The congregants suspended their exertions momentarily as Domingos threw some leaves and black powders into the vessel of water with the knife stabbed through the center. Then he ordered Thereza to call Leonor out of the house. Leonor joined the other women, awaiting her turn to put her finger into the pot of water. After a short time, the congregation resumed moving around the altar in a circular motion. In the middle of the circle was a black woman "dancing and jumping like she was possessed by the Devil."[36] Making his way to the center of the circle, Domingos cast some black powders at the woman he called "Captain," prompting her to fall to the ground "like a dead person." Domingos walked up to the prostrate woman and, with a staff in his hand, rapped the ground next to her head. The woman immediately arose, taking on a different persona, speaking in unintelligible languages. Then Domingos took a calabash and, placing his finger over the mouth of the vessel, clapped the bottom with his other hand and hit it against his thigh. After he removed his finger from the hole, a cloud of smoke emerged. Domingos commanded the woman to inhale the smoke. He also wafted some toward her ear and her head, which "provoked and infuriated her further." Domingos placed his finger on the back of her head and began asking the Captain questions "to learn what made the others ill." The Captain proffered her divinations, answering that some had *feitiços*, others "suffered from this or that illness," and so on. Domingos responded to the Captain's divinations by choosing the appropriate herbal remedy for each of his patients. He then ordered another of his disciples, a man named Barbaças (Long-Bearded One), to administer the medicines.

When it came time for her to diagnose Leonor de Oliveira's illness, the Captain suddenly became agitated. She claimed that she had gone "blind" and could no longer see. The Captain ordered Leonor to leave the ritual ground, admonishing that she was not one of them but rather from the wealthy and elite.[37] Angered by this revelation, the other members of the *terreiro* began throwing rocks at Leonor. Fortunately, Domingos came to her rescue, ordering her to retreat to the safety of the house where she could eat a meal while passions calmed. While Leonor was in the house, Domingos confided to Thereza in the Mina language that "that *mulata* [Leonor] needed to know who he was," and he was going to make her "show him everything God gave her."[38] A short time later, Leonor returned to the ritual proceedings, and the Captain began proffering new divinations. When prompted by Domingos, she revealed news from distant lands. For example, she told of a schoolmaster in Coimbra who split the head of one of his students. The Captain also described three ships leaving Portugal, one of which was lost at sea during a storm. Finally, Domingos asked the woman, "Captain, are we friends?" And the Captain responded, "We are." Then Domingos asked, "Am I in hell?" To which the Captain responded, "No, because you all are more able than I, and where you all walk, we are not able to walk."³⁹ Seeing these things, Leonor de Oliveira was "astonished and terrified." Despite her fears, Leonor stayed late into the night, hoping to find the cause of her illness. When they finally returned home, Thereza revealed to Leonor that "in order to seek revenge on her," Domingos "wanted to ensorcell her and introduce the Devil into her body and make her run around the countryside nude, and that was the end he was trying to achieve."⁴⁰

The following morning, Domingos walked across the city, arrived at Leonor de Oliveira's door, and "with great affection" told her that he had a cure that would "heal her immediately."⁴¹ Ignoring Thereza's warnings from the previous night, Leonor once again submitted to Domingos' charisma, inviting him into the house. To achieve his cure, Domingos announced that he needed "some shrimp, and with them he wanted to make her some mush [*papas*] or porridge [*mingau*]." Leonor immediately dispatched the slave Caetano to purchase the shrimp. When Caetano returned, he, Domingos, and Thereza prepared a shrimp and manioc porridge (*angu*) in the kitchen. Domingos announced to Leonor that he threw "seven things" into the porridge, presumably the medicines that would heal her. However, after eating the porridge, Leonor felt "very bad, . . . afflicted, pained, and perturbed." Domingos quickly went to her aid, arriving at her bedside to administer his black powders. But as soon as Domingos touched the back of Leonor's head, she immediately jumped out of bed in her night clothes, screaming furiously and running "like a crazy person" out of the house and into her backyard. There, she remained in a state of madness, shouting hysterically "from morning until midday." Leonor's husband, Manuel Pereira da Fonseca, tried to calm her by showing her an image of Our Lady of the Conception. He also attempted to restrain her with a Cord of Saint Francis, but she violently rejected both holy objects, throwing them to the ground.⁴² Leonor's only relief from this episode came when Domingos eventually grabbed her. Evidently, his touch alone returned her to her senses.

In the aftermath of these disturbing events, Leonor de Oliveira's health continued to worsen. Suspicion fell on the young slave Caetano, whose friendship with Domingos marked him as a likely source of malevolence. Fonseca ordered Caetano placed in chains, torturing him until he elicited a confession.⁴³ Caetano eventually admitted that he and Domingos buried various things in strategic places around the house—under all of the doors, under the bench on the veranda where Leonor did her needlework, and under Leonor's bed—in order to bring her "misery and ultimately to kill her."[44] Digging in these places, Fonseca found human bones, animal bones, fish skeletons, pig's teeth, rattles, pins, hairs, peels, and roots of various types. Some of this "filth" was tied in bundles; other pieces stood apart on their own. Because of Caetano's complicity in the production of this evil, Fonseca ordered him to be sold more than 250 miles south in the city of Santos. Fonseca remitted Caetano to the custody of an agent, whose task it was to escort Domingos' young protégé to market. Unfortunately, Caetano did not fare well on the journey; Fonseca's envoy reported that the young man died before he could be sold, perhaps partly as a result of the injuries he suffered at the hands of his master.

THOUGH THE DOCUMENTS provide numerous examples of Domingos' ritual practices, this series of exchanges between Domingos and his former masters perhaps best illustrates the complex cultural, social, and political tensions engendered by his healing. Despite suspecting that Domingos was the source of her torment when he was her slave, Leonor de Oliveira still traveled to Domingos' ritual space on the pretense that he would cure her chronic illness. Leonor harbored misgivings about Domingos, but these were tempered by her husband's insistence that she seek all available avenues for a cure. Their decision to submit to Domingos' healing demonstrates just how deeply implicated Brazilians of all backgrounds were in African forms of healing. Domingos' powers to cause mayhem and death, the very traits that compelled Leonor de Oliveira and Manuel Pereira da Fonseca to sell him, emanated from the same set of powers they hoped would cure her. Portuguese-born, just as much as African-born, believed in these powers, placing their faith, and their lives, in the hands of African healers. The result was a remarkable convolution of the racial and social hierarchy, one in which a Portuguese man insisted that his *mulata* wife yield to the power of an African man, his former slave.

After several years of suffering her hubris, Domingos knew exactly what ailed Leonor de Oliveira. The only "cure" for her illness was public humiliation and social censure. Racial, social, and cultural animus tinged their conflict. Clearly, Domingos resented the conditions of his earlier enslavement and the continued enslavement of his comrades, Caetano and Thereza. But it is telling that Leonor de Oliveira was the target of his hostility and not her Portuguese husband, Manuel Pereira da Fonseca. The thirty-eight-year-old Leonor was perhaps only one or two generations removed from her own enslavement, which still marked her as *"parda"* or *"mulata."* Leonor consciously distanced herself from her African past, marrying a Portuguese man more than thirty years her senior, owning multiple African slaves, and heaping scorn on Domingos' "repugnant" ritual practices. Leonor's self-loathing became a source of misery and suffering for Domingos, Caetano, and even Thereza, who, though she seemed to be her mistress's closest confidante, was also complicit in some of the machinations against her. Ultimately, Domingos forced Leonor to confront her "ills" at the ritual space in Glória, and he was determined to "heal" her.

The cures performed for Leonor de Oliveira at Domingos' ritual space in Glória and at her house in Santa Rita acted as "a résumé of the whole social order," a public performance of simmering conflicts over social status, race, and gender.[45] When the Captain went "blind," she claimed she could no longer divine because Leonor was not one of them. The message was clear enough: The invoked spirit could not see Leonor de Oliveira because she was a traitor, a wealthy slaveholder and tormentor of Africans. This public upbraiding and the subsequent rock-throwing incident illustrated the vast social gulf that separated Leonor from her African slave past. As a result, she could not access the salutary powers of the African healer and would continue to suffer. Later, when Domingos told Thereza that "that *mulata*" needed to know who he was, he revealed a racial dimension to his diagnosis. The scorn of the *"mulata"* epithet underscored Domingos' belief that Leonor's sense of superiority was largely tied to her mixed racial heritage. By forcing Leonor to yield to his powers, he would demonstrate that power came in many colors. Eventually, Leonor succumbed to the fortified porridge and black powders administered at her house on Largo de Santa Rita. What Leonor and her husband interpreted as Domingos putting an evil spirit into her body was more likely his drawing the evil out of her body, just as he had done on other occasions with other people.[46] Regardless of intent, Domingos demonstrated mastery over Leonor's will and volition. His "black" African medicines controlled her *"mulata"* body, inverting the social order in such a way that she was now, in essence, his slave.

Perhaps the most telling revelations that emerged from these healing sessions were the rather transparent sexual tensions that existed between Leonor and Domingos. Even when Domingos was Leonor's slave, their interactions alternated between uncomfortable familiarity and outright hostility. The process of healing Leonor's illnesses created physical intimacies normally prohibited between mistress and male slave. The herbal drinks, purgatives, and baths that Domingos administered over the course of the six months he was Leonor's slave would have drawn them perilously close to one another. The fact that Leonor's husband was an old man while Domingos was her contemporary probably only exacerbated these tensions. Leonor publicly repudiated the idea that she, as a slave master, could be attracted to her slave, yet she still seemed drawn to Domingos.

Just before her conflicts with Domingos reached their apex in mid-1737, Leonor de Oliveira fell pregnant. Shortly thereafter, the governor intervened to aid in the sale of Domingos. Might the paternity of the child have been in question? On March 29, 1738, Manuel Pereira da Fonseca appeared at the baptismal font to claim his son, José.[47] We will never know whether he was actually the father. What we do know is that sexual tensions between Leonor and Domingos simmered, boiling over into public performance during the two days that Domingos healed Leonor in Glória and Santa Rita. On the evening they departed the ritual space at Glória, Thereza warned Leonor that Domingos had spoken some "indecent" words and wanted to "make her run around the countryside nude." Thus, the idea was firmly planted in Leonor's head. When Domingos arrived at her door the next morning, Leonor did not turn him away, as one might expect of an "honorable" married woman.[48] Instead, she almost magically succumbed to his "charm." Then, as if to fulfill the prophecy, Leonor rose from her bed "discomposed," wearing only a night shirt, running about like a mad woman. She rejected all of her husband's entreaties. The old man and his holy objects were impotent in the face of the African's power. Ultimately, only Domingos' touch could bring Leonor relief and calm. For Domingos, Leonor's physical submission represented the remedy for her arrogance and contempt. Manuel Pereira da Fonseca saw things very differently. Not only was his wife possessed by the Devil; she was now seemingly the subject of another man.

We will never know the extent to which Leonor de Oliveira actually resented her African past or yearned for Domingos' affections. In fact, she was probably deeply ambivalent on both of these topics, perhaps even unconsciously so. Nevertheless, Domingos' divinations and healing laid bare ambiguities and tensions that were very real, exposing them as public "truths." In this way, his rituals worked to excavate hidden, unspeakable conflicts that were often at the very core of society. The actual contents of the rituals—the Captain's possession and divination, the medicinal porridge, the black powders—were much less important than the revelations that emerged from them. Some of these revelations were purely physical; for example, the demonstration that *melão de São Caetano* relieved the symptoms of certain New World illnesses. Others were deeply psychological. We can question the efficacy of particular cures or the reality of spirit possession, but this would be to lose sight of the broader meanings of African forms of healing. The question is not do you really believe that Domingos had the power to channel spirits or remove hair, bones, and insects from people's bodies? Rather, the question is do you believe that these rituals revealed a wide array of social, political, economic, physical, and psychological ills that otherwise would have remained hidden? If so, then one must recognize that the revelations were themselves a significant aspect of the cure. When Paula Rosada vomited hair and expelled chicken bones and hawk talons from her rectum, these were the corporeal expressions of an unknowable illness whose symptoms were alleviated by Domingos' medicinal infusions. Likewise, when Leonor de Oliveira lost her faculties, she finally acknowledged the psychological burdens of her life between disparate worlds—master/slave, rich/poor, white/black, Catholic/non-Catholic. Not all of Domingos' cures worked, but those that did were rarely just a simple transaction between an individual healer and an individual patient. They were almost always a broader commentary on the collective health and well-being of society.

If healing operated partly as a tool to diagnose broader social and political ailments, how do we assess these global revelations that emerged from individual therapeutic interventions? Were they simply interesting, isolated critiques, divorced from political action and empowerment? Or did the sum of these individual critiques form the foundation for larger political challenges against the economic exploitation and physical violence associated with imperialism and slavery? Could these peculiarly African forms of revelatory politics translate into new networks of empowerment in Atlantic slave settings? Earlier chapters have demonstrated that some of the most illuminating new sources for West Africa might actually emanate from places of enslavement like Brazil. For example, we know the Portuguese accused Domingos Álvares of using *gbo* to delay the progress of a slave ship traveling from Recife to Rio de Janeiro. This evidence not only corroborates Dahomean oral tradition that suggests some *gbo* were a direct response to the slave trade but also reinforces the common thread of African-Portuguese responses to new, Atlantic imperatives such as capitalism and slavery. After all, it was the Portuguese who accused Domingos of using "fetishes" to stop the wind, signaling their own belief in the African's power to blunt economic "progress." Similarly, Leonor de Oliveira and Manuel Pereira da Fonseca demonstrated their belief in the power of *gbo* when they discovered the bundles that Domingos and Caetano buried around their house.

In these instances and others, the broad and durable links between healing in Dahomey and healing in Brazil could not be clearer. The genius of Domingos Álvares and others like him was the social and political commentary embedded in each cure, each revelation. The power of healers lay in their ability to point out the tensions, conflicts, and hypocrisies of ruptures, like illegitimate warfare and plundering in Dahomey or enslavement and forced exile in Brazil. These ruptures were the bricks and mortar of history, the catalysts for change that linked hundreds of years of transformation in Africa, in some cases extending into the diaspora. Internal African struggles over kinship, kingship, and spirits did not so much shift as become interconnected to Atlantic ones like exile, slavery, capitalism, and colonialism. Thus, healing actually became a crucial tool for rendering new Atlantic categories, making them more comprehensible and ultimately more African.

6

The Politics of Healing

The King . . . hated this *gbo* because it permitted too many alliances against him.
—Dahomean oral history, recounting why Agaja outlawed
certain powerful ritual implements in the eighteenth century, quoted in
Melville J. Herskovits, *Dahomey: An Ancient West African Kingdom*

For Domingos Álvares, the structure, symbolism, and ritual of his healing
practice were thoroughly etched in his African past; however, by necessity, he adapted these familiar forms to accommodate new social and political conditions. From a purely cultural perspective, Domingos replicated
much of the ritual symbolism and practice from his Dahomey homeland.
The principal ritual catalyst at his shrine—the earthen vessel of water with
the knife through the middle—reflected similar shrine objects found in
Dahomey in the eighteenth century. Around 1714, an anonymous Frenchman visiting Savi noted that "the higher-ranking Negros each have in their
home their own God. . . . These are pieces of iron . . . that they stick in the
ground; some earthen pots and other similar things."[1] These shrine objects
represented what Suzanne Blier calls the "alchemy" of *gbo* (empowerment
objects). Blier notes: "Factors of selection are important in *bo* and *bocio*
alchemy not only because the materials themselves have religious and/or
medicinal attributes, but also because of the powerful ontological properties they are believed to possess. Both in their own right and when manipulated and conjoined in certain ways, these properties are thought to create
a dynamic or field of power which can then be employed to offset, coun-
terbalance, or oppose other forces or powers at play in the world."[2] For Domingos, the "hot" knife of Gu, god of war, penetrating the "cool" waters of
the *amasi* (leaf bath) likely symbolized complementary powers—the knife
destroying malevolent forces; the leaf bath soothing and restoring positive
energy (*axé*).[3] Meanwhile, the activating forces of the knife (iron) and the
bath (leaves) emanated from the power of the earth, thereby rendering the
"whole" an object of the earth god's healing power.

Each of the activating ingredients of Domingos' empowerment object was ambiguous. The knife could kill, slaying malevolent forces, but it could also cut through the forest, helping the healer find lifesaving medicines. Furthermore, the knife could cut the cords of attachment and confinement, opening paths to freedom. For Dahomeans, the symbolism of Gu's ability to open new paths began at birth, when the midwife used the knife to cut the umbilical cord.[4] Curses that resulted in illness were also seen through the lens of "binding" and "tying." Perhaps most evocative, slaves were bondage personified. The Fon word for slave (*kannumon*) translates literally as "person in cords."[5] Thus, the knife of Gu simultaneously represented the power to destroy one's enemies (Agaja, slave masters, and so on) and the power to liberate onself from the confines of powerful, usually malevolent, forces (slavery, illness, disease, hunger, and so on).

Just like the knife, the leaves and powders that Domingos threw into the ritual bath embodied both positive and negative forces. We have already seen how the power of plants cured and killed, either as "medicines" or as "poisons." Western doctors conceive of medicine as curing disease and illness; yet, counterintuitively, too much medicine (overdose) results in poisoning and death. If medicine is a curative, how can too much ever be a bad thing? Likewise, how can some lethal poisons be considered medicines? On its face, the logic of the medicine/poison dichotomy is faulty and often contradictory. Medicines and poisons really are one and the same. For Fon speakers, there are no such qualitative distinctions between "medicinal" and "poisonous" plants. They are simply empowered. Hence, the Fon word for powder (*atin*) translates as both "medicine" and "poison."[6] Domingos' black powders—black representing fertile earth, family, and ancestors, as well as darkness, death, and mourning—simultaneously performed the function of healing and purging.[7] The powders worked as a catalyst for activating the desired result, whether empowering a ritual bath, sealing and protecting from *feitiços* when rubbed into wounds, or expelling and destroying the forces of malevolence like bones, hair, and pins when taken in a drink.

The calabashes that formed a part of Domingos' shrine also carried important symbolic and ritual meaning. In the first place, calabashes were considered the birth canal of the voduns, the "womb" of their empowerment. The activation of any vodun shrine required the employment of calabashes.[8] In all of the ritual practices at his *terreiro*, Domingos utilized calabashes as crucial tools of invocation. Furthermore, Domingos carried a calabash with him wherever he went. According to some observers, he kept the "Devil" inside his calabash, and that was how he made his cures.[9] Though it might be tempting to dismiss these references, a closer examination of the "Devil's" meaning reveals an alternate explanation for the power in the calabash. Peixoto's *Língua geral de Mina*, the Mina-Portuguese dictionary written in eighteenth-century Brazil, translates "Devil" as "Leba," or Legba, the temperamental messenger of the voduns whose blessings are required to activate any ritual object or setting.[10] For Domingos, Legba opened the path to spirit possession and divination. This is particularly evident in his interactions with the Captain, whose divinations Domingos provoked when he uncorked the calabash and fumigated her with "smoke of various colors."[11] Gnanwisi Ayido, a contemporary diviner in Benin and informant of Suzanne Blier, explained, "The . . . calabashes of Legba contain good and bad powders. When Legba is dancing he . . . takes the powder and blows it. Even if he does not say anything, that which he said on the powder previously will begin to happen. If [offerings are made and] Legba eats well in it, he will blow white powder and things will work well for you; or he can blow the red powder and negative powers will return to the one who sent it."[12] Though we do not know exactly what color powder emerged from Domingos' calabash, we can surmise that Legba was satisfied by his offerings since the invocation resulted in the appearance of the Captain and her subsequent divinations.

Legba was equally important as a catalyst in activating the power of ritual medicines. According to Fon oral tradition, Legba was the first to reveal *gbo* to man. As such, "Legba has many *gbo* for headache, for colic, for dysentery, for leprosy, for eye trouble, for rheumatism, and for all other kinds of illness. No one is stronger in *gbo* than Legba."[13] In this way, Legba would have been a logical companion for Domingos, one who could accompany him and show him the path to various medicinal remedies. As Domingos carried his calabash throughout the city, some of his African compatriots seemed to understand the mercurial, ill-mannered trickster capacity of the force inside the vessel. When slave children cried, it was customary for their mothers to warn, "Watch out, there comes Father Domingos with his little calabash!" Apparently, the prospect of Domingos and his calabash was frightening enough to shut up even the most wayward of wailing children.[14]

The universality of this humorous admonition illustrates perhaps the most important aspect of Domingos' public healing practice in Rio—that of community building. Though the slave women who made these comments may not have been among Domingos' followers, they constituted a significant slice of a broader community of knowledge that naturalized vodun to urban Rio de Janeiro. On the one hand, Domingos and his cala-bash were quite clearly dangerous forces to be feared. On the other hand, "Pai Domingos" was the "father," the widely acknowledged leader of a heal-ing community. The title "father" was at once an implicit reference to the kinship ties that bound members of his community and a reference to the broader sense of deference and respect that his position commanded. In this way, he was not unlike the "fathers" of the Catholic Church.[15] Even in their most flippant references, slave women passed on to their children knowledge of the powerful links between kinship, power, and healing.

Another, more proximate, layer of community building is represented by people like Paula Rosada and Caetano, each of whom was touched deeply by Domingos' healing powers. Even though they formed strong bonds with Domingos, neither of them became initiates of his healing community. Paula evidently made this decision of her own accord, yet she remained "faithful" to Domingos in the broadest sense. Caetano, because of his en-slavement, simply did not have the freedom to commit himself fully to his mentor. Like dozens of other enslaved Africans that Domingos counseled, Caetano was still a "person in cords," subject to the will and caprice of his master. Clearly, Domingos did not form such solid bonds of sympathy and friendship with every enslaved person he encountered; however, there can be little doubt that there were other Caetanos, some of them perhaps even Domingos' own countrymen, who constituted an eager community of fol-lowers and who were the direct beneficiaries of Domingos' healing powers. All they required to become full-fledged initiates of his *terreiro* was freedom of movement and association.

The locus for greatest kinship and community building was Domingos' *terreiro* in Glória. In the African context, this ritual space was "the unifying center of the cult-group, a place in which the personal associations clus-tering about initiation are interwoven with the emotions of identification with the deity and the collective membership, all of whom have shared common experiences of initiation and worship. It symbolizes, therefore, the security of a spiritual home."[16] In Brazil, the attraction of such a space for those who were forcibly uprooted from their natal homelands, or who were otherwise marginalized or enslaved, was powerful indeed. We know of at least three of Domingos' followers who were almost certainly initiates of his healing community—Capitão (Captain), Barbaças (Long-Bearded One), and Velho (Old Man). Several of these figures appear repeatedly in eyewitness descriptions of Domingos' ritual performances.[17] Moreover, their names seem to reflect ritual symbolism and esoteric knowledge that only "insiders" could understand thoroughly. Though it is difficult to be sure, the names also might have been a rough approximation of the internal hierarchy of the community, rendered as Portuguese colloquialisms that could be readily understood by noninitiates who traveled to the *terreiro* to be healed. The Bearded One and the Old Man, for instance, appear to be generic, age-specific designations suggesting wisdom and ritual knowledge, while the title "Captain" invokes a high-ranking official or commanding officer of the congregation.

Even as these ritual names were made comprehensible for a Portuguese-speaking audience, they almost certainly reflected some of the qualities of the new personas adopted by the initiates, whose old, earthly identities symbolically died during the initiation process. It seems likely that all of Domingos' devotees dedicated themselves to the earth vodun. As such, they would have been "reborn" as a quality of that divinity, taking on its name, attributes, and so on.[18] The African iterations of these qualities would have been obscured to most Portuguese listeners, who simply noted that many of Domingos' ritual invocations and conversations were in "the Mina language." However, the actual Fon-Gbe initiatory names no doubt persisted, alongside "Captain," "Bearded One," and "Old Man," with the Portuguese versions standing as markers of rank, as well as shorthand descriptive traits of particular Sakpata deities, in much the same way that "Devil" held the place of "Legba" in eighteenth-century Brazil.

Because Sakpata pantheons in Dahomey consisted of dozens of "family" members, varied from village to village, and were often contradictory in their hierarchies, it is impossible to determine the exact correlations between Domingos' followers and their patron deities.[19] Nevertheless, for purposes of illustration, one might suggest that the martial title "Captain" corresponded to Keledjegbe, "who bears the reputation of having outwitted the mother of Death, and who is regarded as a warrior."[20] Likewise, the Old Man and the Bearded One could have been either Dada Langa or Dada Zodji, both of whom are attributed elder status in the Sakpata family.[21] Regardless of our imprecision in identifying these deities, it is clear that Domingos viewed the Captain, the Bearded One, and the Old Man as particular expressions of vodun qualities. In the same way that he used his calabash to blow smoke in the ear of the Captain, he did the same for the Bearded One and the Old Man, provoking their particular deities to come into their heads.[22]

The ritual practices of Domingos' healing community served to draw initiates closer to one another, as well as to the vodun. Meeting every Saturday, the *vodunsi* aided Domingos in his healing, administering the infusions and purgatives he prescribed. Most of these remedies were made from roots, leaves, and powders that Domingos collected from the forest. In order for the medicines to become empowered, the vodun required offerings of *aguardente*, chickens, and so on. In the most extreme cases, when a patient arrived at the *terreiro* "convulsing and in great pain," Domingos sacrificed a black chicken, "and with the blood of the chicken, he anointed the person on the head and chest, rubbing it all the way down to the legs, and also throwing some herbal powders."[23] These offerings of food and drink to the vodun eventually became sustenance for his followers, yet another way that kinship and reciprocal relationships facilitated community cohesion.

Perhaps the most spectacular forms of ritual practice in Domingos' community were spirit possession, divination, and prophecy. According to anthropologist Bernard Maupoil: "The essential character of the divinity seems to be its claim to possess the one that serves it, 'to mount the head,' as the Fon say: *vodu-wa-ta-towe.*"[24] When Domingos' followers "danced" in a circular motion, they maintained a steady beat until the voduns came down to enter the heads of the devotees. Domingos cast black powders over the fontanel of the Captain to act as a catalyst to possession, nourishing the vodun and inviting it to ascend. In Fon thought, the fontanel is the locus of spiritual power and authority. It is the place where the soul resides. This idea is expressed in various ways. Sorcerers take possession of an individual's life force by passing their hands over the fontanel. Young children are particularly susceptible to such nefarious maneuverings; hence, great suspicion arises when strangers touch a child's head. Similarly, anthropomorphic empowerment figures (*bochio*) sometimes have holes carved in the tops of their heads so they can be "fed" medicines.[25] Once the Captain's head was properly "fed," the vodun mounted the Captain and she fell to the ground "like a dead person," indicating her transformation as a vehicle for the spirit. Rising from the floor, she took on the persona of the divinity, adopting its mannerisms and even its voice. According to Thereza Arda, when the Captain entered her trance, she spoke in Latin and some other "language she did not understand."[26] Given Thereza's fluency in the Mina language, we might speculate that this other language was the arcane form of Yoruba that was the preferred ritual language of Sakpata devotees in Dahomey.[27] Proffering her divinations, the Captain answered Domingos' questions on a range of issues, from the source of illness to news of events in Portugal.

Although similar forms of divination and prophecy had been relatively common in Brazilian slave communities since at least the early seventeenth century, they almost always emanated from Central African *calundus*. The *calundeiros* performed ceremonies to draw a recently deceased ancestor into their heads, nourishing the spirit with offerings of food, alcohol, blood, and so on, in order to divine the causes and cures of illness. The choreography of *calundu* rituals and those performed by Domingos were similar—dancing in a circle, giving offerings to the spirit, falling to the ground "like a dead person," and taking on the persona of the spirit.[28] However, there were also important differences. First, *calundeiros* did not build permanent grounds, shrines, or altars; they normally remained itinerant in their healing practices. Second, they usually called upon the aid of their most proximate, direct ancestors—parents, grandparents, and especially children—as opposed to more distant ancestral deities like voduns. And finally, although a *calundeiro* almost always worked with a retinue of singers, dancers, and musicians, only the *calundeiro* could be possessed by the divinity.

As one of the first congregations to move beyond itinerant ritual to a more stable institutional structure, Domingos' *terreiro* stands as a significant early achievement in Afro-Brazilian religious history. The presence of the permanent ritual space, the altar, and the initiates who acted as mediums of the vodun point to the existence of an "ecclesiastical" structure far earlier than generally has been accepted up to now.[29] The timing of the emergence of Domingos' congregation was not mere coincidence; it was directly tied to the turmoil and conflicts that racked Dahomey during the late 1720s and 1730s. As noted in chapter 1, under the reign of Agaja, Dahomean religion and healing transformed as Agaja sought to defend himself from perceived challenges to royal authority. Spiritual leaders asserted their authority as the legitimate redeemers of the land, while Agaja attempted to tear down the institutional and ritual bases of independent healing communities. In some cases, Dahomey succeeded in co-opting voduns into the official pantheon at Abomey, integrating the deities and their devotees as imperial subjects. In other cases where the political threat was judged to be acute, the monarchy took more drastic measures. Agaja banished Sakpata priests, Fa divination replaced divination with *gbo*, and so on. The monarchy even attempted to curtail spirit possession. According to oral tradition, in these "early times, when the gods came into the head of the *vodunon*, and even *vodunsi*, they would prophesy. But the kings did not want this. A man or a woman in any village in Dahomey might then rule in the name of God."[30] The only apparent solution was to enslave these perceived threats and send them into exile.

One important outcome of this Dahomean purge of powerful healers was the spread of these banned ritual practices to places like Brazil, where some of the most obstinate, committed, politically savvy diviners and healers ended up as slaves. It seems likely that many of the former follow-ers of these healers—all enemies of Dahomey, many of whom were ex-iles prior to their enslavement—joined their mentors as slaves in Brazil. This, in part, explains the particular resonance of Domingos' healing in the African slave community of Rio. It also goes some way toward explaining the very particular pre-Dahomean rituals practiced in other parts of Bra-zil during the same time period. For some healers, the heightened social and political consciousness evoked by Dahomean censure simply carried over into Brazilian slavery, as an almost-seamless struggle for community well-being. Of course, the definition of "community" transformed in ac-cordance with the new environment. Some, like Domingos, reconstituted vibrant and powerful African-centered communities. Other Gbe-speaking healers were more isolated, relegated to healing mostly Portuguese strang-ers. In these interactions between Gbe healers and their Portuguese clients, we can see how very specific precolonial African ritual forms were utilized as tools for mediating peculiarly Atlantic and Brazilian problems. On the one hand, these rituals corroborate and extend even further the hypoth-eses that healers were particular targets of enslavement in Dahomey and that their ritual practices became ways of addressing the conditions of exile and enslavement. On the other hand, the Portuguese embraced these spe-cific pre-Dahomean forms as an effective means of translating their own struggles with isolation, anxiety, and illness, indicating the adaptability of these forms and their continued salience in a rapidly expanding and mod-ern world.

Between 1742 and 1744, at practically the same time that Domingos was building his congregation in Rio, at least three other Africans in nearby Minas Gerais engaged in ritual practices that, according to oral tradition, were proscribed in Dahomey. For example, in 1742, in the small town of Barra do Brumado in the district of Rio das Velhas, a slave named Manuel Cata divined using metal tubs and mining pans. Cata, who was from Savalu in the northern part of Mahi land, performed his divinations by turning the metal vessel upside down, rubbing it with corn husks, and chanting, "Asió bosu bosu." After a short time, a "frightful, horrible voice" came from underneath the pan. Cata responded to the voice, asking it questions in "the Mina language." Among other things, the voice revealed the sources of ill-ness and news of events in Portugal and Spain. Cata claimed that the voice was that of his deceased grandfather, who had been "diviner of the king of his land."[31]

What concerns us here is not so much the outcome of the divination, although we clearly see African ritual addressing Portuguese anxiety about new, colonial problems. Rather, we want to focus on the content, the choreography, and the ancestral spirit invoked. If we are to believe oral history, the form of divination described here is one of the very ones that Agaja banned during the 1720s and 1730s. According to an account taken from Dahomey in the 1930s:

> Fá is a vodun who, originating with the Nago [Yoruba], came to Dahomey in the time of Agadja. In those days, when a man died, it was necessary to go to a . . . man who divined *gbo*, by using a kind of pottery in which the pot was turned upside down and rubbed with [a string of] cauries until a voice was heard from within. . . . The voice of the dead man, when called, would tell what was to be done with his property, and . . . the voice would also tell the cause of his death—whether he had been killed by an animal, or by some man or woman with whom, for example, the dead had had difficulties over a lover. All this, which was what used to be done before Fá came, made for much hatred among the people.
>
> Now there were people who had little faith in this system, and the time came when the King, who hated this *gbo* because it permitted too many alliances against him, looked about for something which was truly a thing of the gods. Thus, when some time later a man . . . came to tell the King of the existence of Fá . . . , he was given the opportunity to spread this new form of divination.[32]

Missing from the Dahomean oral history is a clear explanation for why the king "hated this *gbo*" and the nature of the "alliances against him." These ideas receive greater clarity with Manuel Cata's revelation that the voice emanating from under the tub was his grandfather's, the former "diviner of the king of his land." The ability to channel another sovereign, or a proxy of that sovereign, was more than an expression of spirituality and healing; it was a direct political threat to Agaja. This threat was made all the more salient by persistent opposition and unrest in Savalu during the 1730s.[33] Indeed, in 1733 Agaja ordered the execution of the second-in-command of his army on suspicion that he planned to desert to Savalu.[34] Temporal kings, claims makers, and traitors might easily be dispatched by the powerful Dahomean army, but the military could not kill those who were already dead. Nor could the army harness people's desires to reclaim legitimate rulers, even those from the world of the dead. Nowhere in the oral history do we find direct references to *gbo* diviners being targeted for the slave trade, but it seems likely that the most powerful, most persistent diviners would have met this fate. Certainly the presence of Manuel Cata in Brazil would suggest as much. At the very least, Cata's Brazilian divinations confirm the Dahomean oral history: Agaja's determination to reform the system of divination was a direct response to political threats, not at all dissimilar to his decision to enslave Sakpata priests and send them into permanent exile.[35]

Interestingly, the symbolism and words of Manuel Cata's ritual also point to an invocation of the earth vodun. The corn husks that Cata rubbed on the tin basin took the place of the string of cowries utilized in the pre-Dahomean ceremony. In the absence of actual cowries, the husks that "wrapped" and "tied" corn kernels sufficed to catalyze the power of the *gbo*. Among the Fon, these individual kernels were themselves symbolic of the pustules created by smallpox.[36] The words that Cata chanted, "Asió bosu bosu," were almost certainly an invocation of Sakpata. The Portuguese transcription, "Asió," is likely a corrupted version of a Fon word for Sakpata. According to Segurola, Aihosu is "king of the land, title given to Sakpata."[37] Meanwhile, Bosu is the actual name of a particular quality of the vodun. Bosu features prominently in lists of Sakpata divinities across the Gbe-speaking region.[38] In fact, oral history holds that when the founder and first king of Savalu, Ahosu Soha, led his people on their northern migration to their new homeland, they encountered the Kadja people along the Ouémé River. The Kadja, who were themselves migrating from a Yoruba-speaking region near Badagry, carried with them their patron god, Sakpata Agbosu (Aihosu Agbosu). The Kadja joined Ahosu Soha's people in their northward migration, and they subsequently established Sakpata at Savalu, Manuel Cata's homeland.[39] Hence, Manuel Cata's words of empowerment, necessary to draw his grandfather's spirit into the *gbo*, were very likely a reference to Savalu's founding Sakpata quality, Agbosu. Ultimately, Manuel Cata's linking of ancestral divination with invocations of the earth vodun represented a powerful antidote to Dahomey's illegitimate assertions of power. That Savalu was a cradle of Mahi resistance against Dahomey in the 1730s only reinforces the links between political opposition, public divination and healing, and the African slave trade.

Other Africans in Minas Gerais also combined ancestral divination, healing, and the worship of voduns. In 1743, in Rio das Pedras, the freed

Mina João da Silva made "divinations with his ancestors . . . and cured the *feitiços* of those who payed him." Silva used a range of baths, purgatives, infusions, and drinks to perform his cures. Like Domingos Álvares, Silva often concluded his healing sessions by taking a "small piece of glass," cutting his clients, and then putting black powders into the incisions. His remedies also included the roasted, powdered remains of the hummingbird and squirrel cuckoo, which he gave to men "to attract apprehensive women for dishonest acts" and "to invoke the goodwill of their masters."[40] Silva used various bundles and pots of *gbo*—made from frogs, snakes, lizards, chicken feathers, herbs, roots, and leaves—that he buried under doorways and at crosswalks, as well as in the gold mines, in order to leverage influence over people, increase gold production, and so on. Finally, Silva also owned a piece of iron, "hollow on the inside in the manner of a pike," which he called "the saint of his land."[41] Silva guarded the pike closely, moving it "all the time" so it would not be discovered and profaned. In order to "sustain his saint," Silva sometimes unveiled the iron pike, sticking it into the ground and "putting the blood of chickens inside it, speaking some words in the Negro Mina language." He also offered the pike some cooked chicken and other foods, which he subsequently ate, saving the chicken bones to bury in a separate ceremony.[42]

At roughly the same time that João da Silva made offerings to the "saint of his land," another African healer from the Mina Coast, Francisco Axê ("*axê*" meaning "power" in the Fon-Gbe language),[43] also paid reverence to a "knife like a pike, about one and a half feet [*palmos*] in length with a little ball on the end made from the same iron, hollow on the inside like a cow bell." Axê insisted that "nobody should touch his pike." He carried the iron object with him when he healed several men in Rio das Pedras in 1744. In each instance, Axê followed the same ritual process. Sticking the pike in the ground, he "fell to his knees and prayed to the pike, giving it devotion and speaking in the Mina language." Axê then ordered his patient to get 4 oitavas of gold and hold it in his hand. After sprinkling *cachaça* (sugarcane liquor) over the top of the iron altar, Axê asked the patient if he wanted the 4 oitavas or his health. The patient responded that he wanted his health, in exchange for which Axê immediately claimed the gold. Axê then took a white rooster and ran it up and down his patient's body, sweeping away the noxious spirits. Meanwhile, he continued "speaking with the pike in his language," eventually motioning with it "as if he were ringing a bell," blessing his patient's bed. Finally, Axê washed his patient with a bath made from *melão de São Caetano* root, the same root Domingos Álvares utilized to cure

Paula Rosada's foot ailments. Axê also gave his patients various drinks and infusions made from leaves and roots.

Months later, Axê returned to his patient's house, claiming that the "father of the *feitiços*, with a great beard" had appeared to him "from the other world." And the father brought with him "his wife and many children." When Axê asked the "father of the *feitiços*" what caused his patient's illness, the father answered that it was "Moquem" and that he was "going around still alive because they had not fed him." After describing this revelation to his patient, Axê ordered him to shave his beard and his head. While the patient shaved, Axê dug a hole in the ground. Then he fashioned out of the clay and dirt a "statue or doll" that had the body of a man but no head. Axê constructed a head out of the same clay material and then cast it into the hole, where he also put the shaved hair of his client. The patient washed his head with water so that it drizzled into the hole. Then Axê requested a white cloth, which he used to wrap the clay doll before also putting it into the pit. Finally, Axê asked the ailing man for one of his bedsheets, which Axê wrapped around himself in "the manner of a priest's tunic [*sobrepeliz*], saying he was performing the burial of the doll." Together, Axê and his patient then proceeded to fill the hole with dirt.[44]

The ritual practices of Silva and Axê demonstrate the extraordinary depth of devotion of Gbe-speaking Africans to their ancestral traditions in the face of persistent persecution, enslavement, and forced migration. Perhaps the most remarkable aspect of their healing was the use of the iron altars in their ceremonies. Though it might be tempting to conclude that Silva's and Axê's iron pikes were simple invocations of the vodun Gu, in fact, the descriptions adhere very closely to ancestral altars known as *asen*. According to anthropologist Paul Mercier, the *asen* is a "portable altar, generally of metal. It is planted in the ground at the ceremonial location, and one pours in offering, on the plateau that crowns it, sacrificial blood and alcohol."[45] The earliest surviving examples of *asen* come from mid-nineteenth-century Dahomey, including exquisitely decorated ones produced in honor of the Dahomean royal family. Today, these *asen* are highly sought after as objects of art in the West and can be found in museums around the world, but the precise origins of these portable altars remain shrouded in uncertainty.

Oral histories recorded in the mid-twentieth century suggest that the *asen* evolved from offerings of food and drink made to ancestors in calabashes (*sinuka*). The earliest *asen* adapted the calabash form into a permanent iron altar consecrated to a particular ancestor or group of ancestors. This evolution in form is reflected in the semantic history of the object.

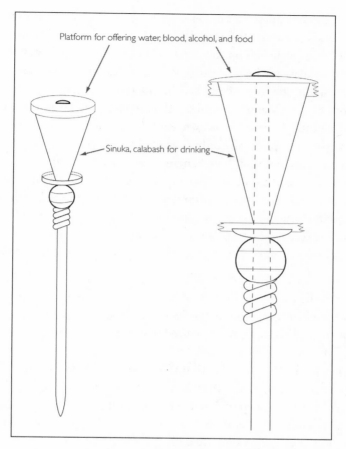

Platform for offering water, blood, alcohol, and food

Sinuka, calabash for drinking

Aladasen. Drawing by the University of Wisconsin Cartography Lab.

Even today, the word "*sinuka*," which literally translates as "a calabash for drinking," is utilized to describe *asen* in ceremonial settings.[46] According to Mercier's informants, the altar itself consisted of an iron post with a closed metal funnel, similar to a calabash or a "cow bell," sitting atop the post. These earliest forms were known as *asen godokponon*, literally "*asen* that has a calabash." They were also known as *aladasen*, pointing to a provenance in Allada, the ancient and venerable kingdom whose overthrow by Dahomey in 1724 engendered resentment and hatred of Agaja across the region.[47]

While Mercier's compelling oral sources tell us much about the possible origins of *asen*, "unfortunately, written sources prior to the nineteenth century neither support nor refute [his] evidence, while contemporary oral sources are silent on the question."[48] In fact, it now seems that the eighteenth-century documents from Brazil corroborate Mercier's findings and expand upon them. The style of "pikes" used by Silva and Axê was remarkably similar to those described by Mercier's informants. Axê's staff with the "little ball on the end made from the same iron, hollow on the inside like a cow bell," mirrors Mercier's description of the *aladasen*. Moreover, the offerings of chicken blood and *cachaça* are precisely the kinds of offerings Mercier describes. The frequency of Silva's and Axê's ancestral invocations through the *asen* would seem aberrant in contemporary Benin since *asen* are usually only consulted and "fed" sporadically, during yearly rituals or important life-changing events such as births, deaths, poor harvests, illnesses, and so on. The continuous invocations Silva and Axê conducted for strangers once again draw our attention to the prohibitions enforced by Agaja during the time period.

It will be recalled that Agaja ordered Fa divination to replace divination with *gbo* in the 1720s and 1730s. According to yet another oral tradition:

> When Fa first came to the world, he requested a slave to work on his farm. So he went to market and bought a slave named Asen acrelele. Fa immediately sent him to the farm to cut the bush, but when it was time to start his work, Asen realized that he was going to cut the herb that cures fever. He exclaimed: "It is impossible to cut this plant! It is too useful." The second herb that he saw cured headaches. He also refused to destroy it. The third herb got rid of colic. . . . "In truth," he said, "I cannot pull up such much needed herbs." Fa, quickly noticing his slave's refusal to cut some herbs, requested that he show him those that possessed great value and contributed to maintaining the body's good health. And once he understood, he decided that Asen would no longer work in the field but would remain with him in order to explain the virtues of plants, leaves, and herbs. Since this time, Fa and Asen have been inseparable, and whenever Fa leaves home, he is always accompanied by Asen. And when one consults Fa, Asen acrelele is always there during the consultation.[49]

For the most part, the tradition glosses the relationship between Fa and Asen as a mutually beneficial partnership. Fa divined; Asen provided knowledge of medicinal plants. Yet Asen was Fa's slave. Fa literally owned Asen acrelele's medicinal knowledge and put it to his own use. This subordination of Asen to Fa calls to mind Agaja's proscription of *gbo* diviners in favor of Fa diviners. Is it possible that Agaja believed the use of ancestral *asen* "permitted too many alliances against him" in the same way that divination with *gbo* did? Just as Agaja prohibited divining with empowered objects, he no doubt would have feared the continuous revelation of powerful ancestors through *asen*. It would have made perfect sense for Agaja to naturalize "Asen" to the more stable and controllable Yoruba form of divination. As a result, *asen* could be reduced almost solely to the "servitude" of Fa diviners. Even today, "each Fon diviner owns an iron staff (the *asen acrelele*), which is present when he consults Fa and is used to lead processions into the sacred forest."[50]

If Asen acrelele became the servant of Fa, Agaja apparently appropriated older ancestral and vodun forms of *asen* into the service of royal dynastic empowerment. As already noted in chapter 1, during Agaja's reign sacrifices were made not to the voduns but rather to Agaja's deceased royal ancestors. According to accounts taken in the 1850s and 1870s, Agaja introduced a new ritual known as "Se-que-ah-hee" (Sin Kwain) in order to accommodate these sacrifices.[51] During this ritual, "the spirits of the deceased monarchs are invoked and solicited to lend their aid to the living representative, by the sacrifice of men and animals, whose blood is sprinkled not upon the tombs, but upon the mysterious fetiche-irons . . . of each of the kings."[52] Supposedly, Agaja sacrificed "upwards of 200,000 human beings" before these "fetiche-irons" for the purposes of maintaining this "frightful blood fête."[53] Perhaps not coincidentally, the oral history of the Hountundji family of royal blacksmiths maintains that one branch of the family migrated from Allada to Cana, about five miles southeast of Abomey, at the request of Agaja in the eighteenth century.[54] If Agaja indeed appropriated the ancestral *asen* to empower the royal dynasty, it bears to reason that any other use of *asen* would have been proscribed. The invocation of ancestral powers outside of the royal lineage would have been a political threat worthy of enslavement and expulsion.[55]

Whether or not these oral traditions accurately reflect political conflicts during the reign of Agaja, tensions between royals and healers around the issue of harnessing ancestral power continued deep into the nineteenth century. When artisanal innovations in *asen* construction occurred in the late eighteenth century with the introduction of the spoked cone, and again in the late nineteenth century with lost-wax brass casting, the Dahomean royal family apparently tried to monopolize the most exquisite decorative forms.[56] Once again, these attempts by the monarchy to control empowered objects were more than mere assertions of spiritual authority; they were also a calculated response to the political threats exerted by powerful healers.

Beyond the expressions of healing power inherent in the *asen* of Silva and

Asen used in Sin Kwain ceremony in the nineteenth century marking the graves of Dahomey's former kings. Lithograph from J. A. Skertchly, *Dahomey as It Is; Being a Narrative of Eight Months' Residence in That Country* . . . (London: Chapman and Hall, 1874).

Axê, as well as in the "knife" at Domingos' shrine, we must also recognize that these objects were almost certainly manufactured in Brazil, perhaps even by freed Gbe-speaking ironsmiths. In order for the *asen* to be properly consecrated to an ancestral spirit, it first had to be ritually freed from the heat of Gu. This ceremonial cooling of the iron required specific offerings to the vodun. Otherwise, the *asen* would have been ineffective in attracting the ancestral spirit. In modern-day Benin, the person commissioning the *asen* offers gin and money, while the ironsmith provides a calabash of water, into which are thrown Gu's three sacred leaves. Cooled by the leaf bath and sated by the liquor and money, "Gu gives way and the asen is complete, its essence ready to be consecrated to the spirit of a family member."[57] Assuming that similar ritual preparation of *asen* was required in Brazil, the successful commissioning of these objects suggests a much broader proliferation of the ideas that informed their empowerment. Whether through Gbe-speaking ironsmiths or through the education of others by Gbe healers, the production of *asen* in Brazil points to a community of knowledge that naturalized Gbe therapeutic forms to the diasporic context, a process that necessarily resulted in subtle transformations in the political outcomes of healing. Whereas the Dahomean variant focused on the ills caused by an illegitimate monarchy and its imperial designs, Brazilian healing concentrated on the new ailments of colonial slave society. In some instances, Afro-Brazilians utilized their powers to address slavery and the slave trade directly. In other instances, they treated the broader set of ailments that emanated from slavery. Ironically, new Brazilian disorders often manifested similar symptoms to those encountered earlier in Dahomey—illness, disease, hunger, isolation, and so on—symptoms that were shared in Brazil by Africans and Europeans, slaves and slaveowners alike.

If Axê's use of *asen* to cure illness represented old ways of addressing new maladies, so too did the second part of his ritual cures. The revelation from the "father of the *feitiços*," who was accompanied by his wife and multiple children, seems to be yet another example of a powerful ancestor speaking through a human medium. The doll that Axê constructed was actually a physical representation of Moquem, the wandering spirit that plagued his ill clients.[58] When Axê's patients threw their hair into the grave with the head of Moquem, they symbolically transferred their illness back to his head. At the same time, Moquem's severed body represented his final demise. Francisco Axê's donning of the priest's garb to bury the hair and the doll brought a solemn and "official" end to both the illness and Moquem's malevolent wanderings. The imitation of the priest was a cultural cue for Axê's Catholic patients, an ingenious way of conveying distinctly African messages in Portuguese form.

ALL THREE OF THE CASES described briefly here, as well as the case of Domingos Álvares, illustrate the confluence of divinatory, spiritual, and ancestral invocations that were prohibited in Dahomey. It seems quite likely that each of these men was enslaved and sent to Brazil largely as a result of his divining and healing powers. The replication of fragments of these divination and healing forms would not be at all surprising to most people. What is surprising is the apparent widespread appeal in Brazil of very specific, fully articulated healing practices that were outlawed in Dahomey. The persistent devotion to Sakpata, divination with *gbo*, and ancestral invocations with *asen* suggest a large concentration of Gbe speakers in Brazil who, despite their persecution and enslavement for these practices in Dahomey, continued to view public healing as the most effective means of addressing physical, social, and political ills. Resistance to the conditions of enslavement in Brazil was, in many respects, a continuation of similar struggles against Agaja. In this way, Brazilian history very much became the history of the Gbe-speaking region, at least during the 1730s and early 1740s.

Portuguese slaveholders were often implicated in this continuing Gbe-Brazilian history. Even as slave masters embraced African authority over disease and illness, they feared this power, isolating their diviner/healer slaves as much as possible from the vehicles of spiritual sustenance, especially kith and kin. Many of the same proscriptions that existed in Dahomey continued in Brazil. Those healers who gained their freedom constantly found themselves harassed and under surveillance. Manuel Cata was denounced to the Inquisition dozens of times between 1742 and 1748. Authorities also closely monitored João da Silva, who eventually "absented himself" from Rio das Pedras, abandoning his clients and whatever semblance of community he had been able to develop there. By threats and intimidation, Brazilian colonial authorities sought to insure that Gbe-speaking healers would remain isolated, unstable, and, if all else failed, exiled and on the run.

Ultimately, what separated Domingos Álvares' *terreiro* from other African healing sites in Rio de Janeiro and its hinterlands was that it was a sustainable, collective endeavor. Just as would have been the case with his ritual ground in Naogon, Domingos' *terreiro* in Rio represented a space where refugees and strangers could reconstitute kinship ties under the banner of public healing. This new community redefined each member's "personhood," linking him or her to an ancestral vodun (Sakpata), a "father" *vodunon* (Domingos), brother and sister *vodunsi* (fellow initiates), and other congregants. As in Naogon, this community was far more than a palliative for "family"; it was also a vehicle for social and political empowerment. Women, in particular, found a strong voice in Domingos' community. Though references to male devotees can be found in some of the documents, the vast majority of Domingos' adherents are described as women. Given the various ways that women asserted power through vodun in Dahomey, their prominent roles in Brazil should not surprise us.

Across the Gbe-speaking region, women held positions of esteem in healing communities from at least the early eighteenth century. These women's ability to harness the power of the voduns apparently neutralized even the sharpest gendered social distinctions. Describing Dahomey in 1705, the Dutch trader Willem Bosman observed:

> The Women which are promoted to the degree of Priestesses, tho'
> some of them were perhaps Slaves before, are yet as much respected

as the Priests, or rather more . . . ; and as all other Women are oblig'd
to a slavish Service to their Husbands, these, on the contrary, exert an
absolute Sway over them and their Effects, living with them perfectly
according to their arbitrary Will and Pleasure; besides which, their
Husbands are obliged to shew them so much Respect, as they receiv'd
from their Wives before their becoming Priestesses, which is to speak
to, and serve them upon their Knees. For this Reason, the most sen-
sible Negroes will neither marry a Priestess, nor easily consent that
any of their Wives be rais'd to that Honour: But if notwithstanding it
happens, they must not oppose it; for if they did, they would be call'd
to a severe Account for it, and look'd upon as Men who endevour'd to
stop the common Course of Divine Worship.[59]

Apparently, some priestesses were more feared than others. A popular Fon
proverb states: "A man fires a rifle shot at a Sakpata priestess and runs to
take refuge in the royal palace. There, for sure, is a shortage of refuge!"[60]
The proverb points to two overlapping layers of conflict, one spiritual and
the other gendered. Implicit is the universal fear of a wrathful Sakpata, especially among the Dahomean monarchy. However, the primary source of
tension is the woman's ability to contest male dominance. Neither a man
with a gun nor the king of Dahomey possesses the power to challenge such
a woman. Thus, devotion to Sakpata quite literally becomes a pathway to
social and political liberation for some Dahomean women.

In the late nineteenth century, Richard Burton estimated that roughly a
quarter of Dahomean women were vodun initiates. Whether this preponderance of female power held true in the eighteenth century is difficult to
know; however, Burton hinted in this direction when he wrote: "The old
travellers inform us that in their days these ladies used to lord it over their
lords to such an extent, that to espouse a sancitifed woman was like marrying an heiress in civilized lands."[61] If anything, it seems that women's roles
in vodun were declining in Dahomey over the course of the nineteenth
century. Burton's estimate that a quarter of Dahomey's women were initiates in the late nineteenth century actually might have been higher in the
eighteenth century.

Whatever the actual numbers, it is clear that women almost always
played crucial roles in the ritual world of vodun. Melville J. Herskovits
speculates that the overrepresentation of women was due to their easier
separation from the "everyday duties of life than a man."[62] Given women's
primacy in agricultural and child-rearing duties, this is an entirely unsatisfy-

ing interpretation. A more compelling explanation for women's prominent roles in Dahomean vodun is the actual cosmology, which emphasizes harmony and balance between male and female. This ideology is succinctly summarized in one version of the Fon myth of origins, which begins: "The world was created by one god, who is at the same time both male and female." This androgynous creator gave birth to twins, one male (Lisa) and one female (Mawu), who were given equal domains—sun/moon, day/night, hot/cool.[63] Though this creation myth likely did not enter into Dahomean monarchical "orthodoxy" until after Agaja's death in 1740, the monarchy's embrace of these ideas was a reflection of existing realities of a gender-balanced priesthood and a broader cosmology that placed women at the center of the belief system. Moreover, it was a woman, one of King Tegbesu's wives, Kpojito Hwanjile, who is credited with introducing the Mawu/Lisa myth into the Dahomean cosmos in the 1740s.[64] In practical terms, sexual balance and gender fluidity characterized most congregations in the 1720s and 1730s. Domingos' parents, Afnage and Oconon, shared leadership over their ritual community. In addition, male voduns regularly mounted female initiates, and vice versa, rendering initiates their sexual opposites, at least in their ritual guises. In many respects, androgyny was the ideal expression of balance and reciprocity exemplified in the concept of axê, the life-giving force of empowerment desired by most vodun communities. Male and female had to share equally in order for this power to be achieved.

Many of the same ideas that informed vodun ideology in the Gbe-speaking world carried over to eighteenth-century Brazil; however, the demography and social structures of Brazil's slave societies impacted deeply how and where women might forge new vodun congregations. Overall, the Gbe-speaking population of Brazil reflected the sex ratios of the slave trade from the Bight of Benin, roughly two men for every woman; however, there were regional variations. In mining areas, the sex imbalance was especially acute, reaching ratios of more than ten men for every woman in some places.[65] Obviously, in these demographic circumstances, women had difficulty congregating, let alone forming congregations. As we have already noted, sugar planters were intolerant of any perceived threats to their patriarchal authority. African women ranked firmly at the bottom of this social hierarchy, their freedom of association often strictly curtailed. Unlike agricultural and mining regions, however, urban environments afforded African women a combination of relative sexual balance, adequate population density, and freedom of movement that at least allowed for the conditions to build new healing communities. Given that freed African women far outnumbered their male counterparts, they had the social and economic wherewithal to commit to a congregation and support it with offerings of time and money. The Catholic hierarchy did little to dissuade Gbe-speaking women from remaining devoted to the voduns, excluding women not only from the priesthood but also from any positions of ritual importance in the Church. Meanwhile, women like the Captain exerted remarkable influence over the ritual and social life of Domingos' healing community. In this way, vodun represented one of the few outlets of genuine institutional empowerment for women in Brazil, making it attractive even to some white Portuguese women.[66]

The obvious question is why women did not simply form their own ritual grounds in Brazil.[67] As already suggested, harassment by Catholic priests made the establishment of *terreiros* unlikely even under the best of circumstances. Neither African men nor African women had much success in creating ritual spaces during these early years. Domingos Álvares was therefore exceptional, regardless of his sex. Still, Domingos succeeded in building his ritual space in no small part because of the system of patriarchy and patronage that characterized colonial Brazil. In the minds of European slave masters, African men could access wellsprings of power, both physical and spiritual, that African women generally could not. Of course, this idea of African male power was largely a self-fulfilling prophecy since the Portuguese insured that African men were numerically dominant in Brazil's enslaved population. However, even in their own ideological world, the Portuguese viewed healing as the distinct purview of educated males, especially Catholic priests, doctors, and pharmacists. The idea of female "healers" (as opposed to unsanctioned "sorcerers" who performed folk remedies) was simply not a part of the Portuguese mental universe. The Portuguese imposed this gendered optic onto African healing, assuming that the "art" was largely the preserve of powerful men. As a result, the feared and respected African male *"feiticeiro"* emerged as an iconic figure in colonial Brazil, one who was an expert in the realms of herbal healing and the supernatural.[68] By the early nineteenth century, the Portuguese male elite naturalized African healing power to its own "legitimate" and highly gendered medical establishment, licensing large numbers of African men, but no women, as barber/bleeders.[69]

It did not take a great leap to conclude that a particularly knowledgeable, charismatic, and powerful healer like Domingos Álvares might be capable of generating a lucrative market for his services, especially in an urban space like Rio. It will be recalled that no less a figure than the governor of the captaincy recommended Domingos to work in precisely this capacity. José Cardoso de Almeida's decision to invest in Domingos' skills relied on the governor's good endorsement and protection. Meanwhile, by sanctioning and supporting Domingos' vocation as a healer-for-hire, Almeida afforded Domingos the opportunity to create an extensive infrastructure and network of clients. As a slave, Domingos earned social prestige and a significant economic headstart on his future, opportunities that were contingent on a distinct set of patriarchal ideas and relationships that were unavailable to most people, let alone African female healers. Ultimately, Domingos took full advantage of Portuguese notions of the African *feiticeiro*, as well as the hierarchy of patronage that extended up to the governor, constructing the institutional foundation for the healing community he continued to build as a freedman.

Despite the Portuguese elite's refusal to recognize female healers, once Domingos earned his freedom and established his own ritual space, his community probably could not have functioned without the significant inclusion and leadership of women. The role of the Captain seems particularly significant here. As her title suggests, the Captain held a position of extraordinary ritual importance and power in Domingos' community. Indeed, her role seemed to adhere to that of the *hungan*, literally "chief of the divinity."[70] In vodun, the *hungan* was the ranking member of a healing community, second only to the *vodunon*. If, for some reason, the *vodunon* was absent from the ritual space, the *hungan* took over leadership of the *vodunsi*. As the primary vehicle for the divinity, the *hungan* also was responsible for much of the ritual choreography—dancing, sacrifices, and so on—that drew the vodun into the ritual space for consultation.[71] These were precisely the roles the Captain played in Domingos' *terreiro*, as clearly demonstrated by her actions during the "healing" of Leonor de Oliveira Cruz. The Captain played a similar pivotal role in other ritual performances and invocations in Domingos' healing community, yet another hint of her permanent place of respect among the congregation.[72]

Given the Captain's signal importance to the community, one wonders if Domingos viewed her as an equal partner in his therapeutic enterprise, in similar fashion to the way his parents and other male/female couples presided over vodun congregations in his homeland. We have no way of knowing the Captain's actual name; nor do we know the full contours of her relationship with Domingos outside of the ritual setting. What we do know is that by the early 1740s, Domingos claimed to be "married" to a freedwoman named Maria da Rocha who was "from Allada on the Mina Coast." I have pored over parish marriage records for the entire period of Domingos' time in Rio de Janeiro, and there is no record of his marriage to Maria da Rocha. Nor is there a record of the baptism of their daughter, born in 1741.[73] The absence of Domingos from the official Church record should not surprise us given his ideological alienation from the Church and his renegade status in his home parish of Candelária. Like many other Africans, he probably never married in the Catholic Church at all.[74] This raises the intriguing question of whether his claim to "marriage" with Maria da Rocha was a euphemism for their shared leadership over the family of *vodunsi* at Morro da Glória. If Domingos actually married, it seems inconceivable that his partner would not have played an integral role in his congregation. Moreover, Maria da Rocha, hailing from a kingdom conquered by Dahomey in 1724, probably shared with Domingos a common history in opposition to illegitimate usurpers and enslavers. Perhaps Maria da Rocha was the Captain, a vodun devotee with ritual knowledge gained in Allada and shared with Domingos as his new ritual and life partner in the *terreiro* at Glória. At the very least, the common threads that tied Domingos, Maria da Rocha, their daughter, the Captain, and the *vodunsi* should draw our attention to the varying ways that Africans reconstituted "family" and kinship in the diaspora.

The lines of reciprocity between vodun, vodunon, and vodunsi in Domingos' ritual community mirrored those between ancestors, powerful men, and wives/children in his homeland. In both vodun and kinship idioms, the pathway to empowerment ran through people. The number and quality of people in the ranks of Domingos' ritual family defined its strength and prosperity. Likewise, the largesse of the ritual family defined each individual member. Thus, Domingos' "marriage" and the birth of his daughter were not his alone; they belonged to everyone in his ritual space, as well as to the vodun. To be sure, natal ties mattered, but where social conditions prevented the health and prosperity of birth families, ritual families could act as crucial proxies, ultimately facilitating the construction of new blood ties and the creation of new peoples. With a "wife," a baby daughter, and a group of ritual disciples, Domingos Álvares remade himself into a prosperous man by 1741, not so much because he was economically wealthy but because he once again commanded the deference, respect, and service of an extended family that offered the promise of collective health and well-being, the platform for a new start, to a new people in Brazil.

7

Dislocations

But whatever I may believe, don't you begin to think that
Portugal is rather too much in the neighbourhood of Africa?
—Italian literary critic Giuseppe Baretti, describing his
travels through Portugal in 1760, in *A Journey from London
to Genoa, through England, Portugal, Spain, and France*

Holding onto his hard-earned freedoms proved to be an enormous challenge for Domingos Álvares. When Catholic priests raided his healing center shortly after he had gained his freedom, Domingos barely avoided capture, yet he refused to go into permanent hiding. If anything, the raid seemed to bolster his fame and notoriety in the city, allowing him to expand his healing practice to other parts. Perhaps Domingos became overly complacent, or perhaps he simply had faith that his medicinal and spiritual arsenals were stronger than any other. Either way, brazen public episodes like the one with his former mistress, Leonor de Oliveira Cruz, only drew greater scrutiny from loyal Catholics, who were frequently reminded of their obligation to denounce crimes against the faith. At least once a year, parish priests read Inquisitorial "edicts of faith" from their pulpits before posting them permanently in the sacristy of the church. These edicts reminded parishioners of their obligation to report any known breaches of the faith, including blasphemy, heresy, superstition, and witchcraft. According to canon law, Catholics had thirty days to report the transgressions of their neighbors, friends, and relatives. Failure to denounce sinners in a timely manner could result in excommunication from the Church. Generally, these edicts were ignored; however, some Catholics took them seriously, including several people Domingos encountered in his travels across Rio de Janeiro.

One of the witnesses to the raid on the healing center, Ignácio Correa Barbosa, demonstrated a particularly keen interest in Domingos. As Domingos' neighbor, Barbosa spent many evenings watching the comings and goings at the "public house" and was disturbed by the "great public scandal" that it provoked. When Catholic priests in Candelária failed to find Domingos in the immediate aftermath of their raid, Barbosa took the investigation into his own hands, monitoring rumors of Domingos' whereabouts and chasing promising leads. After learning that Domingos healed in Glória, Barbosa traveled across the city "to certify what Domingos did in his cures, in order to denounce him." Accompanied by his friend, the thirty-one-year-old soldier Manuel da Assumpção de Andrade, Barbosa arrived at Domingos' ritual ground around nine o'clock on a Saturday morning in early 1741. At first, the two men hid outside the gate "to see who entered and to see if they would be able to observe something." Moving in for a closer look, Barbosa went toward the back of the house where Domingos performed his cures. There, he hid in a thicket and waited. Meanwhile, back at the gate, Andrade grew impatient, eventually walking straight up to the veranda of the house, where he saw "various hammocks and many white, *parda*, and *negra* women." Andrade tried to enter the kitchen, but Domingos immediately slammed the door and locked it. Shouting through the closed door, Andrade asked Domingos if he lived in the house. Domingos responded no, he lived in Prainha, in the northern part of the city. Andrade then asked why Domingos was there. Domingos answered that he wanted to close the bodies of those women who were sick. When Andrade asked him why he was closing their bodies, Domingos replied that it was best if he did not know that. At this, Andrade abandoned his inquiries and departed.

A short time later, Barbosa's patient surveillance paid off. Peering from behind the bushes where he was hiding, Barbosa saw Domingos exit the house with a vessel of water, which he put in the middle of the gathered people. Domingos then took a calabash and tapped it on the bottom. He also asked each of the congregants to tap the calabash. Eventually, Domingos pulled the cork from the gourd, and "smoke" emerged. He immediately called "three names: Captain, Old Man, and Long-Bearded Man," and then he announced that he was the "true God and Christ and all should obey him and do as he orders." Arriving at his feet were "a black man on one side and a black woman on the other." Domingos ordered them to inhale the smoke from the calabash. Eventually, each of the people gathered around to put their hand into the vessel of water. Upon seeing this, Barbosa fled immediately to report everything he had witnessed, first to a secular justice official, and later in a denunciation to the Portuguese Inquisition.[1]

Barbosa was not the first to suspect Domingos of witchcraft. As early as 1737, the captain of the slave ship that delivered Domingos to Rio denounced him for controlling the movement of the ship with his *feitiços*. Later, Manuel Pereira da Fonseca denounced Domingos for putting an evil spirit into his wife, Leonor de Oliveira Cruz. Several others accused Domingos of performing "superstitious cures" at the house on Rua da Alfândega and at the ritual ground in Glória. By June 1741, the Inquisitorial commissioner of Rio de Janeiro, Gaspar Gonçalves de Araújo, possessed sufficient evidence to forward Domingos' case to Lisbon for review by the Portuguese Holy Office. Included in the documents were six denunciations, laying out the individual eyewitness accounts of Domingos' crimes. In his summary, the Inquisitorial commissioner concluded that Domingos "had a pact with the Devil, being publicly known as a *feiticeiro* with notorious scandal all over this city." The commissioner explained that he had no "hatred or malice" against Domingos. He was simply obeying the charge of his office, so that "a crime so prejudicial to the service of God, and to the good spiritual habits of the many Souls tricked by the accused, would not remain unpunished." For the commissioner, the evidence was overwhelming and incontrovertible. He requested that the Holy Office "proceed against the accused with all the penalties of law." These penalties included arrest, transport to Lisbon, and a full Inquisitorial trial. But before the commissioner could act, he had to wait to hear back from his superiors in Lisbon.[2]

The administrative structure of the Portuguese Inquisition played a key role in determining where, when, and how Domingos Álvares might be brought to justice.[3] Unlike the Spanish Inquisition, which established permanent tribunals in Mexico City (1570), Lima (1570), and Cartagena (1610), the Portuguese Inquisition had no fixed institutional presence in Brazil. Instead, the tribunal at Lisbon maintained jurisdiction over all of Portugal's overseas colonies. The Portuguese appointed *comissários* (commissioners), *familiares* (lay officials), and *notários* (notaries/scribes) to administer and enforce ecclesiastical justice in Brazil. Generally, each major city received one or two commissioners and an equal number of scribes, along with dozens of lay officials who assisted the commissioner by tracking down witnesses, apprehending suspects, accompanying prisoners in their travels, and so on. The commissioner's primary charge was to investigate crimes against the Catholic Church and carry out orders sent from Lisbon. Only under extraordinary circumstances could the commissioner arrest a suspect without first receiving orders from overseas. If a commissioner arrested a suspect independent of Lisbon's demands, he was required to show that 1) the case was within the Inquisition's jurisdiction; 2) there was sufficient evidence of crimes against the faith; and 3) the suspect was a serious flight risk. Otherwise, he had to await word from Lisbon, a process that could take many months or even years, depending on the Lisbon tribunal's caseload and the vagaries of transoceanic travel.

Inquisitorial commissioners sometimes abused their powers, arresting suspects without Lisbon's consent; however, Gaspar Gonçalves de Araújo was a devoted servant of due process. In fact, just as Domingos' case emerged, Araújo accused another Rio commissioner, Manuel Freire Batalha, of breaching procedural and jurisdictional requirements. In a petition to Lisbon, Araújo complained that Batalha was "exercising his ordinary occupations of contentious jurisdiction," arresting people for crimes not pertinent to the Inquisition. Araújo feared that such undisciplined behavior on the part of commissioners undermined the Inquisition's authority among Brazilian Catholics; he also worried that Inquisitors might lose confidence in more diligent commissioners like himself.[4] For Domingos, Araújo's strict adherence to the bureaucratic procedures of the Portuguese Holy Office spelled a short respite before the inevitable. On March 31, 1742, more than nine months after Araújo sent the package of denunciations, the Inquisitors finally issued a warrant for Domingos' arrest and demanded that he be sent to Lisbon for trial. They also ordered Araújo to reconvene all of the witnesses, have them swear on their original testimonies, and add any new evidence that might have surfaced since the previous June.

Even before the Inquisition's arrest order could make its way back across the Atlantic, the bishop of Rio intervened, ordering Domingos' apprehension.[5] Though the exact date and details of Domingos' arrest are unclear, one witness, Maria de Jesus, described how "various sergeants and soldiers and other people" gathered on her street with such commotion that she wondered aloud if someone had been killed. Her domestic servant, who had just come in from the street, responded that nobody had been killed. Rather, "they were surrounding Domingos' house to capture him and they said he was a *feiticeiro* and for that reason they were going to arrest him."[6] This time, Domingos could not evade his captors, whose planning and coordination must have taken him by surprise. The small army of secular and Church officials captured Domingos at his healing center in São José, bound him in chains, and marched him across the city to the ecclesiastical jail, only two blocks from where he had first lived in Rio as a slave.

Domingos was familiar with the conditions in Brazilian penal institutions. Like the Recife jail, the ecclesiastical jail in Rio was always "overflowing with people." The cells sometimes held as many as 400 prisoners, crammed into compartments built to accommodate only twelve to fifteen. According to one witness, these "dens of infection" were "true cesspools,

where the criminals rotted alive."[7] The local church provided little maintenance for the prisoners. Generally, food and water were the responsibility
of inmates' families and friends. Though the Inquisition allotted a stipend
for upkeep and transport of its prisoners—60,000 réis in the case of Domingos—corruption and graft meant that inmates did not always receive
their daily sustenance.[8] To make matters worse, unlike Recife, it appears
that there were few, if any, charitable efforts to support those in Rio's jails.
In the early 1740s, one prisoner accused of bigamy wrote a letter to the Inquisitors in Lisbon complaining of the conditions in Rio. He noted that "in
this prison many suffer in misery without mercy." He lamented that nobody
came to the prison to relieve their suffering, as people did in other jails, not
even "to provide a cup of water or food." The man concluded that people in
uncivilized, pagan lands (*terra do gentio*) received greater sustenance than
that provided to the prisoners in Rio.[9] Domingos endured these dire conditions for at least a month, awaiting news of his fate.[10]

As Domingos sat in his fetid cell, Commissioner Araújo duly followed
the orders of the Holy Office, collecting evidence for the case against the
accused. Beginning on August 18, 1742, and stretching over several days,
Araújo recorded the testimonies of twelve people. First, he went about the
task of certifying the initial denunciations taken in 1741. Araújo easily found
four of the original witnesses, but two were missing. A brief investigation
revealed that Manuel da Costa Simões had died in December 1741, and Manuel da Costa Soares, the slave ship captain, was away in Pernambuco. After
certifying the absences of the two men, Araújo gathered eight new denunciations. Altogether, then, fourteen different witnesses provided testimony
describing Domingos' activities in Rio, Pernambuco, and at sea. The witnesses included nine men and five women; ten whites, three *pardas*, and
an African woman. Their occupations included slave trader, brass worker,
soldier, farmer, businessman, priest, street hawker, and slave. Except for the
relative absence of African slaves, the witness list was a remarkably representative cross section of urban, colonial Brazilian society.

Despite their demographic dominance in Brazilian slave society, Africans appeared before the Inquisition with striking irregularity. The Inquisition, and the Church more generally, viewed African slaves as redeemable
yet unreliable servants of God. Most Africans were baptized in the Catholic
Church and therefore obliged to abide by its laws and precepts. According
to the faith, converted Africans were just as much God's children as those
Portuguese born into the Church. Nevertheless, operating side by side with
these doctrines of equality were deeply held assumptions that Africans

were incapable of completely grasping Church tenets. In his 1742 letter of summary to his superiors in Lisbon, Gaspar Gonçalves de Araújo clearly revealed these contradictory tensions. On the one hand, Araújo noted that among "the named witnesses . . . there is a slave [Thereza Arda], who despite the defect of her condition, because of her good intelligence and the way that she swore her oath, seems credible in her testimony." On the other hand, in closing his letter, Araújo stated the following: "The *preto* Domingos is without doubt . . . reputed as a curer of *feitiços*, which one suspects in this kind of people, principally those from the Mina Coast, who are most cunning, and brought from there as adults they do not easily forget the superstitions with which they were raised in that paganism."[11] Thereza overcame her "condition" as a Mina slave through "intelligence" and the good fortune of having lived most of her life in Brazil. But the very fact that Araújo felt compelled to justify Thereza's testimony indicates that he considered her the exception rather than the rule. Meanwhile, Domingos shared Thereza's "defects" of birth and status, but he more closely adhered to the Church's expectations of adult Africans since he remained a "cunning" *feiticeiro* who retained the "superstitions" of his homeland.

Araújo understood clearly that Domingos' beliefs and practices were tied to the age at which he was enslaved. In fact, most Africans arrived in Brazil as young adults, and very few of them forgot "the superstitions with which they were raised." Nevertheless, the Church hierarchy demanded the same level of devotion from someone like Domingos as it did from any other Catholic. Domingos' baptism and confirmation in Pernambuco years earlier cemented his obligation to comply with Catholic doctrine and gave the Church jurisdiction to judge his adherence. Yet, in the majority of instances, the Church simply ignored African "superstitions," preferring to concentrate its efforts on maintaining the devotion of those born into the faith. Between the early sixteenth and late eighteenth centuries, the Portuguese Inquisition tried nearly 40,000 cases from across the empire; only 46 of these involved African-born defendants accused of witchcraft.[12] Nevertheless, some Catholic priests called for more thoroughgoing institutional oversight of African practices. In 1742, the year Domingos was arrested, the archbishop of Bahia pleaded for a permanent Inquisitorial tribunal to be established in Salvador "because beyond the negros who are already innumerable, not a month passes without arriving at this port two or three ships full of these people from the Costa da Mina and others, not only practicing their barbarous and diabolical rites, but they excite those who were already here, almost forgotten, who then accompany them."[13] Lisbon received these complaints, but the pleas fell on deaf ears. Only in rare instances when African practices impinged directly on Catholicism, threatening the institutional authority of the Church, did the Inquisition intervene to prosecute African *feticeiros*.

Whether or not Domingos actually uttered the words attributed to him by Ignácio Correa Barbosa—"I am the one true God . . . and all should obey me"—his immense popularity and growing congregation of followers in Rio de Janeiro endowed the statement with a deep and disturbing resonance for Portuguese authorities. Domingos posed a formidable challenge to the institutional authority of the Catholic Church, and just like in Dahomey and Pernambuco, spiritual threats had profound political implications. Indeed, Domingos' therapeutic activities in the tightly knit world of urban Rio were as much an affront to King João V as similar practices had been to Agaja in Dahomey or to sugar planters in Pernambuco. The absolutist Portuguese Crown owed its worldly power to the Catholic Christian God. In turn, the Crown bore the burden as propagator of the Catholic faith, with the Inquisition as its primary instrument of justice. The king maintained ultimate authority and control over the Portuguese Church, almost always selecting members of the royal family for high positions like Inquisitor general. Because Crown and Church were so intertwined, a threat to one was implicitly a threat to the other. When a popular and charismatic leader like Domingos challenged God's power on earth, he also challenged the authority of King João V. Ultimately, then, it was not so much Domingos' "superstitions" that drew the attention of the Inquisition; rather, it was the broader political threat that they represented. Just as with Agaja and the sugar planters of Pernambuco, the Portuguese king could brook no competitors.

In mid-September 1742, an Inquisitorial *familiar* escorted Domingos from Rio's ecclesiastical jail to a Portuguese merchant vessel waiting in Guanabara Bay. The *familiar* relinquished custody of Domingos to the ship's captain, along with pertinent paperwork—Commissioner Araújo's letter of summary and remittance and the new eyewitness testimonies—to be delivered to the Inquisitors in Lisbon. Portuguese law required that ship captains transport accused criminals and exiles across the empire and remit them to appropriate judicial or ecclesiastical authorities. Failure to accommodate these requests could result in Crown seizure of the ship.[14] Loath to transport such potentially dangerous cargoes, ship captains often treated Inquisitorial prisoners as virtual slaves, locking them in chains and isolating them from passengers and crew in order to ensure that they would not corrupt the innocent with their heretical ideas. Food and fresh water were always in short supply, especially for prisoners. Disease was endemic. And if misfortune struck the ship during the ocean crossing, passengers and crew often unleashed their frustrations on Inquisitorial prisoners, whose grave sins were believed to invoke the wrath of God.[15] As we have already seen, captain and crew genuinely feared the powers of African captives. Domingos himself was subject to physical abuse in his passage from Pernambuco to Rio de Janeiro because he was judged to control the winds. Though we lack any account of what happened on Domingos' Atlantic crossing to Lisbon, we can assume that the ship's captain took all necessary precautions to protect his passengers and crew from the perceived threats posed by Domingos.

On September 22, 1742, the ship on which Domingos was sequestered, along with more than a dozen other merchant and naval vessels, lifted anchor and set sail for Lisbon. For Domingos, the physical suffering of the seaborne journey was by now familiar, but the crossing to Lisbon would have been no less traumatic than his passage from Africa to Brazil more than ten years earlier. Alone with his thoughts in the isolation and daily monotony of the sea, Domingos must have come to realize that he would never again see his wife, his infant daughter, and his family of devotees. Just as Agaja and the Pernambuco sugar planters had done years earlier, the Catholic Church forcibly removed Domingos from the social structures that gave his life meaning.

The impacts of this social unmooring went well beyond the bitterness of Domingos' individual suffering. Domingos' ritual family in Rio also must have felt a deep sense of loss upon his departure. Indeed, if we conceive of the ritual community as a singular, living entity, the removal of its spiritual leader was a form of vivisection, the excision of spiritual knowledge and empowerment that were at the very heart of the community. We have no way of being certain, but it seems likely that Domingos' *terreiro* and healing centers ceased to exist in the absence of his intellectual leadership. If so, an important source of sustenance and therapy was lost to a broad cross section of colonial society in Rio de Janeiro, not just his immediate kin. Domingos would have been acutely aware of the circularity of loss, of the implications his absence had on the larger community of Africans in Rio de Janeiro. How he carried these losses, and the accompanying guilt, is impossible to know, but the psychological wounds must have cut deeply. Overcoming almost insurmountable odds to build a vibrant and productive therapeutic community in the heart of the Portuguese colonial world, one that addressed so many pressing needs of poor and enslaved Africans, was a supreme accomplishment. To have these achievements so swiftly and cru-elly dashed by yet another corrupt and illegitimate power must have been a devastating blow indeed.

ON DECEMBER 11, 1742, after eighty-one days at sea, a fleet of sixteen Por-tuguese merchant vessels, accompanied by two war ships, sailed up the Tejo River and into the port of Lisbon.[16] Normally, the Portuguese wel-comed more than fifty ships a year from various Brazilian ports, but 1742 had been unusually slow. The ships from Rio de Janeiro represented the first, and only, fleet to arrive during the year.[17] Given Portugal's economic dependence on Brazil, the contents of the fleet were always much antici-pated. Aboard the vessels arriving from Rio were various trade goods, in-cluding sugar, hides, ivory, whale whiskers,[18] fish oil, and dye woods.[19] Also onboard were large sums of silver, around 500 pounds of gold, and a signifi-cant quantity of diamonds. One of these diamonds, a remarkable specimen of 87 ½ carats, prompted gossip among Lisbon's high society and perhaps resulted in the manumission of the lucky slave who discovered the stone in Minas Gerais.[20] By the early nineteenth century, any slave working in the mining district who found a diamond of at least 1 oitava (17 ½ carats) re-ceived public accolades, a new suit of clothes, and his *carta de alforria* (let-ter of manumission).[21] Similar rewards existed in the eighteenth century, although they do not appear to have been extended as a uniform custom. For example, in 1739, Domingos Jorge de Sintra, a miner working in Goias, offered manumission to his slave Maria, but only on condition that she first extract a pound of gold on his behalf.[22] In this way, the "alchemy" of trans-forming enslaved bodies into trade goods on the African coast could, on occasion, be reversed through the productive capacities of those bodies in the colonies.[23] In the social and cultural "purgatory" of colonial Brazil, the clearest path to bodily "salvation" was through a strict devotion to the pro-ductive universe, with its gaze across the Atlantic, toward the metropole's accumulative "paradise."[24]

If the landing of the magnificent jewel on Lisbon's docks represented "paradise" in the form of financial and, perhaps, human redemption, then the arrival of Domingos Álvares on the fleet's ships was the embodiment of African "hell," brought forth from the colonial "purgatory" to be disci-plined by God's earthly agents, the Portuguese Catholic Church and King João V. Domingos was not alone in representing the face of African "hell." At least two African-descended women accompanied him from Rio on the 1742 fleet, also ordered to appear before the Portuguese Inquisition. One of these women, Luzia Pinta, was a freedwoman from Angola accused of performing *calundu* rituals in Sabará, Minas Gerais. As mentioned earlier, *calundu* was the principal form of ancestral consultation for Central Africans.[25] Like Domingos, Luzia Pinta commonly gathered a small contingent of her enslaved countrymen to aid in her rituals. Two Angolan women sang and a man played an *atabaque* (small drum) in order to stir the "winds of divination." As the volume of the music rose, Luzia's ancestors ascended into her head, causing her to jump around "like a goat." Upon entering a trancelike state, Luzia continued to be racked with "great tremors." Dressed in ritual garb that included ribbons in her hair, rattles around her wrists and ankles, and a dagger in her hand, Luzia eventually offered remedies for people's illnesses.[26]

The other Inquisitorial prisoner aboard the fleet from Rio was an African-descended, Brazilian-born *crioula* named Luzia da Silva Soares, accused of various crimes in a small mining settlement near the present-day city of Mariana, Minas Gerais. Among other things, Soares' master and mistress accused her of placing a curse on the mines, halting the extraction of gold. They also held her responsible for the deaths of their two children. According to various denunciations and subsequent confessions, Soares murdered her master's newborn baby by "flying through a hole in a window, in the ... form of a butterfly" and sucking blood out of the baby's nose and mouth. After the baby was buried, Soares allegedly dug up the corpse and used the body parts to wreak havoc on her enemies. The infant's arms and legs were put in an oven in the slave quarters. The child's intestines were preserved in jars and stirred into the mistress's porridge. Finally, Soares allegedly burned the placenta and buried the remains under the threshold of the main entry to her master's house.[27]

Through the lens of the Portuguese, the horrendous acts of barbarism committed by Domingos Álvares, Luzia Pinta, and Luzia da Silva Soares were the result of "pacts" that each of them made with the Devil. Only by confessing to the pacts, renouncing them, and submitting to Inquisitorial justice could these wayward souls be brought back into the Christian fold. Ironically, the institutional mechanism by which Satan's Afro-Brazilian agents would be brought to justice sat in the heart of the metropole. In this way, the Lisbon tribunal operated as a sort of magnet for the most diabolical elements of the colonies, literally bringing hell to heaven's doorstep. Of course, Africans constantly flowed in and out of Portugal with their Brazilian masters, and thousands of other enslaved and freed Africans and their descendants lived and toiled in Portugal. The Inquisition was by no means the only purveyor of things African; however, in its role as arbiter of the faith, the Inquisition inadvertently introduced the sins of "purgatory" (Brazil) and "hell" (Africa) into Portugal itself.[28]

The presence of Africans in Portugal represented much more than the physical embodiment of "paradise" lost; Africans were a constant reminder that the Portuguese were deeply implicated in the psychological terror of colonialism and enslavement. Nowhere was this clearer than in the case of Luzia da Silva Soares. Though Soares confessed to several heinous crimes in Minas Gerais, she did so under extraordinary duress. When Soares initially denied her role in the illnesses and deaths of her masters' children, her master and mistress subjected her to days of unrelenting torture. They heated blacksmith's tongs until they were red hot, pinching Soares' flesh, leaving open sores all over her body. They stuck a needle through her tongue. They tied her to a ladder and set it near a raging fire. They dripped hot wax on her genitals. They jabbed her in the eye with a sharp stick until the eye eventually came out of its socket, leaving Soares blind. They put her toes on the firing pin of a shotgun and dropped the hammer, breaking the bones one by one. They beat her with fists and blunt objects, breaking her shoulder. Finally, they ordered her flogged until she was covered with blood. She was then tied up and left in the sun to be bitten by insects and vermin. According to Soares, if not for the charity of other slaves, who washed her wounds and gave her sustenance, she would have died.

As a consequence of this systematic torture, Soares eventually confessed that she made a pact with the Devil, resulting in her arrest by the Inquisition and her subsequent transport to Lisbon. Only after she arrived in Portugal, out of her masters' reach, did she reveal that her confession was elicited under torture. The Inquisitors ordered a new investigation and found that Soares' claims of coercion were true. Remarkably, they ruled that "she should be set free, and sent in peace to wherever it be well for her." The Inquisitors were no doubt vexed that Soares' masters usurped their judicial authority. They also may have concluded that Soares was sufficiently purged of any alliance with the Devil when she was so brutally tortured.[29] Whatever the intellectual rationale of the Inquisitors, Soares stood before them as the mirror image of Portuguese colonialism, a stark reflection of metropolitan complicity in the worst horrors of enslavement and colonial exploitation. Seeing the Portuguese face of "hell" staring back at them from the colonial mirror, the Inquisitors blinked, a fleeting recognition of the terror and inhumanity wrought by the Portuguese in their colonial possessions. As much as they might have tried, Portuguese authorities could not contain the miserable effects of African slavery to the colonies; these corrosive impacts were always intertwined with even the most hallowed of metropolitan institutions, including the Catholic Church.

WHEN DOMINGOS disembarked along the Lisbon waterfront on December 13, 1742, he still carried with him the ritual knowledge and ancestral powers that had sustained him wherever he went. To this end, he was never "alone," at least in a spiritual sense. However, he once again faced the daunting prospect of not knowing if, or how, he might reconstitute "community" and, hence, a socially embodied "self." Solitude meant social alienation in the temporal world, but just as important, it represented the abandonment of communal obligations to deceased ancestors and voduns. Failure to give appropriate praise and offerings could draw their ire, bringing greater hardship, illness, or even death. In this way, the imperative to reconstitute community was as much about survival as about social connection; the "self" could not continue without the reciprocity of ancestors, family, and kin.

As Domingos was marched the twelve blocks inland to the Inquisitorial jails in the city's central square, the Rossio, he must have searched the cityscape for resonant points of connection—sights, sounds, smells—particularly those with an African flavor.[30] From Domingos' perspective, Lisbon would have appeared a vibrant, cosmopolitan city. With a population of around 200,000, it was one of the largest cities in Europe and almost ten times larger than Rio de Janeiro.[31] During the day, the streets teemed with activity. Along the waterfront, the king's galley slaves loaded food, cargo, and ballast onto awaiting ships.[32] Likewise, fishermen, boat pilots, and laundresses engaged in their daily labors. Stretching along the narrow streets and up into the city's steep hills were markets and artisan shops— for fish, meat, grains, flowers, vegetables, cloth, shoes, iron, and gold.[33]

In addition to those gainfully employed, the indigent were everywhere. According to one scholar, Lisbon's eighteenth-century streets were a "veritable ant hill of beggars," thieves, and idlers.[34] It was not uncommon to see people sitting in the streets, alternately putting their heads in one another's laps for delousing. At least one man earned his livelihood hiring out baboons to sit on people's shoulders and dexterously remove the "vermin" that "swarmed" the heads of the "lower class."[35] Every so often, the horse-drawn carriage of a nobleman or woman charged through the crowded streets, sending pedestrians scurrying for safety. Slow movers were simply trampled.[36] The streets themselves were notoriously filthy, allegedly cleaned only once a year, prior to the festival of Corpus Christi.[37] "Rotten shoes," "dead cats," and other garbage presented obstacles for all passersby.[38] The acrid odors of decomposition filled the air, "the olfactory nerves being every moment saluted with the most disagreeable sensations."[39] To make matters worse, those walking the streets risked "being soiled with filth . . . throw[n] out the [upstairs] windows, into the street, since the houses do not have latrines. The general obligation is to carry this waste to the river. . . . This order, however, is not rigorously observed, principally by the common people."[40]

According to European travelers of the period, the "common people" who clogged the streets, filling them with garbage and human waste, were a racially mixed amalgam of poor whites, Africans, and Jews. Through the visitors' optic, Africans and their descendants were ubiquitous in Lisbon. In 1760, an Italian traveler noted:

> One of the things that most surprises a stranger as he rambles about this town, is that great number of Negroes who swarm every corner. Many of these unhappy wretches are natives of Africa, and many born of African parents, either in Portugal or in its ultramarine dominions. No ship comes from those regions without bringing some of either sex, and, when they are here, they are allowed to marry not only among themselves, but also with those of a different colour. These cross-marriages have filled the country with different breeds of human monsters.[41]

Though the precise number of Afro-Portuguese residents is impossible to determine, one English observer in the 1770s estimated that "about one fifth of the inhabitants of Lisbon consists of blacks, mulattoes, or of some intermediate tint of black and white."[42] This figure might be inflated, but the African influence was, nevertheless, palpable. Ultimately, the Italian concluded: "These strange combinations have filled this town with such a variety of odd faces, as to make the traveller doubt whether Lisbon is in Europe; and it may be foreseen, that in a few centuries not a drop of pure Portuguese blood will be left here, but all will be corrupted between Jews and Negroes."[43]

The African slaves Domingos encountered in the streets engaged in a variety of forms of urban labor. Slave women cleaned and whitewashed houses, carried human waste to the river, and hauled water from the public fountains to their masters. Slave men carried sedan chairs and pushed carts through the streets, acted as personal body servants for the wealthy, hauled wood to the shipyards, cleaned sewers, and worked as apprentices

The corner of Jewish Crossing and Street of the Blacks' Pit in Lisbon's old Mocambo neighborhood (today Santa Catarina). The "Blacks' Pit" refers to the old slave burial ground that existed there from the sixteenth century. Photograph by the author, 2008.

for artisans. In general, the Portuguese associated slavery with the filthiest forms of labor. A common insult was to pretend to sneeze whenever a slave passed in the streets.[44] While African-descended slaves often worked side by side with white servants, the Portuguese preferred to employ slaves because they were considered "more docile, cowed by the fear of being sold to work in the mines" of Brazil.[45] The threat of colonial rendition loomed large in the daily lives of Lisbon's slaves, a constant reminder that they were partible chattels, unlike their white compatriots.[46]

This specter of colonial banishment probably led some Lisbon slaves to imagine themselves as genuinely privileged, at least relative to their African brethren in the mines and cane fields of Brazil.[47] Whether slavery in Lisbon actually represented an "easier" form of servitude is debatable. The contrivance of metropolitan culture and refinement, combined with urban intimacies between masters and slaves, no doubt presented expanded opportunities for some. In 1743, eighteen-year-old Antônio Mina had already learned to read and play the trumpet, privileges that would have been unthinkable for the vast majority of young Africans growing up in Brazil during this period.[48] Despite his apparent good fortune, on November 27, Antônio ran away from his master, Francisco Roberto. Nearly a month later, Antônio remained at large, prompting Roberto to post a runaway slave notice in Lisbon's weekly newspaper.[49]

Ironically, it was probably the very "privilege" of slavery in the metropole that rendered Antônio's situation so intolerable. His education and musical skills opened up a world of promise, but slavery stifled creativity and crushed aspirations. This inability to realize the full potential of one's talents bred frustration, resentment, and contempt. Like Antônio, Luís São Tomé, a domestic slave and cook, fled his master's house in the Benfica neighborhood of Lisbon in June 1742. According to Luís' master, Dom Afonso Manuel de Meneses, Luís "bakes very well," but "when he walks and talks he sticks his chest out, and he is very easily angered." By adopting the bearing and posture of a free man, Luís publicly defied his social status. Meneses no doubt considered such behavior intolerable, demanding, instead, head-bowing deference and docility. A defiant Luís refused to accept these daily indignities, eventually abandoning his servitude altogether. He was still on the run six months later when Domingos arrived in Lisbon.[50]

For better or worse, Lisbon's enslaved lived in intimate, urban confines with their masters. Slaves might form genuinely warm relations with their masters. In the 1780s, members of the Portuguese royal family "vied with each other in spoiling and caressing, Donna Rosa, her majesty's black-skinned ... favourite."[51] Yet these same paternalistic intimacies could easily turn abusive, especially in an atmosphere where slaves and masters alike frequently imbibed colonial horrors. The constant threat of Brazilian exile allowed Portuguese slave masters to manipulate and take advantage of their bondsmen's worst fears. The sight of African Inquisitorial prisoners like Domingos Álvares only confirmed the dreadful conditions that might await the enslaved if they were banished to the colonies. Haggard and emaciated from the nearly three-month journey, Domingos no doubt drew curious stares, jeers, and insults as he made his way, bound in chains, to the jail.[52] The hostility that Domingos likely encountered in Lisbon's streets, however disorienting and surreal, was fleeting since he quickly arrived in the solitary confines of yet another jail. Five days later, he was joined in the public jails by Luzia Pinta, the *calunduzeira* from Minas Gerais. It is doubtful that they ever saw each other, however, since men and women were segregated in separate corridors.

The public jails represented a sort of liminal space in the Inquisitorial process. When the accused arrived in Lisbon, they were held until the Inquisitors reviewed their cases and determined whether they should be sent to the "secret jails." During this time, the new prisoners' only communication was with jailers and guards. Often, the accused remained unaware of the charges lodged against them. In Domingos' case, there is little doubt that he understood the basic logic of his incarceration. After all, he had been on the run from Catholic authorities in Rio for months before they finally caught up with him. Domingos knew that the Portuguese feared his powers and sought to contain them. He was once again a slave (*kannumon*)—a "person in cords"—because this was the only way they could harness his spiritual strength and neutralize his political power.

Domingos sat in the public jails for three months before the Inquisitors determined that the testimonies against him warranted a full trial. Such administrative delays were common due to the heavy caseloads of the judges. When they finally issued their report on March 12, 1742, the Inquisitors concluded that Domingos had been "called publicly to cure *feitiços* and that in the said cures he employed totally superstitious means, divining hidden things that naturally could not be known and proffering words that result in a presumption of a pact with the Devil." As a result, these were "sins enough for the accused to be imprisoned in the secret jails of this Inquisition."[53] This ruling prompted Domingos' transfer to a different section of the Inquisitorial compound. Escorted by guards, Domingos crossed an outdoor courtyard, passed through a heavy iron door, and entered the corridors of the secret jails.

The secret jails of the Inquisition were the official holding pens for those enduring the Inquisitorial process. The jails consisted of hundreds of tiny cells, each often shared by four or five men. These cells were "without sun, nor light, nor air, with a bad smell, humidity and decay in everything, [and the] danger of plague and illness."[54] Each cell contained a communal waste bucket that was emptied only once a week. During the winter, the cells were dank and frigid. In the summer, Lisbon's stifling heat exacerbated the fetid smells, inviting all manner of insects and vermin into the narrow cubicles. Silence and secrecy were to be maintained at all times. According to regulations, jailers were "never to put in the same cell, nor even the same corridor, persons who were related to one another, nor persons who knew one another or were from the same land, nor those who had committed the same crime, or new prisoners with old ones."[55] Prisoners were prohibited from speaking to one another about their cases or about the Inquisition more generally. Those who defied the code of silence were subject to beatings by the guards. As a result, the jails were eerily silent, the hush broken only by the opening and shutting of cell doors, the shuffling of feet up and down the corridors, and the occasional screams of those being tortured in the Sala do Tormento, deep in the bowels of the three-story compound.[56]

Some prisoners found ways of circumventing these inhumane conditions. Cellmates communicated by whispering to one another or by using sign language. Messages passed from cell to cell and corridor to corridor by a system of tapping the alphabet on the walls, ceilings, and floors.[57] In addition, jailers and guards were subject to a variety of bribes. Prisoners paid cash and tobacco to have guards carry their dirty clothes to relatives for laundering. Some prisoners took advantage of this opportunity by placing notes in the hems and cuffs of their clothes, thereby communicating with kin on the outside.[58] In other instances, guards charged prisoners a 100 percent markup for higher-quality food rations.[59] Of course, these illicit "privileges" required some point of connection to the world outside the walls of the jail. Africans like Domingos Álvares simply could not access the resources of friends and family in the same way that Portuguese prisoners could. In this respect, the corruption of the jails only amplified the isolation and alienation suffered by African prisoners.

In the absence of friends or family on the outside who might ameliorate their condition, African prisoners sometimes bartered the only commodity available to them—their bodies. In late 1725, Portuguese detainee Matheus Orobio was in his cell in the secret jails when, on several occasions, he heard what he "presumed was some of the guards having carnal access with some black woman [*preta*]."[60] One day,

> he heard some footsteps, which he perceived to be those of a woman . . . and . . . a man, who went in her company. Hearing the woman laugh, the man made a hushing sound, like when someone puts their hand over their mouth, indicating to shut up. And he heard a voice that he understood poorly, but seemed to be that of a man, who said that she should speak more softly. Continuing to take some steps, he heard the voice of the woman, who from her speech indicated that she was *preta* and she said, "Not here; in the courtyard." . . . And after some time passed, the same two people returned . . . who in their whispers, were gasping for air and breathing as if they were fatigued . . . and they were laughing.[61]

Another time, he heard the woman's voice coming from the outdoor courtyard, saying, "Enough, enough, I don't want it." Finally, on yet another occasion, he heard the same voice saying, "It hurts, but you know that."[62] Obviously, there was a coercive element to these encounters between Portuguese guard and black female prisoner; however, the woman's laughter and her reluctant complicity suggest that she received some benefit in return for her sexual favors. The record is silent on what these privileges might have been. Whatever the arrangement, these sexual exchanges once again highlight the isolation, desperation, and social subjectivity of African prisoners. Removed from the material and corporeal protections of kin, Africans sometimes resorted to the most basic survival strategies.

If physical deprivation and abuse were daily reminders of one's vulnerability as an alienated "individual," the Inquisitorial process itself reinforced the psychological traumas of social dismemberment. Three days after arriving in the secret jails, Domingos received an audience with the Inquisitor, Manuel Varejão e Tavora. After more than three months of solitude in the public jails, Domingos' initial interrogation must have come as some relief, although the content of Varejão's questioning served as a painful reminder of Domingos' fractured pasts. When Domingos arrived before Varejão, the Inquisitor asked his name, age, social status, birthplace, and place of residence. Domingos answered that "they should call him Domingos Álvares . . . slave of José Cardoso de Almeida, married to Maria da Rocha, freed black woman, born in Nangô on the Mina Coast, and resident in Rio de Janeiro, thirty-four years old more or less." Varejão then asked if Domingos knew why he was called before the Inquisition and if he had anything to confess. Domingos replied that he had no sins to confess and nothing to report to the Inquisitors. The series of questions that followed required Domingos to outline his family history, as well as his history in the Catholic Church. For the Inquisitors, this "genealogical" inquiry represented the starting point of every trial, providing crucial background and contextual evidence for the sins committed by the accused. For Domingos, the act of "remembering" (and "forgetting") his various pasts laid bare the chronic dismemberment that characterized his life history:

> He said that his name is Domingos Álvares, black slave of José Cardoso de Almeida, born in Nangon on the Mina Coast and resident in Rio de Janeiro. And his parents are already dead and they were called in the language of his land, the father Afnage, and the mother Oconon, both born and raised in Nangon on the Mina Coast. And he does not know who his paternal and maternal grandparents were, nor where they were born or raised. And he is married to Maria da Rocha, who was born in Allada on the Mina Coast and resident in the same city of Rio de Janeiro, from whom he has one little girl who would

be two years of age. And he is a Christian baptized in the Church of Nossa Senhora da Conceição of Engenho Tapirema, parish of Goiana, bishopric of Pernambuco, by the priest of the same church named Gaspar Pereira. Correction: baptized by Father Antonio, whose last name he does not know, resident in the same parish and his godfather was the above-mentioned Gaspar Pereira. And he is confirmed and it was in the Church or Chapel of Engenho Monteiro in the bishopric of Pernambuco by the bishop of the same, and he does not know his last name. And his godfather was Jerónimo Arre. And in the lands of Pernambuco and Rio de Janeiro he went to church and heard mass and preaching and confessed and took communion and performed the other rituals of Christians. And immediately he was ordered to fall to his knees and recite the Christian doctrine: to wit, the Our Father, Hail Mary, Apostles Creed, Hail Holy Queen, the Ten Command-ments, and the laws of the Holy Mother Church. And out of every-thing he knew only the Our Father and the Hail Mary. And he does not know how to read or write. And he has lived in Pernambuco and its outskirts, in the city of Rio de Janeiro, and in the above-mentioned his native country [*pátria*], and in all these lands he spoke with all castes of people who presented themselves to him. And he has never been jailed nor presented to the Holy Office until now.[63]

Less a linear autobiography than disconnected starts and stops, Domin-gos' genealogy reads as a series of incomplete narrative fragments, each fro-zen in time, scattered across several continents.[64] To some extent, this lack of continuity owes itself to the formulaic structure of his interrogation. Yet the halting description of people "already dead," never known, or forgotten suggests that Domingos struggled to reconcile his present circumstances with the compartmentalized, spatially disparate memories of his past. In a material sense, the past was indeed "dead," erased by the serial dislocation of enslavement, arrest, imprisonment, and exile. Nevertheless, memories of social connection and belonging were indelibly linked to Domingos' definition of self and were a crucial source of empowerment. The act of "re-membering" resurrected the filiative bonds that endowed Domingos with social context and history. At times, these memories of past relationships could confound other historical "realities," demonstrating just how con-tingent history was on different forms of memory. Nowhere is this clearer than in Domingos' silencing of his status as a freedman. In both his open-ing introduction to Varejão and his formal genealogical presentation, Do-

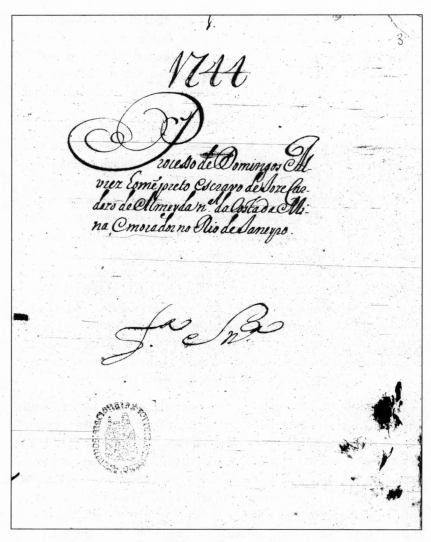

The administrative cover page that begins Domingos' Inquisition case file. It reads: "Trial of Domingos Alvares, black slave of José Cardoso de Almeida born on the Mina Coast and resident in Rio de Janeiro." Tribunal do Santo Ofício, Inquisição de Évora, Processo 7759, fl. 3. Courtesy Arquivo Nacional da Torre do Tombo, Lisbon, Portugal.

mingos claimed he was still the slave of José Cardoso de Almeida. Though he clearly identified his wife, Maria da Rocha, as freed, nowhere in the record does Domingos mention his own manumission. The Inquisitors easily could have corrected this error through a close reading of the materials and testimonies from Rio. Instead, they apparently took Domingos at his word, reinforcing his "slave" status throughout the case file.[65]

Why Domingos chose to present himself as enslaved might seem curious at first glance; however, read as a sociopolitical claim, it makes perfect sense. Domingos remembered Almeida through an idiom of slavery that cohered with broader understandings of patronage and kinship. The insistence that he was still a slave highlighted his connection to a socially and politically powerful Portuguese "big man." It was also an appeal to the freedoms and protection he enjoyed as Almeida's vassal. As Almeida's slave, Domingos was essentially free—free to heal, free to build therapeutic communities, and so on. It was his manumission, the severing of his social connection to his master, that made him vulnerable to a far worse form of enslavement by the Inquisition. By claiming to be Almeida's slave, Domingos might have believed he was contesting the Church's right to imprison him. At the very least, Domingos signaled an affiliation and allegiance to Almeida that transcended the Portuguese definition of "slavery," suggesting kinlike ties and reciprocal obligations that accorded far more closely with African understandings of patron-client relationships.

Domingos' emphasis on the broken bonds of kinship persisted throughout his genealogical presentation. His parents, Afnage and Oconon, were "already dead"; his wife, Maria da Rocha, and young daughter abandoned in Rio de Janeiro; his godfathers, Gaspar Pereira and Jerónimo Arre, still toiling on sugar plantations in Pernambuco. Along with his master/patron José Cardoso de Almeida, each of these figures represented dislocation, fragmentation, and community dismemberment, yet they became a collective whole in Domingos' memory, embodied as kin and, ultimately, as self. Domingos remembered their names and their places because, altogether, they constituted his very being. They, along with a handful of other unnamed friends and ritual adherents, were his only source of social mooring, the essence of his individual history and identity. Meanwhile, the full names of priests and bishops were forgotten, probably never committed to memory in the first place. Likewise, much of the Catholic doctrine escaped his notice. Ultimately, then, those who formed the core of Domingos' historical memory were the same patrons, friends, and family who were the sources of therapy and community well-being in Naogon, Pernambuco, and Rio de Janeiro. Even though these kinfolk were temporally "dead," Domingos continued to honor and serve them in his memories, expressing his individual identity as an extension of the social relationships from his past. When Varejão dispatched Domingos back to the solitude of his cell, these memories, at once painful and uplifting, were all that sustained him.

8

Inquisition

The Devil is in the details.

—Anonymous

Six weeks after his initial genealogical presentation, Domingos finally delivered his first confession in front of the Inquisitor, Manuel Varejão e Tavora. As in his earlier appearance, Domingos tied his individual history and ritual practices to other people—friends, family, and those seeking therapy. Though lacking in depth or detail, Domingos' testimony gives us the first glimpse of how he conceived of and explained his healing practices. After Domingos was sworn in, the scribe recorded his confession as follows:

> Finding himself resident in Pernambuco and in Rio de Janeiro he was publicly procured by various people in order to cure diverse diseases that they understood to be *feitiços*, which he made by applying some remedies that were composed of various herbal roots and tree leaves, that in his land they had taught him, and with these the people to whom they were applied felt better. And he worked everything naturally, as they had taught him in his homeland, without making use of words or any mixture in the said remedies and cures. . . . And he was not sure if in reality the people suffered from *feitiços*, and he only understood this to be the case through the same ones who told him that was what they had.
>
> Moreover he said that he was accustomed to making some powders from the said herbal roots, which he kept in a little calabash, and he carried them into the woods where he made his cures. And when the occasion arose to remove some powder from the calabash, the people who were there were accustomed to saying that he was looking inside the calabash for the Devil, by virtue of everything that he worked . . . , however it is certain that there was nothing else in the calabash except for the referred powders; nor did he use any other thing beyond that which he has already revealed. . . .

Moreover he said that on repeated occasions he was procured in order to divine some hidden things, especially some stolen things, and sometimes he discovered the people who had made the said thefts, not by his own virtue, but only because the same people who had committed the thefts had beforehand helped him discover the crime they had committed and the persons against whom they were committed. And in order to persuade the people who procured him that he possessed hidden virtues, he did not reveal to them the means by which he had known. Thus, they might expect that he was entirely capable of everything he worked, and that he had the virtue to divine hidden things that naturally he could not know. And these are his sins that he has to confess in this Mesa which he makes to discharge his conscience without impediment, that he understood not to have worked evil in that which he has confessed, and that having committed some sin in the referred facts . . . he is very repentant and for everything he requests pardon and mercy. . . . And saying that he had no more sins to confess . . . he was ordered back to his cell, being his first pass this session.[1]

Domingos' confession, skillfully delivered, demonstrates that he was keenly aware of the potential "criminality" of his behaviors. He very consciously and deliberately denied possessing any hidden "virtues" that might have been interpreted as emanating from the Devil. The Inquisition held that any such supernatural powers necessarily came through diabolical channels.[2] According to Domingos, the power of his cures derived from the natural properties of the herbs, roots, and leaves he used to treat the sick, taught to him by people "in his homeland." He admitted that some of his Brazilian clients believed he carried the Devil in his calabash, but he insisted that he only carried powders inside the vessel. Finally, he confessed that he sometimes pretended to divine the location of hidden objects and the identity of thieves but that he actually possessed no real powers to reveal hidden truths. Rather, he talked to people and carefully read the social terrain in order to determine probable perpetrators, victims, and locations of stolen property. It was in his interest to have his clients believe he possessed the power to see into the past, but in fact, his only "virtue" was the charismatic ability to gain people's trust and elicit their hidden secrets.

In Varejão's estimation, Domingos failed to deliver a full and true confession. As a result, he sent him back to his cell. Thirteen days later, Varejão again called Domingos and asked him if he had anything new to confess.

Domingos responded that "he could not remember anything more than that which he had declared in the previous session." Unable to extract any new information from Domingos, Varejão began to interrogate him. He first asked if Domingos had ever abandoned the Catholic faith or his belief in the teachings of the Church. Domingos replied that he had not. Varejão followed with a series of repetitive, hectoring questions about Domingos' relationship with the Devil—whether he worshipped the Devil as God; whether the Devil ever appeared to him, what form he took, and what they talked about; whether he ever made a pact with the Devil; whether through the Devil's intervention he caused harm to people. Domingos replied "no" to each question.

Then Varejão shifted tactics. Returning to Domingos' original confession, he asked whether Domingos remembered saying that he was frequently called upon to cure *feitiços*, applying diverse herbal remedies that made people feel better. Domingos replied "yes." Asked how he made his cures, Domingos responded that he made infusions by cooking various herbs and leaves, prescribing them to the ill until they were healed. Domingos added that the cures came from the "natural" powers of the plants and not by any "virtue" of his own. Varejão then asked if the Devil intervened to make the medicines efficacious. Domingos replied "no." His patience wearing thin, Varejão asked how it was possible that what Domingos said was true since, given the "extraordinary" effects of his remedies, all evidence pointed to a pact with the Devil. Domingos replied that there was no pact with the Devil in his remedies. Varejão became more insistent: If the Devil did not teach him the remedies, who did, and how could these "natural" remedies possibly address the "diversity of complaints" to which he applied them? Domingos explained that "various *pretos* in his land taught him the virtue of the said herbs and that when he applied some and they did not produce the desired effect, he used others until the sick felt better."

Having elicited from Domingos a series of explanations about the "natural" properties of his remedies, Varejão now seemed poised to drive him into a conceptual corner. "Did Domingos remember that in his confession he claimed that he was commonly procured to divine some hidden things, like the location of stolen items and who had stolen them?" Domingos responded "yes." "How then," Varejão asked, "could he discover these thefts, if not by some extraordinary virtue?" Expanding on the explanation he gave during his confession, Domingos answered that "since he had fame as a diviner, the same people who committed the thefts would come to him to prevent him from revealing their identity, requesting that he not solve the case for which he was called to divine, and in this form he came to the knowledge of the referred facts."

Though Domingos apparently revealed the trick behind his divination powers, Varejão refused to believe him. Whether or not Domingos' explanation was truthful is not so important (although surely he had to earn his "fame" as a diviner before people were willing to spontaneously confess to him). What matters most is that Varejão firmly believed Domingos possessed supernatural "virtues" that emanated from the Devil. Meanwhile, Domingos denied having any such powers. Ironically, it was the university-educated Portuguese Catholic priest who rejected Domingos' reasoned, "rational" explanation of his divination practices. In his unyielding quest to reveal the Devil, Varejão implicitly affirmed Domingos' "extraordinary" powers, as well as his own belief in the African supernatural. By the end of the interrogation, Varejão's and Domingos' positions were practically reversed, demonstrating just how close their belief systems actually were. The only difference was that Domingos claimed his powers emanated from communal imperatives, while Varejão insisted that such powers could only come from the Devil. By shining the mirror on the colonial "other," the Portuguese once again revealed himself. Thwarted in his attempts to extract the confession of a pact with the Devil, a frustrated Varejão ordered Domingos back to his cell.[3]

One week later, Varejão tried yet again. Determined to increase the pressure on his African nemesis, the Inquisitor initiated a line of questioning drawn directly from the denunciations made against Domingos in Rio de Janeiro. This was Domingos' first opportunity to answer his accusers. As such, the interrogation is worth quoting at length. In some instances, Domingos was forthcoming in his responses, but he steadfastly continued to deny any suggestion that his ritual practices were supernatural:

VAREJÃO: Asked if at any time [Domingos] was procured by a certain person to cure an ailment . . . and persuaded her she should go to a certain place where he would cure her with drinks made from fresh herbs picked with the morning dew. And this person, going to the site, found many others in a circle [roda] with a pot of water with a knife in it and in the middle a possessed woman he called Captain, who was dancing and jumping, and the accused threw some black powders at her, putting them together with his fingers over her forehead, and then asked her various questions he needed answered in order to make his cures and also to know what happened in distant parts. To which the possessed one responded, giving news of what happened on the seas with ships and in other very remote lands. And the possessed one suddenly fell to the ground like a dead person, and the accused went to assist her, giving a smack on the ground next to her head, which immediately caused her to rise and she continued to respond to the questions he was asking.

DOMINGOS: Said with respect to everything asked in the question, nothing is true except to say that when some of the people were suffering from ailments, he rubbed them on the chest and head with some powders he had in his calabash, which he mentioned in his confession, and with respect to everything else, it is false.

VAREJÃO: Asked if at any time he had asked the following questions to a possessed woman: Captain, are we friends? And she responded to him: We are. And he continued saying the following: Am I in hell? To which she responded: No, because you all are more able than I, and where you all walk, we are not able to walk. And immediately the accused pulled out a little calabash, put his finger over the mouth and hit it with his left hand and then a plume of smoke emerged from the calabash, which he gave to the possessed woman to smell, also putting it on her face and head, which sent her into a fury.

DOMINGOS: Said the only thing true in the question is that he used a small calabash in which he had some powders made from roots and herbs, which he rubbed on the face and head of the people suffering illness; however, this did not result in any reaction, because the people remained calm and in the form they were, and as for the rest of the question, everything is false.

VAREJÃO: Asked if he remembered applying certain remedies made of porridge in which he threw various ingredients which caused the person to feel very bad and suffer such affliction and perturbation that she jumped out of the bed confused, running like a crazy person, without being able to calm her by any means, and that only the accused was able to calm her, and that the accused buried in three parts the bones of dead people and some animals, needles, hairs, peels, and roots.

DOMINGOS: Said that it is true that he gave a purgative of porridge to Leonor de Oliveira, resident of Santa Rita, and the force of her vomit was the remedy, and she jumped out of bed and ran like a crazy person, and after returning to a calm state, she said to him that the perturbation was born of her monthly menstruation, which was going on at the time he applied the purgative. And the malicious objects they found buried were made by Jacinta, slave of Leonor de Oliveira, as she had declared to him.

VAREJÃO: Asked if another time he went to cure a certain person who he found totally mistrusting of doctors, and the accused grabbed her wrist, put his hand on her head, and pulled out some powders that he rubbed on her forehead, saying they were to see if she had *feitiços*, which immediately sent the person into a frightened and deformed state.

DOMINGOS: Said that he did not proffer that which was said in the question and to say the contrary is false. And it is only true that he took the pulse of some sick people; however, this was to see whether or not the person had a weak pulse, and not for any other motive.

VAREJÃO: Asked if another time a person arrived at his site and asked what he planned to do there, and the accused said he wanted to close the bodies of these people who were sick, and the person then asked what this was for, and the accused responded that it was best for him not to know.

DOMINGOS: Said that everything in the question is true; however, everything he did was done naturally, including when he put powders in the cuts on the arm and foot. And the reason the powders disappeared was because they became very fine from beating them.

VAREJÃO: Asked if he gave sick people drinks from roots, over which he made a blessing with his right hand, which resulted in the vomiting of hairs and the defecation of bones that appeared to be chicken and hawk talons, making the people feel better from the great pains they suffered earlier. And the accused predicted the success of the remedy before applying it.

DOMINGOS: Said that he never divined anything like that, and it is false that he predicted anything, and it is only true to say that he announced his intentions when he gave the remedies he proffered in order to facilitate the healing of the people who took them.

VAREJÃO: Asked if another time he cured various people from the spirits that plagued them, using various black chickens that he removed from a house he had there, and the chickens were passed over the heads of the sick people along with some black powders, and all of this resulted in the people suddenly falling on the ground like they were dead, and the accused said they had the cult spirit. And immediately leaving for another place nearby, he ordered a pot of water with a knife and some calabashes. And then he ordered all of the people to put their fingers in the pot, which caused some of them to convulse and snort like filthy animals, and they ran all over the field until they fell to the ground like dead people. And the accused put his hand on the chest, at the same time saying various words, and breaking one of the calabashes he immediately said that the spirit had gone away. And so the spirit would not return to give *feitiços*, the accused cut the arm and sole of the feet and put black powders in the cuts, saying he was closing the bodies so the spirits would not return to cause trouble.

DOMINGOS: Said that everything in the question is true. That when a sick person arrived at his property convulsing and in great pain, he went to find a black chicken he had there. And with the blood of the chicken he anointed the person on the head and chest, rubbing it all the way down to the legs, and also throwing in some herbal powders, everything for the end of seeing the person return to health, and without any other intention than to understand that the said remedy would be naturally good for the said complaint. And afterward, he ordered the person to wash his head in a bowl of water which he always had prepared for everything that would be necessary. And this is the only thing he has to declare that he did with respect to what is contained in the question, and everything else imputed in the question is false.

VAREJÃO: Asked if another time, beyond that which the accused has already confessed, he was called to cure various people and he ordered everyone to appear before him and he began to call out their names without previously having news or knowledge of them. And shortly thereafter the accused was at a certain place where ordering to dig, there was found a calabash with bones, roots, and many other things inside, which the accused said was what made the people sick. And then, putting a pot of water on a fire, the accused threw in various roots that he removed from a sack, and casting a little of this water on one of the people, the person fell to the ground like a dead person. And the accused went to his aid, saying he was not dead, and grabbing him, the person arose alive, like nothing had happened.

DOMINGOS: Said that everything in the question is true, which happened in the following form: He was called by one Francisco Rodrigues, resident in São João de Meriti, next to Prainha on his *roça*, in order to cure various *pretos* he had on that farm. And arriving at the said place, he ordered to appear before him all the *pretos*, and it is true he called some of them by their names, however, only those he knew by sight and dealings in the city of Rio de Janeiro, where Francisco Rodrigues also has a house. And the accused immediately ordered them to dig in a particular place on the farm, and in it was found a calabash with all the ingredients mentioned in the question that was asked. And the accused discovered that a *preta* of Francisco Rodrigues named Justa was who had made that evil, and she had buried them in that spot together with another *preto* who was already dead. And Justa requested that the accused not discover it so her master would not know the person who made the crime. And it is also true that the *preto* who dug up the calabash immediately fell to the ground like a dead person, and then the accused threw a little water at him and he rose to his feet, and the falling to the ground was the effect of the evil that he discovered. And this is all that happened with respect to the content of the question.[4]

Faced with detailed descriptions of his ritual practices, Domingos stood fast to his original story: All of his cures were natural, he possessed no hidden virtues, and he never parted from the Catholic Church. From a narrow, functionalist perspective, Domingos might very well have understood his remedies to emanate from the "natural" properties of roots, herbs, plants, and even animal blood. Of course, the Inquisitor never asked Domingos how the natural world came to be endowed with such properties. His implicit assumption was that God provided these remedies. Yet Domingos would have attributed "natural" powers to ancestors and voduns. The closest he ever came to revealing an alternate worldview was when he earlier admitted that he learned the properties of leaves and plants from people in his homeland. Silenced in his testimony was the broader cosmological vision that explained these "natural" powers. In this way, Domingos deftly avoided Varejão's persistent attempts to reduce him to the Devil's pawn.

Ultimately, intellectual jousting like that between Domingos and Varejão allowed Africans to insinuate themselves into Portuguese religion and society in ways that braided Africa ever more tightly into Portugal itself. Even as Varejão searched for evidence of extraordinary powers that could only emanate from the Devil, he winnowed out other "natural" African remedies that the Church hierarchy implicitly acknowledged as acceptable. Likewise, in his insistence that Africans possessed supernatural powers, Varejão viewed African ritual practices in the context of Christian cosmology, as part of the parallel world of darkness and evil empowered by the Devil. By definition, the work of ancestors and voduns became the work of the Devil. Thus, the Catholic hierarchy often facilitated the Africanization of Portuguese religion and healing practices, providing an intellectual and conceptual framework for interpreting African ritual power. The reduction of ancestral invocation to the Devil's work only affirmed the extraordinary power of African rituals in Christian eyes, essentially putting African divination and spirit possession on the same therapeutic plane as the rituals of the Catholic Church.

At the same time, these Inquisitorial interrogations reveal just how savvy Africans could be in navigating the traps and pitfalls of Catholic canon law. Domingos clearly understood that Varejão wanted to elicit from him a particular type of confession. After nine long weeks and four different appearances before the Inquisitor, a stubborn Domingos still would not break under Varejão's questioning. He denied invoking spirits for divinatory purposes, predicting past and future events, and using ritual prayers or words in his healing. In short, he avoided any suggestion that he channeled the powers of ancestors or voduns. Domingos was acutely aware that the Catholic hierarchy reduced these powers to the workings of the Devil. Sadly, he may have been a victim of his own intellectual and cultural acumen. Had Domingos made a full confession of his transgressions, admitting that his divination and healing powers emanated from the Devil, he might have saved himself from the torture that was to follow.

Yet it is precisely Domingos' intractability that should give us pause, lest we conclude that he was a mere "victim" of a cruel and overzealous Inquisition. Domingos would not subject his faith to facile Christian reductions. Nor would he reveal his faith's secrets. Instead, he used his skills to draw the hidden truths out of his Inquisitorial adversary, just as he had done numerous times for his clients. Varejão's insistence that Domingos' ritual practices were the work of the Devil was an admission of his belief in Domingos' extraordinary powers. This belief in the power of African malevolence was a refraction of Portuguese assumptions about the redemptive power of God through colonialism and slavery. Africans like Domingos could be rescued from the Devil's clutches only through the intervention of the Catholic Church. When Domingos argued away the presence of the Devil in his cures, he exposed the hypocrisies of the divide between Portuguese "good" and African "evil." Indeed, with the Devil removed from the equation, Varejão faced the heretical prospect of a much more universalist spectrum of therapeutic possibilities. That the powers of African healers might be on the same moral and spiritual plane as those of God and the Catholic Church was simply unimaginable to him. Domingos may have won the larger philosophical argument, but in Varejão's eyes, he was an inveterate liar. Behind the mask of intellectual agility and superior logic, the Devil surely resided. Refusing to cede to Satan's trickery, Varejão accused Domingos of criminal libel and once again ordered him to return to his cell.

Six weeks later, the Inquisitors offered Domingos yet another opportunity to confess his pact with the Devil, advising him that failure to make a "full and true" confession would result in the reading of criminal charges against him. When Domingos responded that he had nothing more to confess, the prosecutor called him to his desk and read aloud a summary of his crimes. He began: "The accused, being a baptized Christian, and as such, obliged to have and hold all the beliefs and teachings of the Holy Mother Church of Rome, to give a good example in his life and customs, not to depart from the ways of life of faithful Catholics, to recognize God Our Father as author of all good and reject the Devil as author of all evil . . . has forgotten his obligation . . . doing many things contrary to Our Holy Catholic Faith, publicly curing *feitiços*, divining hidden things, and working other extraordinary things that he could not achieve without a pact with the Devil." After outlining the details of his crimes, the prosecutor concluded: "For the receipt and necessary proof of Domingos Álvares as heretic apostate of Our Holy Catholic Faith, fictitious, false, insufficient confessant, and unrepentant, he will be declared as such, and incur the sentence of major excommunication and the rightful penalties thereof."[5]

The reading of the criminal libel was the final warning in the Inquisitorial process prior to the application of torture. When the Inquisitors summoned Domingos to the Room of Torment six weeks later, they offered one last opportunity to make a "full and true" confession. He again refused, and the torture began. Only when the pain of the rack's straps digging into flesh and bone became unbearable did Domingos shout out for Jesus and the Virgin Mary. Though his cries for mercy fell short of the full confession they demanded, the Inquisitors judged them a sufficient step toward cleansing him of the Devil and reconciling him with the Church. After fifteen minutes of torture, the Inquisitors relented and once again dispatched Domingos to his cell. The following day, they handed down his sentence: "Because the accused has lived apart from Our Holy Catholic Faith and has made a pact with the Devil . . . and divined hidden things that naturally he could not know, and made superstitious cures that result in him being suspect of having made the said pact, he will go to the Auto Público da Fé in the accustomed form, and there he will hear his sentence, renounce all of his sins, and be exiled for four years to Castro Marim, and never again enter Rio de Janeiro, and he will have spiritual penitence and ordinary instruction and pay the costs."[6]

Domingos heard his crimes and sentence read aloud at the Auto Público da Fé of June 21, 1744. The "Public Act of Faith" was an all-day affair, beginning at six o'clock in the morning and lasting until late afternoon.[7] It consisted of a procession through the city's streets, a mass, and a public presentation of Inquisitorial criminals. The day ended with the punishments of the condemned, the most egregious offenders being burned alive before thousands of onlookers. For the residents of Lisbon, the Auto da Fé was a grand, carnivalesque spectacle—a mix of well-choreographed, sober piety and raw, Church-sanctioned violence. Eight days prior to the ceremony, the Inquisition announced its intentions in edicts sent to all parish churches. When the day arrived, the city came to a standstill. Thousands of people jammed the streets; others hung out of their second- and third-story windows, all hoping to catch a glimpse of the apostates. The wealthy dressed in their finest attire, adorned with jewels and accessories "as if it were Corpus Christi day or the Easter processions."[8] Laborers and serfs, who dominated the throngs, "seemed to forget . . . their usual reverence and servility, for they jostled and shouldered the titled nobles who were scattered here and there among the crowd."[9] These common folk "snarled their teeth" and rained curses on the condemned. When not hurling abuse, the "little people" shouted out "zealous exclamations like: What great mercy! Praise be the Holy Office!"[10] Robberies were common; people were trampled to death; smoke and oppressive heat choked the bystanders.[11]

In June 1744, the ceremony unfolded in Lisbon's central square, the Rossio. The proceedings began with a solemn procession that departed from the Inquisition Palace. At the front of the procession appeared a large standard with the emblem of the Holy Office on one side and an image of Saint Peter the Martyr on the other. Following the banner were Dominican priests and members of the brotherhood of Saint George, some carrying crosses. Then came the 41 condemned, 27 men and 14 women, each dressed in penitential garb indicating their crimes, each accompanied by two agents of the Inquisition. At the rear of the procession were guards who insured that the hoards of onlookers did not interfere. Once the procession reached the Church of Saint Domingos and everyone settled into their seats, King João V, the three young princes, other high nobility, and the Inquisitors arrived. Following mass, the Inquisitor general read aloud the crimes of each

Procession of the Auto da Fé through Lisbon. Lithograph from Esteves Pereira and
Guilherme Rodrigues, *Portugal: diccionario historico, chorographico, biographico . . .*
(Lisbon: João Romano Torres, 1907), 3:983.

condemned. Those penitents who reconciled with the Church, like Domingos, were required to approach the pulpit on their knees, heads bowed, candle in hand, to hear their sentence and publicly renounce their sins. They
then kissed the crucifix and returned to their bench. Thirty-three people
reconciled with the Church in this fashion. The other eight were remitted
to secular authorities to be burned at the stake.[12]

Including Domingos, nine of the forty-one who marched in the Auto da
Fé of 1744 hailed from Brazil. Six of these were sentenced for bigamy and
three for witchcraft. The three witchcraft penitents bear particular attention.
In addition to Domingos, there was Luzia Pinta, the Angolan *calunduzeira*
from Sabará, and Miguel Ferreira Pestana, a Tupinambá Indian, originally
from Espírito Santo.[13] Pestana's case, like those of Domingos and Luzia,
was etched partly in the beliefs of his indigenous past, although greatly embellished with Catholic and African elements. Pestana was born and raised
on the Jesuit mission settlement (*aldeia*) of Reritiba in Espírito Santo.

AJURAÇAM DE LEVE.

EU *Domingos Alvres* que presente estou ante vòs Senhores Inquisidores, contra a heretica parvidade, & apostasia, juro nestes santos Evangelhos, em que tenho minhas mãos, que de minha propria, & livre vontade anathematiso, & aparto de mi toda a especie de heresia que for, ou se levantar contra nossa S. Fè Catholica, & Sè Apostolica, especialmente estas que hora em minha sentença me foraõ lidas, & de q̃ me houveraõ por de leve sospeit*o* na Fè, as quaes aqui hei por repetidas, & declaradas: & juro, & prometto de sempre ter, & guardar a S. Fè Catholica que ensina a S. Madre Igreja de Roma; que serei sempre muito obediente ao nosso muy Santo Padre o Papa *Benedito XV.*

hora Presidente na Igreja de Deos, & a seus Successores; & confesso que todos os que côtra esta S. Fê Catholica vierem, saõ dignos de condemnaçaõ, & prometto de nunca com elles me ajuntar, & de os perseguir, & descobrir as heresias q̃ delles souber aos Inquisidores, & Prelados da Igreja. E juro, & prometto quanto em mi for cóprir as penitencias, que me saõ, ou forem impostas: & se contra isto, ou parte dellas em algum tempo vier (o que Deos naõ permitta) quero cair na pena, q̃ por direito em tal caso merecer, & me sobmetto à severidade dos sagrados Canones. E requeiro a os Notarios do S. Officio que disto passem certidaõ, & instrumento, & aos q̃ estaõ presentes sejaõ testemunhas, & assinem aqui comigo. *Com os testemunhas abaixo Manoel da Silva Deniz Sobraria*

D Domingos X Alvres

Anto. X de Sanigz Fernandes de Lopes Lemos

Ajuraçam de Leve, Domingos' written promise to abandon all heresies against the Church, swearing to comply with the penitence imposed upon him. Domingos signed X at the bottom of the page. Tribunal do Santo Ofício, Inquisição de Évora, Processo 7759, fl. 104. Courtesy Arquivo Nacional da Torre do Tombo, Lisbon, Portugal.

Apparently, he grew up speaking a variant of the Tupi language. Years later, when asked to recite the laws of God and the Church for the Inquisition, he claimed that he "did not know them very well in the Portuguese language . . . but he knew them in the language of his country." He then proceeded to make a recitation "in a language so obscure [the Inquisitor] could not understand a single word." Since the Jesuits often taught non-Portuguese speakers the rudiments of the Catholic faith in their native languages, it is not surprising that Pestana remembered Church law in this manner. However, the fact that Pestana had to rely on the rote memories of his youth to invoke his knowledge of Catholicism indicates just how far removed he was from his Jesuit upbringing.[14]

As a young man, Pestana abandoned the *aldeia*, leading the life of a "renegade" Indian, outside the purview of Jesuit control. In this respect, Pestana shared much in common with runaway slaves, with whom he forged a series of friendships and alliances. Years later, he testified that these runaways taught him the virtues of the African-derived talismans, *bolsas de mandinga*. Pestana eventually settled on a farm owned by a *pardo* in Inhomerim, Espírito Santo. There, he gained renown as a purveyor of *mandingas*. Usually, *mandingas* were packets that included some combination of substances from the natural world, as well as handwritten orations. These *mandinga* pouches were worn around the neck or wrist, performing some virtue for the wearer, much as Domingos had been accused of using a *bolsa de mandinga* to control the winds on the passage from Recife to Rio de Janeiro. Like dozens of other *mandingueiros* in the Atlantic world, Miguel Pestana trafficked in a genre of *bolsa de mandinga* that purportedly prevented knives from penetrating the body. In the mid-1730s, he performed public demonstrations in front of "some negros," during which he requested that another acculturated Indian (*índio caboclo*) stab him with a sharpened knife. The Indian stabbed Pestana "with all his might," but the knife "broke into pieces."[15]

Interestingly, when the Inquisition arrested Pestana in 1737, witnesses claimed that it was Pestana who "taught *mandingas* to the negros" rather than the other way around. These eyewitnesses understood that blacks "ordinarily are the ones who trade in *mandingas*." Pestana, however, breached this racial and ethnic order. Moreover, he gained sufficient expertise in the manufacture of *mandingas* that Africans sought him out to purchase his particular variant of the good luck charms, demonstrating the remarkable circularity of culture among marginalized peoples in Brazil—from African, to Indian, back to African. This circularity is also manifest in the mixture of Native American and African substances Pestana utilized in his *mandingas*. For example, one Spaniard testified that Pestana sold a combination of ground corn powder (indigenous to the Americas) and burned banana peels (indigenous to Africa) to give "good fortune." Among his customers were black slaves, who used the powders to "tame" their masters. Even after his arrest, Pestana persisted in selling *mandingas* from inside the jail. The head jailer in Rio de Janeiro testified that, despite increased patrols around the grated bars that opened onto the outside, "negros, mulattoes, but also white women" gathered there to purchase Pestana's talismans. Some of Pestana's fellow inmates resented his fraternization with slaves and freed blacks. On several occasions, angry prisoners beat him severely because he insisted on sharing his *mandingas* with blacks.

Pestana remained jailed in Rio de Janeiro from 1737 to 1743, overlapping with the period of Domingos' time in the city. Would they have learned about each other's practices through the exchanges taking place between Pestana's jail cell bars and the outside world of Rio's streets? Perhaps. Would they have encountered one another in jail once Domingo was arrested in 1742? Almost certainly. Domingos may not have been one of Pestana's African-descended allies; indeed, they very well could have been rivals in the city's competitive world of therapy and healing. Nevertheless, as they marched together in the Auto da Fé in Lisbon, the objects of humiliation before the Catholic Church, the Crown, and an angry Portuguese mob, they must have shared at least a moment of recognition—a glance, a nod, or some other gesture of reassurance. Along with Luzia Pinta, Domingos and Miguel Pestana stood apart from the other penitents as colonized/enslaved subjects and racialized "others"—the natural allies of the Devil. There, in the very heart of the Portuguese metropole, perhaps more than at any other time, the Tupinambá, the Angolan, and the man from Naogon recognized the tragic similarities that made them all "Brazilian."

IF THE THREE convicted Brazilian "witches" stood before King João V and his subjects as the embodiment of superstition and sin, the broader metropolitan Portuguese perception of Africans and Indians was only somewhat more complex. The Crown promoted attempts to integrate colonial subjects into the reign, so long as these subjects submitted to Portuguese institutional control. Some of these subjects played their roles willingly, even with alacrity. Just two months prior to the Auto da Fé, in April 1744, the king and queen had attended a feast-day celebration for Saint Benedict the Moor at the Franciscan convent in Lisbon. There, the black brothers of the Irmandade de Nossa Senhora de Guadalupe extended the king all the courtesies of a permanent honorary officeholder (*perpétuo juiz*) in their brotherhood.[16] In exchange for their fidelity, the king indulged his colonial subjects with symbolic, paternalistic gestures of noblesse oblige, like consecrating their feasts with his presence. Perhaps the most potent royal gesture was a long-standing commitment to manumission for the black brotherhoods' enslaved members. From the sixteenth century, the Portuguese monarchy had issued a series of provisions that obliged slave masters to negotiate a manumission price with the officers of the black brotherhoods in Lisbon and Évora. Once a price was agreed upon, the brotherhoods would raise funds to purchase the freedom of their enslaved members.[17] Of course, the king had no control over financial negotiations in which slaveowners always had the upper hand. Nevertheless, for those slaves who earned their manumission in this manner, it was understood that their freedom emanated from the grace of the king and the Catholic Church. In this way, conversion to Catholicism and loyalty to the king marked the dividing line between those "capable" of freedom and those who deserved to remain in slavery. Even in freedom, however, Africans and their descendants remained subordinate to the Portuguese, segregated in their own racially defined brotherhoods. Ultimately, fawning slaves, "reduced" Indians, and segregated religious brotherhoods were testaments to the king's absolutist power and the empire's ability to subdue its colonial subjects. The message was clear: African and Indian subjects were "Portuguese" only insofar as the king was willing to grant them his mercy and grace. They "belonged" to the metropole but were never truly "of" it.

Another episode, some years later, illustrates the metropolitan attitude toward Africans and Indians even more explicitly. In 1760, King José I, who had witnessed the 1744 Auto da Fé with his father, King João V, attended a bullfight at Campo Pequeno in Lisbon. As the king made his way into the arena prior to the bullfight,

> two triumphal cars entered the area, each drawn by six mules. Eight black Africans were upon one, and eight copper-coloured Indians upon the other. They made several caracoles round; then all leapt from the cars and bravely fought an obstinate battle with wooden swords one band against the other. The Indians were soon slain by the Africans, and lay extended a while on the ground, shaking their legs in the air as if in the last convulsions, and rolling in the dust before they were quite dead. Then . . . both the dead and the living

went to mix with the croud, while the cars drove away amidst the acclamations of the multitude, and made room for the two knights that were to fight the bulls.[18]

In the metropolitan imaginary, Africans and Indians were often little more than actors in a grand imperial spectacle, to be gazed upon alternately with horror and delight. The underlying message of the theatrical public roles played by Africans and Indians in the Auto da Fé and mock battles like the one at Campo Pequeno was that colonized subjects needed redemption from heathenism, anarchy, and violence. The Crown and the Church presented themselves as benevolent caretakers of their less fortunate subjects, taming the natural instincts of Indians and Africans through pious Christian charity.

Of course, some African and Indian subjects were more willing to play their roles than others. Domingos Álvares, Luzia Pinta, and Miguel Pestana all went through the charade of publicly renouncing their sins in the Auto da Fé, but none of them was content to reconcile himself or herself to the Church and become a "good" Christian. As punishment for his crimes, Miguel Pestana received a five-year sentence to work in the king's galleys. Less than two years into his sentence, one of the galley guards reported that Pestana had escaped.[19] Similarly, Luzia Pinta received a four-year sentence of banishment to Castro Marim. Shortly after her arrival in the town, she abandoned the Inquisition's order and traveled to Tavira, where she continued to heal. There, Juliana Maria de Aragão submitted a denunciation against "a *preta* they say is named Luzia, who . . . exited the tribunal of the Holy Office, banished to Castro Marim for witchcraft." Aragão invited Luzia into her house to perform a cure for a sick man. According to Aragão, Luzia "passed over [the man] three times and afterward turned her head to the sky and made gesticulations with her eyes and said that she knew well the evil that he had." Luzia then prepared an herbal mixture that she gave the man to drink.[20] Though Luzia clearly continued to work cures similar to those she had performed in Sabará, her transgressions in the Algarve were not deemed sufficient to demand another full Inquisitorial trial. She remained at large in southern Portugal, presumably sharing Angolan *calundu*, as well as other Central African and Brazilian therapies, with Portugal's rural population.

As for Domingos Álvares, he remained in custody of the Inquisition four more days after the Auto da Fé. The day following the ceremony, he signed a document swearing that he would "keep secret everything he saw and heard inside the jails," as well as "everything that happened with his case."[21] These oaths of secrecy were one of the many ways the Inquisition maintained the aura of terror and fear surrounding the institution, an unambiguous assertion of the Holy Office's impenetrable power. Three days later, Domingos again swore "on penalty of grave punishment" that he would "live a life of good custom and example," confess on the four major holy days, pray the Rosary every week, and say five Our Fathers, five Hail Marys, and five Wounds of Christ every Friday. Moreover, he promised to comply with all the terms of his banishment order. Domingos again put his mark on the Inquisitorial document and was finally freed from the custody of the Inquisition jails.

Altogether, Domingos spent more than eighteen months in the Inquisitorial jails in Lisbon. Including his time in custody in Rio and in the passage to Portugal, it had been more than two years since he had known anything resembling freedom. Given the paltry rations and pestilent conditions of the jails, he must have been in miserable physical condition. Likewise, the loneliness, isolation, and silence surely affected his mental health. To expect that Domingos would emerge from these experiences unscathed would be to ignore the limitations of body and mind. Being set free in Lisbon, just four days after the humiliation of the Auto da Fé, only added to his disequilibrium. He knew nothing about the basic geography or social landscape of the city—where to eat, where to sleep, where to take shelter. It seems logical that he would have wanted to move far away from the city center, the setting for so much of his misery over the past several years. Like all condemned exiles, Domingos had thirty days from the time of his release from prison to depart Lisbon for the village where he was to serve his sentence, in his case Castro Marim.[22] Rather than linger in the city where the stigma of his Inquisitorial conviction loomed so large, he decided to leave immediately to begin serving out the term of his banishment order.[23]

Banishment was one of the most common forms of punishment employed by both secular and Church authorities in the Portuguese empire from the sixteenth through the eighteenth century. Convicted criminals could be sentenced to overseas colonies such as India, Angola, or Brazil, as well as to internal Portuguese destinations like Viseu, Miranda, or Castro Marim. The logic of banishment mirrored that of purgatory: Once cleansed of one's sins after a period of strict penance, a convict could reenter society and live an upright, godly life. When a convicted exile arrived at his destination, he had one major restriction placed on him: He could not leave the district to which he was confined. Most Inquisitorial exiles received sentences of less than five years.[24] However, the penalty for leaving the district before one's sentence expired was a doubling of the original sentence. Repeat offenders could be sentenced to death.[25] Exiles were free to seek employment and, indeed, were encouraged to do so. However, the Church and Crown prohibited Inquisitorial convicts from working in certain prestigious professions, such as doctor, lawyer, pharmacist, and bleeder. Penitents also faced certain social sanctions: They could not wear gold, silver, or precious stones; they could not dress in silk; and they could not ride on horseback.[26]

Domingos would have depended on his own guile or the charity of others to find food and shelter on his passage to Castro Marim. The Inquisition provided no escort or funding for those it banished internally. It expected convicts to make their own way, requiring them to register their legal papers (*carta de guia*) with a notary upon arrival in their designated village.[27] The roads that carried Domingos to Castro Marim, like those that ran throughout much of rural Portugal, were the vestiges of old passageways built by the Romans more than a thousand years earlier. These roads were isolated, dangerous, and poorly maintained. Robberies, and even murders, were not uncommon. In March 1742, Portuguese priest and diarist Father Luiz Montez Mattozo, describing the perils of the country's roadways, wrote: "The thieves are so impudent that each day they invent new ways of robbing." Just five months later, he recorded the robbery and stabbing death of an innocent herdsman on a rural path near Braga, in northern Portugal. He concluded ruefully: "There are so many thieves that they are robbing everywhere."[28] Domingos probably encountered some of these opportunistic characters on his passage to Castro Marim; however, as a destitute African Inquisitorial convict, he made an unlikely target.

Domingos initially traveled east, quickly leaving behind the cosmopolitan world of Lisbon and proceeding in the direction of the Spanish border. When he arrived in the city of Évora, he was required to present himself before an Inquisitorial notary. Since the Évora tribunal handled all Inquisitorial business in southern Portugal, Domingos was no longer subject to Lisbon's jurisdiction. The notary in Évora registered Domingos' arrival and provided him with the paperwork and information necessary for the final leg of his trip. Having dispensed with the bureaucratic formalities of Inquisitorial jurisdiction, Domingos resumed his journey, turning south toward the Mediterranean. Once he forged the small mountains of the Lower Alentejo and entered the Algarve region, isolation from the rest of Portugal became more pronounced. Domingos continued along the remains of the

Roman road, paralleling the Guadiana River, passing through the towns of Beja, Mértola, and Alcoutim, before finally reaching his final destination. Altogether, the 150-mile trek from Lisbon to Castro Marim normally took from two to three weeks; Domingos took six weeks to make the journey.[29]

Castro Marim was a medieval walled city in the far southeast corner of the country. Strategically located on the border with Spain at the Mediterranean Sea, it served as an important military outpost, especially in the fight against North African piracy during the sixteenth and seventeenth centuries. Despite its importance, the town had difficulties supporting a stable population, mostly due to its remote, frontier location. In an effort to sustain the region while at the same time providing "purification" for its convicted criminals, the Crown began sending exiles to the town in 1524. From that year forward, a steady stream of convicts arrived yearly to serve out the terms of their sentences. Geraldo Pieroni and Timothy Coates estimate that around 100 exiles arrived in the village annually from 1550 to 1755. Roughly a quarter of these were condemned by the Inquisition and the remainder by the Crown.[30] By the middle of the eighteenth century, the population of Castro Marim had grown to nearly 1,500, in part due to the diverse group of Africans, Brazilians, Jews, witches, sodomites, and thieves dispatched there by criminal and Inquisitorial courts.[31] Though the Crown intended to "purify" its criminals, the banishment of convicts from the colonies to Portuguese towns like Castro Marim also served to spread the "hellish" influences of the colonies to Portugal itself, even to its most rural outposts.

Despite the cosmopolitan flavor of Castro Marim, it was still a decidedly Portuguese town, made even more so by its strong culture of penance. Most Portuguese viewed internal exile to Castro Marim as an act of "divine mercy" on the part of the Crown, infinitely preferable to banishment to Brazil or one of the other overseas colonies. Portuguese convicts so dreaded the prospect of colonial rendition that many requested the Crown to commute their overseas sentences to Castro Marim instead. Indebted to the Crown for its "mercy," these metropolitan convicts took seriously their obligations to perform penance lest the Crown change its mind. The presence of small numbers of colonial convicts in Castro Marim, many of them accused of witchcraft, only reinforced what might be in store if one were sent overseas.[32] As Pieroni put it, "Castro Marim was a purgatory with amenities, a place of expiation closer to heaven than to hell."[33] While this may have been true for internal exiles from Portugal itself, for Africans like Luzia Pinta and Domingos Álvares, Castro Marim was tantamount to hell. Not only were they marked by their convict status, but they were much more discernibly "colonial" and "black" in southern Portugal than they were in Brazil. In this way, they were triply marked as criminals, colonial subjects, and African-descended, former slaves.[34] Their possibilities for transcending their marginal status were almost zero in the penitential atmosphere of Castro Marim. As we have already seen, Luzia Pinta abandoned the terms of her banishment shortly after arriving there. Domingos would soon follow suit.

9

Algarve

The scalded cat fears cold water.
—Portuguese proverb

When Domingos presented himself to Inquisitorial authorities in Castro Marim on August 15, 1744, the notary, João Lopes Ignácio, described him as a *preto buçal*, indicating an uncultured, unrefined black man. Ignácio also noted that Domingos was the "slave of José Cardoso de Almeida, born on the Mina Coast, and resident in Rio de Janeiro." After linking Domingos' blackness to colonial servitude and lack of metropolitan sophistication, Ignácio recorded other physical traits that set Domingos apart from the Portuguese—his filed teeth, the piercings on his nose and ears, and his crippled right hand. Despite nearly fifteen years as a Portuguese subject, Domingos was still a visibly discernible "outsider," even to the supposedly neutral and dutiful notary. Unaware of the ways he was already being corporally surveilled, Domingos promised Ignácio that he would adhere to the terms of his exile and live an honest, upright, Catholic life in Castro Marim.[1]

Unlike most criminal exiles, Domingos could not simply blend into the social and cultural fabric of Castro Marim. His difference—his criminality—was marked on his very body. As he ventured out into the village, he encountered withering hostility. He later testified that "the residents there abhorred him . . . calling him a *feiticeiro*."[2] This reduction of blackness to criminality was not at all uncommon in eighteenth-century Portugal, especially in the south. In the rustic villages of the Algarve, the social hierarchy was relatively flat, with the exception of a thin layer of nobility at the top. As a result, large numbers of middling folk "pursued the desire of being noble . . . living according to the style and law of the nobility: participating in the governance of the city, in a confraternity or on the board of the local almshouse . . . boasting their prestige and, above all, their blood purity [*limpeza de sangue*]."[3] These assertions of "blood purity" were invariably couched in racial terms. An Italian traveler of the period noted that "to be white . . . is a title of honor: so that when a Portuguese says he is a Blanco, you are not to understand that he is a white man, which is the real signification of the word; but that he is an honest man, a man of honour, a man of family, a man of consequence and importance."[4] Implicit in such reductions was the understanding that blackness represented the opposite—criminality, dishonor, philandering, and so on—in short, the uncivilized *buçal*. In a setting where blood purity was the basic marker for an aspiring upward mobility, Domingos' *lack* of blood purity would have been exaggerated, all the more so in an exile town like Castro Marim. For those who sought to "invent" their noble status, racially marked people like Domingos became obvious targets for scorn and abuse. Indeed, ascension of the social hierarchy depended on distancing oneself from such obvious stains of racial impurity.

Beyond the bitter social rejection, this racial animus also had economic consequences: Domingos could not find work in Castro Marim. Shortly after arriving, "obliged by hunger and unable to sustain himself in that city," Domingos abandoned the terms of his exile.[5] Coming on the heels of his prison experiences, the rejection and deprivation of Castro Marim were simply intolerable. If he could not earn respect in the city of his exile, he would command it elsewhere, even if it meant breaking the terms of his banishment and risking further punishment. Striking out to find reliable sources of food and shelter, Domingos trekked west along another Roman road, this one paralleling the Mediterranean coastline. After walking about thirteen miles, he arrived in the town of Tavira. There, he resumed his healing practice and began developing new social networks.

Among those he attempted to cure was forty-year-old Feliciana Thereza da Silveira, who "had a growth on her face that they said was cancer." Consulting a surgeon, Silveira learned that the growth was not cancerous but rather some other kind of tumor that the surgeon could not heal. Shortly thereafter, Domingos arrived, explaining that "with God's favor" he could provide a remedy. Over the course of several sessions, Domingos applied various medicines to the growth on Silveira's face. These included crushed plants with honey, as well as cooked herbs and powders. According to Silveira, when Domingos applied the medicines, he "made the sign of the cross with his hand without saying any other word, nor other ceremony. Nor did she hear him boast of removing *feitiços*." Silveira admitted that she felt some relief in the days immediately following her consultations with Domingos; however, the tumor eventually grew larger and more painful than it had been before.[6] In these early days in southern Portugal, Domingos tried to accommodate his healing practice to the cultural expectations of his clients, carefully avoiding any suggestion that he was a *feiticeiro*. For

Silveira, his healing amounted to little more than natural remedies and the exaggerated gestures of the Catholic Church. Over time, however, Domingos expanded his repertoire to reflect some of the same practices that had landed him in trouble in Brazil.

In July 1745, a woman named Domingas de Andrade called on Domingos to perform a cure for her. Andrade had been bedridden for six weeks with a mysterious illness. After several unsuccessful consultations with Portuguese barbers, presumably using bleedings and purges, her condition worsened. By the time Domingos met her, Andrade was paralyzed from the waist down. In addition, she had "great pain and fire in her heart."[7] Domingos ordered Andrade's husband, Antônio Viegas, to rub her "from her head to her feet," first with a chicken and then with a 10-réis coin.[8] Domingos later claimed both the chicken and the coin as part of his payment. After sweeping away any external malevolence, Domingos went about the more serious business of diagnosing her illness. First, he took some white powders that "smelled like incense" and threw them into a cup of water. He then took out a cane tube and, approaching the cup of water and powders, hit it on the floor, causing smoke to emerge from the top of the tube. Next, he peered into the cup and announced he saw the *feitiços* that caused Andrade's illness. He immediately burned half of the powders that were floating on top of the water. Then he removed the remaining powders from the water and put them into a small *bolsa*, which he ordered Andrade to wear around her neck. Upon completing the ceremony, Domingos explained that the powders he burned were for the woman who cast the *feitiços* on Andrade. Later, he ordered Andrade to remove the *bolsa* from her neck. Taking the powders from inside the *bolsa*, Domingos mixed them in a bowl with water and cow dung. He then used a small broom to spread the mixture on the floors of Andrade's house, explaining that this was necessary because her house was also bewitched. After cleansing the house, Domingos wrapped Andrade's head in a towel and turned over a full cup of water on top of it, allowing the water to soak slowly into the towel, a remedy Domingos later confessed he learned in Brazil, "where the whites are accustomed to doing it."[9] Domingos then prescribed some infusions made from herbs he gathered in the countryside. Finally, he cut a small cross on Andrade's arm and put in two powders, "some black and the others that appeared to be auburn or brown." As he administered the medicines, he recited aloud, "In the name of God and the Virgin Mary." He then took his cane tube and shook it over the cut, prompting the emission of more "smoke." According to Andrade, when the smoke cleared, the powders had disappeared from the cuts. Domingos then repeated this ceremony, rubbing powders into cuts on her other arm and both ankles.[10]

As a result of this elaborate set of cures, Domingas de Andrade "in a short time felt better and could soon walk and take care of her house." Evidently, Andrade was well-satisfied with both the content and the outcome of Domingos' interventions. She later invited Domingos back to her house to cure her cousin, Eufemia Viegas, who had traveled ten miles from the village of Monte Gordo to consult with Domingos about her stomach ailment. In addition, Andrade introduced Domingos to several other ailing family members. Altogether, nearly a half dozen of Andrade's family and friends eventually consulted Domingos. On the surface, it seemed that Domingos was beginning to build a new therapeutic community, not unlike the ones he presided over in Dahomey and Brazil. Yet the financial and social reciprocity that had characterized relationships in his homeland and in Brazil simply did not exist in southern Portugal. On the contrary, despite Domingos' widely acknowledged successes in healing the people of Tavira, its residents refused to grant him even a modicum of the respect he commanded in Brazil. There, he earned upwards of 25,000 réis for a consultation; in Tavira, he eked out an existence, earning only around 1,000 réis for most of his cures, plus the chicken and 10-réis coin he demanded as part of his healing ceremonies. Some of his patients seemed to resent even these meager offerings. Domingas de Andrade, for instance, complained when Domingos took the coin and chicken after performing his cure for her. The chicken and 10 réis became a customary offering for all of the people that Andrade sent to Domingos; however, in every instance, it seems that Domingos had to wrest these small payments away from his clients under the pretext of the ceremonies themselves. Ultimately, both Domingos and his poor, rural clients felt they were being exploited.

Domingos' activities in Tavira did not escape notice by authorities. In the fall of 1745, just one year after Domingos' arrival in the Algarve, the dutiful notary of Castro Marim, João Lopes Ignácio, reported to his superiors in Évora that Domingos had fled to Tavira "immediately after presenting himself," thereby abandoning the terms of his banishment order. To make matters worse, he resided in Tavira "with notable scandal among the residents," publicly curing. Among the handful of residents who lodged complaints was the vicar of the local parish church. Eventually, the notary of Tavira, Antônio Martins Vieira, approached Domingos and "personally cautioned him that if he did not want to be arrested, he should immediately return to Castro Marim and remain there for the duration of his exile." Ignoring the notary's stern warning, Domingos "stayed in that city, continuing with the same scandalous cures."[11]

Even as reports of Domingos' wayward behavior reached Évora, his situation in Tavira began to unravel. On the morning of October 20, Saint Iria's feast day, Domingas de Andrade and her husband, Antônio Viegas, awoke before dawn to prepare for the day's celebrations. Viegas departed in the early-morning darkness to attend a fair in the city of Faro, almost twenty miles from Tavira. A few hours later, Andrade stepped outside her front door and immediately flew into a terrified frenzy. According to witnesses, Andrade ran about, "disturbed and acting like she was crazy." The cause of her hysterics? A bundle of objects left on her front doorstep consisting of "a doll with thirty-nine pins; human hair, some blonde, and others black; dog hair; snake skins; sulfur; chicken feathers; pieces of glass; half a bottle with two packets of pepper and corn kernels . . . some bones . . . and grave dirt." Andrade immediately set out to find Domingos, who told her that the things at her door were *"feitiços* for her, for all the people in her house, and for the cattle and farm." Domingos promised Andrade that he would remove the malevolence from her property, but in order to do so, he would need salt water and *aguardente,* crucial substances in the fight against witchcraft. Andrade purchased the materials for the remedy and waited for Domingos at her house, but he never showed up.

Later that evening, Andrade's husband returned from Faro and learned what had happened. Together, the couple went in search of Domingos. When they found him, they accused him of leaving the bundle at their door. Domingos denied the accusations, but Viegas and Andrade told Domingos that five people had seen him on the path near their house just before Andrade discovered the bundle.[12] Domingos admitted that he had been outside their house, but he insisted that he was not responsible for placing the objects there. He tried to allay the couple's fears, again promising that he would come to their house and fix everything. He also boasted that he was an expert at removing *feitiços,* claiming he knew all the *feiticeiros* in the region, including one woman "capable of killing all the people from Lisbon to the Algarve."[13] As proof of his extraordinary knowledge, Domingos showed the couple two books he had in his house, which he claimed were on the subject of *feitiços.* Andrade testified that one of the books contained a figure with horns on its head wearing a crown. By brandishing the books, Domingos feigned authority not only over the world of *feitiços* but also over the "magical" world of literacy. If the drawings in the books symbolized the power of devils and kings, one could only imagine what the writings might hold. By pretending to be literate, Domingos asserted yet one more layer of power and authority over his rustic clients. Despite his strong assurances that he would use his powers to remedy their situation, Domingos never returned to the house of Andrade and Viegas. As a result, the couple denounced him to the Inquisition.

In his denunciation, Viegas admitted that Domingos probably wanted to injure them "because he was not satisfied with the payment for [his wife's] cure." Domingas de Andrade had been bedridden for more than six weeks when Domingos brought her back to health. According to Viegas, he gave Domingos 12 tostões (1,200 réis) for healing his wife's paralysis, no small sum for a rural Portuguese farmer. Nevertheless, Domingos wanted more. When Viegas refused to pay him, an angry Domingos threatened that they should never call him to cure again.[14] Yet precisely because of his desperate financial straits, Domingos attended to Andrade and her extended family on multiple occasions. Each time he did, his resentment against the family no doubt deepened. After all, he restored their health, perhaps even rescuing them from death; meanwhile, he barely survived. This economic suffering mirrored broader social suffering. Domingos became the vehicle for the continued health and vitality of Andrade's family, even as he remained an isolated, marginal outsider. His only weapon against these gross disparities was the very same therapeutic power that allowed him to heal.

Domingas de Andrade and Antônio Viegas understood the bundle of materials left by Domingos purely as an act of vengeance—"witchcraft" aimed to harm and destroy them. Certainly this was one possible interpretation; however, the stark visual power of the objects also reflected "the social and personal impact . . . of insecurity and disempowerment" on Domingos Álvares.[15] As therapeutic objects, the items in the bundle represented specific solutions to the maladies that plagued Domingos. Aggression and violence were one set of possible solutions, as Domingos was quick to remind his antagonists, but they were not the only ones. By examining the precise contents of the bundle, we can begin to understand its full range of meanings and intentions.

To begin, the sculptural figure was not simply a "doll" but an anthropomorphic representation known as *bochio*. These *bochio*, or "empowered cadavers," were common across the Fon-Gbe-speaking region of West Africa. As art historian Suzanne Blier has noted, *bochio* functioned simultaneously as "counterfoils and complements" to the psychological traumas that accompanied social disorder.[16] Threats of death and destruction could be projected onto the symbolic cadaver and away from its owner. The *bochio* could relieve the profound anxieties of dire poverty and social marginalization, but only if it was properly empowered. Domingos activated his *bochio* with a range of substances designed to address the specific attributes of his suffering. Perhaps the most visually disturbing of these empowerment objects were the thirty-nine pins stuck into the "doll"-like figure. Each of these pins represented an oath. As Blier puts it, "The act of piercing (and then filling) a hole . . . suggests . . . getting at the root of an issue, difficulty, or dilemma, then actively responding to it."[17] Usually, the owner of the *bochio* would pierce the object, put the needle in his mouth (or spit into the hole), announce his remedy aloud (for example, "Andrade will pay her debt"), and then stick the needle into the hole, thereby "locking" the action of the verbal pronouncement into the very object. Domingos no doubt would have demanded fair payment for his cures, respect for his powers, social inclusion, and so on. Thus, the pins were as much about coercing the wills of Andrade and Viegas as they were about harming them. Of course, the pins also had the effect of imprisoning their intended targets, subjecting them to great pain, and even death, if they did not follow the manufacturer's injunctions. In this way, the *bochio* acted as a progressive remedy, one aimed primarily at curbing others' behavior but with the equal potential to injure them.

The other substances that made up Domingos' bundle had similar ambiguous aims. The sulfur and pepper were powerful powders (*atin*) that might be used as medicine or poison. Pepper, in particular, was used to both activate and alleviate "hot," traumatic situations.[18] Snakes, especially the python, usually were associated with well-being and being "cool." Thus, their skins could be added to *bochio* as a calming substance. However, venomous snakes were considered "hot," their parts believed to invoke fury.[19] Pieces of dog sometimes represented the loyalty dogs show to their owners. The dog hair in Domingos' *bochio* likely signified the demonstrations of respect and reciprocity he expected from his clients.[20] Bones and grave dirt invoked the significant, if unpredictable, power of the dead. And, finally, feathers often were applied to sculptures as representations of both death and rejuvenation, a signal that the empowerment of the object was complete.[21] Altogether then, one can see in the "alchemy" of these various objects a full résumé of the social disorder and alienation Domingos was attempting to address.[22] As with other forms of divination and healing, *bochio* objects could be read as social texts, although the manufacturers and the recipients often read them in significantly different ways.

By drawing his rural clients into the world of vodun, Domingos could demonstrate the spectacular range of his powers. Like many rustic Portuguese folk, Andrade and her family already shared many of the same broad ideas and beliefs as those held by Domingos, in particular, the belief that illness could emanate from *feitiços* sent by one's enemies.[23] Yet the bundle of empowered substances left at the doorstep of Domingas de Andrade was of another order altogether. As Domingos himself defined it for Andrade, it would destroy everything associated with her household. Domingos maintained that he alone had the power to remove this deadly curse, if only Andrade and her family would show some inclination toward relieving his own economic and social suffering. Otherwise, they would suffer the dire consequences. Apparently, Domingos perceived no change of heart on the parts of Domingas de Andrade and Antônio Viegas, a hunch borne out by their subsequent denunciations of Domingos before the Inquisition. Domingos never returned to Andrade's house to remedy the effects of his *gbo*. He no doubt hoped it would produce its intended widespread suffering. In the end, Domingos' calculated gamble to reclaim social standing failed miserably. He was as isolated and poverty-stricken as ever; he was also once again a wanted man, on the run from the Inquisition.

In January 1746, just a month after Andrade and Viegas offered their denunciation, the tribunal at Évora wrote to the Inquisitorial commissioner in Tavira: "There is information that Domingos Álvares . . . can presently be found in the village of Tavira. . . . We order that he go immediately to the village of Castro Marim to comply with his exile where he is not to leave without our order . . . on pain of being punished with all rigor."[24] The commissioner responded that Domingos was no longer in Tavira, and "it is said he is in Beja, because he has been seen on the road to that city."[25] This prompted a series of inquiries from Évora to various villages in the interior hinterlands of the Algarve, including Espírito Santo and Mértola. Yet, despite the Inquisition's best attempts to ascertain Domingos' whereabouts, he successfully avoided detection by remaining constantly on the move.

Domingos must have known that his time in Tavira had come to an end. Almost immediately after his conflict with Andrade, he fled southwest, eventually making his way to the village of Faro, where he found refuge in a hostel owned by forty-seven-year-old Bras Gonçalves. Domingos had known Gonçalves for several months, having first stayed in his hostel during the summer of 1745.[26] Gonçalves, "seeing at this time that Domingos . . . suffered great need because of his poverty," offered him food and shelter in exchange for his labor in the daily upkeep of the inn. Over the course of his initial stay at the hostel in 1745, Domingos related to Gonçalves the many

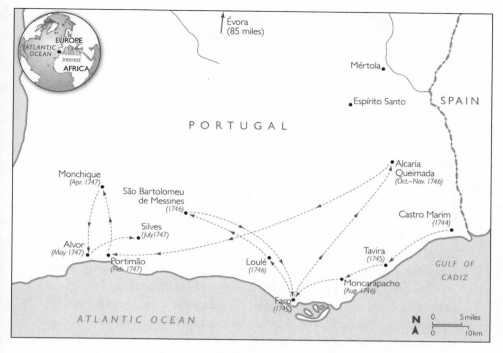

MAP 9.1 Domingos' travels through the Algarve, 1744–1749. Map created by the University of Wisconsin Cartography Lab.

"vexations of justice" that had landed him in such dire straits. Gonçalves, himself a humble, illiterate man, sympathized with Domingos' plight and later claimed that he "cared with great particularity for the *preto*."[27]

During one of their early conversations, Gonçalves revealed that a Spanish treasure hunter was coming to Faro. Knowing that Domingos had been exiled as a *feiticeiro*, Gonçalves "assumed that Domingos must be familiar with the gold in the countryside and how to divine hidden treasures."[28] Domingos explained that indeed he knew about the treasures, and that "if [Gonçalves] would guard the secret, he would discover the treasures because he knew where there were many riches in this Algarve."[29] A few days later, Gonçalves accompanied Domingos to the small village of Beira Mar. There, Domingos lifted his eyes to the sun and threw a rock into the air. Domingos told Gonçalves that they would find four loads of silver and diamonds on the spot where the rock landed. Marking the spot, Gonçalves was eager to begin digging. However, Domingos informed him that they needed to wait sixty days before uncovering the treasures because the person who buried it there had not yet died.[30]

In the meantime, Domingos left for Tavira. When he failed to return to Faro after sixty days, Gonçalves went to search for him, during precisely the time that the conflict with Domingas de Andrade reached its apex. Domingos successfully put off Gonçalves' persistent inquiries about the buried treasures, forcing Gonçalves to return to Faro empty-handed. Then, some time in early 1746, Gonçalves heard rumors that Domingos had fled north. Gonçalves followed Domingos' trail until he finally caught up to him in the village of Loulé. From there, he accompanied Domingos to the town of São Bartolomeu de Messines. Domingos continued to heal people, but he also claimed that buried treasures could be found on the farm of a man named Domingos Lopes. There, more than a half dozen men gathered to dig a massive trench. Once they completed their work, Domingos stood next to the hole and announced, "Now we are going to have a great smell in this hole." Shortly thereafter, a pleasant smell arose from the trench. Then Domingos said, "Now we are going to have a great wind." Almost immediately, a stiff wind began to blow. Finally, Domingos placed two pieces of cane, in the shape of a cross, next to the hole and called for the wind to stop blowing, which it did. Despite his many gesticulations and impressive command of the elements, Domingos did not elicit any treasure from the hole.[31] According to Gonçalves, Domingos was frustrated by the unavailability of the spell-breaking herb "mil homens" in the region.[32] Unable to successfully complete his work in São Bartolomeu, Domingos departed for Faro with Bras Gonçalves still in tow.

Arriving in Faro, Domingos moved back into Gonçalves' small inn. He also kept his promise to help Gonçalves uncover the treasures at Beira Mar. In May 1746, Domingos and Gonçalves, along with two other men, arrived at the site and dug for an entire night without discovering any treasures. The men reconvened the following night and continued digging until they were interrupted by the police. Running from the authorities, they sought shelter on a nearby property. Unbeknownst to the four men, their chosen place of refuge belonged to a Catholic priest.[33]

Scrambling onto the property, the men encountered Father João de Oliveira Delgado, who offered them a temporary hiding place. Upon realizing that he was in the house of a Catholic priest, Domingos became visibly frightened. As a pretext for leaving the house, Domingos explained that he needed to go back and retrieve the magical herb he had lost when fleeing the police. The confused priest asked why Domingos could not simply find the herb growing in the nearby countryside. Domingos replied that he had only been able to find the herb in Mértola. At this, the skeptical priest warned that Domingos "should only be fearful of him and not the lack of an herb." Gonçalves quickly intervened to defend Domingos, explaining that he was no mere "trickster [*patarata*]." In fact, Gonçalves claimed he had recently witnessed Domingos use his extraordinary abilities to extract a large "load" of buried treasures. When the Catholic priest suggested that the only way someone could make such discoveries was through the "art" of the Devil, Gonçalves explained that Domingos possessed "virtues" that allowed him to discover "what was in the interior of the earth and in the body of the creature."[34]

Gonçalves had little way of knowing that the Catholic Church was increasingly rejecting the idea that God might endow mere mortals with such powers. Indeed, by the eighteenth century, claims of divine virtue were seen as largely human inventions, affronts to God worthy of criminal prosecution.[35] His curiosity piqued by Gonçalves' explanation, the priest pressed Domingos for answers, insisting he wanted to know more about what he did. But an evasive Domingos sarcastically spurned the priest's entreaties. "You are very subtle," he joked with the priest. This effectively ended the conversation, as Domingos refused to offer any further information. Months later, after learning that Domingos was an Inquisitorial convict, the outwitted priest offered a Portuguese proverb to explain Domingos' evasive and suspicious behavior that night: "The scalded cat fears cold water."[36]

This somewhat opaque episode reveals crucial tensions, as well as fascinating entanglements, in the worlds of the African healer, the Catholic priest, and the humble innkeeper. On the one hand, Domingos recognized the danger in sharing such intimate quarters with a Catholic priest. After all, the institutional power of the Church had been the source of much of his misery. His immediate reaction was to flee. On the other hand, Domingos engaged the priest as an intellectual equal, fielding his questions with an expert's knowledge of Catholic doctrine, skillfully avoiding any suggestion that his "virtues" were anything other than God-given. For his part, Bras Gonçalves allied himself with Domingos, demonstrating a firm faith in his ability to see "in the interior of the earth and in the body of the creature." Gonçalves' endorsement and eyewitness accounts no doubt mitigated in Domingos' favor. As a white Portuguese Christian, his strongly held belief in Domingos' powers influenced the Catholic priest just enough that the priest was willing to entertain the possibility that the African was something other than a *feiticeiro*. In a final bit of irony, the Catholic priest utilized a common African idiomatic form—the proverb—as a retrospective explanation for Domingos' nervous behavior and clever sidestepping of his probing questions. The Portuguese proverb "The scalded cat fears cold water" is best translated in English as "Once bitten, twice shy." Given the universality of the sentiment and the African propensity for proverbial expression, perhaps Domingos invoked the very same maxim, only in the Fon-Gbe idiom, as he endured the uncomfortable interrogation in the house of the Catholic priest. As one Fon proverb says, "A snake bit me; I see a worm, I am afraid."[37] Whether or not such an idea leapt to Domingos' mind we will never know, but he embodied the pithy meaning of both proverbs. In any idiom, Domingos did not fall into the trap a second time.

This narrow escape did not deter Domingos from continued attempts to divine the location of buried treasures. Indeed, all of Portugal seemed to be obsessed with the fever of treasure hunting. In 1744, just months before Domingos' arrival in the country, the official Crown newspaper, the *Gazeta de Lisboa*, reported that, outside the city of Braga, treasure hunters had discovered almost 300 gold coins, each weighing a quarter of an ounce. The coins, which reflected the "ultimate Roman perfection," bore the images of various ancient emperors—Nero, Trajan, Marcus Aurelius, and others. The majority of the coins ended up in the hands of an English merchant, who immediately sent them to England "to embellish that nation's museums of curiosity."[38]

If the occasional discovery of Roman coins inspired some treasure seekers, even more pervasive was the belief that Islamic "Moors" had buried unimaginable riches when they retreated from the country hundreds of years earlier during the Catholic Reconquest. According to Portuguese legend, these treasures were guarded by enchanted Moors who could take the form of giant snakes.[39] In the 1720s, a French traveler dismissed the "ridiculous superstition of the Portuguese that there are hidden treasures and spirits that guard them."[40] Still, the Frenchman needed a letter of safe-conduct to travel into the interior "because the Portuguese are convinced that their country is full of treasures and that foreigners have ways of removing them."[41]

The idea that "foreigners" possessed powers to remove treasures might be understood on two levels. In the broadest sense, such a belief could be interpreted as a thinly veiled critique of the Portuguese Crown's economic policies. Portuguese subjects witnessed the arrival of fabulous Brazilian treasures—diamonds, gold, and silver—on the docks of the Rio Tejo in Lisbon. But these riches seemed to "magically" disappear into the hands of British merchants, whose eighteenth-century commercial colonization of Portugal drained wealth out of the Portuguese royal coffers and sent it to England.[42] In this way, the legend served to express often-hidden macro-level economic anxieties. At the same time, however, the very real successes of Spanish, English, and other "foreign" treasure hunters in Portugal only reinforced the perception that outsiders possessed unique powers to locate and haul away Portuguese wealth. As the Frenchman's comment reveals, such perceptions stirred Portuguese enmity toward foreign visitors. Just beneath the surface of this anger was a deeper uncertainty about the Crown's protection of Portuguese economic interests. If the Crown could not prevent Portuguese treasures from fleeing the country, the people would take matters into their own hands to protect and claim what was rightfully Portugal's.

The Portuguese Crown and the Catholic Church did not sit idly by in the face of these challenges to their economic and political power. Just as Agaja targeted vodun priests claiming to redeem the land in Dahomey, so too the Portuguese Crown blunted the similar desires of unsanctioned, "superstitious" treasure seekers. During the seventeenth century, the Portuguese Inquisition prosecuted only two cases involving treasure seekers. By the eighteenth century, however, this number increased dramatically, as the Inquisition systematically targeted treasure hunters as "*feiticeiros*."[43] In 1735, the Lisbon tribunal even took the extreme measure of turning one of these convicted treasure seekers over to secular justice. Francisco Barbosa, who claimed he discovered buried treasures guarded by twelve Moorish men and twelve Moorish women, was publicly executed by garroting in Lisbon's Rossio. His strangulation represented one of the rare instances in which convicted *feiticeiros* were remitted to secular justice for punishment, a stark reminder of the intertwined power of Church and Crown and a gruesome public example for any others intent on searching for buried Moorish treasures.[44]

As an African diviner exiled by the Inquisition, Domingos was particularly well-situated to take advantage of the opportunities offered by the legend of the Moorish treasures and Portuguese assumptions underlying it. During his travels through the Algarve, he quickly learned the details of the legend and began integrating them into his divination repertoire. Indeed, Domingos was eager to let the Portuguese harness his "foreign" magical powers to recover their buried treasures. Interestingly, the Portuguese myth may have cohered with some of Domingos' own understandings of the subterranean world. According to the Dahomean creation myth, when Mawu began constructing the earth, she was carried from place to place in the mouth of a serpent, Aido-Hwedo. Wherever they rested, the snake's excrement created mountains. As a result, "when a man digs into a mountain slope, he finds riches." Once Mawu completed her work, she ordered Aido-Hwedo to reside under the earth to help support the weight of her creations.[45] Though the Dahomean myth says nothing about seeking the serpent's permission to remove treasures, the proximity of the snake to earth's buried riches might very well have resonated with Domingos.

In August 1746, Domingos traveled to the small settlement of Moncarapacho, between Faro and Tavira. He had passed through the region about nine months previously, teaching a remedy for roundworm to the son of Maria Nesta da Palmeira and providing cures for the slaves of Maria da Graça and Domingos Coelho Vasconcellos.[46] On this second trip, Vasconcellos called on Domingos to search his farm for buried treasures. When Domingos arrived at the farm, he took a small cup of wine, threw some powders into it, and drank the mixture. He then set out to begin his search. Surveying the property, Domingos assured Vasconcellos that there were "many buried treasures and that in just one of these spots there were more than fifteen loads of gold coins and diamonds." In yet another place on the property, there were "three pots of money." Unfortunately, none of these treasures was easily accessible. In fact, at least nine enchanted Moors guarded over the treasures, including one family made up of a father, mother, and daughter. Vasconcellos asked Domingos if he dared to disenchant the Moors and remove the treasures. Domingos responded, "We will see. The Moorish woman is amenable, but her husband does not want to respond." Domingos claimed he spoke to the woman, who agreed to give over the treasures if he would disenchant her and her daughter "because she wished to return to her homeland" in North Africa. The man, however, was not available to confirm his wife's wishes; he was off visiting some of the other enchanted Moors on the same farm.[47]

Guarding another of the treasures was a giant Moor, half man and half serpent. In order to disenchant the "monster," Domingos revealed that he would have to hug and kiss it. The prospect of embracing the creature terrified Domingos because he feared it would squeeze him to death. Nevertheless, Domingos resolved to go and try to remove the treasures. One night, he went out alone, carrying only a torch. He returned after a short time, apologizing that he could not carry out his work because people were leading their cattle to pasture. Another night, Domingos asked for 3 vintéms to buy a candle. He then set out to speak to the enchanted Moorish family, but he again returned empty-handed. Eventually, he departed for Castro

Marim, promising Vasconcellos that he would return to extract the treasures, but he never followed through on the promise.[48]

Domingos soon reunited with his friend Bras Gonçalves, this time to uncover treasures at Rio Seco, just outside of Faro. According to Domingos, enchanted Moors also guarded these treasures. For two straight nights, Domingos wrapped himself in a white bed sheet, carried a lit candle, and performed certain gesticulations—speaking in an indecipherable language, dancing, and laying prostrate with the candle at his feet. On the second night, stones suddenly rained down on Domingos and Gonçalves. A startled Gonçalves asked who threw the rocks. Domingos replied that it was the Devil. Gonçalves declared that he wanted nothing to do with the Devil. But Domingos bravely stood firm, ordering Gonçalves to find him a tree branch. Gonçalves quickly found a branch, to which Domingos attached two smaller branches. Taking the rod, Domingos walked purposefully in a circular motion, praying. Then, just as suddenly as the rocks fell from the sky, they stopped.[49]

Though Domingos once again failed to uncover any treasures, Gonçalves remained deeply impressed with his powers to control forces beyond human control. He held tightly to his faith in Domingos until one day when he was approached by a stranger, a Frenchman who went by the nickname São Penha. São Penha revealed that Gonçalves was the victim of an elaborate fraud. He explained that everything Domingos did was "a ruse in order for him to get something to eat." He also confessed that he and two other men were responsible for the hail of rocks at Rio Seco. Domingos had asked them to hide in the woods and launch the rocks on his cue, helping him trick Gonçalves. On hearing this news, Gonçalves admitted that he felt like a "fool." Embarrassed and angered by the betrayal of trust, he promptly threw Domingos out of his house.[50] Apparently, Gonçalves was not content just to rid himself of Domingos. One night shortly after his eviction, several men unknown to Domingos approached him in the street and gave him a "good beating." Domingos later attributed the beating to the lies and tricks he played on Gonçalves.[51]

Eventually, Gonçalves carried his grudge to the Inquisition, denouncing Domingos as a "*feiticeiro* . . . a fine trickster and a liar." In addition to providing the Holy Office with detailed information on Domingos' divining and healing practices, Gonçalves turned over to the Inquisitorial notary a letter that Domingos had given him. According to Gonçalves, Domingos told him that if he carried the letter with him at all times, he would be protected from harm. Neither Gonçalves nor Domingos could read, so their inter-

Justo Juiz, the prayer of the "Just Judge" that Domingos gave to Bras Gonçalves. Gonçalves submitted the prayer to the Inquisition as evidence of Domingos' *feitiçaria*. Tribunal do Santo Ofício, Inquisição de Évora, Processo 7759, fl. 156. Courtesy Arquivo Nacional da Torre do Tombo, Lisbon, Portugal.

pretations of the letter's power are a fascinating case study of the "magic" of the written word. Domingos likely paid someone to prepare the letter or received it as payment in kind for one of his own cures. Thus, there is no reason to doubt his faith in the letter's powers. Likewise, Gonçalves also believed in the letter, trusting Domingos' interpretation of it as a force for good. For both men, the strength of the epistle lay partly in its unknowability, the object power of a piece of paper endowed with indecipherable "strong" words. However, as soon as Gonçalves learned of Domingos' lies about the treasures, he deduced that the letter was also a ruse. Gonçalves had no sure way of knowing the scripture's contents. It might have been a Christian prayer or, just as easily, an appeal to Satan. By the time he remitted the letter to the Inquisition, Gonçalves concluded that it did not protect him from harm. In fact, he said he had "experienced the contrary," implying that the letter was an object of malevolence.[52]

Actually, the letter contained the Oration of the Just Judge, a Catholic prayer used to protect the carrier from enemies, illness, and other forms of harm. It was, and continues to be, used as a protective prayer among Catholics.[53] Copies of the prayer were also utilized by Africans in Brazil and Portugal as powerful talismans.[54] This apparent confluence of beliefs served African and Portuguese alike, although not always in the same ways. For Gonçalves, the power of the oration came from the particularity of the words—the presumption of an appeal to God's mercy. For Domingos, the distinctions between prayers to God, Legba, Satan, and Sakpata were probably not as important as the powers that emanated from them. All were strong oaths, endowed with particular qualities. In this way, the consecration of the paper with a Catholic prayer was one of many possible prescriptions, not unlike other empowered medicines that could variously "heal" and "harm." Whereas Gonçalves viewed the letter through the prism of "good" versus "evil," Domingos saw it simply as empowered. Perhaps the written words rendered the paper more powerful than a similarly spoken oath, but the object itself was still the vessel for that empowerment. The key to unlocking the object's hidden powers was a kind of literacy that neither man possessed. Ironically, the modern magicians who held the power to read and write—the Catholic priests—revealed that the African's letter was a thing of God and not the evil curse Gonçalves believed it to be.

Having thoroughly alienated Bras Gonçalves, Domingos once again set himself in motion. This time, he traveled fifty miles north to the village of Alcaria Queimada. There, he suspended his treasure-hunting exertions in favor of more familiar healing practices. In October and November 1746, he performed cures for at least four people. These cures ranged from herbal baths for general illness to infusions of *aguardente* and pepper for fevers.[55] They also included the remedy of towels and water on the head (learned in Brazil) and the liberal use of Catholic holy water, prayers, and the sign of the cross. All of Domingos' clients claimed that their health improved significantly as a result of his interventions. However, Domingos shared troubling news with each of them. He discovered that the source of all the illnesses in Alcaria was a powerful *feiticeira* living in the village. Domingos "expressly refused to name" the evildoer, claiming that she already had knowledge of his presence in the village. If he revealed her identity, she would have him arrested by the Inquisition. According to Domingos, the woman knew an oration that could "attach and bind" the *familiares* of the Inquisition, thereby shaping their behavior.[56] Here, Domingos projected his own fears and anxieties onto a purported rival. He knew that he was being pursued by the Inquisition, yet he believed that it was only through the hidden, malevolent powers of others that the Inquisitors would succeed in catching him.

Domingos insinuated that the author of the village's widespread suffering was a woman named Domingas Dias, along with her daughter and apprentice Luzia. Whenever the two women passed in the street, Domingos told his clients, "There they are" or "Here come my godmothers."[57] Domingos' strong suggestion that Dias was the culprit did not surprise the residents of the village. Manuel Mestre, for example, suspected Dias of ensorcelling people in the past. She had threatened his sister's children on several occasions. Dias also allegedly gave poisoned milk to a mother and her small daughter, causing the death of the infant and a lengthy illness for the mother.[58] As he had done elsewhere, Domingos successfully diagnosed deep social tensions and tied them to physical ailments. By also expressing his own apprehensions and fears through the divisive presence of Domingas Dias, he embedded himself ever more deeply into the social world of his clients. Altogether, Domingos and the residents of Alcaria shared a common interest in eliminating this powerful threat to health, reproduction, and group stability. As the self-designated protector of the community, Domingos turned Dias into his fiercest enemy.

One day, while Domingos was curing Maria Mestra, Domingas Dias arrived at Mestra's front door. Domingos was sitting by the fire when Dias entered the room. The two exchanged hostile glances but did not say a word to each other. As Domingos sat eyeing the woman, he fashioned a cross out of two small sticks, tying them together with a piece of string. He then threw the cross into the fire. An indignant Dias rose from her seat and demanded to know what "that *preto*" was doing with the crosses.[59] As she fled to the safety of her own house, Dias accused Domingos of being a *feiticeiro*. She also warned Mestra that she should kick Domingos out of her house. Dias clearly interpreted Domingos' gesture as a threat, perhaps even a curse aimed at causing her harm. If Domingos' intent was to strike fear into Dias, it worked. Dias never again returned to Mestra's house as long as Domingos was there.

The deep social tensions Domingos uncovered in Alcaria meant that he could not linger there for long. After less than two months, he fled once again, this time heading west. The pace of his movement and the distance he traveled suggest that he must have suffered deep anxiety over the prospect of arrest. He left Alcaria in November 1746. Just three months later he re-emerged more than eighty miles away in the coastal village of Portimão, where he continued healing, administering infusions, and giving herbal baths. In one instance, he treated a gravely ill woman named Catharina Varella. Varella had been suffering for almost seven years with an ailment that had suddenly taken a turn for the worse. Her chest pains were especially unbearable. Domingos tried several approaches to her treatment, but nothing seemed to work. Eventually, he asked Varella's husband to catch a fish and bring it to his wife's sickbed. On two different occasions, Domingos asked Varella to spit into the mouth of a live toadfish (*xarroco*). The fish was then released back into the ocean with the expectation that it would carry away the evil that plagued Varella. Domingos later confessed that he had learned this remedy "in his homeland, where he was accustomed to using it . . . for tuberculosis or consumption [*tísico ou etico*]."[60] Unfortunately, the remedy failed and Varella died a short time later.[61]

Despite this minor setback, some people in Portimão seemed to have great respect for Domingos. Varella's husband, José Pacheco, was careful not to blame Domingos for his wife's demise, noting that her death was caused solely by her "great weakness." In Pacheco's estimation, Domingos "lived a clean, judicious life . . . and always seemed to be in his right mind."[62] Another of Domingos' clients, Leonor Alonso, called Domingos by the deferential title "Father [Pai]," just as his loyal followers in Brazil had done. Alonso's proximity to the more cosmopolitan and democratic world of seafaring folk might explain her willingness to see Domingos as more than a simple fetisher. Her husband was a ship's captain; she also named at least one other seaman among Domingos' clients.[63] Unfortunately, not all of Portimão's residents were so open in their worldviews. Less than two months after Domingos' arrival in the village, Inquisitorial agent Manuel de Andrade Carvalho learned of Domingos' activities and sent a letter of denunciation to authorities in Évora.[64] This letter, outlining Domingos' healing practices in Portimão, finally prompted the Holy Office to issue an order for his arrest.[65] However, once again, Domingos managed to stay one step ahead of his pursuers. By the time the arrest order arrived in Portimão, Domingos had departed for the village of Monchique, some fifteen miles into the northern interior.[66]

Since at least Roman times, Monchique's hot sulfur springs had been widely renowned for their therapeutic properties in treating rheumatism, respiratory problems, backaches, and many other ailments. In 1495, shortly before his death, King João II sought treatment in Monchique.[67] Similarly, when King João V suffered a series of illnesses in the mid-1740s, he spent time at the baths, accompanied by his sons.[68] While Domingos' precise motivations in going to Monchique are unclear, perhaps he anticipated a large and sympathetic audience for his own therapeutic practices. If so, this was yet one more demonstration of Domingos' keen intuition and ability to read the social landscape. Whatever his intentions, Domingos did not stay in Monchique for long. In May 1747, while traveling back toward the coast, he encountered a man named Florencio Rodrigues. Rodrigues informed Domingos that his wife, Theadora Gonçalves, had been suffering from an illness for more than six months. Domingos offered to consult with the woman, following Rodrigues to their house in the village of Alvor.[69]

Arriving at the couple's house, Domingos sat down and ordered Theadora Gonçalves to walk into the sunlight. He immediately announced that he did not know how she was still alive "since the evil she suffered came from witches and *feiticeiros*." Domingos then proceeded to describe "all of the illnesses and pains" that plagued Gonçalves. After divining her ailments, Domingos offered to return Gonçalves to health. The frightened woman eagerly agreed. Domingos administered some infusions, made from powders he carried in a wrapped paper. He also ordered a series of herbal baths. Gonçalves followed Domingos' directions carefully, claiming that after washing with the herbs the pain in her head immediately felt better. But Domingos warned that her relief was only temporary. The "pin pricks" she felt in her head would return even stronger since those responsible for her illness knew that he was there trying to cure her. Just as Domingos predicted, Gonçalves' head pains returned with a vengeance.

Domingos advised Gonçalves to continue with her baths. He also revealed that the perpetrator of her illness was a neighboring woman. The next day, the woman appeared at Gonçalves' front door and made her way to the kitchen. Domingos suspected she wanted to steal his medicines. He also thought she was trying to frighten and intimidate him, hoping he would abandon his attempts to heal Gonçalves. The woman brusquely asked Domingos, "If you are the virtuoso, can you see what I am suffering?" Domingos answered, "You have nothing; nor do I know anything I could teach you." At this, the woman departed. After she was gone, Domingos told Gonçalves that the woman "knew more than he did because she was a witch and a *feiticeiro* and that seven years ago she had slept with the Devil." Moreover, he said that the Devil had given the woman *feitiços* and ordered her to put them in Gonçalves' body. Skeptical of Domingos' story, Gonçalves asked when the woman had first implanted the *feitiços* in her. Domingos answered that it had been about three years ago. According to Gonçalves, Domingos had no way of knowing that this was precisely the time she first began suffering so much pain.[70]

Impressed by Domingos' clairvoyance, Gonçalves invited her close friend Maria da Silva to come to her house for a consultation with Domingos. Silva had also been suffering from a long-term illness. Domingos again claimed that he could "see" the *feitiços* inside Silva's body and advised her to let him administer his cures. Silva agreed, but she needed to consult with her husband first. After she left, Domingos confided to Theadora Gonçalves that Silva's case was even more dire than hers. Returning later in the day, Silva submitted to a more extensive examination. According to the sick woman, Domingos divined "all the ailments that she suffered, better than she herself could explain them."[71] Domingos ultimately determined that Silva was infected with two different sets of *feitiços*. One consisted of some malevolent materials, half of which were burned. The remaining half were put in Silva's food, served on a plate that had chips around the edges. In fact, Silva owned a plate with precisely such faults. The second set of *feitiços* consisted of a "doll" that had been cast into the sea. Domingos offered to remove both sets of *feitiços* but warned that retrieving the ones in the ocean would cost Silva and her husband dearly.

Addressing the terrestrial malevolence first, Domingos ordered his usual regimen of herbal baths and infusions. Silva assiduously followed his directions and, as a result, "immediately felt better." Domingos assured Silva that she no longer needed to worry about these *feitiços* since they were now completely removed. Turning his attentions to the seaborne *feitiços*, Domingos demanded 180 réis, claiming that he needed to purchase a balm to rub on the doll when he recovered it. Around nine o'clock that evening,

Domingos left the house of Theadora Gonçalves and headed toward the beach to search for the *feitiços*. Returning the following morning, Domingos announced that his search had been unsuccessful. He claimed that whenever he approached the *feitiços* "a great windstorm" arose, preventing him from recovering them. Domingos attributed the inexplicable shift in weather to the holy objects he wore around his neck—rosary beads, scapulars, veronicas, and a Cord of Saint Francis. He told Silva he would leave these objects behind and try again later that night.

On the second night, Domingos achieved greater success. He removed the *feitiços* from the sea. However, in order to do so, he needed to enlist the help of seven *feiticeiros*, all at great expense. With the group's assistance, Domingos recovered a bundle of substances that included a "doll" made from black cloth, a little piece of the broken plate from Silva's house, some earth that she walked on, blood taken from her laundered clothes, hairs from her head, saliva, fourteen needles, and fifteen pins. Having finally recovered the malevolent objects, Domingos ordered Silva to bring him a cup of water. Domingos cast some powders into the water, and peering into the mixture, he explained to Silva that he was seeing who had given her this evil. If she wanted, he could make her something to avenge her enemies, but Silva declined his offer, responding that "God should help them." Finally, Domingos asked Silva to bring him a full glass of water. Wrapping towels on her head and turning the glass of water over on top of the towels, he administered the Brazilian remedy, telling her that this would remove any evil remaining in her head. As a result of Domingos' therapies, Maria da Silva later testified that she quickly regained her health and remained free of illness for months to follow.[72]

Domingos performed his cures in Alvor through the month of June 1747. By July, he was once again on the move, this time tracking northeast. As he passed through the town of Silves, secular authorities apprehended Domingos. Though the exact circumstances of his arrest are not spelled out in the documentary record, his initial detention may have been for something as simple as vagrancy. He would have been a truly odd spectacle in the rural areas of the Algarve—a tattered, hungry African man, embellished with *bolsas*, beads, and veronicas, carrying a cane tube full of medicines and a sack with various other healing implements. Among the strange objects found in the bag was a "small rock" taken from the head of a jackfish (*xaréu*). Domingos later confessed that he threw this rock into herbal baths as part of the treatment for kidney stones, another cure he learned in Brazil.[73] Whatever the precise circumstances of his arrest, the Holy Office in

Évora had been pursuing Domingos for almost two years and was closely monitoring news of his whereabouts. On July 15, the Évora tribunal issued an order requesting that Domingos be turned over to its jurisdiction. It also ordered that he be confined in the Inquisitorial jails in that city.[74] Less than a month later, Domingos arrived in Évora, where he once again faced a judicial inquiry before the Portuguese Holy Office.[75]

By the time of his arrest, Domingos had been in the Algarve for nearly three years. During that time, he traveled hundreds of miles on foot, moving frequently from place to place, trying to eke out a living wherever he could. In Mértola, he sold sardines. In Faro, he worked in Bras Gonçalves' inn. But mostly he divined and healed. Domingos' position in Portuguese society scarcely resembled the elevated status he enjoyed in his homeland, or even in Brazil. In those places, his skills were widely acknowledged as crucial to the maintenance of community well-being. Ties of reciprocity between Domingos, the local community, and the world of the spirits were recognized and respected. In this way, Domingos became an integral force in the creation and continued vitality of social networks that defined individuals by their temporal and spiritual relationships.

Despite his best efforts to serve new communities and forge new social networks in Portugal, nothing could transform his singular status as an exile, outcast, and social pariah. Everywhere he went, people recognized him as a colonial convict. Some people abhorred him, while others selfishly sought to capitalize on his purported powers. As a result, Domingos constantly remade himself in order to curry favor and adhere to Portuguese expectations. He was variously a healer, a virtuoso, and a *feiticeiro*. In one town, he cured illnesses with herbal baths, Catholic prayers, and the sign of the cross. In the next, he peered inside the earth, spoke to enchanted Moors, and discovered incredible riches. He conspicuously wore holy objects, yet he also carried a sack full of *feitiços*. Most of his clientele knew he was from the Mina Coast and had spent time in Brazil, yet he allegedly told some people that he was from Angola.[76] Whatever the social context, Domingos seemed to have an appropriate answer.

It is tempting to see these various transformations in the Algarve as ingenious, resistant, even heroic. They were, of course, all of these things, but we must temper the urge to celebrate Domingos' extraordinary adaptability. The image of Domingos as the polymorphous, triumphant trickster belies a starker reality of surviving by one's wits, constantly fleeing the specters of temporal and social death. Struggling daily against the threats of homelessness, hunger, and physical violence, Domingos suffered a profound alienation from Portuguese social life. The basic narrative of his confession before the Inquisitors in Évora spells out this painful quest for survival. Near Mértola, he healed Maria Mestra with herbal baths, infusions, and balms made from sheep's lard. Though he knew "that her illness was syphilis, in order that she would better reward him, he told her that her pains were *feitiços*." When she recovered from her illness, she gave him "lots to eat and drink and 1 quarto de ouro [1,200 réis]." In Alcaria, he provided cures "only for some things they gave him to eat, which he requested . . . for the love of God." In Faro, he "faked" his ability to find buried treasures "because he did not have anything to eat and they could give him something." In Portimão, he unsuccessfully attempted to cure Catharina Varella, but Varella's husband, José Pacheco, still "rewarded him with some money and something to eat."[77] Altogether, these explanations suggest that abject poverty and desperate hunger drove Domingos to perform whatever roles were necessary to elicit compensation from his clients, even if this meant forsaking his own vast body of knowledge and beliefs.

Domingos' quest for sustenance, along with his fear of individual and Portuguese institutional recriminations, also guided his frequent, frenetic movements. This chronic instability eventually took a toll on Domingos. For every new destination, every new incarnation of "self," some part of him died. This was as true in Dahomey and in various Brazilian settings as in the Algarve, but the pace of serial alienation accelerated in southern Portugal. By the time of his arrest, Domingos was a remarkably hybrid cultural composite, but the crushing violence of everyday life also rendered him a humiliated caricature of the proud and powerful figure he had once been. Without the fortifying sustenance of family or friends, he was isolated and alone, scarcely a "person." In the social realm, as well as in the physical one, Domingos hung onto the very precipice of existence.[78]

To be sure, even in this most meager, bare-bones survival, Domingos continued to grow and refine his healing practices. He was not always "performing" solely for Portuguese consumption. His knowledge of the medicinal properties of various flora and fauna, for example, never waned. In fact, his arsenal of medicines expanded significantly in Portugal. In his confession, he recited no fewer than ten different local roots and herbs that he utilized in his cures.[79] These were not random choices. Some he no doubt recognized as akin to those he used in Africa and Brazil. Others he probably learned from the Portuguese. Whatever the case, many of them proved effective. For example, he confessed that in Alcaria he treated an open ulcer on a woman's finger with the herb black nightshade (*Solanum nigrum*, or *erva Mouros* in Portuguese). Though he may have claimed to be curing *feiti-ços*, the beneficial qualities of black nightshade as a treatment for ulcers has since been proven scientifically.[80]

Domingos also frequently invoked memories of past practices, though sometimes with an eye toward his present, impoverished condition. He continued to carry his medicines in a cane tube in Portugal "because it cost him nothing and because the papers ripped apart when he put them in his pocket."[81] He also persisted in sweeping away evil spirits with black chickens. In those instances where a chicken was unavailable, a rooster sufficed—not so much for ritual purposes but to eat afterward.[82] Finally, his use of complex bundles of empowered substances, *bochio* "dolls," and strong oaths reflected directly on his African past, as did his belief that threats of illness and death could be projected onto empowered cadavers, toadfish, and even other people.

When the Inquisitor, Luís Antônio Fragoso de Barros, interrogated Domingos about his healing practices in the Algarve, he asked "if after renouncing his sins [in Lisbon] he had some revelation giving him the grace to cure, or if he learned medicine . . . what person taught it to him?" Domingos once again reverted to his African past to explain his gifts. He said that nothing had been revealed to him in Portugal; nor had he learned medicine. Rather, "in his land, through experience and knowledge they teach one another the natural virtue of herbs, and they cure their infirmities, and it is in this way that he knows some countervenoms and virtues of herbs . . . which are used in this way in his land."[83] Though separated from his African homeland by nearly twenty years and two continents, Domingos still clung to a set of core understandings passed along to him by his ancestors. By invoking "his land," his people, and their ways of teaching and healing one another, Domingos not only memorialized his past, asserting his true sense of place and belonging. He also positioned that past as central to the pursuit of health and well-being, ahead of Catholic "revelation" and European "medicine." As the vehicle for a system of collective knowledge gained through years of experience, Domingos constantly reiterated links to family and kin through his healing practices. In the hostile environment of southern Portugal, these healing practices, no matter how diluted or corrupted, still served as a vital source of social sustenance, tethering him to a world that remained vital and alive, even if only in his memory.

Curiously, Domingos' recollection of his first Inquisition case was not nearly as complete as his memory of his homeland. The Inquisitor in Évora reminded him that after his first trial he was "warned that his mode of curing was illegal . . . and gave birth to the presumption that he was suspect in the faith and had some pact or alliance with the Devil." In response, Domingos replied that he did not "remember what was asked of him at his first case." Nevertheless, "neither before nor after he renounced his sins did he have any pact or alliance with the Devil." In that case, the Inquisitor wondered, how did his healing in Portugal differ from his healing in Brazil? Domingos explained that in Portugal, "he did not use any mode of curing that was accused of him in his first case: he did not speak with any man or woman possessed by the Devil; nor did he use the little calabash; nor other circumstances that were stated in his first case." In other words, he engaged in none of the behaviors that required a broader community of believers— spirit possession, invocations of Legba, and so on. Instead, he only "applied some remedies composed of herbs harvested publicly, without using words or ceremonies . . . obliged by the hunger and poverty in which he found himself."[84]

Domingos held firm to his story that his cures were natural, learned in his homeland, and necessary for his survival. But the skeptical Inquisitor reminded Domingos that he had already confessed to using live fish, chickens, and ceremonies with cups of water and towels wrapped around the head. Thus, it was not true he cured only with herbs; he also performed "false and useless actions" that were "the work of the Devil." Domingos denied the charges. He claimed that he learned the cures with the fish and the cup on the head in Brazil, "where, generally, all the Christians make it, without words or any actions, and he never heard nor understood that there was anything evil in the cure."[85] As for the cure with the chicken and the 10-réis coin, he claimed that he heard a Portuguese "white woman" originated it, and "it seemed to him a good way to get the chicken and the money, and for this reason he used it and not because he wanted to make some superstitious thing by intervention of the Devil."[86]

The Inquisitor remained unimpressed, asserting that natural remedies worked only through direct application to the sick, not separate from them in other living creatures. Therefore, the remedies Domingos described could only work by virtue of some pact or friendship with the Devil. Again, Domingos objected vigorously. He reiterated that "he learned the cures of spitting in the mouth of a fish and putting a cup with water on the head in Brazil, where all castes of people are accustomed to using it, and not even the priests know whether they work by natural virtue or superstition. And he applied them without malice and never made a pact, nor had friendship with the Devil." Frustrated, Domingos concluded that he "did not know what more to say."

Nevertheless, the Inquisitor continued badgering him. If Domingos understood that he was convicted of curing feitiços in his first trial, how could there be so many accusations against him in the Algarve if he was not continuing to cure in the same way, by virtue of the Devil? If he was warned in his first case that curing feitiços made him suspect in the faith and suspicious of having made a pact with the Devil, why did he continue involving himself in these things unless he wanted the Devil's friendship? Did he think it was acceptable for him to break the promise of his abjuration, relapsing in his sins and refusing to comply with the punishment they imposed on him? Domingos responded that it seemed to him that the cures he made in the Algarve were not similar to those he made in Brazil. Still, the cures he performed in Portugal "weighed heavily" on him, and he made them "obliged by hunger . . . out of necessity and misery . . . and not for ill will toward Our Holy Catholic faith, nor because he wanted something from the Devil." Desperate, Domingos threw himself on the mercy of the Inquisitor, confessing that he now recognized his error in departing the place of his exile but that he did so only out of "extreme necessity, because nobody would favor him." He swore that he did not intend to repudiate the orders of the Inquisition, to which "with many tears he begs for pardon."[87]

Ultimately, the tribunal at Évora showed some mercy toward Domingos. On September 19, 1748, a little over a year after his arrest, the Holy Office handed down its sentence. In their ruling, the Inquisitors concluded that Domingos did not cure by "virtue" because in his cures with chickens, fish, and cups of water on the head, "some of the sick people did not return to health, nor in their application did he use words indicating a pact with the Devil." Domingos' other remedies with herbal baths, balms, and infusions, while containing "some unusual actions," were "natural remedies without vain observance or mixture of holy or sacred things, orations, or words." The Inquisitors also determined that there was no evidence of divination "because from the exposition of the facts his ruse and tricks are known." In the end, it was clear that there was "not a second lapse of feitiçarias, sortileges, or divinations." As such, the Inquisitors ruled that Domingos "should not be punished in accordance with the penalties" normally associated with such relapses, a judgment that probably spared Domingos his life. Nevertheless, they judged that he was a "liar and a trickster of people, a vile man, and transgressor of the orders of the Holy Office." The Évora tribunal found him guilty of departing the place of his exile before complying with the entire period of his sentence.[88]

As punishment, the Inquisitors passed down a sentence strikingly similar to the one Domingos received in Lisbon. They once again forced him to submit to the public humiliation of the Auto da Fé. On October 20, 1749, Domingos endured this excruciating process in the city of Évora, far removed from the familiar African and Brazilian actors who formed a significant minority of those marching in Lisbon's Auto da Fé five years earlier. This time, there would be no visibly recognizable colonial faces, no knowing glances, no clearly discernible social lifeline. Domingos walked alone. At the conclusion of the procession and the mass, Domingos again approached the pulpit to hear his sentence and publicly renounce his sins. There, he learned that his sentence included whipping in the streets "without the spilling of blood [*citra sanguinis effusionem*]." In addition, the Inquisitors sentenced him to another four years of banishment, this time to the small town of Bragança in the mountains of far northeast Portugal. On November 4, 1749, after nearly fifteen months in jail, Domingos was released from the custody of the Évora tribunal. In their release orders, the Inquisitors required that Domingos present himself to the tribunal at Coimbra within twenty days. The distance from Évora to Coimbra was 140 miles. After that, he was to continue on to Bragança, a further 175 miles. Adding insult to injury, and seeming to ignore the economic desperation and misery he expressed during his trial, the Inquisitors concluded: "Seeing that he is now unable to satisfy the costs of his trial and the provisions for his time in prison, he should take great care to satisfy them immediately."[89] At that, Domingos made his mark, agreeing to comply with the orders, and he was again set free. As he embarked on his sixth forced migration in twenty years, wandering in solitude across the plains of central Portugal, he no doubt reflected on his life history and his seemingly singular fate. He could scarcely imagine that, in Dahomey, preparations were under way to send an official diplomatic mission to Brazil, one that would reinforce the very imperial and commercial links that had landed him in this painful predicament.

Obscurity

As he is about to be sacrificed to the ancestors, a slave is entrusted to carry a load
of powder from King Agaja to the late kings of Dahomey. Angry, the man screams
out: "What? After a life of toil, you want to take away from me the rest that every
man enjoys in the land of the dead? No! Has the Creator denied me rest forever?"
— Gabriel Kiti, Fon proverb, first recorded in 1927, in
Gérard Guillet, *Regards sur la litterature Dahoméenne: Les Proverbes*

On October 22, 1750, exactly one year and two days after Domingos Álvares
marched in the Auto da Fé in Évora, an odd yet fabulous sight appeared in
the streets of Salvador, Bahia. At the head of an official procession, traveling from the Jesuit College to the viceroy's palace, appeared a well-built
African man "dressed in a red garment, embroidered with gold, arranged
like a woman's skirt, but without a waistline . . . embellished with silk fringes
. . . and [over this], a robe with a long train, like royal clothing, of multi-
colored cloth lined with lustrous white silk and strips of different colors."
Embellishing this sartorial splendor, the African also wore "a magnificent
and costly turban, and high-laced golden boots." Accompanying the man
were two other African gentlemen dressed in a similar fashion but donning
different colors than their leader. All three men rode through the streets of
Salvador on sedan chairs, followed on foot by their servants and four ten-
year-old girls "dressed in the manner of their country with wraps on their
heads, but without shirts." Rounding out the procession were a number
of curious onlookers, fascinated by this rare spectacle of African "royalty"
traveling through the streets.[1]

When the African arrived at the viceroy's palace, he did not seek any
form of mercy, charity, or even patronage. On the contrary, Ambassador
Churumá Nadir represented the powerful Dahomean King Tegbesu (1740–
74) on a diplomatic mission of peace, goodwill, and free trade. Over the
previous seven years, relations between Dahomey and Portugal had dete-
riorated. During the early 1740s, as Dahomey struggled to consolidate its
military victory along the coast of the Bight of Benin, Portuguese traders

conspired to return Dahomey's exiled Hueda enemies to power. In response, Dahomean troops arrested the director of the Portuguese fort at Ouidah in 1743, eventually sending him into exile in Bahia. The Dahomean army then proceeded to burn the fort to the ground, massacring its residents, including a number of Hueda refugees. Devastated by this thrashing at the hands of the Dahomean army, the Portuguese contemplated their revenge. In 1747, the secretary of state wrote that Tegbesu deserved "some punishment that would oblige him to show more attention and respect to the [Portuguese] nation, because among such people fear works better than reason, and tolerance and pretense make them more insolent."[2] The viceroy of Bahia answered three months later that indeed the "Negros" of Ouidah were "insolent and great thieves, who do not protect the loyalty or word of anyone." However, punishment seemed impractical and "difficult . . . without prejudicing the extraction of slaves, who are so crucial to us for the agriculture of Brazil."[3] Abandoning Ouidah for nearby ports represented one option, but the Portuguese determined that they "would experience the same inconvenience, insolence, and incivility from similar kings."[4] Anger and mistrust persisted on both sides in the years that followed until, finally, King Tegbesu sent his emissaries to Bahia to try to ease the diplomatic stalemate. Of particular interest to Tegbesu was the resumption of the once-vibrant trade, so necessary for the prosperity of both nations.

It was in the context of these strained relations that Ambassador Churumá Nadir sought an audience with the viceroy. From the day of his arrival in Bahia, the ambassador made clear that he would not bow to Portuguese custom or law. When the viceroy offered him the use of his sedan chair, Churumá Nadir refused, arguing that such forms of travel should be reserved for the day of their official meeting. Later, when the viceroy insisted on outfitting the ambassador in Portuguese-style dress, made from the richest velvet and damask cloths, the ambassador again rejected the offer, preferring to wear clothes in "the style of his country, in order to represent the king, for whom he was minister."[5] Finally, during the days leading up to the official meeting, Churumá Nadir orchestrated a celebration in accordance with "the pagan rite that they profess." As a part of this festival, the participants performed a ceremony in which "they killed many birds, and anointed themselves with their blood." They then feasted on a banquet of African foods, offering toasts to "the health of their king and to the felicity of his governance."[6]

Upon finally receiving an audience with the viceroy some three weeks after his arrival in Salvador, Churumá Nadir continued to challenge Portuguese diplomatic protocol. Entering the room where the viceroy sat with other ministers and officials, the ambassador asked his interpreter which one was the viceroy. He immediately walked up to the viceroy and bowed three times in the fashion of the Portuguese, "with many airs." He then dropped to the floor "in the fashion of his country, prostrating himself . . . with arms extended, the hands one over the other, snapping his fingers like castanets, a ceremony which in Dahomey . . . they use to show veneration for their kings." When the ambassador rose from the floor, the viceroy offered him the distinguished seat next to him. Again, the ambassador refused, saying that "the seat was made for extended conversation and thus had no use in the Court of Ambassadors, whose communications are always brief."[7]

Standing, Churumá Nadir delivered his message on behalf of King Tegbesu. Translating for the viceroy were a Portuguese man who had worked in Dahomey and the mulatto son of a Mina woman, both of whom spoke the Mina language "elegantly." According to the interpreters, Churumá Nadir relayed Tegbesu's directives as follows:

> That High and Sovereign Master, king of all Gentile Nations, including those that inhabit the Ocean Coasts, as well as those who live in the extended backlands, of which the ends have still not been discovered, whom people of great esteem fear, among whom all are exceeded by Dahomey; wishes to ally himself and treat with great friendship the great Master of the West, the illustrious king of Portugal; and . . . ordering me to Brazil and conceding to me all the powers of his royal personage, he ordered me to make for Your Excellency in this rough representation the affirmations of his desire. Wishing good health to Your Excellency, despite the difference that religion has made between Christian and Gentile; because that Highest Power, who, without any doubt, created this earth and the immensity of the heavens, . . . does not prohibit communication between those who live in different laws, nor the peace and goodwill that so corresponds with the commerce between men. This friendship, which he desires with the Portuguese Crown, the king promises with his word to observe faithfully, and in the absence of his personage, he bequests this friendship to his successors. The proof of the truth of my expressions Your Excellency will see signed with the Royal Sign from his eminency.[8]

At that, the ambassador removed from his tunic a letter addressed to the Portuguese king. Churumá Nadir urged the viceroy to protect the secrets of the letter and the packages that would follow. Then, just as quickly as he had entered the palace, he departed.

Arriving back at the Jesuit College, the Dahomean ambassador ordered his assistants to pay twenty gold coins to the enslaved porters who had ferried them through the city in sedan chairs. The Portuguese military officers who accompanied the entourage convinced the slaves that they should not accept the money. However, the ambassador insisted, arguing that "nobody has jurisdiction to limit the actions of princes." A short time later, the ambassador dispatched gifts to the viceroy's palace on behalf of King Tegbesu. These included two iron trunks, one each for the viceroy and Portuguese King João V,[9] filled with fine cloths from the African coast. In addition, the ambassador sent the four young girls to serve as slaves for the Portuguese king. Finally, the ambassador designated 100 Mina slaves for the viceroy's personal use.[10] Six months later, Churumá Nadir and his two assistants returned to the Mina Coast on the Portuguese ship *Bom Jesus d'Além e Nossa Senhora da Esperança*. Onboard the ship were 8,101 rolls of Brazilian tobacco, which were eventually traded for more than 900 Dahomean slaves.[11] On June 27, 1752, 834 of these enslaved Africans disembarked in Salvador, the immediate bounty of improving relations between Dahomey and Portugal.[12]

From the perspective of the Dahomean and Portuguese Crowns, Churumá Nadir's diplomatic mission succeeded in defusing political tensions, facilitating economic expansion on both sides of the Atlantic. However, the voiceless victims of this imperial "friendship" were thousands of enslaved Africans who constituted the bulk of the "commerce" binding the two nations. Some of these slaves, like the young girls Tegbesu sent to Portugal, were lucky enough to escape the arduous labor of Brazil's cane fields or gold mines. Yet even these "privileged" Africans were not impervious to the hardship and disease that plagued Atlantic circuits. Three of the African girls eventually made it to Lisbon, becoming the personal chambermaids of the Portuguese queen. However, one of the girls, apparently suffering from ophthalmia contracted onboard the ship from Dahomey to Bahia, went blind during her stay in Salvador. When her compatriots departed for Portugal, she was left behind in Bahia to an uncertain fate, the useless refuse of imperial comity.[13]

AT FIRST GLANCE, it might not appear that Domingos Álvares shared much in common with the blind girl in Salvador. To be sure, both were victims of the Dahomean-Portuguese imperial alliance, enslaved and forcibly removed from their homelands to serve unknown masters in faraway places. Yet Domingos built a vibrant new life for himself in Brazil, while the blind girl had her possibilities cut short almost before they ever began. Domingos' remarkable achievements in Brazil, along with his defiant, steadfast quest for survival in Portugal, contain all the ingredients for a heroic narrative of "triumph over tragedy." In spite of the continuous hardships that he faced, his was a life extraordinarily well-lived. Meanwhile, the blind girl's tale bespeaks nothing but tragedy. Despite the very real differences in their trajectories, by the early 1750s, they stood on opposite sides of the Atlantic, far removed from their homelands, sharing the same basic existential condition. Both were isolated and alone, removed from "sight." For Domingos, this process unfolded over many years; for the blind girl, a matter of weeks. But together, along with countless other Mina slaves scattered across the Portuguese world, their struggles were the same: How were they to contest the relentless forces of individuation borne of imperial institutions—in Dahomey, in Brazil, and even in Portugal? In all of these settings, the forces of imperialism wrought for its victims loneliness, solitude, and social invisibility, which were tantamount to blindness.

The metaphor of "losing sight" captures well not only the broad experiences of enslaved Africans in the Atlantic world but also the efforts of those historians trying to recover their pasts. As soon as the young African woman descended into blindness, she disappeared from the European historical record, no longer worthy of comment. For most Africans, like the 900 Dahomean prisoners loaded onto the *Bom Jesus d'Além e Nossa Senhora da Esperança*, plunging into the darkness of the ship's hold represented the permanent erasure of familiar sights in their homeland. It also marked the only time that most of these anonymous individuals would appear in the historical record, as part of an aggregate "cargo." On arrival in the Americas, some would gradually discover new ways of "seeing," converting to Christianity, forging Western-style families, earning manumission, and contributing to broader emancipatory movements. Not surprisingly, these Africans and their descendants are the ones historians most often discover in the documentary records.

For those Africans who remained in "darkness," unable or unwilling to be led toward European-style "enlightenment," the record is much less complete. Many died quick and brutal deaths. Others, like Domingos Álvares, claimed the darkness as their advantage, offering familiar glimpses of the African past to those who could not comprehend their present circumstances. These glimpses—through divination, healing, and the construction of new communities—remained mostly the preserve of enslaved Africans and their allies. In this way, African healers sometimes became sharp critics of European ideologies, inverting assumptions about "enlightenment." Africans simply could not "see" those who identified most closely with the divisive individualism that exemplified Portuguese imperial power. It will be recalled, for example, that the Captain suddenly went "blind" when asked to divine the illness of Leonor de Oliveira Cruz in Rio de Janeiro. Leonor's position among Rio's wealthy elite rendered her invisible to the powerful spiritual quality possessing the Captain. Yet the same Captain offered diagnoses and solutions to a range of ailments that plagued a larger, subject community consisting mostly of Africans.

As long as Domingos Álvares successfully shined the light of therapy, health, and healing onto the symptoms of Portuguese colonialism and slavery, he offered a competing vision of redemption, a way of addressing isolation and alienation through the prism of a more stable and comprehensible deep past that emphasized communal well-being. Wealthy planters, the Church, and the Crown could not tolerate the challenges that such a collective vision implied. As such, they systematically condemned Domingos to darkness—in ship holds, in jails, in the sociocultural vacuum of southern Portugal. In this way, he experienced a sort of serial isolation, repeatedly rendering him sightless and invisible to the world. Yet even in the darkness, he managed to retain his singular focus, undaunted by attempts to naturalize his vision to Portugal's colonial myopia. This was a testament both to Domingos' dogged persistence and to the resilience of his beliefs and practices in an ever-changing world.

Unfortunately, by the time Domingos reached the Algarve, Portuguese institutional might finally succeeded in extinguishing his communal vision. Domingos walked hundreds of miles across southern Portugal, desperately seeking social visibility. But he could never rekindle the light in the same ways he had in Dahomey or Brazil. Lacking a community that shared in the history and memories invoked by his ritual practices, Domingos was effectively reduced to a solitary oblivion, not that far removed from the one suffered by the blind girl in Salvador. And just like the blind girl, at the moment of his most profound isolation, upon exiting the Inquisition tribunal at Évora, he abruptly disappeared from the documentary record.

Domingos never made it to Bragança to serve out the terms of his exile, or at least that is the way it appears in the documents. Under normal circumstances, the tribunal at Coimbra would have sent a note to Évora acknowledging that he arrived there safely. Likewise, the Inquisitorial notary at Bragança would have sent a note to the tribunal at Coimbra confirming Domingos' arrival to serve the terms of his exile. No such records exist. Nor does Domingos' name appear again in the records for any of the Portuguese Inquisition tribunals in the years immediately following his exile order.[14] If, indeed, he remained in Portugal, he ceased his healing practices or concealed them well, neither of which seems likely. Nevertheless, it is possible that the documentary records from Coimbra were simply misplaced and Domingos lived out the rest of his days in Bragança in quiet, solitary misery. Even more improbable, Domingos might have absconded from his penitential obligations, fleeing toward the coast and out into the relative safety of the Atlantic. For those insistent on holding onto the image of a defiant, irascible Domingos, this ending holds great appeal. Unfortunately, history rarely adheres to such uncomplicated romanticism. The likeliest scenario explaining Domingos' fate is far grimmer. At around forty years old, he was no longer a young man. He had suffered more than ten grueling years of slavery and spent more than half of his seven years as a "freed" man in ecclesiastical jails. This accumulation of hardship and physical abuse may have finally taken its toll. Given the apparent absence of any record of Domingos in Portugal after his release from jail in Évora in November 1749, it seems most likely that he perished before arriving in Coimbra, unaccounted for and unrecorded.

Whatever Domingos' ultimate fate, it seems appropriate that he disappeared into obscurity, for that is precisely the condition to which he had been reduced. He and the blind girl in Salvador shared in the same existential dilemma at the same time on different continents. They, along with thousands of other Africans from the Bight of Benin, were the subjects of interconnected imperial processes that repeatedly and systematically plunged members of families and communities into empty solitude—as displaced refugees in war-torn Dahomey, as beasts of burden on Brazilian sugar plantations, as criminal exiles in Portuguese backwaters. The imperial designs of Dahomey and Portugal worked together with remarkable synergy in the eighteenth-century Atlantic world. In the context of broader Atlantic studies, it is crucial to recognize the extent to which Dahomey's diplomatic, economic, and military strength rendered it a vital imperial player alongside Portugal and other European powers. To ignore African imperial expansion is to neglect an important aspect of Atlantic history. At the same time, we must recognize that for the displaced, diseased, and famished victims of empire, it was difficult to disentangle the ruptures of warfare in Dahomey from those of enslavement in Brazil or even criminal exile in Portugal. Each of these ruptures had its own particular, devastating impacts, but the symptoms of social alienation, physical hardship, and hunger were strikingly similar in all of these places. The question of how to solve these widespread ailments was one that, for the sake of survival, consumed nearly all imperial subjects.

Most people from the Bight of Benin understood community health to emanate from a unity of ancestors and kin, offering reciprocal benefits to all who sacrificed for the greater good. The seat of worldly power resided in those who could most effectively harness the powers of the living *and* the deceased, relieving people of their most pressing physical and social ills. Dahomean Ambassador Churumá Nadir underscored the crucial ties between spiritual propitiation and temporal political legitimacy when he made public sacrifices of "birds" (chickens?) to King Tegbesu, highlighting the "felicity of his governance." Yet as was the case under Tegbesu's father, Agaja, these sacrificial offerings were made solely on behalf of the king and his royal descendants. Instead of appealing to the spirit world for the prosperity of its subjects, the Dahomean monarchy attempted to monopolize this power for its own political purposes. In essence, the monarchy hijacked ancestors and voduns to serve the narrow interests of imperial expansion. One way for Dahomey's alienated subjects to restore their communities was to reclaim their histories, seizing outlawed forms of spirit possession, divination, therapy, and healing from their imperial usurpers.

This imperative for regeneration did not die during the Middle Passage. If anything, the atomizing impacts of enslavement reinforced the necessity of creating new communities out of the ashes of the old. Domingos Álvares came of age in a world charged with social and political strife—a world where imperial expansion collapsed into warfare, displacement, famine, and slavery. The kings of Dahomey were illegitimate, not because they ruled ruthlessly, enslaving thousands, but rather because they violated the principles of hierarchy, community building, and spiritual reciprocity that had defined generations of history in the Bight of Benin. These had been unceremoniously replaced by a politics of royal greed and expansion. Instead of "healing the land," Dahomean kings were systematically polluting it.[15] When Domingos was forcibly removed from Dahomey to Portugal, he found little to distinguish the two empires in terms of their impacts on subjects and slaves. The daily struggles to survive Portugal's voracious economic appetite remained virtually the same as the struggles to survive the expansionist appetite of Dahomey. And just as in Dahomey, the solutions to these afflictions were circumscribed by imperial institutions—monarchy, mercantilism, and centralized religion. For Domingos and others like him, the best way to regenerate communities and restore rightful rulers was through divination and healing.

The broader implications of histories of African healing like that of Domingos can be found in their presumed conflicts with Western and Atlantic "modernities"—capitalism, colonialism, monotheism, state formation, biomedicine, and so on. Recent scholarship on Africa demonstrates that healing and spirit mediumship are deeply implicated in historical ruptures covering hundreds, even thousands, of years of history. For example, there have been at least four reconfigurations of healing practices in the Great Lakes region of East Africa going back to the first millennium, each informed by a shifting constellation of environmental, economic, political, and social forces. Healing retains its salience and remains thoroughly "modern" through negotiation and adaptation to the changing world; yet as a part of these transformations, certain "bundles of meaning and practice" from the deep past survive across the *longue durée*, providing a persistent and durable resource for mediating change. Thus, the assumed boundaries between the modern and the premodern, the colonial and the precolonial, become conflated in ways that demand a fuller understanding of the earliest histories. In this formulation, healing emerges as a critical prism for translating African histories writ large.[16]

These regional approaches to healing in Africa across long swaths of time can be fruitfully compared to the shifts demanded by the Atlantic enslavement of Gbe-speaking healers in eighteenth-century Dahomey. In many respects, the experiences of diaspora healers in the Middle Passage represent a sort of "superconductor" for the dialogic tensions and ruptures outlined in the linking of Africa's deep past to its more recent histories. Literally in a matter of weeks, healers could be thrust from the chaos and warfare of imperial Dahomey to forced labor and enslavement in colonial America, as unnatural and abrupt a departure as one might imagine. Joining these enslaved healers were dozens, even hundreds, of their allies and followers who shared in the tumultuous history that led to their enslavement.[17] Arriving in the Americas, many healers found that their influence faded quickly under the crushing pressures of slavery and European colonial structures. Some became the victims of physical assault, maiming, and death. Others were forcibly isolated from the groups of Africans and their descendants that might provide the foundation for new communities. However, others refused to be vanquished, carrying with them crucial "bundles of meaning and practice," endowing them with new relevance and urgency, sometimes even reconstituting therapeutic communities in their new American homes.

The decision of slaves to draw upon African discourses of health and healing was neither arbitrary nor rote. Enslaved Africans inherited these discourses from the past, but they made "an active decision to say that they are meaningful at this moment, to select a particular form of discourse as opposed to other possible forms, and to shape the inherited language anew to explain current problems."[18] African healing transcended the simple treatment of individual physical ailments, encompassing collective ideas about a wide range of human conflicts and interactions—cultural, social, economic, and, of course, political. By tracing the movement of this capacious conceptual category across various African, American, and European borders, we can more easily discern complex ambiguities in the *processes* of historical transformation. In this way, the Atlantic world becomes an ideal laboratory for gauging what was durable and what was not in the transformations wrought by the imperial forces of warfare, capitalism, and the Atlantic slave trade. As the receptacle for this accumulated knowledge of health and healing, Domingos Álvares was uniquely qualified to interpret and make sense of the radical transformations of his time.

In Dahomey, healing transformed in response to Dahomean brigandage and warfare. Adherence to local spirits, like Sakpata, expanded and strengthened as the Dahomean military drove people into flight and exile. Fearing the growing power of certain displaced healers and vodun priests, Dahomean King Agaja banished people like Domingos Álvares to the Atlantic slave trade in the 1720s and 1730s. Persistent devotion to Sakpata, divination with *gbo*, ancestral invocations with *asen*, and so on suggest a large concentration of Gbe speakers in Brazil who, despite their persecution and enslavement for these practices in Dahomey, continued to view healing as the most effective means of addressing physical, social, and political ills, including those associated with enslavement. Resistance to everyday conditions in Brazil was at once new and a continuation of similar struggles against Agaja. In this way, the history of the Gbe-speaking region became integral to the history of Brazil and the broader Atlantic world.

Of course, Portuguese slaveholders were also implicated in this continuing Gbe-Brazilian history. Slave masters embraced African authority over disease and illness, calling upon Gbe healers to cure their slaves and even their loved ones. Yet slaveholders understood and feared the implications of Gbe power, isolating their diviner/healer slaves as much as possible from the vehicles of spiritual sustenance, especially kith and kin. Individual cures on the master's behalf were one thing; collective therapies for groups of enslaved Africans were quite another. In much the same way that King Agaja feared the political power of healers, slave masters also believed that their authority could be undermined by popular, charismatic healers. This was especially true in rural, sugar-growing regions, where a planter's ability to control his slaves was considered essential to social order. Thus, planters tried to isolate enslaved healers, containing their power. Where these attempts failed, slave masters either jailed them or sold them away, fearing their potential challenges.

In urban areas like Rio de Janeiro, where social boundaries were often more fluid than in rural areas, new possibilities emerged. Because healing skills were potentially lucrative in the urban setting, relationships between masters and slaves were sometimes more akin to those of patrons and clients. Indeed, no less a figure than the governor of the captaincy brokered Domingos' sale to a master eager to capitalize on his skills. Domingos gained the freedom to travel the city healing, collecting medicines, and building a clientele. His master even arranged for him to have his own house, a rented dwelling in the western part of the city. In return, Domingos earned his master a healthy sum of money. Eventually, Domingos saved enough on his own account to purchase his manumission, but freedom under the law meant the loss of his master's patronage and protection. As a result, Domingos became more vulnerable to prosecution by Church authorities, who viewed his increasing social and political power as a threat. Ironically, Domingos possessed greater "freedom" when he was the slave of a powerful, politically connected master than when he was legally freed and subject to the unimpeded surveillance and harassment of Church officials, who eventually placed him in shackles and dispatched him to Portugal. In this way, even the borders between slavery and freedom were sometimes blurred in the Atlantic world.

Domingos' arrival in Portugal in 1742, along with two other African-Brazilian exiles, reminds us of yet another way that the presumed borders of the Atlantic and colonial worlds were sometimes porous. As much as they tried, the Portuguese could not contain the miserable effects of African slavery to the colonies; these corrosive strands were always intertwined with the most hallowed of metropolitan institutions, including the Catholic Church. The Inquisition perpetuated the "sins" of Africa and Brazil onto Portugal, embodied by the African-Brazilian criminal exiles that arrived in Lisbon in a small but steady stream over the course of the colonial period. Those who were healers continued to heal. While in Portugal,

Domingos fused his African understandings of divination and healing onto Portuguese folk remedies and myths, thoroughly convincing some of his clients of his powers, while at the same time nourishing his desperate bid to survive.

In the end, Portuguese institutional power managed to neutralize Domingos and many others like him, but not before these Africans made a profound impact on the intellectual discourse of the Atlantic world. These African intellectuals offered an alternative language of health and healing that simultaneously defied the socioeconomic outcomes of imperialism and sought ingenious translations of them. The ambiguities and apparent contradictions embedded in this discourse were the natural outgrowth of political conflict and compromise that emerged in new communities. By challenging the mercantilist and expansionist expressions of imperialism, while at the same time weaving itself into the fabric of colonial slave society, this alternative political discourse of health and healing revealed that the "capitalist empire . . . turned out not to be so consistently capitalist after all, bureaucratic rule not so consistently bureaucratic, the making of colonial subjects not so consistent in their ideas of what kind of subject was to be produced."[19] These conclusions are not meant to endorse healing as the most viable solution to the historical problems of capitalism, slavery, and colonialism. Rather, they are meant to show that through the lens of health and healing we can witness the fragmentation of European colonial ideologies, as well as African communal ones. These ideologies were never pristinely European or African so much as they were Atlantic, braided together in ways that made them both mutually distinctive and mutually constitutive of one another.

Where Africans figure in Atlantic world histories, emphasis generally rests on their adoption of European and American legal mechanisms, commercial forms, and revolutionary ideas. To be sure, many Africans applied their creative energies to making these categories their own. Yet such emphases often rest on the a priori assumption that African categories would become folded into Atlantic and American ones rather than constituent of them. Regardless of intent, these approaches reify the idea that Atlantic "modernity" was contingent on a sort of untrammeled civilizing process in which individual rights replaced those of ancestors and kin, capital accumulation replaced reciprocal exchange, states replaced statelessness, monotheism (God) replaced polytheism (ancestors/spirits), biological science replaced herbal remedies, and so on. In fact, as the history of Domingos' healing practices demonstrates, African and European-

American categories of meaning were often part of the same modernizing thread.[20]

Arguably, discourses of nation-state, capitalism, Christianity, and science eventually won out over others in the broader Atlantic world. But the competition over which discourses would emerge as authoritative was always fiercely contested. Through the Fon-Gbe lens, health and healing amounted to a bundle of powers that Europeans often reduced to "witchcraft." Yet Europeans clearly understood the ways these powers challenged their understandings of religion, science, economy, and politics. As these competing discourses entangled, African ideas became etched into Atlantic ones, informing the development of revolutionary and Enlightenment ideas, so often understood to be derived from a uniquely European "intellectual" heritage. Domingos' sustained attempts to eradicate the afflictions caused by empire, slavery, and mercantilism anticipated the "modern" European anticolonial, abolitionist, and socialist movements by decades, if not centuries. Yet his opposition to these Atlantic ills was not driven by modernist "humanitarian" impulses or ideas of individual "liberty." On the contrary, he persistently sought to reconstitute the "self" through the collective power of ancestors and kin. In this way, the artificial boundaries between "imaginary" spiritual power and "real" social power blurred into a political system with divination and healing firmly at its center.[21]

Unfortunately, the condescension of Atlantic history as enlightened, democratic triumphalism often obscures African epistemologies and ways of being, reducing Africans either to "resistant" cultural anachronisms who fought slavery from essentialist, ethnic barricades or to "finished" Americans who miraculously adapted their African pasts to liberal, revolutionary principles. Each of these approaches represents a neat "modern" morality tale, but neither reflects the chronic vulnerability, serial dislocation, or episodic histories that plagued most Atlantic Africans. To tell these fitful, fragmented stories, one would need to tap into alternate epistemologies of violence, rupture, memory, and the quests for spiritual and communal redemption. These epistemological strands are sewn deeply into the fabric of Atlantic history, yet they remain mostly obscured in the broader tapestry of European and American exceptionalism.

Domingos' ability to collapse time and space into a unity of human and spiritual power defies our understanding of history as chronologically ordered and geographically bound. Yet it was precisely through these epistemologies that he and his followers made sense of Atlantic-world anomie. Whether appealing to Sakpata to deliver his countrymen from the depravities of Agaja or utilizing *gbo* to address the ills of enslavement, Domingos generated sociopolitical power out of seamless dialogues between the living and the dead, staving off the isolation and loneliness wrought by the forces of the Atlantic world. For Domingos and his devotees, the Atlantic became an integrated memoryscape of voduns, deceased ancestors, and living kin whose power could be called upon to repair the broken shards of diaspora. This collective, regenerative power was their Atlantic history.

Africans experienced vulnerability and chronic dislocation more often than others, but they were never alone in these experiences. The alienating forces of empire also impacted soldiers, planters, merchants, ship captains, governors, and even kings. Thus, Domingos divined news from Spain and Portugal, offered good luck charms for those traveling to university in Coimbra, and remedied unknown illnesses for slave masters. In none of these instances did Domingos' clients share in his communal ethos. On the contrary, they reduced African understandings of reciprocity to the crass anonymity of monetary transactions, underscoring their allegiance to the empire of capital. Nevertheless, their use of Domingos' services betrayed uncertainties and fears about the deeply isolating effects of life in the colonies. Some, like his *mulata* mistress Leonor de Oliveira Cruz, seemed to invite African communal censure upon themselves almost as a form of penance, a public acknowledgment of the bitter and corrosive social divisions caused by their inner turmoils. In this way, Domingos not only served as a savvy, charismatic, and efficacious interpreter of the modernizing Atlantic but also held a critical mirror to it, reminding imperial power brokers that they too shared in the "darkness" of the modern world.

In the end, it was Domingos' extraordinary ability to adapt divination and healing to new circumstances—to translate his knowledge to a world of violent and unrelenting change—that is perhaps his most enduring legacy. Imperial power brokers wanted to dismiss him as a superstitious anachronism, but he consistently proved himself to be a socially relevant, progressive, and thoroughly modern figure. Indeed, some of his ideas seem as pertinent today as they were nearly 300 years ago. In a gesture of "modern" religious tolerance, he embraced the healing power of the Catholic Church. He manipulated the "modern" cash economy, healing for slave masters in order to serve the interests of his spiritual community. Embedded in his healing rituals were "modern" scientific and biomedical practices that proved to be efficacious years before Western medicine discovered them. In his lengthy exchange with Inquisitor Manuel Varejão, he proved himself a virtuoso of "modern" philosophical debate, forcing the Catholic priest to consider a spiritual universalism that included African ancestors and deities. Altogether, Domingos' dazzling skills as a priest, psychologist, physician, philosopher, historian, and sociologist placed him at the very forefront of the incipient modern world. At the same time, as the intellectual catalyst and mediator for a diffuse community of African slaves and freedpeople, he embodied the stunning and terrifying potential of their spiritual and social unity. Domingos was quite literally power incarnate. That is why he survives in Portuguese archives—as an exemplar of modernity but also as its fiercest opponent.

There is a strong temptation to reduce Domingos' powers to his remarkable individual skills. To be sure, his story contains elements of an epic, even heroic, history of a "self-made" man. Yet the teleology of the biographical narrative laid out in his Inquisition case, or even in this book, obscures broader imperatives of communal empowerment that structured Domingos' life. Domingos' individual powers derived from his ability to cultivate a collective historical consciousness through language, proverbs, rumors, and jokes, as well as through divination, healing, initiation rituals, and invocations of ancestors. Such expressions often seem contrived, contradictory, or downright illusory. But the "truths" of Atlantic history cannot be confined to a single genre of linear narrativity. Embedded in the convoluted poetics of spirit possession, magic, rumor, and so on were "realities" that powerfully explained the modernizing world. These realities were generated from a wider historical consciousness that bound the natural with the supernatural, the living with the dead, the material present with the imagined past. In the Atlantic, violence, alienation, and individuation reinforced the importance of these connections to other worlds and other times, providing dislocated Africans with the discursive tools to resurrect lost family and friends. Domingos Álvares possessed the specialized knowledge to coordinate this regeneration of kin and community, but the actualization of this knowledge depended entirely on others. In this way, his individual story is the product of a collective historical consciousness, reflecting the struggles, aspirations, successes, and failures of voduns, ancestors, family, and friends across three continents and over many generations. His history ultimately belongs to all of them and to the broader intellectual history of the Atlantic world.

Notes

ABBREVIATIONS

The following abbreviations are used throughout the notes.

ACMRJ
Arquivo da Curia Metropolitana do Rio de Janeiro

ADB/UM
Arquivo Distrital de Braga/Universidade de Minho

AHU
Arquivo Histórico Ultramarino

ANRJ
Arquivo Nacional do Rio de Janeiro

ANTT
Arquivo Nacional da Torre do Tombo, Lisbon

CSB
Congregação de São Bento

TSTD
Eltis et al., Trans-Atlantic Slave Trade Database

INTRODUCTION

1 ANTT, Inquisição de Évora, Processos, No. 7759, ff. 98–98v.
2 See, for example, Dubois, *A Colony of Citizens*; Bennett, *Africans in Colonial Mexico*; de la Fuente, "Slave Law and Claims-Making in Cuba"; Scott, "Public Rights and Private Commerce"; and Landers, *Atlantic Creoles in the Age of Revolutions*.
3 Cañizares-Esguerra, "Entangled Histories," 794. For a similar sentiment, see Games, "Atlantic History." Perhaps the best critique of Atlantic history, generally, is Coclanis, "Drang Nach Osten."
4 The most forceful articulations of Europeanization among coastal Africans can be found in the works of Ira Berlin, Linda Heywood, and John Thornton, although the idea now proliferates across the literature on the Atlantic world. See, for example, Berlin, "From Creole to Africa"; Berlin, *Many Thousands Gone*; Berlin, *Generations of Captivity*; and Heywood and Thornton, *Central Africans, Atlantic Creoles, and the Foundation of the Americas*.

5 Eltis, "Free and Coerced Migrations," 36.

6 Feierman, *Peasant Intellectuals*, 18. Many of the ideas on health and healing that follow in these pages draw on the theoretical insights of Feierman.

7 The meaning of "Mina" identity becomes more salient as Domingos moves forward into the Atlantic world. See chapter 2 for more on "Mina."

8 ANTT, Inquisição de Évora, Processos, No. 7759, ff. 45–48v, testimony of Thereza Arda (August 21, 1742). The ethnonym "Cobú" is a corruption of the Fon "Covénu," meaning "Cové people." Castro, *A língua Mina-Jeje no Brasil*, 131–33.

9 ANTT, Inquisição de Évora, Processos, No. 7759, ff. 59–61, Genealogia (March 15, 1743). It is tempting to conclude that "Nangon" was an expression of Yoruba identity since the term "Nagô" would eventually come to be synonymous with "Yoruba" in the Americas. However, the first use of the term "Nago" occurred in Africa in 1725, just years before Domingos was enslaved. Moreover, Domingos consistently claimed that he was "from Nangon," "born in Nangô," and so on, leaving the strong impression that "Nangon" was a place name rather than an expression of group identity. On the first use of "Nago," see Labat, *Voyage du chevalier Des Marchais*, 2:125–26. Some scholars now argue that the ethnonym "Nagô" emerged only as a refraction from Brazil. See, for instance, Law, "Ethnicity and the Slave Trade," and, more recently, Matory, "The English Professors of Brazil." Biodun Adediran challenges the notion that Yoruba identity only emerged in the nineteenth century, instead arguing that the Yoruba subgroups of the precolonial period consciously shared linguistic, religious, and historical similarities. See Adediran, "Yoruba Ethnic Groups or a Yoruba Ethnic Group?" and, more recently, Adediran, *The Frontier States of Western Yorubaland*.

10 For more on Domingos' various and shifting identities, see Sweet, "Mistaken Identities?"

CHAPTER 1

1 Cowries imported from East Africa were a standard form of currency along the coast. Snelgrave gives the value of the prisoners in shillings. I have converted his estimates to cowries: 5 shillings = 200 cowries, based on Law, *The Slave Coast*, 176. In 1727, the Royal African Company paid the equivalent of 60,000 cowries for a slave. Ibid., 174. Around the same time, an egg cost 20 cowries and a banana 30 cowries on the coast at Jakin. Harms, *The Diligent*, 81.

2 The preceding discussion is based on Snelgrave, *A New Account*, 15–110.

3 Law, "Further Light on Bulfinch Lambe," 216–17; Harms, *The Diligent*, 171.

4 In addition to Snelgrave, see the accounts of Agaja's English slave, Bulfinch Lambe, in Law, "King Agaja of Dahomey."

5 For the social and political history of Dahomey, see Akinjogbin, *Dahomey and Its Neighbors*, and Law, *The Slave Coast*.

6 For a brief description of Tado's history as the cradle of Adja civilization, as well as a summary of the pertinent literature, see Law, *The Slave Coast*, 26–27. The term "Gbe-speaking area" was first coined by Hounkpati B. C. Capo in 1980. See Capo, "Le Gbe est une langue unique." More recently, it has been adopted in Law, *The*

Slave Coast, 21–32, and Parés, *A formação do Candomblé*, 31–38. For the argument that the so-called Slave Coast constitutes a single cultural area, see Lepine, "As metamorfoses de Sakpata," 122.

7   Estimates for the 1710s and 1720s actually ranged as high as 21,500 in a single year. My estimate of 18,000 is a conservative peak figure. For an analysis of the estimated volume of the slave trade during this time, see Law, *The Slave Coast*, 165.

8   Eltis, "The Transatlantic Slave Trade." The TSTD shows 293,269 slaves departing the Bight of Benin in 1700–1725, more than twice any other region. The next closest region, the Gold Coast, sent 123,011 people into slavery. TSTD (accessed on April 27, 2009).

9   Labat, *Voyage du chevalier Des Marchais*, 2:276.

10 Law, *The Slave Coast*, 189.

11 Norris, *Memoirs of the Reign of Bossa Ahádee*, 138; Snelgrave, *A New Account*, 148.

12 On the "Mahee" as a powerful confederacy, see Norris, *Memoirs of the Reign of Bossa Ahádee*, 138.

13 On the meaning of "Mahi," see Anignikin, "Histoire des populations mahi."

14 The first document describing the "Maillais" comes from the French in January 1732; another, referring to the "Maquis," was written by a Portuguese official in September 1732. We can presume that the term was just coming into vogue in the early 1730s since Snelgrave, in his 1732 account of the fall of Jakin, labeled the Mahis "Yahoos." Law, *The Slave Coast*, 19; Snelgrave, *A New Account*, 148.

15 On Mahi as slave territory, see Bergé, "Étude sur le pays Mahi," 723.

16 Akinjogbin, *Dahomey and Its Neighbors*, 83–99; Adediran, *The Frontier States of Western Yorubaland*, 102–10; Adediran, "Ìdáìsà."

17 Bergé, "Étude sur le pays Mahi," 723.

18 On the idea of "meta-ethnicity," see Parés, *A formação do Candomblé*, chapter 1, and for the relationship of meta-ethnicity to "Mahi" more particularly, see ibid., 38–42.

19 Anignikin, "Histoire des populations mahi," 252–53. On the importance of overlapping political, religious, and commercial networks in Mahi, especially in the twentieth century, see Le Meur, "State Making and the Politics of the Frontier in Central Benin."

20 Soares, *Devotos da cor*, 201.

21 For the Russian dolls reference, see Parés, *A formação do Candomblé*, 15.

22 For a fascinating discussion of the etymology and meaning of "vodun," see Blier, *African Vodun*, 37–47.

23 In the 1930s, Bernard Maupoil estimated that between 200 and 600 voduns were worshipped in Dahomey. Maupoil, *La géomancie*, 55.

24 Bosman, *A New and Accurate Description*, 368a.

25 For the reference to the trees, see ibid. These trees, or Loko, were later associated with the medicines that derived from trees. For the thunder vodun, Hevioso, see Anonymous Frenchman, "Relation du Royaume de Judas" (ca. 1715), quoted in Law, *The Slave Coast*, 111.

26 Law, *Ouidah*, 23.

27 Bosman, *A New and Accurate Description*, 369.

28 Snelgrave, *A New Account*, 11–12.

29 Law, "'My Head Belongs to the King.'" Likewise, sacrificed slaves were expected to serve and nourish Agaja's ancestors in the next life, as suggested in the Fon proverb: "As he is about to be sent to the ancestors, a slave is entrusted with a load of powder from King Agaja." This proverb survived into the twentieth century as a statement on the extreme tyranny of Agaja, who fortified his royal ancestors at the expense of servants and, arguably, voduns. See Vignondé, "Slaves and Slavery in the Study of Fon Proverbs."

30 On this myth, see Herskovits and Herskovits, *Dahomean Narrative*, 167–68.

31 See *Doctrina Christiana*. For a general discussion of Christian missions to the Bight of Benin, see Law, "Religion, Trade, and Politics."

32 Herskovits, *Dahomey*, 2:151.

33 On the devotion to the thunder god in early eighteenth-century Ouidah, see Anonymous Frenchman, "Relation du Royaume de Judas" (ca. 1715), quoted in Law, *The Slave Coast*, 111. The migration of voduns was not at all unusual. In another work, Law shows how Hu, the vodun of the sea, was established in Ouidah in the 1680s or 1690s. Forced to flee the Dahomean conquest, Hu was resettled in Ouidah in the 1720s by one of the most prominent families of the region. Law, *Ouidah*, 22–23.

34 The centralization of religious ideas echoed broader attempts to centralize political organization beginning in this period. See Akinjogbin, *Dahomey and Its Neighbors*, and, more recently, the archaeological findings in Monroe, "Dahomey and the Atlantic Slave Trade."

35 On the policy of religious assimilation by Dahomey, see Law, *The Slave Coast*, 332–34.

36 It should be noted that Agaja also eventually adopted Dangbe, the snake, into the pantheon of voduns worshipped at Abomey. See Le Herissé, *L'Ancien Royaume du Dahomey*, 102–3, 110, 243.

37 Snelgrave, *A New Account*, 154.

38 Claude Lepine claims that the first recorded outbreak occurred in 1613. Lepine, "As metamorfoses de Sakpata," 135.

39 On Europeans bringing smallpox to the region, see Parés, *A formação do Candomblé*, 107. For a description of the earliest evidence of smallpox in Egypt, see Hopkins, *Princes and Peasants*.

40 Snelgrave, *A New Account*, 75.

41 Le Herissé, *L'Ancien Royaume du Dahomey*, 128. The exact location of this major shrine in Mahi is uncertain. Differing versions of the story place its origins in Savalu, Dassa Zoumé, or Vedji. It is worth noting that Vedji is less than fifteen miles northeast of Cové, near the city of Ketu. On the origins of the Sakpata shrine in Benin, see Parés, *A formação do Candomblé*, 295–96.

42 Lepine, "As metamorfoses de Sakpata," 135.

43 On the famine that resulted from Dahomey's invasion of Ouidah, see Snelgrave, *A New Account*, 15.

44 On the growth of Sakpata, see Lepine, "As metamorfoses de Sakpata," 135.

45 Bosman, *A New and Accurate Description*, 369.

46 Anonymous Frenchman, "Relation du Royaume de Judas" (ca. 1715), quoted in Law, *The Slave Coast*, 112.

47 Herskovits, *Dahomey*, 2:137.

48 Ibid., 1:289.

49 "*Lecumies barbas*" refers to the Bariba people of Borgu in present-day northern Benin. Sandoval, *De instauranda*, 95–96.

50 Dalzel, *The History of Dahomey*, xviii. Mahee nose piercing was also noted by Portuguese writer Luiz Antonio de Oliveira Mendes in the 1790s. See the transcription in Silva, "A memória histórica," 278.

51 Bosman, *A New and Accurate Description*, 353.

52 Dalzel, *The History of Dahomey*, xviii.

53 Domingos' parents' names are rendered twice in the Inquisition documents by different scribes, once during a genealogical examination in Lisbon on March 15, 1743, and again during a similar examination in Évora on October 25, 1747. Domingos' mother's name is consistently written as Oconon in both documents; however, his father's name is somewhat less clear. In the earlier document, the scribe appears to have hesitated over the spelling. The first two letters, "Af," are easily discernible, as are the last three, "age." In between is a malformed, ink-blotted letter that could be an "m," "n," or "u." In the later document, the father's name is more clearly written. At first glance, it appears as Afnaje; however, upon closer examination of the scribe's writing style, the "n" may just as easily be a "u." Whether Afnaje or Afuaje, the Portuguese phonetic renderings of Domingos' spoken words are strikingly close to Avimanje. ANTT, Inquisição de Évora, Processos, No. 7759, ff. 59–61, Genealogia (March 15, 1743), and ff. 260–261v, Genealogia (October 25, 1747).

54 Herskovits, *Dahomey*, 2:140 (n. 1).

55 Ibid., 142.

56 The meaning of "Avimanje" and the explanation for its connection to Sakpata come from Luis Nicolau Parés' oral interviews and field notes from Benin. Parés generously shared his notes with me in an email (November 21, 2008).

57 See, for instance, the fascinating exchange between priests, Pai Euclides of Brazil and Avimandje-non of Benin, in the award-winning Brazilian documentary, *Atlântico Negro—Na Rota dos Orixás* (1998), directed by Renato Barbieri.

58 On Bahia, see Parés, *A formação do Candomblé*, 297, and Carvalho, *Gaiaku Luiza*, 85, 124, 152, 154. In oral history of Candomblé Jeje in Rio de Janeiro, an enslaved woman from Allada, Gaiaku Rosena, founded the Terreiro do Pó Dabá in the Saúde neighborhood. Leadership then passed to her daughter, Adelaide do Espírito Santo, and eventually to a woman named Joana de Cruz de Avimadjé, who transferred the *terreiro* to the neighborhood of Coelho da Rocha.

59 Herskovits, *Dahomey*, 2:187–88.

60 In Fon, one often places the letter "O" in front of words beginning with consonants. The word "*kó*" = "earth," and "*nŏ*" = "mother of" or "possessor of." Segurola, *Dictionnaire Fon-Français*, 2:448, 1:298, 2:408. Also, in a 1934 list of principal deities worshipped in the Agonli-Cové region, a French colonial observer noted that Sakpata was also known as "Docounon." Mensan, "Le culte des fétiches dans la région de Zagnanado," 19.

61 "*Bo*" from "gbo" = "empowerment object." "*Kóo*" = "earth." "*Non*" = "possessor/mother of." Thus, the literal translation of "Bokonon" is "possessor of empowered

objects from the earth." For "Bokónò" as "diviner," see Segurola, *Dictionnaire Fon-Français*, 1:95.

62 Herskovits, *Dahomey*, 2:208–12.

63 Ibid., 259–60.

64 As we will see in chapter 6, there is strong evidence to suggest that enslaved *gbo* diviners continued to ply their trade in Brazil.

65 Parés, *A formação do Candomblé*, 135.

66 Herskovits, *Dahomey*, 2:175. See also the 1797 account of Father Vicente Ferreira Pires, who wrote that the "office of Fetisher Parents" passed "from husband to wife, from father to children, in a manner that it always stays in one family." Pires, *Viagem de África*, 93.

67 Herskovits, *Dahomey*, 2:188.

68 Snelgrave, *A New Account*, 129.

69 Dalzel, *The History of Dahomey*, v.

70 Herskovits, *Dahomey*, 2:63.

CHAPTER 2

1 Harms, *The Diligent*, 229–30.

2 Bosman, *A New and Accurate Description*, 489. Snelgrave also observed that "these poor People are generally under terrible Apprehensions upon their being bought by white Men, many being afraid that we design to eat them." Snelgrave, *A New Account*, 163.

3 Harms, *The Diligent*, 252.

4 Iroko, "Cauris et esclaves," 199. For an expanded examination of the economic meanings embedded in such an interpretation, see Austen, "The Moral Economy of Witchcraft."

5 In a similar fashion, traders "read" the bodies of female slaves to determine their ages. In Portuguese documents, women who had a "fallen breast [*peito caido*]" were considered the age equivalents of "bearded" men. For designations of "fallen breast" women, see the inventory of the Portuguese slave ship *Nossa Senhora da Thalaia e Santo Antônio* in Filho, *Negócios coloniais*, 2:170–84. This slave voyage is described in further detail below.

6 Labat, *Voyage du chevalier Des Marchais*, 2:131–32. English slave trader John Atkins also noted the Portuguese preference for child slaves. In 1735, he wrote: "The Portuguese, who trade hither from Brasil, chuse their Cargoes all Boys and Girls, if they can." Atkins, *A Voyage to Guinea*, 177.

7 On Dahomey's preference for gold after 1727, see Law, *The Slave Coast*, 307–8. In 1731, Brazilian sugar and tobacco planters in Pernambuco complained bitterly about the trade in gold and diamonds on the Mina Coast. See, for instance, AHU, Conselho Ultramarino, Pernambuco, Caixa 42, Documento 3767 (October 28, 1731).

8 Thomas Wilson, quoted in Law, *The Slave Coast*, 308.

9 French, Dutch, and English traders recognized "Portuguese slaves" as superior in quality. See Harms, *The Diligent*, 248, and Law, *The Slave Coast*, 204–5. On Agaja's preference for gold, see ibid., 307–8.

10 Law, *The Slave Coast*, 205; Law, *Ouidah*, 130; Harms, *The Diligent*, 152, 248.

11 Letter from viceroy of Brazil, Vasco Fernandez Cesar de Menezes, April 29, 1730, quoted in Verger, *Fluxo e refluxo*, 148.

12 Snelgrave, *A New Account*, 125. Snelgrave later reiterated that "the Dahomes using no Trade but that of War, few Negroes are now brought down to be sold to the Europeans." Ibid., 130.

13 Viceroy of Brazil, October 12, 1728, quoted in Verger, *Fluxo e refluxo*, 146–47.

14 Thomas Wilson, quoted in Law, *Ouidah*, 140.

15 West India Company 111: Des Bordes to Assembly of X, September 17, 1738, quoted in Van Dantzig, *The Dutch and the Guinea Coast*, 338.

16 AHU, Conselho Ultramarino, Pernambuco, Caixa 39, Documento 3477 (July 11, 1729), Carta do provedor da Fazenda Real da Capitania de Pernambuco, João do Rego Barros, ao rei (D. João V) remetendo relação do que renderan os direitos das embarcações que vieram da Costa da Mina ao porto de Pernambuco.

17 Viceroy of Brazil, April 29, 1730, quoted in Verger, *Fluxo e refluxo*, 148–49. In fact, some of the voyages from Bahia approached two years in length. See, for instance, the journey of the *Nossa Senhora da Piedade e São Felix*, which departed Bahia on June 23, 1729, and returned on May 25, 1731. See also the *Santo Inácio e São Francisco Xavier*, which departed Bahia on February 20, 1730, and returned on December 15, 1731. TSTD (accessed on April 22, 2009).

18 West India Company 138: Hertogh Correspondence, Hendrik Hertogh to Jan Pranger, June 12, 1730, and June 26, 1731, quoted in Van Dantzig, *The Dutch and the Guinea Coast*, 249, 255–56.

19 The pioneering study on social death is Patterson, *Slavery and Social Death*.

20 For a fine critique of the scholarly focus on social death, see Brown, "Social Death and Political Life."

21 Snelgrave, *A New Account*, 58–59.

22 Skertchly, *Dahomey as It Is*, 6.

23 Harms, *The Diligent*, 228.

24 For the most recent scholarly treatment, see Smallwood, *Saltwater Slavery*. Slave narratives include those of Olaudah Equiano, Ottobah Cuguano, and Mahommah Buquaqua. The best-known film depiction of the Middle Passage is Steven Spielberg's *Amistad* (1997).

25 For example, the French ship *Diligent* departed Jakin on November 27, 1731, and only arrived in Martinique on March 14, 1732, a journey of some fifteen weeks. Harms, *The Diligent*, 264, 333. Snelgrave's 1727 trip to Antigua lasted seventeen weeks. Snelgrave, *A New Account*, 109–10. According to the TSTD, the average number of days for the Middle Passage from the Bight of Benin to the Caribbean in the years 1726–50 was 105.6, or roughly three and a half months. TSTD (accessed on June 8, 2009).

26 Mendes, *Discurso academico*, quoted in Conrad, *Children of God's Fire*, 22.

27 Storms could also cause severe interruptions to the trade, as was the case in 1730 when two Brazil-bound slave ships (one from Pernambuco) were blown from their anchors, forcing the ships to sail prematurely, leaving their captains and some crew

members in tents on the Jakin coast. Hertogh to Pranger, June 12, 1730, quoted in Van Dantzig, *The Dutch and the Guinea Coast,* 250.

28 Verger, *Fluxo e refluxo,* 690.

29 For example, in 1731 the *Diligent* took twelve days to pass from Jakin to São Tomé. Harms, *The Diligent,* 264, 277. See also the description of the *Nossa Senhora da Thalaia e Santo Antônio* below. It is worth noting that the duration of the Middle Passage for Portuguese slave ships leaving the Central African ports of Angola was generally ten to fourteen days less than for those leaving the Mina Coast. This difference is roughly the amount of time it took Mina traders to escape the Guinea Current. On the comparative duration of the passage for slave ships in the nineteenth century, see Florentino, Ribeiro, and Silva, "Aspectos comparativos," 113.

30 Ultimately, only 109 of these slaves sold. One young man was reserved for Pinheiro's personal use in Lisbon. One old man was completely blind and unmarketable. And a third young man died of disease while waiting to be sold in Rio.

31 The most expensive male slaves in this cargo sold for 150 mil-réis.

32 All of the pertinent documents on the slave voyage of the *Nossa Senhora da Thalaia e Santo Antônio* can be found in Filho, *Negócios coloniais,* 2:50–52, 170–84.

33 Average numbers of slaves arriving in Pernambuco can be found in AHU, Conselho Ultramarino, Pernambuco, Caixa 42, Documento 3786 (January 16, 1732), and Caixa 44, Documento 4007 (June 21, 1733). On the *Nossa Senhora da Vida e Santo Antônio,* see AHU, Conselho Ultramarino, Pernambuco, Caixa 39, Documento 3477 (July 11, 1729).

34 Mott, *Rosa Egipcíaca,* 15. For the island of "Sambula" as the equivalent of Sherbro Island and its inhabitants as "Sambores," see Adams, *Heroes of Maritime Discovery,* 68.

35 Mortality rates on the passage from the Bight of Benin to Rio were 8.2 percent. TSTD (accessed on June 8, 2009).

36 For more on European shipboard "order" and "science" versus African disorientation, see Smallwood, *Saltwater Slavery.* The ideas here are drawn from ibid., 98–100, 126–52.

37 TSTD (accessed on April 27, 2009). This 21 percent rate of shipboard revolt on the Slave Coast in the late 1720s was more than double the 10 percent average for the entire trade during its 400-year history. For a more detailed accounting of shipboard revolts, see Richardson, "Shipboard Revolts."

38 On the *Parfait* revolt, as well as other insurrections aboard French slave ships, see Harms, *The Diligent,* 270.

39 See, for instance, the 1731 case of the English slave ship *Katherine,* which reported that two captives were killed and four seriously wounded in an onboard insurrection at Jakin. Richardson, "Shipboard Revolts," 74.

40 The scholarship on children in the African slave trade remains underdeveloped. To my knowledge, none of this scholarship takes into account the developmental impacts of orphanage and enslavement on young children. Though it is beyond the skill set of most historians to address childhood psychology, it seems safe to conclude that the combined effects of witnessing warfare, experiencing orphanage and enslavement, enduring the Middle Passage, and so on were tantamount to the

worst forms of child abuse and must have taken a devastating toll on the psyches of these children, marking them for the rest of their lives. For a recent anthology on the topic of child slavery, see Campbell, Miers, and Miller, *Children in Slavery*.

41 In one of the most remarkable cases of shipboard community building, sixty Africans who arrived in Rio de Janeiro in 1821 aboard the Portuguese ship *Emilia* returned together to Nigeria fifteen years later. See Hawthorne, "Being Now, as It Were, One Family."

42 Koster, *Travels in Brazil*, 182. On *malungos*, see Slenes, "Malungu ngoma vem!" and Sweet, *Recreating Africa*, 33–34.

43 Saint-Méry, *Description topographique*, 1:36.

44 Labat, *Nouveau voyage*, 4:138–41. Other slave ships encountered similar difficulties with African forms of sorcery and witchcraft. In 1751, Englishman John Newton captained the ship *Duke of Argyle* from the Windward Coast to the Caribbean. During the Middle Passage, the enslaved captives "conveyed some of their country fetishes . . . or talismans into [a cask of drinking water], which they had the credulity to suppose must inevitably kill all who drink of it." Newton, *The Journey of a Slave Trader*, 55–56.

45 Suzanne Preston Blier notes that the Fon imagery of the enslaved prisoner is evoked most clearly in the concept of *kannumon*, or "things belonging [in] cords." Antidotes for such terror and helplessness often included powerful objects that were bound or tied (*bocio*). Domingos' predicament in the slave ship must have been doubly frustrating. Not only was he rendered incapable of producing a response to the suffering of slavery, but he was the object of someone else's tying and binding, as Europeans co-opted his corporeal power. Blier, *African Vodun*, 26–27.

46 On the basic outlines of this crisis, see Palacios, "Peasantry and Slavery in Brazil," esp. 33–46.

47 Schwartz, "Plantations and Peripheries," 97.

48 Florentino, Ribeiro, and Silva, "Aspectos comparativos," 83–84.

49 AHU, Conselho Ultramarino, Pernambuco, Caixa 33, Documento 3076 (June 14, 1726). See also AHU, Conselho Ultramarino, Pernambuco, Caixa 42, Documento 3739 (September 4, 1731).

50 AHU, Conselho Ultramarino, Pernambuco, Caixa 42, Documento 3767 (October 28, 1731).

51 AHU, Conselho Ultramarino, Pernambuco, Caixa 45, Documento 4031 (July 4, 1733).

52 AHU, Conselho Ultramarino, Pernambuco, Caixa 43, Documento 3860 (November 23, 1731).

53 For slave trade data for 1726–31, see AHU, Conselho Ultramarino, Pernambuco, Caixa 42, Documento 3786 (January 16, 1732). For 1732, see AHU, Conselho Ultramarino, Pernambuco, Caixa 44, Documento 4007 (June 21, 1733).

54 AHU, Conselho Ultramarino, Pernambuco, Caixa 47, Documento 4194 (August 26, 1734).

55 AHU, Conselho Ultramarino, Pernambuco, Caixa 43, Documento 3860 (November 23, 1731).

56 Costa, *Anais Pernambucanos*, 116.

57 Menezes, "Idéa da população da capitania de Pernambuco," 21–24.

58 AHU, Conselho Ultramarino, Pernambuco, Caixa 31, Documento 2826 (June 30, 1725).

59 AHU, Conselho Ultramarino, Pernambuco, Caixa 37, Documento 3347 (August 4, 1728).

60 Of the 35 *engenhos* in Itamaracá, all 6 on the island were functioning; 7 of the 29 in the inland parishes were inoperable. "Informação geral da capitania de Pernambuco," 478.

61 AHU, Conselho Ultramarino, Pernambuco, Caixa 42, Documento 3738 (September 4, 1731).

62 AHU, Conselho Ultramarino, Pernambuco, Caixa 67, Documento 5683 (March 18, 1748).

63 On the value of sugar *engenhos* in eighteenth-century Brazil, see Schwartz, *Sugar Plantations*, 212–18.

64 On Engenho Tapirema, see AHU, Conselho Ultramarino, Pernambuco, Caixa 20, Documento 1948 (November 19, 1703), and Caixa 42, Documento 3824 (March 26, 1732). The debt on Tapirema remained unpaid into the middle of the eighteenth century. See AHU, Conselho Ultramarino, Pernambuco, Caixa 79, Documento 6590 (May 20, 1755).

65 In addition to performing field labor, slaves who worked on large *engenhos* with mills were often forced to work in the mills at night, even after having toiled in the fields all day. For descriptions of sugar labor, see Antonil, *Cultura e opulência*, and Schwartz, *Sugar Plantations*, 139–49.

66 Costa, *Anais Pernambucanos*, 67. The Crown issued similar orders to planters in Bahia in 1701. See Schwartz, *Sugar Plantations*, 137.

67 Antonil, *Cultura e opulência*, 128.

68 See, for instance, the Royal Letter of April 29, 1719, in which the king ordered that the bishop of Pernambuco be informed of all slaves who had not been indoctrinated or baptized. Costa, *Anais Pernambucanos*, 68.

69 There is a rich literature on the impacts of Catholicism on African slaves, particularly those from Kongo and Angola. See the many works of John K. Thornton, as well as Sweet, *Recreating Africa*. The impacts of Catholic teachings on East and West Africans in the Americas are less well chronicled.

70 ADB/UM, CSB, 321 (unpaginated), Treslado da sindicação que se tirou do Muito Reverendo Padre Mestre ex-Abbe Frei Salvador dos Santos (October 20, 1750). For other examples of cruelty by priests, see Sweet, *Recreating Africa*, 75–76, 222.

71 There are numerous examples of individual priests speaking out on behalf of slaves. The best-known published accounts are Benci, *Economia cristã*; Antonil, *Cultura e opulência*; and Rocha, *Ethiope resgatado*.

72 The king rejected the proposals on two grounds. First, he argued that the masters released their slaves assuming they were incurable and not to kill them. The king concluded that "it was better to remedy something than nothing at all." Second, turning over slaves to those who cured them would create many conflicts. AHU, Conselho Ultramarino, Pernambuco, Caixa 23, Documento 2134 (June 7, 1710).

73 Pereira's race and social status are not delineated in the extant documents; however,

in other regions of Brazil, we know that slaves served as the godparents of adult Africans in more than 70 percent of cases. See Schwartz, *Sugar Plantations*, 411.

74 *Constituições Primeiras do Arcebispado da Bahia feitas e ordinadas pelo Illustrissimo e Reverendissimo Senhor D. Sebastião da Vide* (1707), quoted in Conrad, *Children of God's Fire*, 155.

75 On rituals of initiation in vodun generally, see Herskovits, *Dahomey*, 2:111–27. Blood was also sprinkled on the heads of some initiates. For initiation into the congregation of Sakpata, see ibid., 179–88. It is important to note that instruction in the worship of voduns could take months, and the culminating rituals of initiation an entire week.

76 The full quotation from the Catholic Catechism of the Council of Trent is, "When salt is put into the mouth of the person to be baptized, it evidently imports that, by doctrines of faith and the gift of grace, he should be delivered from the corruption of sin, experience a relish for good works, and be delighted with the food of divine wisdom."

77 On salt as a "necessity of life" in Dahomey, see Herskovits, *Dahomey*, 1:125.

78 *Constituições Primeiras*, quoted in Conrad, *Children of God's Fire*, 156.

79 Antonil, *Cultura e opulência*, 124–27.

80 For more on African responses to Catholicism in Brazil, see Sweet, *Recreating Africa*.

81 It remains unclear exactly why Domingos was sent to Recife. The most logical explanation is that when Lázaro Maciel de Azevedo took possession of his rental portion of Tapirema, some of Carvalho's slaves became superfluous. It is also possible that Domingos was sent to Recife to avoid Tapirema's creditors or was sold to Carvalho's sister in an effort to raise funds for the property. Either way, the exchange illustrates the social and economic ties that bound the "planter nobility" of Brazil's sugar-growing northeast. For the family connections of Domingos' masters, see the entries for the sisters, "D. Sebastianna de Carvalho" and "D. Antonia da Cunha," in Fonseca, *Nobliarchia Pernambucana*, 1:200. For the descendants of Manoel Cavalcante de Albuquerque Lacerda, who continued as owners at Tapirema after Sebastianna Carvalho's death, see ibid., 418–19.

CHAPTER 3

1 Estimates of Recife's colonial population vary widely. In 1749, a Church census of those taking communion in Recife counted fewer than 8,000 people. "Informação geral da capitania de Pernambuco," 407. However, it seems likely that this census excluded children and slaves. By 1774, the population grew to 17,934, but, again, slaves appear to have been excluded. Menezes, "Idéa da população da capitania de Pernambuco," 102. According to Antônio Paul Rezende, in 1711 the actual population of Recife was around 16,000; by 1745, the number had jumped to 25,000. Rezende, *O Recife*, 52.

2 For a description of eighteenth-century Recife, see Menezes, "Idéa da população da capitania de Pernambuco," 40–42.

3 "Bando sobre a proibição das pessoas que vendem fazendas pelas ruas, etc.," Regis-

tro de Previsões 03/1 (1769–97), Arquivo Público Estadual de Pernambuco, quoted in Silva, "Na casa, na rua e no rio," 3.

4   AHU, Conselho Ultramarino, Pernambuco, Caixa 43, Documento 3866 (April 25, 1732).

5   See, for example, copies of two letters from King João V written on October 11, 1721, and September 5, 1722, ordering members of the *câmara* to cease the practice, in AHU, Conselho Ultramarino, Pernambuco, Caixa 60, Documento 5180 (September 29, 1744).

6   AHU, Conselho Ultramarino, Pernambuco, Caixa 59, Documento 5040 (April 4, 1743).

7   For the nineteenth century, see Silva, "Na casa, na rua e no rio."

8   The original donatary captain of Pernambuco, Duarte Coelho, granted the lands of Casa Forte to Diogo Gonçalves and Isabel Fróes as a wedding gift in the mid-sixteenth century. In 1645, Casa Forte was the site of one of the most celebrated battles of the Dutch occupation. Pernambucan forces attacked a Dutch column that had imprisoned some of the captaincy's most illustrious women in the *engenho*'s "big house." The Pernambuco army was victorious, freeing the women and imprisoning their Dutch enemies. On Casa Forte, see Costa, *Arredores do Recife*, 51–58. For more on Jacinto de Freitas, see Fonseca, *Nobliarchia Pernambucana*, 1:200.

9   Anonymous Frenchman, "Relation du Royaume de Judas" (ca. 1715), quoted in Law, *The Slave Coast*, 64.

10 Ibid., 65. For further explanation of male control of female labor, see Law, *The Slave Coast*, 63–66.

11 Santos, *Calamidades de Pernambuco*, 12.

12 AHU, Conselho Ultramarino, Pernambuco, Caixa 33, Documento 3039 (March 28, 1726). Altogether, seven men testified to the same effect. These included two plantation owners (*senhores do engenho*) and five small farmers (*lavradores de cana*).

13 ADB/UM, CSB, 138, Estados do Mosteiro de Olinda, 1657–1756, f. 170. On the efficiency of Benedictine properties and the fair treatment of their slaves, see Schwartz, "The Plantations of St. Benedict."

14 ANTT, Inquisição de Évora, Processos, No. 7759, ff. 45–48v, testimony of Thereza Arda (August 21, 1742).

15 For example, between 1660 and 1666, the Benedictine monastery at Olinda paid 144$120 for "medicines and negro curers." ADB/UM, CSB, 138, ff. 49, 87.

16 Only Chango would have been familiar to Domingos since the others are derived from Central African languages, in particular, Kimbundu. All of these names are drawn from a 1761 census of *engenhos* conducted by the governor of Pernambuco. See AHU, Conselho Ultramarino, Pernambuco, Caixa 95, Documento 7501 (February 15, 1761).

17 During this period, the "Costa da Mina" included ports from Elmina to Badagry. According to the TSTD, roughly two-thirds of all Mina slaves arriving in Pernambuco from 1722 to 1732 hailed from the Bight of Benin, especially Jakin and Ouidah; the other third came from the Gold Coast, particularly Elmina. TSTD (accessed on June 8, 2009).

18 ANTT, Inquisição de Évora, Processos, No. 7759, ff. 45–48v, testimony of Thereza Arda (August 21, 1742).

19 On the shared "*língua geral*" in Benin, see Dalzel, *The History of Dahomey*, v and chapter 1.

20 Peixoto, *Obra nova*. For a recent, critical edition of Peixoto's work, see Castro, *A língua Mina-Jeje no Brasil*. It should be noted that Peixoto's Mina dictionary was not the first of its kind. In 1697, a Kimbundu grammar was recorded in Bahia, reflective of the early dominance of Central Africans in Brazil's slave population. See Dias, *A arte da língua de Angola*.

21 Peixoto, *Obra nova*, 15.

22 For a careful examination of the African languages and concepts described by Peixoto, see Yai, "Texts of Enslavement."

23 Peixoto, *Obra nova*, 20. Both *guno* and *gamlimno* appear in a list of Brazilian ethnoracial designations that also includes whites, mulattoes, creoles, Indians, and Angolas.

24 Cobus represent less than 2 percent of the enslaved population in most extant research samples from eighteenth-century Brazil. In his longitudinal study of the demography of Minas Gerais, Laird Bergad finds only .7 percent Cobus in property inventories between 1715 and 1888. Bergad, *Slavery*, 151. A more narrow sample taken by Moacir Maia finds 1.85 percent Cobus in the tax records of Vila do Carmo in 1723. Maia, "Quem tem padrinho não morre pagão," 44. However, an examination of similar records from Tijuco in 1735–36, chronologically much closer to Peixoto's and Domingos' time in Brazil, reveals that, in a sample of 315 slaves, 7.6 percent were Cobus. Cobus were the fourth most-represented group, trailing only the Mina (46 percent), Angola (9.5 percent), and Courano (7.9 percent). Clearly, the Cobu and Courano represented their own distinct and prominent ethnic groups in the 1730s. Among the eighteen other groups represented in the sample, nearly half were from the Bight of Benin, including the Sabaru (4.4 percent), Fao (3.8 percent), Lada (3.2 percent), Nago (2.2 percent), Jeje (1 percent), Catacori, Chambá, and Ayó. See Arquivo Público Mineiro, Seção Colonial, Documentos Encadernados, Codice No. 51, Registro de escravos, vendas, e licenças em Tijuco (1735–36). These documents can be accessed online at http://www.siaapm.cultura.mg.gov.br/modules/brtdocs/viewcat.php?cid=51 (accessed on July 12, 2009).

25 Parés, "Ethnic-Religious Modes of Identification," 187.

26 Peixoto, *Obra nova*, 20. The translation as "white man's vodun" comes from Yai, "Texts of Enslavement," 108.

27 Peixoto, *Obra Nova*, 20.

28 Ibid., 21.

29 Ibid., 32. In vodun, Legba is the mercurial "trickster," master of the crossroads, and gatekeeper whose blessings are sought before any ritual invocation. Though capricious by nature, Legba is not inherently evil, as the "Devil" translation might imply. Interestingly, even though the Portuguese glossed Legba as the chief spirit of evil, their translation of "hell" was much more literal and spiritually benign. The Christian idea of "hell" translated as "*zoume*," meaning "in the fire." Yai, "Texts of Enslavement," 108. See also "zomè," in Segurola, *Dictionnaire Fon-Français*, 2:640.

30 Peixoto, *Obra nova*, 25, 32. It should be noted that my rendering of this "dialogue" is actually drawn from two different parts of Peixoto's work. The first statement regarding the lack of war in "white man's land" stands alone in a section of words and phrases on war and killing. The last three lines stand together in a separate section. What draws the passages together is the discussion of the value of "white man's land [*terra de Branco*]." Other examples from Peixoto that speak to links with Dahomey include the following: "Where did you get married [*filhàhegulialú*]?" "I got married in the Kingdom [meaning Dahomey] [*hegullialô touboume*]." "I got married in this land [*hègulialò toumefi*]" (22). "Your son is already baptized [*vi ecódugê*]?" "He still is not baptized [*e mácodugehâ*]." "He is already baptized [*ecódugê*]" (23).

31 On the Angolan influences in Brazil during the sixteenth and seventeenth centuries, see Alencastro, *O trato dos viventes*, and Sweet, *Recreating Africa*.

32 For an elaboration of Central African rituals in Brazil, see Sweet, *Recreating Africa*, esp. chapters 6–8.

33 On calundu in Pernambuco, see ANTT, Inquisição de Lisboa, Cadernos do Promotor, No. 86, Livro 279, ff. 232, Olinda (September 23, 1716).

34 To my knowledge, the first reference to "Caçûtû," or "Caçuto," in Brazil occurs in a 1720 list of "Rites from Pagan Angola" from Rio de Janeiro. In describing the Angolans in Rio, the author writes: "They adore the Devil in the figure of a goat that they call Caçuto, many of them gathering at night with great noise from *Atabaques* [drums] in their *Senzallas* [slave quarters]." ANTT, Conselho Geral, "Santo Ofício Tomo XXXI" (1720), Livro 272, ff. 123–123v, 235–235v (two copies of the same document in the livro). The reference to "Caçûtû" in Pernambuco comes from the town of Una, near Serinhaém, in 1761. ANTT, Inquisição de Lisboa, Cadernos do Promotor, No. 124, Livro 818, unpaginated, roughly two-thirds through the volume (February 16, 1761).

35 ANTT, Inquisição de Lisboa, Cadernos do Promotor, No. 91, Livro 284, ff. 535–536v, Recife (March 28, 1721), and Livro 297, f. 42, Recife (October 1743).

36 On Jurema, generally, see Wadsworth, "*Jurema* and *Batuque*." For the spread of Jurema in Paraíba in the 1730s, see AHU, Conselho Ultramarino, Pernambuco, Caixa 56, Documento 4884 (July 1, 1741). Its hybrid ritual expression with *pardos*, whites, and so on at Una can be found in ANTT, Inquisição de Lisboa, Processos, No. 6238. Interestingly, one of the common features of Jurema rituals was the appearance of a goat as the culmination of trance. Just as with Caçûtû, the goat sometimes served as the oracle. The fact that Caçûtû and Jurema each appear in the small village of Una only twenty years apart demonstrates the fascinating and complex evolution of healing rituals in the region.

37 ANTT, Inquisição de Lisboa, Processos, No. 597.

38 On the use of *bolsas* in Portugal and its overseas colonies, see Calainho, *Metrópole das mandingas*. See also Souza, *The Devil and the Land of the Holy Cross*, 130–41; Paiva, *Bruxaria e superstição*, 113–14; and Sweet, *Recreating Africa*, 179–86.

39 ANTT, Inquisição de Lisboa, Processos, No. 597.

40 ANTT, Inquisição de Lisboa, Cadernos do Promotor, No. 79, Livro 272, ff. 397–397v.

41 ANTT, Inquisição de Lisboa, Cadernos do Promotor, No. 101, Livro 294, ff. 415–418,

and No. 112, Livro 304, ff. 98–106v. This case eventually devolved into a dispute between secular authorities and the bishop of Pernambuco. After the seven Africans were arrested, the bishop wanted them remitted to Inquisitorial justice; however, secular authorities claimed that there was only "eating and drinking" going on in the house and the Church was overstepping its jurisdictional boundaries. After spending some months in jail, the seven accused were eventually released, to the great protest of the bishop, who claimed that the slave masters conspired with Crown officials to free the accused.

42 ANTT, Inquisição de Lisboa, Processos, No. 14577.

43 ANTT, Inquisição de Évora, Processos, No. 7759, ff. 262–271, testimony of Domingos Álvares, Évora (November 3, 1747).

44 ANTT, Inquisição de Évora, Processos, No. 7759, ff. 272–276, testimony of Domingos Álvares, Évora (November 10, 1747).

45 Information on the place of Domingos' confirmation comes from ANTT, Inquisição de Évora, Processos, No. 7759, ff. 59–61, Genealogia (March 15, 1743). My description of the ceremony is drawn from the standard ritual and liturgical requirements demanded by the Catholic Church. Though the details of Domingos' actual confirmation may have varied somewhat from my description, the spirit of the ceremony would have been the same.

46 Antonil, *Cultura e opulência*, 84.

47 For a treatment of planter attitudes in the Brazilian northeast, see Schwartz, *Sugar Plantations*, 283–94.

48 On the idea of the "unthinkability" of slave actions against their masters, see Trouillot, *Silencing the Past*, 70–107.

49 ANTT, Inquisição de Lisboa, Cadernos do Promotor, No. 99, Livro 292, ff. 386–387 (September 12, 1738).

50 For other accounts of slave-on-slave violence, see Sweet, *Recreating Africa*, 81–82.

51 AHU, Conselho Ultramarino, Pernambuco, Caixa 52, Documento 4563 (July 24, 1738).

52 On the history of Palmares, see the classic work, Carneiro, *O Quilombo dos Palmares*. The best English-language accounts of Palmares are Kent, "Palmares"; Schwartz, "Rethinking Palmares"; and Anderson, "The 'Quilombo' of Palmares." On runaway slave communities in Brazil more generally, see Reis and Gomes, *Liberdade por um fio*.

53 AHU, Conselho Ultramarino, Pernambuco, Caixa 39, Documento 3465 (July 5, 1729).

54 AHU, Codice 260, f. 200, quoted in Silva, "'Nas solidões vastas e assustadoras,'" 138.

55 ANTT, Inquisição de Évora, Processos, No. 7759, ff. 21v–22v, 29–30v, testimony of Caetana Maria do Espírito Santo, Rio de Janeiro (June 14, 1741, and August 18, 1742).

56 Antonil, *Cultura e opulência*, 124.

57 Here, I acknowledge that the "science" of the Enlightenment had not yet emerged; however, scholars of the day recognized that the "natural" properties of plants resulted in consistent medicinal outcomes.

58 For an outstanding articulation of the circularity of the "hall of mirrors," see Lewis, *Hall of Mirrors*.

59 ANTT, Inquisição de Évora, Processos, No. 7759, ff. 45–48v, testimony of Thereza Arda (August 21, 1742).

CHAPTER 4

1 AHU, Conselho Ultramarino, Pernambuco, Caixa 35, Documento 3192 (February 11, 1727).

2 For the completion of the new jail, see AHU, Conselho Ultramarino, Pernambuco, Caixa 43, Documento 3855 (April 20, 1732). On the continuing problem of over-crowding, see AHU, Conselho Ultramarino, Pernambuco, Caixa 48, Documento 4261 (January 24, 1735).

3 The biblical stories of the Ephesians and the Babylonian captivity resonated deeply among Catholic priests ministering to the enslaved in Brazil. Jesuit priest António Vieira, himself of European and African ancestry, delivered the most famous ser-mon invoking these themes in the middle of the seventeenth century in Bahia. Vieira argued that while slave masters owned African bodies, Africans' souls were free. Suffering on earth in the name of God would result in redemption in heaven: "You do not serve as captives, but as free men, because God will pay you for your labor; . . . and you do not obey as slaves, but rather as sons and daughters [of God], because God, to whom you are similar in that fate which He gave you, will make you his heirs." Father António Vieira, quoted in Conrad, *Children of God's Fire*, 170.

4 ANTT, Inquisição de Évora, Processos, No. 7759, ff. 15–16, testimony of Manuel da Costa Soares (June 14, 1741).

5 In 1740, "Manoel da Costa" captained the *Nossa Senhora do Pilar*, carrying more than 350 slaves from the Bight of Benin to Pernambuco. This is the only reference to a Brazilian ship captain during this period that approximates the name Manuel da Costa Soares. TSTD, voyage ID #41056 (accessed on June 8, 2009).

6 Information on Domingos' passage from Recife to Rio comes from ANTT, Inquisi-ção de Évora, Processos, No. 7759, ff. 15–16, 45–48v, testimonies of Manuel da Costa Soares (June 14, 1741) and Thereza Arda (August 21, 1742).

7 According to F. A. Pereira da Costa, Jacinto de Freitas was born in 1680 and died in 1759. Costa, *Arredores do Recife*, 57.

8 White, *Speaking with Vampires*, 70.

9 ANTT, Inquisição de Évora, Processos, No. 7759, ff. 36v–40v, testimony of Leonor de Oliveira Cruz (August 21, 1742).

10 "Gave thanks to God" from ANTT, Inquisição de Évora, Processos, No. 7759, ff. 45–48v, testimony of Thereza Arda (August 21, 1742).

11 See ibid. for Thereza Arda's description of Domingos as "her partner [*parceiro*] in this city [Rio]."

12 Caetana and Domingos speaking "numerous times" from ANTT, Inquisição de Évora, Processos, No. 7759, ff. 29–30v, testimony of Caetana Maria do Espírito Santo (August 18, 1742).

13 The colonial capital of Brazil moved from Salvador to Rio in 1763, after which Rio grew to be the largest city. On the population of Rio, see the various works of Eulália Maria Lahmeyer Lobo, especially *História do Rio de Janeiro*, 1:55. On the population of Brazilian cities from the mid-eighteenth century, see Alden, "Late Colonial Brazil," 288–89.

14 According to a 1779 census, Rio had a slave population of 34.5 percent. Altogether, 55.5 percent of the city's 43,376 inhabitants were nonwhites. "Resumo total da população que existia no anno de 1779."

15 ACMRJ, Nossa Senhora de Candelária and Santíssimo Sacramento, Óbitos (1737–40). Admittedly, this is a small sample (107 properties); however, Mary Karasch's evidence from nineteenth-century Rio mirrors almost exactly the numbers reported here. In a sample of 10,151 households, Karasch found 36,182 slaves, an average of 3.6 per household. Karasch, *Slave Life in Rio de Janeiro*, 62–63.

16 In addition to the inventory evidence presented in table 4.1, see the Soares sample of 397 burials in Candelária between 1724 and 1736. She finds that Africans represented 73 percent of the enslaved population. Soares, *Devotos da cor*, 147.

17 Goulart, *A escravidão africana no Brasil*, 153, 217.

18 Soares, *Devotos da cor*, 150.

19 Ibid., 83.

20 Klein, *The Middle Passage*, 253.

21 There is suggestive evidence from parish records and manumission records from the early 1750s that Mina slaves were disproportionately represented in the freed African population of Rio. Despite being a distinct minority in the Rio slave population, Minas represented 57 percent of manumitted Africans between 1749 and 1754. See Sweet, "Manumission in Rio de Janeiro."

22 Just over ten years later, in 1751, Largo de Santa Rita would be the home of Rosa Egipcíaca, a Courana slave from the Mina Coast whose continuous visions and heretical claims are chronicled in Mott, *Rosa Egipcíaca*.

23 For descriptions of residential housing in eighteenth-century Rio, see Soares, *Devotos da cor*, 140–41. For Largo de Santa Rita more specifically, see Mott, *Rosa Egipcíaca*, 209–12.

24 Soares, *Devotos da cor*, 143. See also Honorato, "Controle sanitário," 14. For the history of slave burials in Rio more generally, especially after the cemetery moved from Santa Rita to Valongo in 1769, see Pereira, *À flor da terra*.

25 On the significance of burial rites in Dahomey, see Herskovits, *Dahomey*, 1:400–402. For an examination of death and "mortuary politics" in Jamaica, see Brown, *The Reaper's Garden*.

26 On the illicit exchanges, see ANTT, Inquisição de Lisboa, Processos, No. 6982. This case is discussed in greater detail in chapter 8.

27 Caetana testified that she lived "on Rua da Prainha, next to the Benedictine Fathers." ANTT, Inquisição de Évora, Processos, No. 7759, ff. 21v–22v, testimony of Caetana do Espírito Santo (August 14, 1741).

28 The word "*quitanda*" comes from the Central African Kimbundu word "*ki-tanda*," meaning "market." In Brazil, the word also encompassed the goods sold in the mar-

ket. Thus, women who "sold *quitandas*" were purveyors of baked goods, sweets, fruits, vegetables, and so on. ANTT, Inquisição de Évora, Processos, No. 7759, ff. 42v–45, testimony of Paula Rosada (August 21, 1742).

29 Ferrez, "O Rio de Janeiro," 163.

30 Ibid. The fear of being eaten by Europeans persisted until the final moment of purchase in Brazil. See chapter 2 for the ways European cannibal myths proliferated in the Bight of Benin.

31 On the transport of living and dead by hammock in eighteenth-century Rio, see Soares, *Devotos da cor*, 140.

32 Moraes, *Chronica geral e minuciosa do imperio do Brazil*, 119.

33 ACMRJ, Santíssimo Sacramento (Sé), Óbitos, José Dias (February 26, 1740).

34 Soares, *Devotos da cor*, 140.

35 For the smell at Rosário, see ibid., 139. During Domingos' time in Rio, Rua da Vala was still considered the western border of the city "proper." Along the *vala* (drainage ditch) that ran from Carioca to Prainha, people threw "rubbish, trash, sweepings, and filth . . . that hindered the flow of water." In 1735, the town council passed a law that prohibited such pollution, on pain of whipping and two months in the galleys for slaves and a 20,000 réis fine for free people. Ferreira, *A cidade do Rio de Janeiro e seu termo*, 83–84.

36 Soares, *Devotos da cor*, 136–39.

37 Ibid., 139.

38 The history of the brotherhood of Santa Efigênia and Santo Elesbão is recounted in ibid. On the brotherhood's beginning in the Chapel of Saint Dominic, see ibid., 170. By 1747 the brotherhood received a land grant and construction began on its own church, which was completed by the early 1750s, just two blocks from the Chapel of Saint Dominic. Ibid., 191.

39 Oliveira, *Devoção negra*, 269.

40 Karasch, *Slave Life in Rio de Janeiro*, 272.

41 Soares, *Devotos da cor*, 183.

42 On the hierarchy of the brotherhood of Santa Efigênia and Santo Elesbão, see ibid., 181–87.

43 Ibid., 179.

44 ACMRJ, Nossa Senhora da Candelária, Óbitos, Francisco Gomes (January 4, 1741). Gomes' case is fascinating on a number of grounds. In addition to the money he left to the brotherhoods and churches, he willed significant amounts to his stepson, his stepson's daughter, and his own "natural" son, born out of wedlock from an earlier relationship. Unlike most wills, in which Portuguese law dictated that half of community property went to the spouse, Gomes and his wife married under a contract that stipulated the separation of property at marriage. As such, only the community property Gomes accrued after his marriage with Rosa Mendes was subject to her claim. In addition, Gomes' recognition of his "natural" son in his will meant that the son was entitled to one-third of his father's property, including the property he owned before his marriage to Rosa Mendes. The complicated distribution of Gomes' property demonstrates how wealth could be created through webs of kinship that we might not normally associate with "inheritable" family. On the status

of "natural" children and inheritance law in colonial Brazil, see Lewin, "Natural and Spurious Children."

45 See, for instance, the last testament of Branca Ferreira, a freed Angolan who owned a manioc farm in Pacobaiba. Similarly, João Ribeiro Santarem owned a five-*braça* site in Pacobaiba where he grew vegetables. ACMRJ, Nossa Senhora da Candelária, Óbitos, Branca Ferreira (December 13, 1740), and João Ribeiro Santarem (September 7, 1743). Santarem's case is also notable because he had a son who allegedly tried to poison him. In response, Santarem, who was Mina, exiled his son to Angola for four years.

46 Antônio da Fonseca (Mina) was a barber who was training a thirteen-year-old Mina boy, José, when Antônio died in 1740. ACMRJ, Santíssimo Sacramento, Óbitos, Antônio da Fonseca (February 25, 1740). Antônia da Conceição (Mina) was a seamstress. ACMRJ, Santíssimo Sacramento, Óbitos, Antônia da Conceição (February 13, 1738).

47 ACMRJ, Nossa Senhora da Candelária, Batismos (1737–41). Of these 38 freed slave-owners, 27 were "*pretos*" and 11 were "*pardos*" and 31 were women. The implications of the sexual imbalance in the freed community is addressed below and in chapter 5. Santa Rita only became its own parish in 1753.

48 ACMRJ, Nossa Senhora da Candelária, Óbitos, João Ignácio Álvares (November 2, 1738).

49 ACMRJ, Santíssimo Sacramento, Óbitos, Thome da Souza (February 9, 1739).

50 The concept of "wealth in people" originated in Miers and Kopytoff, *Slavery in Africa*. The idea has been replicated in other important works, including Miller, *Way of Death*; Vansina, *Paths in the Rainforests*; and Thornton, *Africa and Africans in the Making of the Atlantic World*.

51 On the idea of "wealth in people as wealth in knowledge," see Guyer and Belinga, "Wealth in People as Wealth in Knowledge." Admittedly, Brazilian slave masters utilized slave knowledge primarily as a tool for capital accumulation; however, distinctions between forms of coercion and dependency based on slave knowledge and those based on raw, physical labor challenge notions of slavery as an undifferentiated social condition. "Slavery" (and "freedom") often operated on a continuum determined, to some extent, by varying regimes of knowledge.

52 The material on manumission is drawn from ANRJ, Segundo Ofício de Notas da Cidade de Rio de Janeiro, Livros de Notas, Nos. 51–54, and Quarto Ofício de Notas, Livros de Notas, Nos. 27–35. The sample includes a total of 266 manumissions between 1738 and 1744. For similar conclusions nearly a decade later, see Sweet, "Manumission in Rio de Janeiro." For a broader overview of manumission trends during the period, see Sampaio, "A produção da liberdade."

53 A total of 57 out of 75 Africans (76 percent) paid for their manumission.

54 There are few reliable estimates for slave prices in Rio during this period; however, Laird Bergad has shown that the average price of healthy African slaves in Minas Gerais was 197,398 réis between 1738 and 1744. Bergad, *Slavery*, 262. Many of these Africans would have arrived in Rio and passed overland to the mines. Scholars have estimated transport costs from the coast to the interior at around 100 percent of the cost of a slave. Thus, average slave prices for Africans in Rio would have been just

under 100,000 réis. Anecdotal evidence is also suggestive. The Benedictine monastery in Rio purchased 23 slaves between 1739 and 1743, at an average cost of 83,478 réis. ADB/UM, CSB, Livro 134, Estados do Mosteiro de Nossa Senhora do Montesserrate do Rio de Janeiro, 1620–1748, f. 215.

55 Here, I am only making reference to the cash transaction in which a slave paid money for his/her manumission. Ascertaining the actual costs of manumission is difficult. Masters often placed conditions on the slave's manumission, the most common of which was service to the master until his death. Determining the cost of a manumission that included a cash payment and continued service is virtually impossible in the absence of data on the timing of the master's death.

56 ANRJ, Quarto Ofício de Notas, Livro de Notas, No. 34, ff. 11–11v.

57 Between 1738 and 1744, at least a half dozen Africans paid 200,000 réis or more for their manumission; several paid 300,000 réis. The average value of a slave here is calculated as 100,000 réis.

58 This was precisely the case at the Benedictine monastery in Rio between 1781 and 1783, when it manumitted four slaves, "and with the product of these another seven were bought." ADB/UM, CSB, 135, Estados do Mosteiro de Nossa Senhora do Montserrate, f. 196.

59 ANRJ, Quarto Ofício de Notas, Livro de Notas, No. 34, ff. 14–14v.

60 ANRJ, Quarto Ofício de Notas, Livro de Notas, No. 27, ff. 61v–62. *Molecona* (young girl) is the feminine form of *moleque*.

61 ANRJ, Quarto Ofício de Notas, Livro de Notas, No. 49, ff. 132–132v.

62 ANRJ, Primeiro Ofício de Notas, Livro de Notas, No. 125, ff. 119v–120.

63 In a sample of 266 manumissions between 1738 and 1743, 71 percent (189) were granted to Brazilian-born slaves. Of these, 64 percent (120) were granted to females. Within the category of African manumissions, 77 percent (60) were granted to females. These figures cohere almost exactly with those found in another sample of 605 manumissions in Rio de Janeiro between 1749 and 1754. See Sweet, "Manumission in Rio de Janeiro," 59.

64 Ibid., 59–60.

65 ANRJ, Quarto Ofício de Notas, Livro de Notas, No. 30, ff. 61–61v.

66 ACMRJ, Nossa Senhora da Candelária, Batismos (May 15, 1737).

67 These figures hold true for both the 1738–43 sample and the 1749–54 sample. For the earlier sample, only 6 percent of manumissions were granted to African men; for the later period, African men represented 7 percent of total manumissions. Sweet, "Manumission in Rio de Janeiro," 60.

68 ACMRJ, Santíssimo Sacramento, Óbitos, Domingas da Cruz (October 9, 1738).

69 ANRJ, Quarto Ofício de Notas, Livro de Notas, No. 34, ff. 18–18v.

70 ACMRJ, Nossa Senhora da Candelária, Batismos (March 19, 1739).

71 On customary rights and slave property in the United States, see the provocative work of Penningroth, *The Claims of Kinfolk*.

72 ACMRJ, Nossa Senhora da Candelária, Casamentos de pessoas livres e escravos (July 20, 1741).

73 AHU, Conselho Ultramarino, Rio de Janeiro, Caixa 31, Documento 7112 (January 8, 1732).

74 For examples of these disputes, see the description of an attack by an African *quitandeira* named Angela, who along with a companion, was accused of maiming a female slave owned by Antônio de Souza Valladares. ANRJ, Segundo Ofício de Notas, Livro de Notas, No. 53, f. 73v, Escriptura de perdao que da Antonio de Souza Valladares a Angella mulher pretta (March 29, 1741). See also Manuel Dines de Oliveira's accusation that the slaves owned by the Convent of Saint Anthony mortally wounded his slave Sebastião. ANRJ, Segundo Ofício de Notas, Livro de Notas, No. 55, ff. 143–143v, Escriptura de perdao que da Manuel Dines de Oliveira aos escravos do convento de Santo Antonio (October 26, 1743).

75 Evidence of the Fonseca boys' departure for Coimbra to study for the priesthood comes from ANRJ, Quarto Ofício de Notas, Livro de Notas, No. 30, ff. 232–234, Escriptura de Patrimonio que faz Manuel Pereira da Fonseca e sua mulher a seu filho Manuel Jose Pereira da Fonseca and Escriptura de Patrimonio que faz Manuel Pereira da Fonseca e sua mulher a seu filho Antonio Joseph Pereria da Fonseca (June 7, 1741).

76 ANTT, Inquisição de Lisboa, Cadernos do Promotos, No. 102, Livro 295, f. 155 (February 19, 1741).

77 On the "six or seven" months that she and her husband owned Domingos, see ANTT, Inquisição de Évora, Processos, No. 7759, ff. 36v–40v, testimony of Leonor de Oliveira Cruz (August 21, 1742).

78 Leonor de Oliveira gave birth to a son, Jozé, on March 29, 1738. ACMRJ, Nossa Senhora da Candelária, Batismos (March 29, 1738).

79 ANTT, Inquisição de Évora, Processos, No. 7759, ff. 50–52, testimony of Padre Salvador Ferreira Mendes (August 21, 1742).

80 ANTT, Inquisição de Évora, Processos, No. 7759, ff. 40v–42, testimony of José Cardoso de Almeida (August 21, 1742).

81 The average price was around 113,000 réis. Again, data is scarce, but the average price of 22 healthy Africans in Minas Gerais was 226,000 réis in 1738. Along the coast, these prices would have been about half. See Bergad, *Slavery*, 262.

CHAPTER 5

1 On the letters of request and the public house, see ANTT, Inquisição de Évora, Processos, No. 7759, ff. 50–52, testimony of Father Salvador Ferreira Mendes (August 21, 1742).

2 On the financial arrangements between slave masters and slaves-for-hire in nineteenth-century Rio, see Frank, *Dutra's World*, 27, 60–69.

3 The exact timing of Domingos' manumission is unclear since none of the documents provides a date or even a year. In August 1742, one witness, Mathias de Almeida, noted that he "had knowledge of Domingos for 2 ½ to 3 years in this part, from the time that he was already freed." This statement suggests that Domingos was freed some time in late 1739. ANTT, Inquisição de Évora, Processos, No. 7759, ff. 25–26v, testimony of Mathias de Almeida (August 18, 1742).

4 ANTT, Inquisição de Évora, Processos, No. 7759, ff. 40v–42, testimony of José Cardoso de Almeida (August 21, 1742).

5 The differences between Domingos' two Rio masters were, in some respects, re-flective of broader debates emerging between an old Portuguese nobility and a newer, "business" class. See Fragoso, "Senhores do Atlântico versus senhores de um negrinho."

6 On slave autonomy in nineteenth-century Rio, see Ferreira, "Autonomia escrava."

7 Walsh, *Notices of Brazil*, 2:20. For a more detailed history of slavery in nineteenth-century Rio, see Karasch, *Slave Life in Rio de Janeiro*. On the crucial place of slaves in wealth building in nineteenth-century Rio, see Frank, *Dutra's World*.

8 This figure is based on an analysis of 898 estate inventories between 1815 and 1825. See Frank, *Dutra's World*, 41.

9 See ANTT, Inquisição de Évora, Processos, No. 7759, ff. 42v–45, testimony of Paula Rosada (August 21, 1742), who reported that Domingos charged slave masters 25,600 réis for each cure he performed at his *terreiro* in 1740. On charging "2 doblas" for a diagnosis, see ANTT, Inquisição de Évora, Processos, No. 7759, ff. 33v–34v, testimony of Maria de Jesus (August 21, 1742).

10 Schwartz, *Sugar Plantations*, 226.

11 The calculation of Domingos' earnings is somewhat speculative; however, if we as-sume that he earned a minimum of 30,000 réis per month (12,800 réis "in very few days") on Almeida's account, we begin to see how truly lucrative his practice was. Rental costs on a dwelling in the western outskirts of the city likely would not have exceeded 1,500 réis per month. Rental rates on small houses in the city ran as low as 800 réis per month in 1749. See, for instance, ANRJ, Primeiro Ofício de Notas do Rio de Janeiro, Livro de Notas, No. 117, ff. 112–113. Food and clothing allowances for plantation slaves during the eighteenth century added up to around 8,400 réis per year. Schwartz, *Sugar Plantations*, 226. Costs in Rio were likely higher, perhaps 10,000 réis. Thus, rental (18,000 réis) and upkeep (10,000 réis) would have added up to no more than 28,000 réis for the year. Removing these costs from the ledger, Domingos still would have earned roughly 332,000 réis in a single year, more than two times his original purchase value of 150,000 réis. One piece of evidence that supports Domingos' tremendous earning power is the very rapidity with which he was able to purchase his freedom. It seems highly unlikely that Domingos would have been able to buy his manumission unless he was earning such lofty sums, and the timing of his manumission within one year suggests that the above calculations are, if anything, conservative.

12 The classic text on the connection between slavery and capitalism is Williams, *Capitalism and Slavery*. Williams argues that the foundations of the English indus-trial revolution were based on profits from slavery. Although Brazil did not achieve such economic ascendancy, scholars are beginning to show the systematic ways that slaveholding created a platform for wealth building in places like Rio, with in-vestments flowing upward from slaves to property to stocks and bonds. See, for instance, Frank, *Dutra's World*, esp. chapter 2.

13 ANTT, Inquisição de Évora, Processos, No. 7759, ff. 16v–18v, testimony of Ignácio Correa Barbosa (June 14, 1741).

14 ANTT, Inquisição de Évora, Processos, No. 7750, ff. 48v–49v, testimony of Rev. Ignácio Manuel da Costa Mascarenhas (August 21, 1742).

15 Alden and Miller, "Out of Africa," 206.

16 AHU, Conselho Ultramarino, Rio de Janeiro, Caixa 46, Nos. 10917–20 (January 24, 1739–November 17, 1740). As a skin disease, leprosy fell under the purview of Sakpata, much in the same manner as smallpox. The fact that Domingos probably "specialized" in curing an epidemic disease might also explain his popularity and his high fees.

17 ANTT, Inquisição de Évora, Processos, No. 7759, ff. 33v–34v, testimony of Maria de Jesus (August 21, 1742).

18 ANTT, Inquisição de Évora, Processos, No. 7759, ff. 34v–36v, testimony of Manuel da Assumpçao de Andrade (August 21, 1742).

19 The history and legends about the church are drawn from its website: http://www .outeirodagloria.org.br/historia.htm.

20 Herskovits, Dahomey, 2:152.

21 Morro da Glória and its associated church remain spiritually important to Rio's African-descended population even today. The Candomblé goddess of the sea, Yemanjá, is directly associated with the saint, Nossa Senhora da Glória. Both deities are celebrated yearly on August 15.

22 On the location of Domingos' altar "in the back of the house at the foot of an orange tree," see ANTT, Inquisição de Évora, Processos, No. 7759, ff. 45–48v, testimony of Thereza Arda (August 21, 1742). See also ANTT, Inquisição de Évora, Processos, No. 7759, ff. 36v–40v, testimony of Leonor de Oliveira Cruz (August 21, 1742).

23 Herskovits, Dahomey, 2:171.

24 On ficus, see Voeks, Sacred Leaves of Candomblé, 164–65, and on jack fruit, see Parés, A formação do Candomblé, 182.

25 Bosman, A New and Accurate Description, 382. For a similar description of patients seeking cures at "Bocó" trees in 1797, see Pires, Viagem de África em o reino de Dahomé, 90.

26 On "compositional" wealth, see the work of Jane Guyer and Samuel Belinga, who argue that the concepts of accumulation and composition "focus on very different dynamics, one quantitative and one qualitative, one additive and the other synergistic, one achieving numbers and the other patterns, one risking loss and isolation and the other courting the dangerous tensions of centrifugality." Guyer and Belinga, "Wealth in People as Wealth in Knowledge," 108. For a further articulation of the idea of market values as complex social processes, see Guyer, Marginal Gains.

27 ANTT, Inquisição de Évora, Processos, No. 7759, ff. 42v–45, testimony of Paula Rosada (August 21, 1742). Subsequent references in the text to Rosada's experiences at the healing center are from this source.

28 There have been dozens of recent studies on the medicinal uses of Momordica charantia. For example, see Srivastava, Venkatakrishna, Verma, Venkaiah, and Raval, "Antidiabetic and Adaptogenic Properties of Momordica charantia"; Chaturvedi, "Role of Momordica charantia"; Ojewole, Adewole, and Olayiwola, "Hypoglycaemic and Hyposensitive Effects of Momordica charantia"; and Beloin, Gbeassor, Akpagana, Hudson, Soussa, Koumaglo, and Arnason, "Ethnomedicinal Uses of Momordica charantia."

29 Voeks, Sacred Leaves of Candomblé, 178.

30 On the relationship between African healing and science, see Horton, *Patterns of Thought in Africa and the West.*

31 Like *melão de São Caetano, pinhão* also has known medicinal properties. In particular, the oil from the seeds is said to relieve constipation. *Pinhão* also continues to be used in Brazilian Candomblé. Voeks, *Sacred Leaves of Candomblé,* 180.

32 On the use of chickens to sweep away evil, see Blier, *African Vodun,* 215. Chickens are understood as the "birds of the ancestors," and utilizing them to remove bad things from the house was a prerequisite to spirit possession and divination. The practice was also common in Haiti, where, after the sweeping, the chickens were shaken "like dusty feather-dusters" in order to remove the evil spirits. Métraux, *Voodoo in Haiti,* 172.

33 In a brief but tantalizing note, Pierre Verger explains that in the Sakpata pantheon at Abomey, Adan Tagni, the oldest son of Da Zodji, was the one who "sent leprosy and who cuts the feet and hands." Verger, *Notas sobre o culto aos orixás e voduns,* 240.

34 ANTT, Inquisição de Évora, Processos, No. 7759, ff. 36v–40v, testimony of Leonor de Oliveira Cruz (August 21, 1742). The slave Thereza Arda offers a somewhat different account. She notes that her mistress was "repulsed" by Domingos, initially refusing his offers. According to Thereza, Leonor only changed her mind after Domingos and Caetano threw black powders all over her house. ANTT, Inquisição de Évora, Processos, No. 7759, ff. 45–48v, testimony of Thereza Arda (August 21, 1742).

35 ANTT, Inquisição de Évora, Processos, No. 7759, ff. 45–48v, testimony of Thereza Arda (August 21, 1742).

36 ANTT, Inquisição de Évora, Processos, No. 7759, ff. 36v–40v, testimony of Leonor de Oliveira Cruz (August 21, 1742).

37 From the testimony of Leonor de Oliveira Cruz: "O grande e a capeluda erão por ella testemunha, e que não erão dos seus." Ibid. And from Thereza: "Não podia ver porque não era dos seus, senão do Grande." ANTT, Inquisição de Évora, Processos, No. 7759, ff. 45–48v, testimony of Thereza Arda (August 21, 1742).

38 ANTT, Inquisição de Évora, Processos, No. 7759, ff. 45–48v, testimony of Thereza Arda (August 21, 1742). For their exchange in the Mina language, see ANTT, Inquisição de Évora, Processos, No. 7759, ff. 25–26v, testimony of Mathias de Almeida (August 18, 1742), who noted that Domingos wanted to introduce a malignant spirit into Leonor, but "Thereza . . . impeded it because she understood the language of the *preto* because they are from the same nation."

39 ANTT, Inquisiçao de Évora, Processos, No. 7759, ff. 36v–40v, 45–48v, testimonies of Leonor de Oliveira Cruz (August 21, 1742) and Thereza Arda (August 21, 1742).

40 The foregoing descriptions are composited from ANTT, Inquisiçao de Évora, Processos, No. 7759, ff. 36v–40v, 45–48v, testimonies of Leonor de Oliveira Cruz (August 21, 1742) and Thereza Arda (August 21, 1742).

41 ANTT, Inquisição de Évora, Processos, No. 7759, ff. 36v–40v, testimony of Leonor de Oliveira Cruz (August 21, 1742).

42 After his conversion, Saint Francis wore a rough cord around his waist in memory of the cords that were used to bind Christ during the crucifixion. Supposedly, Saint Francis also used the cord in rituals of self-flagellation in order to escape the temp-

tation of the Devil. The rope with three knots, representing poverty, chastity, and obedience, eventually became a standard part of the Franciscan habit.

43 Not surprisingly, the precise form of torture exacted upon Caetano is unclear in the documentary record. Fonseca and Cruz cryptically note that they "subdued" Caetano, however, another witness, Mathias de Almeida, admits that he arrived at Fonseca's house to find Caetano "in chains," delivering his confession. ANTT, Inquisição de Évora, Processos, No. 7759, ff. 14v–16, testimonies of Mathias de Almeida (June 14, 1741) and Manuel da Costa Simões (June 14, 1741).

44 ANTT, Inquisição de Évora, Processos, No. 7759, ff. 45–48v, testimony of Thereza Arda (August 21, 1742).

45 On the "résumé of the whole social order," see Junod, *The Life of a South African Tribe*, 571.

46 Think, for instance, of one of the cures performed when Paula Rosada was at his terreiro. His clients ran around "like filthy animals" before falling "like dead people." Domingos brandished his calabash and then cut and sealed each woman with black powders.

47 ACMRJ, Nossa Senhora da Candelária, Batismos (March 29, 1738). This would not be the last child of Manuel Pereira da Fonseca and Leonor de Oliveira Cruz. On March 27, 1741, they called Father Damião Antônio da Silva to their house to baptize their newborn daughter, Anna. The baptism took place at home because the baby was born sickly and was "in danger" of dying before she could be baptized in the Church.

48 On notions of chastity and honor in colonial Brazil, see Nazzari, "An Urgent Need to Conceal."

CHAPTER 6

1 Anonymous, *Relation de Royaume de Judas*, quoted in Bay, *Asen, Ancestors, and Vodun*, 43.

2 Blier, *African Vodun*, 215.

3 On the importance of hot and cold opposites in activating *gbo*, see ibid., 221–23.

4 Ibid., 201–2.

5 Ibid., 244. See also Segurola, *Dictionnaire Fon-Française*, 1:286. "*Kānumò*" (slave) derives from "kānu," which Segurola translates as "at the end of a cord, slavery, under the domination of." Curiously, under the entry for "kānimò" (slavery), Segurola writes: "In the proper sense, slavery is nothing more than a bad memory." This bit of editorializing reveals another way that slavery is "bound"—trapped under layers of memory. For a powerful examination of slavery and historical memory in another African context, see Shaw, *Memories of the Slave Trade*. For the various meanings of cords/tying and their relation to slavery in Fon thought, see Blier, *African Vodun*, 239–70.

6 Segurola defines "*àtí*" as a "medicinal powder made with plants; or from poison." Segurola, *Dictionnaire Fon-Française*, 1:65.

7 On the symbolism of the color black, see Blier, *African Vodun*, 268–69.

8 Brand, "Rites de naissance."

9 See, for instance, ANTT, Inquisição de Évora, Processos, No. 7759, ff. 25–26v, 33v–34v, testimonies of Mathias de Almeida (August 18, 1742) and Maria de Jesus (August 21, 1742).

10 Peixoto, *Obra nova*, 32.

11 On the smoke of various colors, see ANTT, Inquisição de Évora, Processos, No. 7759, ff. 45–48v, testimony of Thereza Arda (August 21, 1742).

12 Blier, *African Vodun*, 91–92.

13 Herskovits, *Dahomey*, 2:259. For Legba's role in the origins of *gbo* more generally, see ibid., 256–59.

14 ANTT, Inquisição de Évora, Processos, No. 7759, ff. 33v–34v, testimony of Maria de Jesus (August 21, 1742).

15 In fact, the word used to describe a Catholic priest, "padre," resonates quite differently than "pai." In Portuguese, "padre" is almost always used as a title, indicating one's membership in the Catholic priesthood, although it also has the meaning "father." The word "pai" is the word most often used to describe male parents. Therefore, "Pai Domingos" was etched more deeply in natal kinship connections. The titles "mãe" and "pai" remain salient for leaders in contemporary Candomblé *terreiros* in Brazil. Officially, these titles are "mãe de santo" and "pai de santo," mother and father of the saint, indicating their "parental" control over the congregation in its worship of the deity.

16 Herskovits, *Dahomey*, 2:174.

17 Capitão is described in ANTT, Inquisição de Évora, Processos, No. 7759, ff. 45–48v, 36v–40v, 16v–18v, 30v–33, testimonies of Thereza Arda (August 21, 1742), Leonor de Oliveira Cruz (August 21, 1742), and Ignácio Correa Barbosa (June 14, 1741, and August 18, 1742). Barbaças is described by Cruz and Barbosa. Velho is described only by Barbosa (June 14, 1741).

18 A detailed description of the initiation process can be found in Herskovits, *Dahomey*, 2:179–90.

19 For the diverse variations on the Sakpata pantheon and descriptions of the deities, see ibid., 139–44, and Verger, *Notas sobre o culto aos orixás e voduns*, 239–40.

20 Herskovits, *Dahomey*, 2:142.

21 According to Herskovits, in the "official" hierarchy of Sakpata at Abomey, Dada Zodji was the oldest member of the family, while Dada Langa was his oldest son. Ibid., 139. However, Verger's Abomey informants contradicted this hierarchy, naming Kohosu as the founding male member of the family. Informants at Vedji and Zagnanado named yet other deities as the oldest males. Verger, *Notas sobre o culto aos orixás e voduns*, 239–40.

22 See ANTT, Inquisição de Évora, Processos, No. 7759, testimony of Ignácio Correa Barbosa, ff. 16v–18v, 30v–33 (June 14, 1741 and August 18, 1742).

23 ANTT, Inquisição de Évora, Processos, No. 7759, ff. 71–78, In Specie e mais exame (May 16, 1743).

24 Maupoil, *La géomancie*, 59. Literally, "vodun come to your head" ("vodu" = "vodun," "wa" = "come," "ta" = "head," "towe = your"). Segurola, *Dictionnaire Fon-Française*.

25 On the importance of the fontanel, see Blier, *African Vodun*, 155–58.

26 ANTT, Inquisição de Évora, Processos, No. 7759, ff. 45–48v, testimony of Thereza Arda (August 21, 1742).

27 Herskovits, *Dahomey*, 2:188.

28 For a more complete and detailed description of calundu, see Sweet, *Recreating Africa*. See also Sweet, "The Evolution of Ritual."

29 In his excellent history of Candomblé, Luis Nicolau Parés hypothesizes that "in the last quarter of the eighteenth century, the *jejes* . . . [in Brazil] already had the capacity to establish incipient religious congregations . . . around a single divinity." Parés, *A formação do Candomblé*, 118. The findings here push Parés backward in time nearly forty years.

30 Herskovits and Herskovits, *An Outline of Dahomean Religious Belief*, 36.

31 ANTT, Inquisição de Lisboa, Cadernos do Promotor, No. 102, Livro 295, ff. 12–17, and No. 107, Livro 299. Cata was denounced first in April 1742 and again in September 1745.

32 Herskovits, *Dahomey*, 2:209.

33 Dahomey's inability to subdue Savalu is captured well in a proverb that states: "The dung beetle rolling balls of excrement toward Savalou is surprised by rain. The hand never benefits from all that it makes." Guillet, *Regards sur la litterature Dahoméenne*, 24.

34 Law, *The Slave Coast*, 294, 325.

35 It bears noting that divination with upside-down pots continued in Dahomey despite the "official" prohibition. Herskovits observed the persistence of the practice in the 1930s. If this type of divination remained illicit or marginal compared to Fa divination, one wonders if its surviving form might have been one of those sites of durable collective memory regarding slavery.

36 Herskovits, *Dahomey*, 2:141. Much later in Brazil, exploding kernels of corn (popcorn) were among the principal offerings to Omolu, Sakpata's equivalent in Candomblé. Voeks, *Sacred Leaves of Candomblé*, 125.

37 Segurola, *Dictionnaire Fon-Français*, 1:77. In another instance, Segurola writes that Aihosu is a "surname for Sakpata." Ibid., 32.

38 See, for instance, Maupoil, *La géomancie*, 73, as well as several lists in Verger, *Notas sobre o culto aos orixás e voduns*, 239–40. In some of these lists, "Bosu" has a slightly different construction or spelling: "Bosu Zoho" (Maupoil), "Bosu Zuhon" and "Bozuhon" (Verger). See also Herskovits, *Dahomey*, 2:140, 142, for "Gbosú."

39 Verger, *Notas, sobre o culto aos orixás e voduns*, 240. The exact timing of the founding of the Kingdom of Savalu is uncertain, although estimates place it sometime around 1650.

40 The powder represents the essential character of the birds transferred to humans. In this case, both the hummingbird and the squirrel cuckoo are birds that jump or flit quickly from plant to plant, in a "flirtatious" and "promiscuous" way. On the metaphorical connections between birds and humans in Fon thought, see Blier, *African Vodun*, 227–28. Blier supplies a half dozen other examples of the ways birds are associated with humans. See also the list of various *gbo* consisting of bird parts in Herskovits, *Dahomey*, 2:264–88.

41 The iron "knife" and the reference to the knife representing the "saint" or "god" of his land indicates the vodun Gu; however, as we will see below, this pike might in fact have been an ancestral *asen*.

42 ANTT, Inquisição de Lisboa, Cadernos do Promotor, Livro 297, ff. 195–214.

43 The name "Francisco Axê," also rendered in the documents as "Ache," is of great significance. In Fon-Gbe, "axê" literally means "to enable, power, jurisdiction; grace," but its larger implications are related to the life force or energy that healers attempted to harness in their cures. The idea of collective *axê* remains crucial to Yoruba and Fon-derived religions even today. Segurola, *Dictionnaire Fon-Française*, 1:3.

44 ANTT, Inquisição de Lisboa, Cadernos do Promotor, No. 108, Livro 300, ff. 52–58.

45 Mercier, *Les ase du Musée d'Abomey*, 7.

46 On the linguistic history, see Tidjani, "Notes sur le mariage au Dahomey," esp. 59; Segurola, *Dictionnaire Fon-Français*, 2:473; and Bay, *Asen, Ancestors, and Vodun*, 34.

47 Mercier, *Les ase du Musée d'Abomey*, 7–9.

48 Bay, *Asen: Iron Altars*, 41. See also Bay, *Asen, Ancestors, and Vodun*, esp. 42–59. Bay's recent book is the most complete history of *asen* in Dahomey and Benin.

49 Maupoil, *La géomancie*, 176.

50 Bay, *Asen, Ancestors, and Vodun*, 32. Bay suggests that the Fon adopted the name "Asen" from the Yoruba *orisha* of medicine, Osanyin. Osanyin is also closely associated with iron staffs known as Opa Osanyin. At first blush, this connection makes sense; however, there is no indication that "Asen" ever implied anything other than an ancestral altar among the Fon. Asen never became a deity among the Fon. Bay admits that Fon-Gbe etymologies of the name "typically suggest the manner of use of ancestral asen." The connection between Fa divination and Asen *acrelele* might explain the gap between the Yoruba version of the myth and the Fon one. Bay, *Asen, Ancestors, and Vodun*, 30–33.

51 Forbes, *Dahomey and the Dahomans*, 2:88.

52 Skertchly, *Dahomey as It Is*, 391.

53 Forbes, *Dahomey and the Dahomans*, 88.

54 In addition to *asen*, the Hountundji also crafted the guns, swords, and other weapons for the Dahomean army. Bay, *Asen, Ancestors, and Vodun*, 60–64.

55 Despite these transformations of *asen* during Agaja's reign, the herbal/medicinal associations of Osanyin never replaced the ancestral ones of Asen. In the same way that *gbo* divination never disappeared among common people, the use of ancestral *asen* continued. Ibid., 33.

56 Ibid., 42–114; Mercier, *Les ase du Musée d'Abomey*, 9; Bay, *Asen: Iron Altars*, 41.

57 Bay, *Asen: Iron Altars*, 29.

58 The significance of "Moquem" is difficult to discern. It could be some manifestation of an ancestor; however, I can find no rough equivalents in Fon-Gbe. More intriguing, in Brazilian Portuguese "moquem" is now associated with a form of barbecue on a spit. The term derives from a Tupi word, "mokaen," which as early as the sixteenth century, Hans Staden defined as "the roasted flesh . . . of Christians." The memory of "moquem" as "roasted flesh" persisted well into the nineteenth century. We might speculate that Francisco Axê's "Moquem" represented the unhappy

souls of those Portuguese who died at the hands of Tupi cannibals. If so, we see the ingenious knitting together of Fon ritual structure and local Brazilian historical knowledge, a necessary adaptation if a healer was to remain salient in the new community. Staden, *The Captivity of Hans Stade*, 104; Souza, *Tratado descriptivo*, 338; Wells, *Exploring and Traveling*, 265.

59 Bosman, *A New and Accurate Description*, 363.

60 Guillet, *Regards sur la litterature Dahoméenne*, 8.

61 Burton, *A Mission to Gelele*, 2:102 (n. 3).

62 Herskovits, *Dahomey*, 2:177.

63 Ibid., 101–5.

64 Bay, *Wives of the Leopard*, 91–96.

65 For example, in 1719, 91 percent of slaves working at Morro da Vila Rica were male. For other examples, see Russell-Wood, *The Black Man in Slavery and in Freedom*, 112.

66 The consistent reference in the documents to "one white woman" in Domingos' ritual space raises the intriguing possibility that this white woman was an initiate. If so, this points to the beginnings of a much more thoroughgoing female gendered space, one that, on some level, privileged female empowerment over the maintenance of other hierarchies, like race and ethnicity (Gbe v. non-Gbe). The fact that there were no white men and only a few black men in Domingos' community also points in this direction. For the descriptions of "one white woman" among a few pardas and "many negras," see ANTT, Inquisição de Évora, Processos, No. 7759, ff. 36v–40v, 42v–48v, testimonies of Leonor de Oliveira Cruz (August 21, 1742), Paula Rosada (August 21, 1742), and Thereza Arda (August 21, 1742).

67 Scholars have for many years debated the origins of Candomblé's "matriarchal" leadership, beginning with Ruth Landes' groundbreaking and controversial *City of Women*. Most authors take it as a given that the overwhelming female leadership in these communities was a postabolition phenomenon. These authors cite a host of reasons why this was the case. Some argue that women gravitated to Candomblé primarily because the Catholic Church prohibited them from attaining positions of meaningful leadership. Harding, *A Refuge in Thunder*, 127. Others argue that the numerically dominant African men controlled vodun spaces in Brazil until the end of the slave trade, at which point their mostly female initiates began entering into positions of leadership. Reis, "Candomblé in Nineteenth-Century Bahia." Finally, there are those who conclude that it was Landes herself who created the Candomblé "matriarchy" with her research findings. Matory, *Black Atlantic Religion*, 188–207.

68 On the African male as the prototypical "fetisher" and "curer," see Marques, *O feiticeiro*; Souza, *The Devil and the Land of the Holy Cross*, 99; and Parés, *A formação do Candomblé*, 136.

69 On the history of African barbers in Rio de Janeiro, see Soares, "African Barbers." See also the biography of a nineteenth-century African-Brazilian barber, Antonio José Dutra. Frank, *Dutra's World*.

70 The root word "hun" has multiple meanings, including "blood," "heart," "drum," and "divinity." Segurola, *Dictionnaire Fon-Français*, 1:233–34.

71 Parés, *A formação do Candomblé*, 318.

72 See ANTT, Inquisição de Évora, Processos, No. 7759, ff. 30v–33, 34v–36v, testimonies of Ignácio Correa Barbosa (August 18, 1742) and Manuel da Assumpção de Andrade (August 21, 1742), discussed in chapter 7.

73 The information on Domingos' "marriage" and his unnamed daughter comes from ANTT, Inquisição de Évora, Processos, No. 7759, ff. 59–61, Genealogia (March 15, 1743). His daughter's birth year is based on his claim that she was "two years old" in 1743.

74 Between 1709 and 1714 in the parish of Santíssimo Sacramento in Rio, 93.4 percent of children born to African mothers were born out of Christian wedlock. In more than a third of these cases, the mothers named the child's father, indicating the likelihood of enduring bonds between the couples. For these and similar statistics, see Sweet, *Recreating Africa*, 35–37.

CHAPTER 7

1 ANTT, Inquisição de Évora, Processos, No. 7759, ff. 16v–18v, 30v–33, 34v–36v, testimonies of Ignácio Correa Barbosa (June 14, 1741, and August 18, 1742) and Manuel da Assumpção de Andrade (August 21, 1742).

2 ANTT, Inquisição de Évora, Processos, No. 7759, ff. 13–14, Traslado da Culpa de Domingos preto liberto de nascam Minna tirado por ordem de Reverendo Padre Doutor Provizor Vigario geral e Commissario do Santo Officio Gaspar Gonçalves de Araújo (June 14, 1741).

3 On the administrative structure of the Inquisition in Brazil, see Novinsky, "A igreja no Brasil colonial," and Wadsworth, *Agents of Orthodoxy*.

4 ANTT, Inquisição de Lisboa, Cadernos do Promotor, Livro 297, f. 112 (September 11, 1743).

5 On Domingos' arrest at the order of the bishop, see ANTT, Inquisição de Évora, Processos, No. 7759, ff. 48v–49v, testimony of Rev. Ignácio Manuel da Costa Mascarenhas (August 21, 1742).

6 ANTT, Inquisição de Évora, Processos, No. 7759, ff. 33v–34v, testimony of Maria de Jesus (August 21, 1742).

7 Edmundo, *Rio de Janeiro nos tempo dos vice-reis*, 451.

8 On the 60,000-réis stipend provided by the Lisbon tribunal, see the arrest order of the Inquisitors in ANTT, Inquisição de Évora, Processos, No. 7759, f. 7 (March 31, 1742). The crimes of jailers will be discussed later in this chapter.

9 ANTT, Inquisição de Lisboa, Cadernos do Promotor, No. 124, Livro 818, f. 8, letter from Francisco da Silva Meirelles (no date, early 1740s).

10 Since we do not know the date of his arrest, we cannot be certain of the exact length of time Domingos spent in the ecclesiastical jail. We know that he was there for at least one month, during which time Araújo collected final depositions. But it is possible that Domingos was in the jail for much longer, perhaps upwards of fifteen months, since the bishop intervened at an indeterminate time after Araújo sent the first denunciations in June 1741.

11 ANTT, Inquisição de Évora, Processos, No. 7759, f. 53, letter from Gaspar Gonçalves de Araújo to Inquisitors (September 11, 1742).

12 Calainho, *Metrópole das mandingas*, appendices, table 10. Though only a handful of cases were ever brought to full trial, the records of the Inquisition include hundreds of witchcraft denunciations against Africans across the Portuguese empire.

13 ANTT, Inquisição de Lisboa, Cadernos do Promotor, No. 110, Livro 302, ff. 41–41v.

14 Coates, *Convicts and Orphans*, 33–34.

15 On the treatment of criminal exiles (*degredados*) in the Portuguese world, see the firsthand account in Dellon, *Relation de l'Inquisition de Goa*.

16 On the arrival of the 1742 fleet, see Mattozo, *Anno noticioso*, 444. See also *Gazeta de Lisboa*, no. 51 (December 18, 1742): 715.

17 Between 1740 and 1744, an average of fifty-seven ships arrived yearly in the fleets from Brazil. The year 1742 was, by far, the slowest year during the period. Delgado, *O jornal manuscrito de Luiz Montez Mattozo*, 124. On the economic aspects of Rio de Janeiro's connections to the Atlantic world, see Santos, *O Rio de Janeiro e a conjuntura Atlântica*.

18 Whale whiskers (*barbas de baleia*) are flexible yet durable protein deposits found on the upper jaw of toothless whales that are used for filter feeding. Prior to the invention of plastics, whale whiskers were used to manufacture umbrellas, women's corsets, and so on.

19 With the exception of the precious metals and stones, the precise contents of the 1742 fleet are unknown. The contents listed here are an approximation based on the products delivered in the previous year's fleet. *Gazeta de Lisboa*, no. 45 (November 9, 1741): 539.

20 On the metals and stones onboard the fleet, see the diary of Jesuit priest Luiz Montez Mattozo: "Na Frota do Rio de Janeyro chegaram perto de 2 milhares em prata, patacas, e peças deste metal, e sem embargo da quantidade ali nam passou o marco de 7 mil reis para bayxo. Tambem veyo hum Diamante, que pezou 5 oytavas, e muytos mais Diamantes, do que na Frota passada: o ouro dizem, que excede pouco de 16 arrobas." Mattozo, *Anno noticioso*, 449–50.

21 Russell-Wood, *The Black Man in Slavery and in Freedom*, 44.

22 ANRJ, Segundo Ofício de Notas do Rio de Janeiro, Livro de Notas, No. 51, f. 53v (January 28, 1739).

23 On the slave trade as "alchemy," see Smallwood, *Saltwater Slavery*.

24 On the compelling and provocative metaphor of economic "redemption" from colonial "purgatory," see Souza, *The Devil and the Land of the Holy Cross*, esp. 78–87.

25 For more on calundu as an integral Central African ritual form in the Americas, see Sweet, "The Evolution of Ritual."

26 ANTT, Inquisição de Lisboa, Processos, No. 252. For more detailed analysis of the case of Luzia Pinta, see Mott, "O calundu angola"; Souza, *The Devil and the Land of the Holy Cross*, 153–54, 170, 233–37; and Souza, "Revisitando o calundu."

27 ANTT, Inquisição de Lisboa, Processos, No. 11163. See also the discussion in Souza, *The Devil and the Land of the Holy Cross*, 228–33.

28 Ironically, this was precisely a period when "the forces of tradition sought to eliminate the channels by which these ideas came to Spain and Portugal." For example, prohibitions on banned books expanded from heretical religious texts to include "books whose content was lascivious or political." Schwartz, *All Can Be Saved*, 215.

29 For this interpretation, see Souza, *The Devil and the Land of the Holy Cross*, 232–33.

30 This walk inland may actually have been as long as fourteen blocks. Prior to the earthquake of 1755, Lisbon's streets were a curvy, hilly maze, not unlike the present-day streets of the Alfama neighborhood. Only after the Pombaline reconstruction did the Baixa take the orderly, grid pattern one sees today. For a map of the Baixa showing both before-and-after renderings of the streets, see Araújo, *Peregrinações em Lisboa*, 12:32–33, figure 3.

31 Estimates of Lisbon's population on the eve of the 1755 earthquake vary, commonly running as high as 275,000. The most reliable figures, based on parish household censuses and confession records, can be found in Pereira, "The Opportunity of a Disaster." Historian Teresa Rodrigues places the figure at around 191,000 for Lisbon and its immediate suburbs. She estimates that the central city had around 168,000 residents. Rodrigues, *Cinco séculos de quotidiano*, 26, 39.

32 Galley slaves included large numbers of "Turks" and "Moors" captured from North African pirate ships in the Atlantic and Mediterranean. African slaves also figured prominently in the king's galleys. When slaves committed infractions like running away, their masters punished them by sending them to the galleys. For a description of galley labor, see Merveilleux, *Memórias instrutivas*, 221, 253 (n. 68).

33 On the street life of Lisbon, see Rodrigues, *Cinco séculos de quotidiano*, 46–70.

34 Ibid., 68.

35 Twiss, *Travels through Portugal and Spain*, 22.

36 For example, in July 1742, five months before Domingos' arrival, a royal carriage ran over a young mulatto (*mulatete*) on one of the city's main thoroughfares, "immediately spilling his brains out." Mattozo, *Anno noticioso*, 227.

37 Merveilleux, *Memórias instrutivas*, 212.

38 Beckford, *Italy: With Sketches of Spain and Portugal*, 2:68.

39 Costigan, *Sketches of Society and Manners in Portugal*, 2:61. On the filth and foul smell of Lisbon's streets, see Fielding, *The Journal of a Voyage to Lisbon*, 197; Dalrymple, *Travels through Spain and Portugal*, 140; and Baretti, *A Journey from London to Genoa*, 1:279.

40 Anonymous Frenchman, *Descrição da cidade de Lisboa*, 39. See also Merveilleux, *Memórias instrutivas*, 216–17, which states that "one runs the danger of being killed by the buckets that many times tumble into the streets with their contents."

41 Baretti, *A Journey from London to Genoa*, 1:273–74. See also Anonymous Frenchman, *Descrição da cidade de Lisboa*, 55.

42 Twiss, *Travels through Portugal and Spain*, 2.

43 Baretti, *A Journey from London to Genoa*, 1:274.

44 Rodrigues, *Cinco séculos de quotidiano*, 67.

45 Anonymous Frenchman, *Descrição da cidade de Lisboa*, 60–61.

46 For enslaved Africans sold away from Lisbon against their will, see Sweet, *Recreating Africa*, 77–78.

47 The attraction of Lisbon over Brazil was such that some freed slaves in Brazil even abandoned family and friends in order to seek opportunities in the metropole. See ibid., 78–79.

48 The overwhelming preponderance of Brazil's enslaved Africans were destined for

agricultural and mining labor. In urban areas of Brazil, slave masters sometimes cultivated their slaves' musical capacities. For example, in Rio in the 1740s, one witness observed that the fiddle could be heard in "almost all the houses," and "each person wants to teach this instrument to their blacks." In addition, the enslaved played wind instruments. Despite these efforts to cultivate music among slaves, literacy remained elusive for all but a select few in Brazil, even among slave masters. On slave musicians in Rio, see Ferrez, "O Rio de Janeiro, no tempo de Bobadela," 163.

49 *Suplemento á Gazeta de Lisboa*, no. 51 (December 19, 1743): 1020.

50 Ibid., no. 3 (January 17, 1743): 60.

51 Beckford, *Italy: With Sketches of Spain and Portugal*, 2:165.

52 On the negative reception for Inquisitorial prisoners, see Mott, *Rosa Egipcíaca*, 633.

53 ANTT, Inquisição de Évora, Processos, No. 7759, f. 56, Order of Inquisitors (March 12, 1742).

54 Letter from Jesuit, Gaspar de Miranda, to Inquisitor General Francisco de Castro (1630), Biblioteca Nacional de Lisboa, Sala do Reservados, cod. 868, quoted in Coelho, *Inquisição de Évora*, 1:34.

55 Silva, *Regimento do Santo Ofício*, Livro I, Título III.

56 For conditions inside the secret jails, see Dellon, *Relation de l'Inquisition de Goa*, 59–60, and Anonymous [Father António Vieira], *Notícias recônditas*.

57 ANTT, Inquisição de Lisboa, Cadernos do Promotor, No. 98, Livro 291, ff. 88–175. See especially the testimony of Manuel de Castro e Peralta (August 26, 1727), who reported that "the jails were completely full of people, and he spoke and communicated with all of them—the men who were on the same corridor as him and on either side of his cell, and with the women who were on the corridor above, and that the said communication was by tapping, which they made on the walls through the alphabet."

58 ANTT, Inquisição de Lisboa, Cadernos do Promotor, No. 98, Livro 291, ff. 88–175, testimonies of Manuel de Castro e Peralta (August 26, 1727) and Marcia Guterres (August 26, 1727).

59 ANTT, Inquisição de Lisboa, Cadernos do Promotor, No. 98, Livro 291, ff. 88–175, testimonies of Catherina Nunes (September 6, 1727), Antonio Cardozo Porto (September 13, 1727), Pedro Lopes (November 24, 1727), and João Pinto Coelho (November 26, 1727).

60 ANTT, Inquisição de Lisboa, Cadernos do Promotor, No. 98, Livro 291, ff. 88–175, testimony of Pedro Broha (May 11, 1726).

61 Ibid., testimony of Matheus Orobio (May 21, 1726).

62 Ibid., testimonies of Pedro Broha (May 11, 1726) and Matheus Orobio (May 20, 1726).

63 ANTT, Inquisição de Évora, Processos, No. 7759, ff. 59–61, Genealogia (March 15, 1743).

64 For a closer analysis of the fragmented narrative of Domingos' life story, see Sweet, "Mistaken Identities?" My thinking on the broken, "jagged" narrativity of slavery is informed by Smallwood, *Saltwater Slavery*.

65 This error in Domingos' social status is most pronounced in the administrative cover

page that begins his case file. Following from his genealogy, it reads: "Processo de Domingos Alvares, homem preto escravo de Jose Cardoso de Almeida natural da Costa da Mina, e morador no Rio de Janeiro" As a result of the mistake, Domingos appears as a "slave" in the Portuguese National Archive's electronic database. Understandably, nearly all of the scholars who have mentioned Domingos' case have repeated this error. See, for instance, Varnhagen, "Excerptos de varias listas de condemnados," 76–77. In the list of condemned for 1744, Domingos is delineated as José Cardoso de Almeida's slave. Meanwhile, in the same list, Luzia "Pinto" is delineated as a "freed black woman." See also Moraes, *Carceres e fogueiras da inquisição*, 108. More recent works that repeat this error include Souza, *The Devil and the Land of the Holy Cross*, 98, 103, 107, 114, 168, 217, 308; Pieroni, "El Brasil colonial"; Walker, "Sorcerers and Folkhealers," 95; and Calainho, *Metrópole das mandingas*, 83.

CHAPTER 8

1 ANTT, Inquisição de Évora, Processos, No. 7759, ff. 63–65, Confissão (April 26, 1743).

2 According to Timothy Walker, Inquisitors viewed those healers who claimed to possess "divine virtue" as among the gravest threats. Not only did these healers present theological competition; they also undermined the growing power of licensed doctors and surgeons, many of whom had direct connections to the administration of the Inquisition. On the importance of "virtues" in Inquisitorial definitions of crime, see Walker, *Doctors, Folk Medicine, and the Inquisition*, 11–13, 46–49.

3 ANTT, Inquisição de Évora, Processos, No. 7759, ff. 66–70, Exame (May 9, 1743).

4 ANTT, Inquisição de Évora, Processos, No. 7759, ff. 71–78, In Specie e mais confissão (May 16, 1743).

5 ANTT, Inquisição de Évora, Processos, No. 7759, ff. 80–85, Admoestação antes do Libello (June 26, 1743).

6 ANTT, Inquisição de Évora, Processos, No. 7759, f. 100, sentence of Domingos Álvares (August 13, 1743).

7 There is a rich historiography describing the Portuguese Auto da Fé, including a scene in Voltaire's *Candide*. For other descriptions, see Merveilleux, *Memórias instrutivas*, 168, 177–79; Pereira and Rodrigues, *Portugal*, 3:982–84; Babo, *A inquisição*, 52; and Woodson, "The Auto da Fé of 1755."

8 Merveilleux, *Memórias instrutivas*, 168. See also Woodson, "The Auto da Fé of 1755," 368.

9 Woodson, "The Auto da Fé of 1755," 368.

10 Merveilleux, *Memórias instrutivas*, 178.

11 Rodrigues, *Cinco séculos de quotidiano*, 81–82.

12 For specific information on the Auto da Fé of 1744, see *Nueva relacion*. For the general choreography of the Auto da Fé, see Pereira and Rodrigues, *Portugal*, 3:982–84.

13 For a list of Brazilians who marched in Lisbon Autos da Fé, see Varnhagen, "Excerptos de varias listas de condemnados," 54–86. Those for the year 1744 appear in ibid., 76–78.

14 For the case of Miguel Ferreira Pestana, see ANTT, Inquisição de Lisboa, Processos, No. 6982. A detailed analysis of the case can be found in Mott, "Um Tupinambá feiticeiro." The article is available at Mott's website: http://luiz-mott.blogspot .com/2006/08/um-tupinamb-feiticeiro-do-esprito-santo.html. My summary treatment below follows Mott.

15 These public demonstrations of the virtues of bolsas de mandinga were common in the Portuguese Atlantic world, from Lisbon to Luanda to Recife. For the most complete study of bolsas de mandinga, see Calainho, *Metrópole das mandingas*. See also Sweet, *Recreating Africa*, 179–86. For a close study of an Atlantic *bolsa* network from the 1730s that included more than two dozen Atlantic Africans, see Sweet, "Slaves, Convicts, and Exiles."

16 *Gazeta de Lisboa*, no. 17 (April 28, 1744): 332.

17 On these royal provisions, see Lahon, *O negro na coração do império*, 65, and Fonseca, *Escravos no sul do Portugal*, 213–15.

18 Baretti, *A Journey from London to Genoa*, 1:125–26.

19 The letter from the guard to the Inquisition announcing Pestana's escape is dated March 22, 1746. See ANTT, Inquisição de Lisboa, Processos, No. 6982.

20 ANTT, Inquisição de Évora, Cadernos do Promotor, No. 70, Livro 271, f. 400.

21 ANTT, Inquisição de Évora, Processos, No. 7759, f. 105, Termo de Segredo (June 22, 1744).

22 *Ordenações filipinas de 1603*, Livro V, Título CXL, "Dos degredos e degredados," quoted in Pieroni, *Os excluídos do reino*, 56–57. The most complete history of Castro Marim is Pieroni and Coates, *De couto do pecado*.

23 Domingos stated that upon his release from jail in Lisbon he went "directly" to Évora. ANTT, Inquisição de Évora, Processos, No. 7759, ff. 260–261v, Genealogia (October 25, 1747).

24 According to Geraldo Pieroni and Timothy Coates, more than two-thirds of those banished to Castro Marim received sentences of three years or less. Fewer than 10 percent received sentences greater than five years. Pieroni and Coates, *De couto do pecado*, 31.

25 Pieroni, *Os excluídos do reino*, 50.

26 *Regimento de 1640*, Título III: "Dos Confitentes," quoted in ibid., 64.

27 Pieroni and Coates, *De couto do pecado*, 117.

28 Delgado, *O jornal manuscrito de Luiz Montez Mattozo*, 115, 298.

29 On the normal time it took to make the trip from Lisbon to Castro Marim, see Pieroni and Coates, *De couto do pecado*, 117. The excessive length of Domingos' passage suggests that he stopped frequently along the way, perhaps spending as much as a week in larger towns like Évora, to rest, eat, and find more reliable shelter. Given the almost-certain ill state of his health, the journey must have been especially challenging.

30 Pieroni and Coates, *De couto do pecado*, 121–23.

31 Estimates of Castro Marim's population vary widely. See ibid., 96, 119–20, and Coates, *Convicts and Orphans*, 52–53.

32 Witchcraft was the number one crime represented in the exile population of Castro Marim. Though the records are incomplete, in a sample of 581 Inquisitorial exiles

remitted to the village, Geraldo Pieroni and Timothy Coates show that 127 (22 percent) were convicted of witchcraft, followed by false testimony (20 percent), blasphemy/sacrilege (15 percent), perturbing the Inquisition (10 percent), Judaism (9 percent), and bigamy (7 percent). Pieroni and Coates, *De couto de pecado*, 30.

33 Pieroni, *Os excluídos do reino*, 271.

34 More accurately, Luzia Pinta was quadruply marked as criminal, colonial, black, and female. Since roughly two-thirds (65 percent) of Castro Marim's Inquisitorial exiles were men, Pinta would have been an especially peculiar anomaly. On the sex ratio of exiles to Castro Marim, see Pieroni and Coates, *De couto do pecado*, 29.

CHAPTER 9

1 ANTT, Inquisição de Évora, Processos, No. 7759, ff. 108–108v, letter of João Lopes Ignácio (August 15, 1744).

2 ANTT, Inquisição de Évora, Processos, No. 7759, ff. 254–258, Confissão (September 11, 1747).

3 Serrão and Marques, *Nova história de Portugal*, 82.

4 Baretti, *A Journey from London to Genoa*, 1:274.

5 ANTT, Inquisição de Évora, Processos, No. 7759, ff. 254–258, Confissão (September 11, 1747).

6 ANTT, Inquisição de Évora, Processos, No. 7759, ff. 138–138v, testimony of Feliciana Thereza da Silveira (February 11, 1746).

7 ANTT, Inquisição de Évora, Processos, No. 7759, ff. 135–137v, testimony of Domingas de Andrade (February 11, 1746).

8 ANTT, Inquisição de Évora, Processos, No. 7759, ff. 129–131, testimony of Antonio Viegas de Mendonça (February 8, 1746).

9 ANTT, Inquisição de Évora, Processos, No. 7759, ff. 262–271, Exame (November 3, 1747).

10 ANTT, Inquisição de Évora, Processos, No. 7759, ff. 135–137v, testimony of Domingas de Andrade (February 11, 1746). Andrade's testimony is corroborated by that of her husband and several others.

11 ANTT, Inquisição de Évora, Processos, No. 7759, ff. 121–121v, Treslado do Capitulo de huma carta que escreveo a esta Mesa o Notario da Villa de Castromarim João Lopes Ignacio a qual anda junta ao Processo de Margarida das Chagas (no date). The notary's commentary on Domingos Álvares was an addendum to the *processo* of Margarida das Chagas. The precise date of the notary's letter is unclear; however, Margarida das Chagas was imprisoned by the Inquisition in Évora on November 6, 1745. The papers for her *processo* would have accompanied her on her journey from Castro Marim to Évora. For the case of Margarida das Chagas, see ANTT, Inquisição de Évora, Processos, No. 7972.

12 ANTT, Inquisição de Évora, Processos, No. 7759, ff. 119–120v, denunciation by Antonio Viegas and Domingas de Andrade (December 13, 1745).

13 Domingos promoted his knowledge of the Algarve's underworld widely. The "boast" that he knew all about feitiços comes from ANTT, Inquisição de Évora, Processos, No. 7759, ff. 135–137v, testimony of Domingas de Andrade (February 11,

1746). The specific claim that he knew all of the feiticeiros of the Algarve, including the woman capable of killing all the way to Lisbon, comes from ANTT, Inquisição de Évora, Processos, No. 7759, ff. 131v–133, testimony of Manuel Viegas (February 8, 1746).

14 ANTT, Inquisição de Évora, Processos, No. 7759, ff. 119–120v, denunciation by Antonio Viegas and Domingas de Andrade (December 13, 1745).

15 Blier, *African Vodun*, 27.

16 Ibid.

17 Ibid., 249.

18 Le Herissé, *L'Ancien Royaume du Dahomey*, 149–51. See also Blier, *African Vodun*, 74–76, 79–80, 226.

19 Blier, *African Vodun*, 408 (n. 38).

20 The dog was also associated with Legba, the mercurial trickster. On dog parts in *bochio*, see ibid., 235.

21 Ibid., 213.

22 On the "alchemy" of objects, see ibid., 205–38.

23 For detailed analyses of Portuguese superstitions, witchcraft beliefs, and rituals, see Bethencourt, *O imaginário da magia*; Araújo, *Magia, demónio e força mágica*; and Paiva, *Bruxaria e superstição*.

24 ANTT, Inquisição de Évora, Processos, No. 7759, f. 172, letter from Luis Antonio Fragoso de Barros (January 21, 1746).

25 ANTT, Inquisição de Évora, Processos, No. 7759, f. 173, letter from Henrique Nunes Leal da Gama (February 14, 1746).

26 In his October 1746 testimony, Gonçalves claimed that Domingos first stayed at his hostel "more than a year earlier."

27 ANTT, Inquisição de Évora, Processos, No. 7759, ff. 154v–158v, testimony of Bras Gonçalves (October 17, 1746).

28 ANTT, Inquisição de Évora, Processos, No. 7759, ff. 254–258, Confissão (September 11, 1747).

29 ANTT, Inquisição de Évora, Processos, No. 7759, ff. 154v–158v, testimony of Bras Gonçalves (October 17, 1746).

30 Ibid.

31 Ibid.

32 Erva mil homens, also known as jarrinha in Brazil, is a part of the Aristolochia family. Medicinally, it is used as a diuretic and a sedative. Teas made from the herb are commonly used to treat asthma, fevers, convulsions, epilepsy, and gastrointestinal problems. It is still widely used today in Candomblé. See Voeks, *Sacred Leaves of Candomblé*, 172.

33 ANTT, Inquisição de Évora, Processos, No. 7759, ff. 149–152v, 154v–158v, testimonies of Father João de Oliveira Delgado (October 17, 1746) and Bras Gonçalves (October 17, 1746).

34 ANTT, Inquisição de Évora, Processos, No. 7759, ff. 149–152v, testimony of Father João de Oliveira Delgado (October 17, 1746).

35 Rural Portuguese folk often explained human healing powers as "divine virtues" emanating from God. However, as Timothy Walker has shown, the Inquisition be-

came more and more intolerant of these defenses over the course of the eighteenth century. On "divine virtues," see Walker, *Doctors, Folk Medicine, and the Inquisition,* 47–49.

36 ANTT, Inquisição de Évora, Processos, No. 7759, ff. 149–152v, testimony of Father João de Oliveira Delgado (October 17, 1746).

37 Herskovits and Herskovits, *Dahomean Narrative,* 57.

38 *Gazeta de Lisboa,* no. 27 (July 7, 1744): 531.

39 Gallop, *Portugal: A Book of Folk-Ways,* 77–80.

40 Merveilleux, *Memórias instrutivas,* 156.

41 Ibid., 152.

42 Yearly trade deficits with England steadily increased over the course of the eighteenth century, reaching as high as 1 million pounds sterling by the 1750s. Marques, *History of Portugal,* 386.

43 Paiva, *Bruxaria e superstição,* 159–61.

44 ANTT, Inquisição de Lisboa, Processos, No. 4222.

45 Herskovits, *Dahomey,* 2:248–49; Herskovits and Herskovits, *Dahomean Narrative,* 135–36.

46 On the cure for roundworm and for the slave of Maria da Graça, see ANTT, Inquisição de Évora, Processos, No. 7759, ff. 145–145v, Treslado do Capitulo de huma carta que escreveo nesta Meza Notario Manoel de Oliveira da Rocha da cidade de Faro (September 5, 1746).

47 ANTT, Inquisição de Évora, Processos, No. 7759, ff. 162–164, 152–154, testimonies of Domingos Coelho Vasconcellos (October 24, 1746) and Vasco Gonçalves (October 17, 1746).

48 Ibid.

49 ANTT, Inquisição de Évora, Processos, No. 7759, ff. 154v–158v, testimony of Bras Gonçalves (October 17, 1746).

50 ANTT, Inquisição de Évora, Processos, No. 7759, ff. 154v–158v, 161–162, testimonies of Bras Gonçalves (October 17, 1746) and José Perilha (a.k.a. São Penha) (October 18, 1746).

51 ANTT, Inquisição de Évora, Processos, No. 7759, ff. 262–271, Exame (November 3, 1747).

52 ANTT, Inquisição de Évora, Processos, No. 7759, ff. 154v–158v, testimony of Bras Gonçalves (October 17, 1746). The original copy of the letter that Domingos Álvares gave to Bras Gonçalves can be found in the Inquisition case file at f. 156.

53 For an example of the Justo Juiz protecting women from abusive husbands in Portugal in the late seventeenth century, see Paiva, *Bruxaria e superstição,* 98.

54 For an example of an enslaved African from Ouidah using the Justo Juiz in eighteenth-century Brazil "to free from thieves and enemies," see ANTT, Inquisição de Lisboa, Processos, No. 11767 (José Francisco Pereira).

55 The use of "hot" substances like *aguardente* and pepper to cure fevers is yet another example of the complementarity of vodun belief systems. See ANTT, Inquisição de Évora, Processos, No. 7759, ff. 249–250, testimony of Domingos Guerreiro (September 9, 1747).

56 ANTT, Inquisição de Évora, Processos, No. 7759, ff. 243v–245, testimony of Maria Mestra (September 9, 1747). The Portuguese language of "oration with which they could attach and bind [*oração con que podião atar e se prender*]" adheres closely to Fon-Gbe understandings of "binding speech [*bla gbe*]" or "knotting of speech [*gbe sa*]." Powerful spoken oaths could shape the "wills" and behavior of others. On Fon-Gbe understandings, see Blier, *African Vodun*, 81–82; for the Portuguese "inclining wills," see Paiva, *Bruxaria e superstição*, 96–103.

57 ANTT, Inquisição de Évora, Processos, No. 7759, ff. 247–248v, testimony of Manuel Martins (September 9, 1747).

58 ANTT, Inquisição de Évora, Processos, No. 7759, ff. 209–210, denunciation by Manuel Mestre (August 9, 1747).

59 ANTT, Inquisição de Évora, Processos, No. 7759, ff. 241v–243, testimony of Manuel Martins (September 9, 1747).

60 ANTT, Inquisição de Évora, Processos, No. 7759, ff. 254–258, Confissão (September 11, 1747), and ff. 262–271, Exame (November 3, 1747). In the interrogation of November 3, 1747, Domingos backtracked on his earlier story about learning the remedy in his homeland. Instead, he claimed he learned it in Brazil.

61 ANTT, Inquisição de Évora, Processos, No. 7759, ff. 181–183v, testimony of José Pacheco (May 15, 1747).

62 Ibid.

63 ANTT, Inquisição de Évora, Processos, No. 7759, ff. 195–197, testimony of Leonor Alonso (May 19, 1747).

64 ANTT, Inquisição de Évora, Processos, No. 7759, ff. 166–167v, letter of denunciation of Manuel de Andrade Carvalho (March 28, 1747).

65 ANTT, Inquisição de Évora, Processos, No. 7759, ff. 204–204v, arrest order from Luis Antonio Fragoso de Barros (April 26, 1747).

66 ANTT, Inquisição de Évora, Processos, No. 7759, f. 205, letter from Manuel de Andrade Carvalho to Évora tribunal (May 25, 1747).

67 Resende, *Chronica de el-rei D. João II*, 3:64.

68 See, for example, *Gazeta de Lisboa*, no. 17 (April 28, 1744): 331, and no. 18 (May 5, 1744). As a result of the baths, the newspaper reported, the king's "precious health" was "much fortified."

69 ANTT, Inquisição de Évora, Processos, No. 7759, ff. 229v–232, testimony of Florencio Rodrigues (September 6, 1747).

70 ANTT, Inquisição de Évora, Processos, No. 7759, ff. 221–226v, testimony of Theadora Gonçalves (September 6, 1747).

71 ANTT, Inquisição de Évora, Processos, No. 7759, ff. 212–213v, testimony of Maria da Silva (July 31, 1747).

72 ANTT, Inquisição de Évora, Processos, No. 7759, ff. 225v–229v, testimony of Maria da Silva (September 6, 1747).

73 ANTT, Inquisição de Évora, Processos, No. 7759, ff. 272–276, In Specie e mais confissão (November 10, 1747). The crucial importance of the jackfish for Brazilian fishermen has spawned a rich set of spiritual and folkloric traditions that can be traced back to enslaved Africans. The celebrations and offerings for the fish tend to revolve

around its alimentary importance. The use of the fish's parts for healing purposes elaborates yet one more reason for its celebration. For a summary of these traditions, see Braga, "Notas sôbre a pesca do Xaréu."

74 ANTT, Inquisição de Évora, Processos, No. 7759, f. 112, letter from Luis Antonio Fragoso de Barros to Dr. Juiz de Fora da Cidade de Sylves (July 15, 1747).

75 ANTT, Inquisição de Évora, Processos, No. 7759, f. 113, Auto de Entrega (August 9, 1747).

76 See ANTT, Inquisição de Évora, Processos, No. 7759, ff. 187v–191, testimony of Catharina Jozepha (May 15, 1747). See also ff. 198v–199, testimony of Constança da Conceição (May 19, 1747), who reported that "she heard it said that [Domingos] was born in Angola."

77 ANTT, Inquisição de Évora, Processos, No. 7759, ff. 254–258, Confissão (September 11, 1747).

78 For the idea of isolation as the defining experience of enslavement, see Miller, "Retention, Re-Invention, and Remembering." Like Joseph Miller, I would emphasize that isolation was not the equivalent of social death. On the contrary, as Vincent Brown has argued, social death was the condition against which the enslaved struggled in order to *live*, even in the barest, most meager ways. In this view, slavery was not a collective condition but a "predicament, in which enslaved Africans and their descendants never ceased to pursue a politics of belonging, mourning, accounting, and regeneration." Brown, "Social Death," 1248.

79 Among these were rosemary, Bishop's weed, sarsaparilla, dwarf elder, lavender, wild thyme, mint, and viper's bugloss.

80 See, for instance, Jainu and Devi, "Antiulcerogenic and Ulcer Healing Effects."

81 ANTT, Inquisição de Évora, Processos, No. 7759, ff. 262–271, Exame (November 3, 1747).

82 Ibid.

83 Ibid.

84 Ibid.

85 Here, Domingos cleverly sidestepped the question about spitting in the fish's mouth. On the one hand, he said he learned it in Brazil. On the other, his explanation makes reference, in the singular, *only* to Brazilian Christians practicing the cup-on-the-head remedy; not the remedy with the fish. Earlier, Domingos had confessed that he learned the remedy of spitting in the fish's mouth in his homeland. It was now more expedient to claim it as a Brazilian remedy, probably because of the association between African practices and the work of the Devil. Just as in his first Inquisition case, Domingos very perceptively adjusted to the intellectual jousting implicit in the interrogations.

86 ANTT, Inquisição de Évora, Processos, No. 7759, ff. 262–271, Exame (November 3, 1747).

87 Ibid.

88 ANTT, Inquisição de Évora, Processos, No. 7759, ff. 292–293, sentence of Domingos Álvares (September 19, 1748).

89 ANTT, Inquisição de Évora, Processos, No. 7759, f. 303, Hida e Penitencias (November 4, 1749).

CHAPTER 10

1 Mascarenhas, *Relaçam da Embayxada*, 8–9.
2 Arquivo Público do Estado da Bahia, Ordens Régias, 44, f. 122 (July 25, 1747), quoted in Verger, *Fluxo e refluxo*, 210.
3 Arquivo Público do Estado da Bahia, Ordens Régias, 44, f. 93 (October 8, 1747), quoted in ibid..
4 Quoted in ibid., 211. Verger does not provide the archival citation for this quote, but he dates the document to March 13, 1750.
5 Mascarenhas, *Relaçam da Embayxada*, 7.
6 Ibid., 7–8.
7 Ibid., 9.
8 Ibid., 9–10.
9 The news of João V's death in July 1750 had not yet reached Brazil.
10 Mascarenhas, *Relaçam da Embayxada*, 11.
11 My calculation of more than 900 slaves is based on a Middle Passage mortality rate of around 10 percent. The entry for the *Bom Jesus d'Além e Nossa Senhora da Esperança* in the TSTD places the imputed number of slaves embarked in Benin at 924. See TSTD (accessed on April 11, 2009).
12 On the travels and trade of the *Bom Jesus d'Além e Nossa Senhora da Esperança*, see Verger, *Fluxo e refluxo*, 285, 308 (n. 13).
13 Ibid., 285.
14 In addition to looking for Domingos in the databases of trial records (*Processos*) for all three Inquisition tribunals, I consulted the prosecutor's notebooks (*Cadernos do Promotor*) for Lisbon (1749–60), Évora (1749–63), and Coimbra (1749–71), as well as the records of correspondence sent from local agents of the Inquisition to their respective tribunals. I leave open the possibility that I missed reference to Domingos; however, as an indication of the care with which I read these records, I found evidence that another penal exile from Brazil, Luzia Pinta, continued healing in the Algarve. See ANTT, Inquisição de Évora, Cadernos do Promotor, No. 70, Livro 271 (1732–52), ff. 400 and chapter 8.
15 Here, I again nod toward Steven Feierman, whose study of "peasant intellectuals" among the Shambaa of Tanzania examines disputes over fertility and community well-being that are strikingly similar to the disputes between kings and healers in Dahomey, Brazil, and Portugal. See Feierman, *Peasant Intellectuals*, esp. 69–93.
16 Schoenbrun, "Conjuring the Modern in Africa." See also Kodesh, *Beyond the Royal Gaze*. Building on the work of Feierman, these scholars have expanded on the temporal and methodological scope of histories of healing significantly.
17 In addition to a shared history of persecution and enslavement, many also shared a mutually discernible Mina language, a shared history of vodun, and so on. There were instances when shared bonds were even stronger. For example, when Dahomean King Agonglo was assassinated in 1797, a succession battle erupted. Some royal family members were killed in the struggle; others were sold into the Atlantic slave trade, along with some 600 of their followers. Pires, *Viagem de África em o reino de Dahomé*, 77–80.

18 Feierman, *Peasant Intellectuals*, 3.

19 Cooper, *Colonialism in Question*, 239–40.

20 Indeed, even in the late twentieth century, the contest for "modernity" was far from complete. See, for example, Comaroff and Comaroff, *Modernity and Its Malcontents*; Geschiere, *The Modernity of Witchcraft*; Moore and Sanders, *Magical Interpretations*; Ashforth, *Witchcraft, Violence, and Democracy*; and Smith, *Bewitching Development*.

21 For a similar rejection of the dichotomies between "religious" power and "political" power and its impacts on the production of history, see MacGaffey, "Changing Representations." See also Feierman, "Colonizers, Scholars, and the Creation of Invisible Histories."

Bibliography

ARCHIVAL SOURCES

Brazil

Arquivo da Curia Metropolitana do Rio de Janeiro
  Nossa Senhora da Candelária
  Santíssimo Sacramento
Arquivo Nacional do Rio de Janeiro
  Primeiro Ofício de Notas do Rio de Janeiro
  Segundo Ofício de Notas do Rio de Janeiro
  Quarto Ofício de Notas do Rio de Janeiro
Arquivo Público Mineiro, Belo Horizonte, Minas Gerais
  Seção Colonial, Documentos Encadernados, Codice No. 51

Portugal

Arquivo Distrital de Braga/Universidade de Minho
  Congregação de São Bento
Arquivo Histórico Ultramarino
  Conselho Ultramarino
    Pernambuco
    Rio de Janeiro
Arquivo Nacional da Torre do Tombo, Lisbon
  Inquisição de Coimbra
    Cadernos do Promotor
    Processos
  Inquisição de Évora
    Cadernos do Promotor
    Processos
  Inquisição de Lisboa
    Cadernos do Promotor
    Processos
  Santo Ofício
    Conselho Geral

NEWSPAPERS

Gazeta de Lisboa
Suplemento á Gazeta de Lisboa

PUBLISHED PRIMARY SOURCES

Adams, William Henry Davenport. *Heroes of Maritime Discovery; or, Chapters in the History of Ocean Adventure.* . . . London: Gall & Ingils, 1882.

Anonymous [Father Antônio Vieira]. *Notícias recônditas do modo de proceder da inquisição de Portugal com seus presos.* Lisbon: Imprensa Nacional, 1821.

Anonymous Frenchman. *Descrição da cidade de Lisboa, 1730.* In *O Portugal de D. João V visto por três forasteiros,* edited by Castelo Branco Chaves, 35–128. Lisbon: Biblioteca Nacional, 1983.

Antonil, André João. *Cultura e opulência do Brasil por suas drogas e minas* (1711). Edited by Andrée Mansuy. Paris: Institut des hautes études de l'Amérique latine, 1968.

Atkins, John. *A Voyage to Guinea, Brasil, and the West-Indies; in His Majesty's Ships the Swallow and Weymouth.* 2nd edition. London, 1737.

Baretti, Giuseppe Marco Antonio. *A Journey from London to Genoa, through England, Portugal, Spain, and France.* 3rd edition. 4 volumes. London: T. Davies, 1770.

Beckford, William. *Italy: With Sketches of Spain and Portugal.* 2 volumes. Philadelphia: Key & Biddle, 1834.

Benci, Jorge. *Economia cristã dos senhores no governo dos escravos* (1700). 2nd edition. Edited by Serafim Leite. Porto: Livraria Apostolado da Imprensa, 1954.

Bosman, Willem. *A New and Accurate Description of the Coast of Guinea Divided into The Gold, The Slave, and The Ivory Coasts.* London, 1705.

Burton, Richard F. *A Mission to Gelele, Kingdom of Dahome.* . . . 2 volumes. London: Tylston and Edwards, 1893.

Chambon, M. *Le guide du commerce de l'Amérique principalement par le port de Marseille.* Avignon: J. Mossy, 1777.

Conrad, Robert Edgar. *Children of God's Fire: A Documentary History of Black Slavery in Brazil.* University Park: Penn State University Press, 1994.

Costa, Francisco Augusto Pereira da. *Anais Pernambucanos, 1701–1739.* 2nd edition. Volume 5. Edited by José António Gonsalves de Mello. Recife: FUNDARPE, Diretoria de Assuntos Culturais, 1984.

———. *Arredores do Recife.* Recife: Fundação de Cultura Cidade do Recife, 1981.

Costigan, Arthur William. *Sketches of Society and Manners in Portugal.* 2 volumes. London, 1787.

Dalrymple, William. *Travels through Spain and Portugal, in 1774.* London: J. Almon, 1777.

Dalzel, Archibald. *The History of Dahomey: An Inland Kingdom of Africa* [1793]. London: Frank Cass, 1967.

Dellon, M. Charles. *Relation de l'Inquisition de Goa.* Paris: Horthemels, 1688.

Dias, Pedro. *A arte da língua de Angola oferecida a Virgem Senhora Nossa do Rosário, mãe e senhora dos mesmos pretos.* Lisbon, 1697.

Doctrina Christiana y explicación de sus misterios, en nuestro idioma Español y en lengua Arda. Madrid, 1658.

Ferrez, Gilberto. "O Rio de Janeiro, no tempo de Bobadela, visto por um padre Francês." *Revista do Instituto Histórico e Geográfico Brasileiro* 264 (1964): 155–70.

Fielding, Henry. *The Journal of a Voyage to Lisbon.* London: A. Millar, 1755.

Fonseca, Antonio José Victoriano Borges da. *Nobliarchia Pernambucana*. 2 volumes. Rio de Janeiro: Bibliotecha Nacional, 1935.

Forbes, Frederick E. *Dahomey and the Dahomans*. 2 volumes. London: Longman, Brown, Green, and Longmans, 1851.

"Informação geral da capitania de Pernambuco, 1749." *Annaes da Bibliotecha Nacional do Rio de Janeiro* 28 (1906): 117–496.

Koster, Henry. *Travels in Brazil*. Edited by C. Harvey Gardiner. Carbondale: Southern Illinois University Press, 1966.

Labat, Jean-Baptiste. *Nouveau voyage aux isles de l'Amerique*. 4 volumes. Paris: G. Cavelier, 1722.

———. *Voyage du chevalier Des Marchais en Guinée, isles voisines, et à Cayenne, fait en 1725, 1726, & 1727*. 4 volumes. Paris: Saugraine l'aîné, 1730–31.

Mascarenhas, José Freire Monterroio. *Relaçam da Embayxada, que o poderoso rey de Angome Kiay Chiri Broncom, senhor dos dilatadissimos Sertões de Guine mandou ao illustrissimo e excellentissimo senhor D. Luiz Peregrino de Ataide, Conde de Atouguia . . . Redindo a amizade, e aliança do muito Alto, e poderoso senhor rey de Portugal nosso senhor*. Lisbon, 1751.

Mattozo, Luiz Montez. *Anno noticioso e histórico 1742*. Edited by Maria Rosalina Delgado. Lisbon: Lisóptima Edições/Biblioteca Nacional, 1996.

Mendes, Luiz Antonio de Oliveira. *Discurso academico ao programa: determinar com todos os seus symptomas as doenças, e chronicas, que mais frequentemente accometem os pretos recem tirados da Africa*. Lisbon: Real Academica, 1812.

Menezes, Jozé Cezar de. "Idéa da população da capitania de Pernambuco, e das suas annexas, extenção de suas costas, rios, e povoações notaveis, agricultura, numero dos engenhos, contractos, e rendimentos reaes . . . desde o anno de 1774. . . ." *Annaes da Bibliotecha Nacional do Rio de Janeiro* 40 (1918): 1–111.

Merveilleux, Charles Frederic de. *Memórias instrutivas sobre Portugal, 1723–1726*. In *O Portugal de D. João V visto por três foresteiros*, edited by Castelo Branco Chaves, 129–257. Lisbon: Biblioteca Nacional, 1983.

Moraes, Alexandre José Mello. *Chronica geral e minuciosa do imperio do Brazil: desde o descoberta do Novo Mundo ou America até o anno de 1879*. Rio de Janeiro: Dias da Silva Junior, 1879.

Newton, John. *The Journey of a Slave Trader, 1750–1754, with Newton's Thoughts upon the African Slave Trade*. Edited by Bernard Martin and Mark Spurrell. London: Epworth Press, 1967.

Norris, Robert. *Memoirs of the Reign of Bossa Ahádee, King of Dahomy, an Inland Country of Guiney, to Which Are Added the Author's Journey to Abomey, the Capital, and a Short Account of the African Slave Trade* [1789]. London: Frank Cass, 1968.

Nueva relacion del auto de fe, que celebro en el Convento de Santo Domingo de la ciudad de Lisboa el dia 21. de junio de este año de 1744: en 41. judios penintenciados, penintenciadas, quemados, quemadas, hechiceros, y hechiceras: sendo inquisidor general el eminentissimo, y reverendissimo señor Nuño de Acuña. Madrid: Juan Perez, 1744.

Peixoto, António da Costa. *Obra nova da língua geral de Mina*. Edited by Luís Silveira. Lisbon: Agência Geral das Colónias, 1945.

Pires, Vicente Ferreira. *Viagem de África em o reino de Dahomé* (1800). Edited by Clado Ribeiro de Lessa. São Paulo: Companhia Editora Nacional, 1957.

Resende, Garcia de. *Chronica de el-rei D. João II*. 3 volumes. Lisbon: Escriptorio, 1902.

"Resumo total da população que existia no anno de 1779. . . ." *Revista do Instituto Histórico e Geográfico Brasileiro* 21 (1858): 216–17.

Rocha, Manoel Ribeiro. *Ethiope resgatado empenhado sustentado corregido instruido e libertado*. Lisbon, 1758.

Saint-Méry, Louis-Élie Moreau de. *Description topographique, physique, civile, politique et historique de la partie française de l'isle Saint-Domingue*. 2 volumes. Philadelphia, 1797.

Sandoval, Alonso de. *De instauranda Aethiopum salute: el mundo de la esclavitud negra en America*. Bogotá: Empresa Nacional de Publicaciones, 1956.

Santos, Manuel dos. *Calamidades de Pernambuco* (1749). Recife: Fundação do Patrimônio Histórico e Artístico de Pernambuco, 1986.

Silva, Manuel da. *Regimento do Santo Ofício da inquisição dos Reynos de Portugal ordenado por mandado do ilustríssimo e reverendíssimo senhor bispo d. Francisco de Castro, inquisidor-geral do Conselho d'Estado de Sua Majestade*. Lisbon, 1640.

Skertchly, J. A. *Dahomey as It Is; Being a Narrative of Eight Months' Residence in That Country. . . .* London: Chapman and Hall, 1874.

Snelgrave, William. *A New Account of Some Parts of Guinea and the Slave Trade* (1734). London: Frank Cass, 1971.

Souza, Gabriel Soares de. *Tratado descriptivo do Brazil em 1587*. Rio de Janeiro: Typographia Universal de Laemmert, 1851.

Staden, Hans. *The Captivity of Hans Stade of Hesse in AD 1547–1555*. Translated by Albert Tootal and annotated by Richard F. Burton. London: Hakluyt Society, 1874.

Twiss, Richard. *Travels through Portugal and Spain, in 1772 and 1773*. London, 1775.

Van Dantzig, Albert. *The Dutch and the Guinea Coast, 1674–1742: A Collection of Documents from the General State Archive at the Hague*. Accra: Ghana Academy of Arts and Sciences, 1978.

Walsh, Robert. *Notices of Brazil in 1828 and 1829*. 2 volumes. Boston, 1831.

Wells, James W. *Exploring and Traveling Three Thousand Miles through Brazil from Rio de Janeiro to Maranhão*. London: Sampson, Low, Marston, Searle, and Rivington, 1884.

SECONDARY SOURCES

Adediran, Biodun. *The Frontier States of Western Yorubaland, 1600–1889*. Ibadan: French Institute for Research in Africa, 1994.

———. "Ìdàìsà: The Making of a Frontier Yorùbá State." *Cahiers d'Études Africaines* 93 (1984): 71–85.

———. "Yoruba Ethnic Groups or a Yoruba Ethnic Group? A Review of the Problem of Ethnic Identification." *África: Revista do Centro de Estudos Africanos da USP* 7 (1984): 57–70.

Akinjogbin, I. A. *Dahomey and Its Neighbors, 1708–1818*. Cambridge: Cambridge University Press, 1967.

Alden, Dauril. "Late Colonial Brazil." In *Colonial Brazil*, edited by Leslie Bethell, 284–343. Cambridge: Cambridge University Press, 1987.

Alden, Dauril, and Joseph C. Miller. "Out of Africa: The Slave Trade and the Transmission of Smallpox to Brazil, 1560–1831." *Journal of Interdisciplinary History* 18 (1987): 195–224.

Alencastro, Luiz Felipe de. *O trato dos viventes: a formação do Brasil no Atlântico Sul, séculos XVI e XVIII*. Rio de Janeiro: Companhia das Letras, 2000.

Anderson, Robert N. "The 'Quilombo' of Palmares: A New Overview of a Maroon State in 17th Century Brazil." *Journal of Latin American Studies* 28 (1996): 545–66.

Anignikin, Sylvain. "Histoire des populations mahi: à propos de la controverse sur l'ethonyme et le toponyme 'Mahi.'" *Cahiers d'Études Africaines* 162 (2001): 243–65.

Araújo, Maria Benedita. *Magia, demónio e força mágica na tradição Portuguesa*. Lisbon: Edições Cosmos, 1994.

Araújo, Norberto de. *Peregrinações em Lisboa*. 15 volumes. 2nd edition. Lisbon: Vega, 1993.

Ashforth, Adam. *Witchcraft, Violence, and Democracy in South Africa*. Chicago: University of Chicago Press, 2005.

Austen, Ralph A. "The Moral Economy of Witchcraft: An Essay in Comparative History." In *Modernity and Its Malcontents: Ritual and Power in Postcolonial Africa*, edited by Jean Comaroff and John Comaroff, 89–110. Chicago: University of Chicago Press, 1993.

Babo, Carlos. *A inquisição: enciclopédia pela imagem*. Porto: Lello & Irmão, 1932.

Baldwin, James. *Nobody Knows My Name: More Notes of a Native Son*. New York: Dial Press, 1961.

Bay, Edna G. *Asen: Iron Altars of the Fon People of Benin*. Atlanta, GA: Emory University Museum of Art and Archaeology, 1985.

———. *Asen, Ancestors, and Vodun: Tracing Change in African Art*. Urbana: University of Illinois Press, 2008.

———. *Wives of the Leopard: Gender, Politics, and Culture in the Kingdom of Dahomey*. Charlottesville: University of Virginia Press, 1998.

Beloin, Nadine, Messanvi Gbeassor, Koffi Akpagana, Jim Hudson, Komlan de Soussa, Kossi Koumaglo, and J. Thor Arnason. "Ethnomedicinal Uses of *Momordica charantia* (Cucurbitaceae) in Togo and Relation to Its Phytochemistry and Biological Activity." *Journal of Ethnopharmacology* 96 (2005): 49–55.

Bennett, Herman. *Africans in Colonial Mexico: Absolutism, Christianity, and Afro-Creole Consciousness, 1570–1640*. Bloomington: Indiana University Press, 2003.

Bergad, Laird W. *Slavery and the Demographic and Economic History of Minas Gerais, Brazil, 1720–1888*. Cambridge: Cambridge University Press, 1999.

Bergé, J.A.M.A.R. "Étude sur le pays Mahi (1926–1928)." *Bulletin du Comité d'Études Historiques et Scientifiques de l'Afrique Occidentale Française* 11 (1928): 708–55.

Berlin, Ira. "From Creole to Africa: Atlantic Creoles and the Origins of African-American Society in Mainland North America." *William and Mary Quarterly* 53 (1996): 251–88.

———. *Generations of Captivity: A History of African-American Slaves*. Cambridge, MA: Belknap Press, 2003.

————. *Many Thousands Gone: The First Two Centuries of Slavery in North America.* Cambridge, MA: Belknap Press, 1998.

Bethencourt, Francisco. *O imaginário da magia: feiticeiras, saludadores e nigromantes no século XVI.* Lisbon: Universidade Nova, 1987.

Blier, Suzanne Preston. *African Vodun: Art, Psychology, and Power.* Chicago: University of Chicago Press, 1995.

Braga, Júlio Santana. "Notas sôbre a pesca do Xaréu: folclore e compromisso religioso." *Afro-Asia* 10 (1970): 43–65.

Brand, Roger-Bernard. "Rites de naissance et réactualisation matérielle des signes de naissance à la mort chez les Wéménou (Bénin/Dahomey)." In *Naître, vivre et mourir: actualité de Van Gennep: essais sur les rites de passage,* edited by Jacques Hainard and Roland Kaehr, 37–62. Neuchâtel: Musée d'Ethnographie, 1981.

Brown, Vincent. *The Reaper's Garden: Death and Power in the World of Atlantic Slavery.* Cambridge, MA: Harvard University Press, 2008.

————. "Social Death and Political Life in the Study of Slavery." *American Historical Review* 114 (2009): 1231–49.

Calainho, Daniela Buono. "Jambacousses e gangazambes: feiticeiros negros em Portugal." *Afro-Ásia* 25–26 (2001): 141–76.

————. *Metrópole das mandingas: religiosidade negra e inquisição portuguesa no Antigo Regime.* Rio de Janeiro: Editora Garamond, 2008.

Campbell, Gwyn, Suzanne Miers, and Joseph C. Miller. *Children in Slavery through the Ages.* Athens: Ohio University Press, 2009.

Cañizares-Esguerra, Jorge. "Entangled Histories: Borderland Historiographies in New Clothes?" *American Historical Review* 112 (2007): 787–99.

Capo, Hounkpati B. C. "Le Gbe est une langue unique." *Africa* 53 (1983): 321–48.

Carneiro, Edison. *O Quilombo dos Palmares.* 4th edition. São Paulo: Companhia Editora Nacional, 1988.

Carvalho, Marcos. *Gaiaku Luiza: e a trajetoria do Jeje-Mahi na Bahia.* Rio de Janeiro: Pallas Editora, 2006.

Castro, Yeda Pessoa de. *A língua Mina-Jeje no Brasil: um falar africano em Ouro Preto do século XVIII.* Belo Horizonte: Fundação João Pinheiro, Secretaria de Estado da Cultura, 2002.

Chaturvedi, P. "Role of *Momordica charantia* in Maintaining the Normal Levels of Lipids and Glucose in Diabetic Rats Fed a High-Fat and Low-Carbohydrate Diet." *British Journal of Biomedical Science* 62 (2005): 124–26.

Coates, Timothy J. *Convicts and Orphans: Forced and State-Sponsored Colonizers in the Portuguese Empire, 1550–1755.* Stanford, CA: Stanford University Press, 2001.

Coclanis, Peter. "Drang Nach Osten: Bernard Bailyn, the World-Island, and the Idea of Atlantic History." *Journal of World History* 13 (2002): 169–82.

Coelho, António Borges. *Inquisição de Évora, dos primórdios a 1668.* 2 volumes. Lisbon: Editorial Caminho, 1987.

Comaroff, Jean, and John Comaroff, eds. *Modernity and Its Malcontents: Ritual and Power in Postcolonial Africa.* Chicago: University of Chicago Press, 1993.

Cooper, Frederick. *Colonialism in Question: Theory, Knowledge, History.* Berkeley: University of California Press, 2005.

Delgado, Maria Rosalina. *O jornal manuscrito de Luiz Montez Mattozo: Anno noticioso e histórico, 1742: estudo crítico*. Lisbon: Lisóptima Edições/Biblioteca Nacional, 1996.

Dubois, Laurent. *A Colony of Citizens: Revolution and Slave Emancipation in the French Caribbean, 1787–1804*. Chapel Hill: University of North Carolina Press, 2003.

Edmundo, Luiz. *Rio de Janeiro nos tempo dos vice-reis*. Rio de Janeiro: Athena, 1935.

Eltis, David. "Free and Coerced Migrations from the Old World to the New." In *Coerced and Free Migration: Global Perspectives*, edited by David Eltis, 33–74. Stanford, CA: Stanford University Press, 2002.

———. "The Transatlantic Slave Trade: A Reassessment Based on the Second Edition Transatlantic Slave Trade Data Base." Unpublished paper delivered at the American Historical Association Annual Meeting, 2006.

Eltis, David, et al. The Trans-Atlantic Slave Trade Database. www.slavevoyages.org.

Feierman, Steven. "Colonizers, Scholars, and the Creation of Invisible Histories." In *Beyond the Cultural Turn: New Directions in the Study of Society and Culture*, edited by Victoria E. Bonnell and Lynn Hunt, 182–216. Berkeley: University of California Press, 1999.

———. *Peasant Intellectuals: Anthropology and History in Tanzania*. Madison: University of Wisconsin Press, 1990.

Ferreira, João da Costa. *A cidade do Rio de Janeiro e seu termo: ensaio urbanologico*. Rio de Janeiro: Imprensa Nacional, 1933.

Ferreira, Roberto Guedes. "Autonomia escrava e (des)governo senhorial na cidade do Rio de Janeiro da primeira metade do século XIX." In *Tráfico, cativeiro e liberdade: Rio de Janeiro, séculos XVII–XIX*, edited by Manolo Florentino, 229–83. Rio de Janeiro: Civilização Brasileira, 2005.

Filho, Luis Lisanti, ed. *Negócios coloniais: uma correspondência do século XVIII*. 5 volumes. Brasília: Ministério da Fazenda, 1973.

Florentino, Manolo, Alexandre Vieira Ribeiro, and Daniel Domingues da Silva. "Aspectos comparativos do tráfico de Africanos para o Brasil (séculos XVIII e XIX)." *Revista Afro-Ásia* 31 (2004): 83–126.

Fonseca, Jorge. *Escravos no sul do Portugal: séculos XVI–XVII*. Lisbon: Editora Vulgata, 2002.

Fragoso, João. "Senhores do Atlântico versus senhores de um negrinho." In *Conquistadores e negociantes: histórias de elites no Antigo Regime nos trópicos. América lusa, séculos XVI a XVIII*, edited by João Luís Ribeiro Fragoso, Carla Maria Carvalho de Almeida, and Antonio Carlos Jucá de Sampaio, 35–120. Rio de Janeiro: Civilização Brasileira, 2007.

Frank, Zephyr L. *Dutra's World: Wealth and Family in Nineteenth-Century Rio de Janeiro*. Albuquerque: University of New Mexico Press, 2004.

Fuente, Alejandro de la. "Slave Law and Claims-Making in Cuba: The Tannenbaum Thesis Revisited." *Law and History Review* 22 (2004): 339–69.

Gallop, Rodney. *Portugal: A Book of Folk-Ways*. 1936. Reprint, Cambridge: Cambridge University Press, 1961.

Games, Alison. "Atlantic History: Definitions, Challenges, and Opportunities." *American Historical Review* 111 (2006): 741–57.

Geschiere, Peter. *The Modernity of Witchcraft: Politics and the Occult in Postcolonial Africa.* Charlottesville: University of Virginia Press, 1997.

Goulart, Maurício. *A escravidão africana no Brasil: das origens á extinção do tráfico.* 3rd edition. São Paulo: Editora Alfa-Ômega, 1975.

Guillet, Gérard. *Regards sur la litterature Dahoméenne: les proverbes.* Cotonou: Pro Manuscripto, 1971.

Guyer, Jane I. *Marginal Gains: Monetary Transactions in Atlantic Africa.* Chicago: University of Chicago Press, 2004.

Guyer, Jane I., and Samuel M. Eno Belinga. "Wealth in People as Wealth in Knowledge: Accumulation and Composition in Equatorial Africa." *Journal of African History* 36 (1995): 91–120.

Harding, Rachel E. *A Refuge in Thunder: Candomblé and Alternate Spaces of Blackness.* Bloomington: Indiana University Press, 2000.

Harms, Robert. *The Diligent: A Voyage through the Worlds of the Slave Trade.* New York: Basic Books, 2002.

Hawthorne, Walter. "Being Now, as It Were, One Family: Shipmate Bonding on the Slave Vessel *Emilia,* in Rio de Janeiro and throughout the Atlantic World." *Luso-Brazilian Review* 45 (2008): 53–77.

Herskovits, Melville J. *Dahomey: An Ancient West African Kingdom.* 2 volumes. Evanston, IL: Northwestern University Press, 1967.

Herskovits, Melville J., and Frances S. Herskovits. *Dahomean Narrative: A Cross-Cultural Analysis.* Evanston, IL: Northwestern University Press, 1958.

———. *An Outline of Dahomean Religious Belief.* Menasha, WI, 1933.

Heywood, Linda M., and John K. Thornton. *Central Africans, Atlantic Creoles, and the Foundation of the Americas, 1585–1660.* Cambridge: Cambridge University Press, 2007.

Honorato, Cláudio de Paula. "Controle sanitário dos negros no Valongo Rio de Janeiro, 1751–1831." In *Doenças e escravidão: sistema de saúde e práticas terapêuticas,* CD ROM, edited by Angela Porto. Rio de Janeiro: Casa de Oswaldo Cruz/Flocruz, 2007.

Hopkins, Donald R. *Princes and Peasants: Smallpox in History.* Chicago: University of Chicago Press, 1983.

Horton, Robin. *Patterns of Thought in Africa and the West: Essays on Magic, Religion, and Science.* Cambridge: Cambridge University Press, 1993.

Iroko, Abiola Félix. "Cauris et esclaves en Afrique occidentale entre le XVIe et le XIXe siecles." In *De la traite à l'esclavage: Actes du Colloque international sur la traite des Noirs, Nantes 1985,* edited by Serge Daget, 193–204. Nantes: Centre de Recherche sur l'Histoire du Monde Atlantique, 1988.

Jainu, Mallika, and Chennam Srinivasulu Shyamala Devi. "Antiulcerogenic and Ulcer Healing Effects of *Solanum nigrum* (L.) on Experimental Ulcer Models: Possible Mechanism for the Inhibition of Acid Formation." *Journal of Ethnopharmacology* 104, nos. 1–2 (2006): 156–63.

Junod, Henri. *The Life of a South African Tribe.* Volume 2, *Mental Life.* 2nd edition. London: Macmillan, 1927.

Karasch, Mary. *Slave Life in Rio de Janeiro, 1808–1850*. Princeton, NJ: Princeton University Press, 1987.

Kent, Robert K. "Palmares: An African State in Brazil." *Journal of African History 6* (1965): 161–75.

Klein, Herbert S. *The Middle Passage: Comparative Studies in the Atlantic Slave Trade*. Princeton, NJ: Princeton University Press, 1978.

Kodesh, Neil. *Beyond the Royal Gaze: Clanship and Collective Well-Being in Buganda*. Charlottesville: University of Virginia Press, 2010.

Lahon, Didier. *O negro na coração do império*. Lisbon: Ministério da Educação, 1999.

Landers, Jane G. *Atlantic Creoles in the Age of Revolutions*. Cambridge, MA: Harvard University Press, 2010.

Landes, Ruth. *The City of Women*. New York: Macmillan, 1947.

Law, Robin. "Ethnicity and the Slave Trade: 'Lucumi' and 'Nago' as Ethnonyms in West Africa." *History in Africa* 24 (1997): 205–19.

———. "Further Light on Bulfinch Lambe and the Emperor 'Pawpaw': King Agaja of Dahomey's Letter to King George I of England, 1726." *History in Africa* 17 (1990): 211–26.

———. "King Agaja of Dahomey, the Slave Trade, and the Question of West African Plantations: The Mission of Bulfinch Lambe and Adomo Tomo to England, 1726–32." *Journal of Imperial and Commonwealth History* 19 (1991): 137–63.

———. "'My Head Belongs to the King': On the Political and Ritual Significance of Decapitation in Pre-colonial Dahomey." *Journal of African History* 30 (1989): 399–415.

———. *Ouidah: The Social History of a West African Slaving Port, 1727–1892*. Athens: Ohio University Press, 2005.

———. "Religion, Trade, and Politics on the 'Slave Coast': Roman Catholic Missions in Allada and Ouidah in the Seventeenth Century." *History of Religion in Africa* 21 (1991): 42–77.

———. *The Slave Coast of West Africa, 1550–1750: The Impact of the Atlantic Slave Trade on an African Society*. Oxford: Clarendon Press, 1991.

Le Herissé, A. *L'Ancien Royaume du Dahomey*. Paris: Emile Larose, 1911.

Le Meur, Pierre-Yves. "State Making and the Politics of the Frontier in Central Benin." *Development and Change* 37 (2006): 871–900.

Lepine, Claude. "As metamorfoses de Sakpata, deus da varíola." In *Leopardo dos olhos de fogo*, volume 6 of *Escritos sobre a religião dos orixás*, edited by Carlos Eugênio Marcondes de Moura, 119–43. São Paulo: Ateliê Editorial, 1998.

Lewin, Linda. "Natural and Spurious Children in Brazilian Inheritance Law from Colony to Empire: A Methodological Essay." *The Americas* 48 (1992): 351–96.

Lewis, Laura A. *Hall of Mirrors: Power, Witchcraft, and Caste in Colonial Mexico*. Durham, NC: Duke University Press, 2003.

Lobo, Eulália Maria Lahmeyer. *História do Rio de Janeiro: do capital comercial ao capital industrial e financeiro*. 2 volumes. Rio de Janeiro: IBMEC, 1978.

MacGaffey, Wyatt. "Changing Representations in Central African History." *Journal of African History* 46 (2005): 189–207.

Maia, Moacir Rodrigo de Castro. "Quem tem padrinho não morre pagão: as relações de compadrio e apadrinhamento de escravos numa vila colonial (Mariana, 1715–1750)." Master's thesis, Universidade Federal Fluminense, Rio de Janeiro, 2006.

Marques, Antonio H. de Oliveira. *History of Portugal: From Lusitania to Empire.* New York: Columbia University Press, 1972.

Marques, Xavier. *O feiticeiro.* São Paulo: GRD-IL, 1975.

Matory, J. Lorand. *Black Atlantic Religion: Tradition, Transnationalism, and Matriarchy in the Afro-Brazilian Candomblé.* Princeton, NJ: Princeton University Press, 2005.

———. "The English Professors of Brazil: On the Diasporic Roots of the Yoruba Nation." *Comparative Studies in Society and History* 41 (1999): 72–103.

Maupoil, Bernard. *La géomancie à l'ancienne Côte des Esclaves.* Paris: Institut d'Ethnologie, 1943.

Mensan, Covi. "Le culte des fétiches dans la region de Zagnanado." *L'Éducation Africaine (Bulletin de l'Enseignement de l'AOF)* 23, no. 85 (1934): 9–23.

Mercier, Paul. *Les ase du Musée d'Abomey.* Dakar: IFAN, 1952.

Métraux, Alfred. *Voodoo in Haiti.* Translated by Hugo Charteris. New York: Schocken, 1972.

Miers, Suzanne, and Igor Kopytoff, eds. *Slavery in Africa: Historical and Anthropological Perspectives.* Madison: University of Wisconsin Press, 1977.

Miller, Joseph C. "Retention, Re-invention, and Remembering: Restoring Identities through Enslavement in Africa and under Slavery in Brazil." In *Enslaving Connections: Changing Cultures of Africa and Brazil during the Era of Slavery*, edited by José C. Curto and Paul E. Lovejoy, 81–121. Amherst, NY: Prometheus/Humanity Books, 2003.

———. *Way of Death: Merchant Capitalism and the Angolan Slave Trade, 1730–1830.* Madison: University of Wisconsin Press, 1988.

Monroe, J. Cameron. "Dahomey and the Atlantic Slave Trade: Archaeology and Political Order on the Bight of Benin." In *Archaeology of Atlantic Africa and the African Diaspora*, edited by Akinwumi Ogundiran and Toyin Falola, 100–121. Bloomington: Indiana University Press, 2007.

Moore, Henrietta, and Todd Sanders, eds. *Magical Interpretations, Material Realities: Modernity, Witchcraft, and the Occult in Postcolonial Africa.* London: Routledge, 2001.

Moraes, Evaristo de. *Carceres e fogueiras da inquisição: processos contra Antonio José, o "Judeu."* Rio de Janeiro: Athena Editora, 1935.

Mott, Luiz. "O calundu angola de Luzia Pinta, Sabará 1739." *Revista do Instituto de Artes e Cultura* (UFOP) (1994): 73–82.

———. *Rosa Egipcíaca: uma santa africana no Brasil.* Rio de Janeiro: Editora Bertrand Brasil, 1993.

———. "Um Tupinambá feiticeiro do Espírito Santo nas garras da inquisição." *Revista de História* (UFES) 18 (2006): 13–28.

Nazzari, Muriel. "An Urgent Need to Conceal." In *The Faces of Honor: Sex, Shame, and Violence in Colonial Latin America*, edited by Lyman L. Johnson and Sonya Lipsett-Rivera, 103–26. Albuquerque: University of New Mexico Press, 1998.

Novinsky, Anita. "A igreja no Brasil colonial: agentes da inquisição." *Anais do Museu Paulista* 33 (1984): 17–34.

Ojewole, J. A., S. O. Adewole, and G. Olayiwola. "Hypoglycaemic and Hyposensitive Effects of *Momordica charantia* Linn (Cucurbitaceae) Whole-Plant Aqueous Extract in Rats." *Cardiovascular Journal of South Africa* 17 (2005): 227–32.

Oliveira, Anderson José Machado de. *Devoção negra: santos pretos e catequese no Brasil colonial*. Rio de Janeiro: Quartet Editora & Comunicação Ltda., 2008.

Paiva, José Pedro. *Bruxaria e superstição num país sem "caça ás bruxas," 1600–1774*. Lisbon: Editorial Notícias, 1997.

Palacios, Guillermo. "Peasantry and Slavery in Brazil: A Contribution to the History of the Free Poor Planters from the Captaincy General of Pernambuco, 1700–1817." PhD dissertation, Princeton University, 1993.

Parés, Luis Nicolau. "Ethnic-Religious Modes of Identification among the Gbe-Speaking People in Eighteenth and Nineteenth Century Brazil." In *Africa, Brazil, and the Construction of Trans-Atlantic Black Identities*, edited by Boubacar Barry, Elisée Akpo Soumonni, and Livio Sansone, 179–207. Trenton, NJ: Africa World Press, 2008.

———. *A formação do Candomblé: história e ritual na Nação Jeje na Bahia*. Campinas: Universidade Estadual de Campinas, 2006.

Patterson, Orlando. *Slavery and Social Death: A Comparative Study*. Cambridge, MA: Harvard University Press, 1982.

Penningroth, Dylan C. *The Claims of Kinfolk: African-American Property and Community in the Nineteenth-Century South*. Chapel Hill: University of North Carolina Press, 2002.

Pereira, Alvaro S. "The Opportunity of a Disaster: The Economic Impact of the 1755 Lisbon Earthquake." Discussion Paper, Cherry DP 03/06, Centre for Historical Economics and Related Research, York, UK, 2006.

Pereira, João Manuel Esteves, and Guilherme Rodrigues. *Portugal: diccionario historico, chorographico, biographico, bibliographico, heraldico, numismatico, e artistico*. 3 volumes. Lisbon: João Romano Torres, 1907.

Pereira, Júlio César Medeiros da Silva. *À flor da terra: o cemitério dos pretos novos no Rio de Janeiro*. Rio de Janeiro: Editora Garamond, 2007.

Pieroni, Geraldo. "El Brasil colonial: ¿tierra de exilio? La Inquisición y la expulsión— siglos XVI–XVIII." *Clío* 18 (2000), http://clio.rediris.es/articulos/pieroni.htm.

———. *Os excluídos do reino: a inquisição portuguesa e o degredo para o Brasil colonial*. Brasília: Editora Universidade de Brasília, 2000.

Pieroni, Geraldo, and Timothy Coates. *De couto do pecado à vila do sal: Castro Marim (1550–1850)*. Lisbon: Livraria Sá da Costa Editora, 2002.

Reis, João José. "Candomblé in Nineteenth-Century Bahia: Priests, Followers, Clients." In *Rethinking the African Diaspora: The Making of a Black Atlantic World in the Bight of Benin and Brazil*, edited by Kristin Mann and Edna Bay, 116–34. London: Frank Cass, 2001.

Reis, João José, and Flavio dos Santos Gomes, eds. *Liberdade por um fio: história dos quilombos no Brasil*. São Paulo: Companhia das Letras, 1996.

Rezende, Antônio Paulo. *O Recife: histórias de uma cidade*. Recife: Fundação de Cultura Cidade do Recife, 2002.

Richardson, David. "Shipboard Revolts, African Authority, and the Atlantic Slave Trade." *William and Mary Quarterly* 58 (2001): 69–92.

Rodrigues, Teresa. *Cinco séculos de quotidiano: a vida em Lisboa do século XVI aos nossos dias.* Lisbon: Edições Cosmos, 1997.

Russell-Wood, A. J. R. *The Black Man in Slavery and in Freedom in Colonial Brazil.* New York: St. Martin's Press, 1982.

Sampaio, Antonio Carlos Jucá. "A produção da liberdade: padrões gerais das manumissões no Rio de Janeiro colonial, 1650–1750." In *Tráfico, cativeiro e liberdade: Rio de Janeiro, séculos XVII–XIX,* edited by Manolo Florentino, 287–329. Rio de Janeiro: Civilização Brasileira, 2005.

Santos, Corcino Madeiros dos. *O Rio de Janeiro e a conjuntura Atlântica.* Rio de Janeiro: Expressão e Cultura, 1993.

Schoenbrun, David L. "Conjuring the Modern in Africa: Durability and Rupture in Histories of Public Healing between the Great Lakes of East Africa." *American Historical Review* 111 (2006): 1403–39.

Schwartz, Stuart B. *All Can Be Saved: Religious Tolerance and Salvation in the Iberian Atlantic World.* New Haven, CT: Yale University Press, 2008.

———. "Plantations and Peripheries." In *Colonial Brazil,* edited by Leslie Bethel, 67–144. Cambridge: Cambridge University Press, 1987.

———. "The Plantations of St. Benedict: The Benedictine Sugar Mills of Colonial Brazil." *The Americas* 39 (1982): 1–22.

———. "Rethinking Palmares: Slave Resistance in Colonial Brazil." In *Slaves, Peasants, and Rebels: Reconsidering Brazilian Slavery,* edited by Stuart B. Schwartz, 103–36. Urbana: University of Illinois Press, 1992.

———. *Sugar Plantations in the Formation of Brazilian Society: Bahia, 1550–1835.* Cambridge: Cambridge University Press, 1985.

Scott, Rebecca. "Public Rights and Private Commerce: A Nineteenth-Century Atlantic Creole Itinerary." *Current Anthropology* 48 (2007): 237–56.

Segurola, R. P. B. *Dictionnaire Fon-Français.* 2 volumes. Cotonou: Procure de l'Archdiocèse, 1963.

Serrão, Joel, and A. H. de Oliveira Marques. *Nova história de Portugal.* Volume 7, *Portugal da paz da restauração ao ouro do Brasil.* Lisbon: Editoral Presença, 2001.

Shaw, Rosalind. *Memories of the Slave Trade: Ritual and the Historical Imagination in Sierra Leone.* Chicago: University of Chicago Press, 2002.

Silva, Alberto da Costa e. "A memória histórica sobre os costumes particulares dos povos Africanos, com relação privativa ao Reino da Guiné, e nele com respeito ao Rei de Daomé, de Luís Antônio de Oliveira Mendes." *Afro-Ásia* 28 (2002): 253–94.

Silva, Kalina Vanderlei Paiva da. "'Nas solidões vastas e assustadoras': os pobres do açúcar e a conquista do sertão de Pernambuco nos séculos XVII e XVIII." PhD dissertation, Universidade Federal de Pernambuco, Recife, 2003.

Silva, Maciel Henriques. "Na casa, na rua e no rio: a passagem do Recife oitocentista pelas vendeiras, domésticas e lavadeiras." *Mneme: Revista de Humanidades* 7 (2005), http://www.cerescaico.ufrn.br/mneme/pdf/mneme15/146.pdf.

Slenes, Robert W. "'Malungu ngoma vem!': África coberta e descoberta do Brasil." *Revista USP* 12 (1992): 48–67.

Smallwood, Stephanie E. *Saltwater Slavery: A Middle Passage from Africa to American Diaspora*. Cambridge, MA: Harvard University Press, 2007.

Smith, James Howard. *Bewitching Development: Witchcraft and the Reinvention of Development in Neoliberal Kenya*. Chicago: University of Chicago Press, 2008.

Soares, Mariza de Carvalho. "African Barbers in Brazilian Slave Ports: A Case Study from Rio de Janeiro." In *Port Cities of the Black Atlantic*, edited by Matt Childs, Jorge Cañizares Esguerra, and James Sidbury. Forthcoming.

———. *Devotos da cor: identidade étnica, religiosidade e escravidão no Rio de Janeiro, século XVIII*. Rio de Janeiro: Civilização Brasileira, 2000.

Souza, Laura de Mello e. *The Devil and the Land of the Holy Cross: Witchcraft, Slavery, and Popular Religion in Colonial Brazil*. Austin: University of Texas Press, 2003.

———. "Revisitando o calundu." In *Ensaios sobre a intolerância: inquisição, marranismo e anti-semitismo (homenagem a Anita Novinsky)*, edited by Lina Gorenstein and Maria Luiza Tucci Carneiro, 293–317. São Paulo: Editora Humanitas, 2002.

Srivastava, Y., H. Venkatakrishna, Y. Verma, K. Venkaiah, and B. H. Raval. "Antidiabetic and Adaptogenic Properties of *Momordica charantia* Extract: An Experimental and Clinical Evaluation." *Phytotherapy Research* 7 (1993): 285–89.

Sweet, James H. "The Evolution of Ritual in the African Diaspora: Central African *Kilundu* in Brazil, St. Domingue, and the United States, Seventeenth–Nineteenth Centuries." In *Diasporic Africa: A Reader*, edited by Michael A. Gomez, 64–80. New York: New York University Press, 2006.

———. "Manumission in Rio de Janeiro, 1749–1754: An African Perspective." *Slavery and Abolition* 24 (2003): 54–70.

———. "Mistaken Identities? Olaudah Equiano, Domingos Álvares, and the Methodological Challenges of Studying the African Diaspora." *American Historical Review* 114 (2009): 279–306.

———. *Recreating Africa: Culture, Kinship, and Religion in the African-Portuguese World, 1441–1770*. Chapel Hill: University of North Carolina Press, 2003.

———. "Slaves, Convicts, and Exiles: African Travellers in the Portuguese Atlantic World, 1720–1750." In *Bridging the Early Modern Atlantic World: People, Products, and Practices on the Move*, edited by Caroline A. Williams, 193–202. Farnham, UK: Ashgate Publishing, 2009.

Thornton, John K. *Africa and Africans in the Making of the Atlantic World, 1400–1800*. Cambridge: Cambridge University Press, 1992.

Tidjani, Abdou Serpos. "Notes sur le mariage au Dahomey." *Etudes Dahoméennes* 6 (1951): 27–107.

Trouillot, Michel Rolph. *Silencing the Past: Power and the Production of History*. Boston: Beacon Press, 1995.

Vansina, Jan. *Paths in the Rainforests: Toward a History of Political Tradition in Equatorial Africa*. Madison: University of Wisconsin Press, 1990.

Varnhagen, F. A. de. "Excerptos de varias listas de condemnados pela inquisição de Lisbôa, desde o anno 1711 ao de 1767 comprehendendo só os brasileiros, ou colonos estabelecidos no Brasil." *Revista Trimensal de Historia e Geographia ou Jornal do Instituto Historico e Geographico Brasileiro* 25 (1845): 54–86.

Verger, Pierre. *Fluxo e refluxo do tráfico de escravos entre o Golfo do Benin e a Bahia de Todos os Santos dos séculos XVII a XIX*. 3rd edition. São Paulo: Corrupio, 1987.

———. *Notas sobre o culto aos orixás e voduns: na Bahia de Todos os Santos, no Brasil, e na Antiga Costa dos Escravos, na África*. 2nd edition. Translated by Carlos Eugênio Marcondes de Moura. São Paulo: Editora da Universidade de São Paulo, 2000.

Vignondé, Jean-Norbert. "Slaves and Slavery in the Study of Fon Proverbs in Benin." In *From Chains to Bonds: The Slave Trade Revisited*, edited by Doudou Diène, 258–66. New York: Bergahn Books, 2001.

Voeks, Robert A. *Sacred Leaves of Candomblé: African Magic, Medicine, and Religion in Brazil*. Austin: University of Texas Press, 1997.

Wadsworth, James E. *Agents of Orthodoxy: Honor, Status, and the Inquisition in Colonial Pernambuco, Brazil*. Lanham, MD: Rowman & Littlefield Publishers, 2007.

———. "*Jurema* and *Batuque*: Indians, Africans, and the Inquisition in Colonial Brazil." *History of Religions* 46 (2006): 140–62.

Walker, Timothy. *Doctors, Folk Medicine, and the Inquisition: The Repression of Magical Healing in Portugal during the Enlightenment*. Leiden: Brill, 2005.

———. "Sorcerers and Folkhealers: Africans and the Inquisition in Portugal (1680–1800)." *Revista Lusófona de Ciência das Religões* 5–6 (2004): 83–98.

White, Luise. *Speaking with Vampires: Rumor and History in Colonial Africa*. Berkeley: University of California Press, 2000.

Williams, Eric. *Capitalism and Slavery*. Chapel Hill: University of North Carolina Press, 1944.

Woodson, W. W. "The Auto da Fé of 1755." *Harper's New Monthly Magazine* 41 (June–November 1870): 368–71.

Yai, Olabiyi. "Texts of Enslavement: Fon and Yoruba Vocabularies from Eighteenth- and Nineteenth-Century Brazil." In *Identity in the Shadow of Slavery*, edited by Paul E. Lovejoy, 102–12. New York: Continuum, 2000.

Index

Abomey, Benin, 13, 15, 16, 18, 19, 20, 59, 129, 137

Adja, 14, 18, 19

Agaja (king of Dahomey), 153, 154; and slave trade, 9, 11–12, 28, 31–32, 71; as war leader, 12–14, 18, 135; and vodun, 18–25, 34, 129, 131–32, 136–37, 203

Agonli-Cové, 7, 15, 16, 22, 24, 25, 57, 59

Akaba (king of Dahomey), 12

Alcaria Queimada, Portugal, 207, 214

Alcohol, 28, 29, 37, 54, 82, 112, 129, 195, 204, 208. *See also* Vodun: sacrificial offerings

Allada, 7, 9, 11–13, 16, 19, 58, 59, 135, 137, 145

Almeida, José Cardoso de, 112, 164, 167; purchase of Domingos, 99–101; business acumen, 101, 103–6, 144

Alonso, Leonor, 209

Álvares, Domingos: tortured by Inquisition, 1, 178; as intellectual, 6, 177–78, 201, 230, 232–33; childhood and adolescence, 7–8, 22; physical description of, 22, 191, 212; father (Afnage), 22–24, 142, 167; mother (Oconon), 22–24, 142, 167; as *vodunon*, 24–25, 55, 59–60; enslavement in Dahomey, 25–26; and Middle Passage, 36–42, 243 (n. 45); and sugar labor, 45–47, 55; and Catholic Church, 47–52, 65, 73–74, 87–88, 106–7, 115, 171, 192–93, 200–201, 208, 212; godfather (Gaspar Pereira), 49, 167; early healing in Recife, 55–57, 64–65; conceptions of freedom, 65–66, 70–71, 98–99, 103–6; conflicts with masters, 68–71, 73, 98–99, 117–20;

passage to Rio de Janeiro, 74–75; reputation, 74–77, 99; friendship with slave Caetano, 77, 115, 117–18, 126; description of ritual healing practices, 98, 99–101, 112–14, 115–17, 123–29, 148, 172–75, 192–94, 207–8, 209, 210, 211–12, 215; earnings potential as healer, 101, 105, 109, 194, 214, 256 (n. 11); manumission, 103–4, 106, 167; and "public house" in Rio, 106–7, 147–48; healing clinics in Rio, 107–9; ritual space (*terreiro*) in Rio, 107–12, 129; conceptions of wealth, 112; sexual tensions with former mistress, 119–20; as beneficiary of patriarchy and patronage, 143–44, 165–67; wife (Maria da Rocha), 144–45, 154, 164, 167; daughter, 145, 154, 164–65; denounced before Inquisition, 148–49, 196, 205–7, 210; jailed by Inquisition, 150–51, 212–13; threat to Portuguese Crown, 153; transported to Lisbon, 153–54; Inquisition testimony, 164–65, 169–78, 215–17; literacy, 165, 195–96, 205–7; explains divination practices, 170, 175–76; sentenced by Inquisition, 178–79, 217–18; banished to Castro Marim, 179, 186–89; marches in Auto da Fé, 180, 183, 218; social alienation in Algarve, 191–92, 213–14, 217, 224, 274 (n. 78); conflicts in Algarve, 194–98, 205, 208–9, 210–11; divines location of buried treasures, 199–200, 203–5; banished to Bragança, 218, 224–25; conceptions of history, 231–32

Álvares, Francisco, 95–96

Calabash, 64, 100, 138, 148, 169, 170, 173, 175–76, 216. *See also* Vodun: shrines

Calundu. *See* Spirit possession: calundu

Cana, Benin, 137

Candomblé, 23, 110–11, 113

Cannibalism, 28–29, 82–83

Cape Verde, 86, 95

Capibaribe River, 53, 55

Capuchins, 19

Carmelites, 44, 48, 63

Carvalho, Manuel Antônio de, 92

Carvalho, Manuel de Andrade, 210

Carvalho, Sebastianna de, 46, 51

Castro Marim, Portugal, 1, 185, 186, 187, 188–89, 191–92, 194, 198, 204–5

Cata, Manuel, 130–32, 140

Catholic Church, 94, 100, 126; as protector of Africans and Indians, 47–49, 185; as slaveowner, 48, 74; as healing community, 49–52, 60, 61–63; translated through vodun, 59–60, 86–87; racial and ethnic divisions in, 85–87, 184; and "divine virtues," 201. *See also* Baptism; Brotherhoods, Catholic; Burials; Churches; Inquisition; Marriage

Cavalcante, Manoel, 46

Children, 29, 38, 40, 240 (n. 6), 242–43 (n. 40)

Churches: Nossa Senhora da Conceição (Tapirema), 47, 49; Nossa Senhora das Necessidades (Casa Forte), 55; Saint Pantelão (Monteiro), 65; Nossa Senhora da Candelária (Rio de Janeiro), 78, 79, 80, 89, 90, 107, 145; Santíssimo Sacramento (Rio de Janeiro), 79; Santa Rita (Rio de Janeiro), 80–82; Convento do São Bento (Rio de Janeiro), 82; São José (Rio de Janeiro), 85; São Sebastião (Rio de Janeiro), 85; Nossa Senhora da Conceição (Rio de Janeiro), 85; Nossa Senhora da Glória (Rio de Janeiro), 85, 107, 109–10; Nossa

Senhora do Rosário e São Benedito dos Homens Pretos (Rio de Janeiro), 85–86; São Domingos (Rio de Janeiro), 85–86, 89; São Pedro (Rio de Janeiro), 88; Senhor Bom Jesus (Rio de Janeiro), 88, 115; Convent of Saint Anthony (Rio de Janeiro), 112; São Domingos (Lisbon), 179

Circumcision, 22

Coates, Timothy, 188

Cobu, 7, 57, 59, 247 (n. 24)

Coimbra, Portugal, 116, 218; university, 98

Colaço, José Rodrigues, 68–69

Costa, Antônio Lopes da, 67

Costa, Bishop Manuel Álvares da, 48

Courana, Eugenia, 94

Cowry shells, 12, 14, 23, 28, 29, 37, 55, 131–32

Creolization, 5

Crime: murder, 67–68, 75–76, 156, 187; robbery, 68, 187; and racial identity, 188–89, 191–92; assault, 255 (n. 74)

Criolla, Dorothea, 92

Cruz, Domingas da, 95–96

Cruz, Leonor de Oliveira, 81, 88, 98–99, 121, 147, 149, 173–74, 224; purchase of Domingos, 76–77; travels to Domingos' *terreiro*, 115–17; psychoses, 117–19, 121; sexual tensions with Domingos, 119–20

Dahomey, kingdom of: warfare, 7–9, 11–13, 15–17, 18, 24, 40, 58, 60, 131–32; and human sacrifice, 11–12, 13, 18, 137; slaving and slave trade, 11–12, 14, 16, 22, 25, 129, 139, 222; military capacity, 12, 20, 21, 32; spiritual beliefs, 17–22, 110, 129, 131; myths and traditions, 18–19, 23, 50, 121, 125, 129, 131, 203–4, 261 (n. 33); as empire, 19, 225–26; diplomatic mission to Brazil, 219–22

Dalzel, Archibald, 22

209; and patron-client relationships, 165–67

Koster, Henry, 40

Kpojito Hwanjile (queen of Dahomey), 142

Labor
—and cash economy, 105–6
—*escravos de ganho* (slaves for hire), 56, 104–5
—and illegal trade, 53–54
—occupations: goldsmith, 53, 78, 90; peddlar, 53–54, 78, 79; *quitandeira*, 66–67, 82, 84, 89, 90, 251–52 (n. 28); cobbler, 73, 76–77, 78, 90; factory worker, 78; farmer, 78; mason, 78; muleteer, 78; tailor, 78; blacksmith, 78, 90, 137, 138; porter, 78, 159; midwife, 79; prostitute, 79; seamstress, 79, 89; laundress, 79, 158; housekeeper, 79, 159; cook, 79, 161; fishmonger, 84, 89, 158; barber/bleeder, 89, 90, 92, 187; carpenter, 96; brickmaker, 96; boat pilot, 158; delousing, 158; musician, 160, 266–67 (n. 48); doctor, 187; lawyer, 187. *See also* Economy; *Engenhos*; Healing; Manioc; Mining; Sugar; Tobacco

Lake Nokoué, 27

Language, 25, 54, 113, 116; Yoruba, 13, 50, 59, 128, 132; Fon-Gbe, 14, 15, 17, 22, 23, 59, 124, 128, 130, 132, 133, 141, 202; ritual (Sakpata), 23, 50, 128; *língua geral* of Mina, 25, 58–61, 116, 127, 128, 130, 133; Portuguese, 47, 50, 93; Latin, 50, 128; Tupi, 182; interpreters, 221

Languedoc, France, 2

Lecumies barbas, 22

Lima, João da Costa, 39

Lisbon, Portugal, 37, 42, 47, 187, 202, 218; Inquisition tribunal, 149, 150, 152, 153, 156, 157; physical description, 158–59; Jews in, 159; African slaves in, 159–61; Inquisitorial processions, 179, 183–84

Lopes, Domingos, 200

Loulé, Portugal, 200

Luanda, Angola, 81

Machado, Antônio Nogueira, 96

Mahi, 7, 15–16, 17, 19, 20, 22, 25–26, 28, 40, 86, 130, 132

Malnutrition, 24, 25, 36, 38, 46–47, 56, 192, 213–14, 217

Malungos. See Kinship: shipmates

Manioc, 43, 54, 89, 117

Manumission, 90–91; as perpetuation of slavery, 91–93; privileging women and Brazilian-born, 93–96; as reward for mining strikes, 155; as grace of Portuguese Crown, 184. *See also* Freedom

Mariana, Brazil, 156

Marques, Jozeph Vieira, 37

Marriage, 33, 145; polygamy, 55

Martins, Silvestre, 94

Mascarenhas, Father Manuel da Costa, 107

Mattozo, Luiz Montez, 187

Maupoil, Bernard, 128

Maurício, Father Joseph, 62

Medicine, 48, 117
—animal parts: jackfish, 65, 212; chicken feathers, 114, 174, 193, 195, 197, 215, 258 (n. 32); fish bones, 118; pig's teeth, 118; hair, 118, 195; frogs, 133; hummingbirds, 133; lizards, 133; squirrel cuckoos, 133; snakes, 133, 195, 197; dogs, 195, 197; toadfish, 209; sheep's lard, 214
—baths, 100, 113, 115, 123, 133, 138, 175, 209, 210, 211
—European versus African, 32, 41, 113–14, 124, 207
—grave dirt, 195, 197
—herbal, 64, 77, 98, 100, 103, 116, 123–24, 128, 136, 169, 170–71, 175, 192, 193, 210,

214, 215; *melão de São Caetano*, 113–14, 133; *pinhão* fruit, 114; mil homens, 200–201; *erva Mouros*, 214–15
—infusions, 100–101, 114, 128, 134, 171, 193, 208, 209, 210, 211
—pins, 195, 197
—Portuguese pharmacists, 76, 187
—powders, 107, 114, 116, 117, 124, 128, 133, 169, 170, 172, 173, 174, 192, 193, 197
—purgatives, 101, 113–14, 128, 173–74
—written prayers, 207. *See also* Disease and illness; Healing; Physicians; Vodun
Mendes, Rosa, 89
Mendes, Father Salvador Ferreira, 100
Meneses, Dom Afonso Manuel de, 161
Mercier, Paul, 134–36
Mértola, Portugal, 198, 200, 213, 214
Mestra, Maria, 208–9, 214
Mestre, Manuel, 208
Middle Passage, 12, 26, 34–42, 46, 73, 74, 81–82, 226, 227
Mina coast, 7, 16, 32, 36, 43, 44, 45, 51, 56, 57, 80, 86, 152, 222; Mina identity, 49, 58–61, 71, 79–80, 84, 85–86, 89, 106, 133
Mina, Antônio, 160–61
Mina, Lucas, 90
Mina, Luís, 90
Mina, Maria, 92–93
Mina, Marianna, 93
Mina, Thereza, 99
Minas Gerais, Brazil, 43, 80, 82, 130, 155–57
Mining, 42–45, 58, 80, 133, 155, 156, 160. *See also* Diamonds; Gold
Miranda, Portugal, 186
Moncarapacho, Portugal, 204
Monchique, Portugal, 210
Monte Gordo, Portugal, 194
Moquem, 134, 139, 262 (n. 58)
Mozambique, 81, 86

Nadir, Churumá (Dahomean ambassador), 219–22, 226
Naogon, Benin, 7, 26, 49, 50, 51, 58, 65, 110, 140, 164, 183
Native Brazilians, 61, 64; as military conscripts, 68; in front of Inquisition, 180–83; as exotic spectacles, 184–85. *See also* Healing: Amerindian; Jurema; Moquem; Pestana, Miguel Ferreira
Niger River, 15

Olinda, Brazil, 44, 48, 53, 56, 64
Orobio, Matheus, 163
Ouémé River, 14, 15, 27
Ouidah, Benin: conquered by Dahomey, 9, 11, 12, 13, 16, 19, 58; as slave-trading port, 14–15, 31–33, 37–38; and snake vodun, 17–18, 64; language, 25; Portuguese fort attacked, 219–20
Òyó, kingdom of, 13, 15–16, 19, 24, 28, 34, 40

Pacheco, José, 209, 214
Palmares, 68
Palmeira, Maria Nesta da, 204
Peixoto, Antônio da Costa, 58–60, 125
Pereira, Angela, 92–93
Pereira, Antônio de Azevedo, 73
Pereira, Duarte Sodré, 43, 68
Pereira, Miguel Leite, 94
Pestana, Miguel Ferreira, 180–83, 185
Physicians, 29, 32, 41, 112–14, 192, 268 (n. 2)
Pieroni, Geraldo, 188
Pinheiro, Francisco, 37–38
Pinta, Luzia, 155–56, 161, 180, 183, 185, 188–89
Poisoning, 208, 253 (n. 45); of slave masters, 41, 66–67, 69–71; as medicine, 124
Portimão, Portugal, 209
Porto Novo, Benin, 59
Proverbs, 201–2. *See also* Dahomey, kingdom of: myths and traditions